Cambridge Studies in Historical Geography 1

PERIOD AND PLACE

Cambridge Studies in Historical Geography

Series editors:
ALAN R. H. BAKER   J. B. HARLEY   DAVID WARD

Cambridge Studies in Historical Geography encourages exploration of the philosophies, methodologies and techniques of historical geography and publishes the results of new research within all branches of the subject. It endeavours to secure the marriage of traditional scholarship with innovative approaches to problems and to sources, aiming in this way to provide a focus for the discipline and to contribute towards its development. The series is an international forum for publication in historical geography which also promotes contact with workers in cognate disciplines.

PERIOD AND PLACE

Research Methods in
Historical Geography

Edited by

ALAN R. H. BAKER
University Lecturer in Geography
and Senior Tutor of Emmanuel College, Cambridge

and

MARK BILLINGE
University Lecturer in Geography, Cambridge

CAMBRIDGE UNIVERSITY PRESS
CAMBRIDGE
LONDON   NEW YORK   NEW ROCHELLE
MELBOURNE   SYDNEY

Published by the Press Syndicate of the University of Cambridge
The Pitt Building, Trumpington Street, Cambridge CB2 1RP
32 East 57th Street, New York, NY 10022, USA
296 Beaconsfield Parade, Middle Park, Melbourne 3206, Australia

© Cambridge University Press 1982

First published 1982

Printed in Great Britain at The Pitman Press, Bath

Library of Congress catalogue card number: 81–12266

British Library Cataloguing in Publication Data

Period and place.—(Cambridge studies in historical geography)
1. Geography, Historical—Congresses
I. Title II. Baker, Alan R.H.
III. Billinge, Mark
911   G141

ISBN 0–521–24272–X

Contents

vi   Contents

Preface

As a result of initiatives taken at the 23rd International Geographical Congress in Moscow in 1976, the Executive Committee of the International Geographical Union established a Working Group on Historical Changes in Spatial Organisation. The Group aims in general to promote international cooperation in the study of historical geography, and the specific tasks which the Group has set itself have been reported in *IGU Bulletin*, vol. 28, no. 2 (1977), pp. 45–8. In addition to coordinating the distribution of information about the activities of historical geographers internationally, the Group has also organized a series of joint projects with other IGU Commissions and Working Groups. Furthermore, in the period 1977–80 leading up to the 24th International Geographical Congress in Japan the Working Group on Historical Changes in Spatial Organisation promoted a number of symposia. The first of these was held in the University of Cambridge, England, in July 1979 on 'Research Methods in Historical Geography'. It was attended by thirty-six geographers from eleven member countries of the IGU, and papers were presented by all of the participants. This volume of essays comprises the revised versions of most of the papers read during the Symposium, together with one paper not read because its author, although intending to come to Cambridge, was unable to do so at the last moment.

We would like to take this opportunity to express our thanks to the following institutions, without whose cooperation and assistance the organization of the Symposium would not have been possible: the International Geographical Union, the British Academy, the British Council, the Department of Geography of the University of Cambridge and Emmanuel College, Cambridge. In addition, we owe our gratitude to Alan Nash, Janet Raper and Charles Withers for their invaluable help with the organization of the Symposium. We also owe warm thanks to the contributors to this volume, for their willing cooperation and patience and to Mark Cleary for compiling the index. As a product of international collaboration in historical geography, this volume will have more than met its aim if it promotes further discussion internationally about the purpose and practice of historical geography.

Cambridge   ALAN R. H. BAKER
Good Friday 1981   MARK BILLINGE

This book is published in association with the International Geographical Union's Working Group on Historical Changes in Spatial Organisation.

PART I

Developments in Historical Geography

Historical geography in Israel: retrospect and prospect

Y. BEN-ARIEH

The term 'historical geography' has been associated with the Holy Land for many decades, thanks to the well-known book by George Adam Smith which he published at the end of the last century.[1] Many other books about the Holy Land–Palestine–Eretz-Israel published in the nineteenth century and the beginning of the twentieth century also contained the term historical geography in their titles. It is surprising, therefore, that the development of historical geography as a sub-discipline in Israel's geographical community had to await the mid-1960s, and that it has only recently acquired any measure of independence. The object of this paper is to trace the development of the term historical geography in what was formerly Palestine, to examine its position within geography in Israel today, and to speculate about its prospects.

Geography behind history

In the foreword to his book, George Adam Smith writes that his object is 'to discover from the "lie of the land" why the history took certain lines'. He refers the reader to A. P. Stanley's important work *Sinai and Palestine*, the preface to which is entitled 'The Connection of Sacred History and Sacred Geography'.[2] He explains his intention to find out how the history of the Holy Land has been affected by its geography. Other scholars of nineteenth-century Palestine expressed similar intentions. When they used the term historical geography, they doubtless had in mind the kind of historical geography that was later to be defined as 'geography behind history'. Such studies used to be associated with physical, environmental, determinism; small wonder, then, that one of the most distinguished exponents of this school, Ellsworth Huntington, when referring to the Holy Land also expressed a clear belief in the impact of climate on its history.[3] This type of historical geography, which had been compatible with the nature of nineteenth-century exploration of Eretz-Israel, was not acceptable in the academic world of the early twentieth century when the country's first university (the Hebrew University) was established in 1925. Instead the term historical geography began to acquire a different meaning among the Israeli historians and archaeologists who started to develop their respective discipines at the university during the British Mandate (1918–48).

Historical topography and toponomy

For archaeologists and historians in Israel the term historical geography is confined to the study of historical topography and toponomy. The Department of Archaeology and the Department of History at the Hebrew University offer courses on topics such as 'the historical geography of Eretz-Israel at the time of the Second Temple', or 'the historical geography of Eretz-Israel at the time of the Crusades'. The substance of these courses is the identification of locations, regions, roads and political boundaries in those periods on the basis of archaeological findings and documentary sources. One of the most distinguished scholars in these subjects, who has written a well-known book on the historical geography of Eretz-Israel in the Hellenistic, Roman and Byzantine periods, opens the preface to his book with the following words:

The very term historical geography indicates that this science touches on the subject-matter of two other sciences, geography and history, which are respectively the science of surface and the science of time; its static geographic part deals with the identification of locations which are mentioned in ancient literature and with the establishment of the boundaries of zones and countries; its dynamic, historical part explains how these facts came into being, and how they changed over time.[4]

This outlook is common to this day also among other historians and archaeologists.[5]

Historical cartography

Following the establishment of the State of Israel, D. H. K. Amiran established the first Department of Geography in Israel at the Hebrew University in Jerusalem in 1950. This remained the only such department throughout the 1950s and most of the 1960s. The first three geography teachers in Israel (Amiran, Schattner and Karmon), who were in this Department, did not call themselves historical geographers, yet a considerable portion of their studies, as well as those of their students, were essentially historico-geographical studies in historical cartography; historical geography of relics from the past; and regional historical geography together with 'changing landscape' studies. The first category includes Y. Schattner's detailed study of the map of Eretz-Israel and its history. There are several other articles on this subject by Schattner,[6] Amiran,[7] and Karmon.[8] This is understandable, since the relation of geography to the cartography of the country was obvious, and the first geographers endeavoured to make their contribution in that direction. The initial tendency in Israeli geography to contribute in the field of cartography was reflected also in the *Atlas of Israel*, and later, the *Atlas of Jerusalem*. But apart from the maps and commentary in the *Atlas of Israel* pertaining to the nineteenth century, and Amiran's essay on the development of Jerusalem 1860–1970 in the supplementary volume to the *Atlas of Jerusalem*, the historical chapters in these two atlases, as well as the maps, were written and arranged by non-geographers. Today Israeli geographers and cartographers do not undertake much historical cartography.

Historical geography of relics from the past

Another kind of research topic which can be related to historical geography and which the first Israeli geographers chose to deal with is the study of relics from the past, notably the traces of ancient agriculture in the Negev. In fact, the very first research project undertaken by the Department of Geography at the Hebrew University in Jerusalem was in this field, and it produced a number of experiments and publications.[9] But as research workers from other disciplines also began to find great interest in this subject, it was gradually abandoned by geographers and passed entirely into the hands of agriculturalists, botanists, archaeologists and hydrologists. Other related subjects investigated by Israeli geographers include the caves and ruins in the area of Bet-Govrin;[10] ancient roads, especially those of the ancient Israeli period and the Roman period; the route followed by the Sons of Israel from Egypt;[11] the remains of agricultural terraces in the mountains[12] and ancient water and agricultural installations.[13] Amiran's attempt to construct a catalogue of all earthquakes that have occurred in the history of Palestine also falls into this category.[14] Research work of this kind is still being conducted by a few Israeli geographers, but on a limited scale. Furthermore, the emphasis has shifted towards biblical geography and, as regards the study of agricultural terraces and installations, to quantitative aspects and cultural facets, and also to the study of the first infiltrations of technology into the country.

Regional historical geography and studies of changing landscapes

Another field of geographical research that flourished in Israel in the late 1950s and early 1960s, and of which historical geography was a prominent component, was that of regional research. An outstanding proportion of the early doctoral dissertations completed in Israel were in this field. The historico-geographical aspect of these works was prominent in two areas: first, the relationship between physical conditions and the way in which the settlement of the region under study had developed throughout the various periods in its history; secondly, changes affecting the settlement landscape of this region during these periods, with special emphasis on the modern era and on changes in the agricultural land uses in different regions. This last subject was especially popular, and in turn prompted the study of rural and agricultural settlements, together with their location and pattern. This kind of study has long ceased to be at the heart of Israeli geographical research, even though there remain a few Israeli geographers who pursue it, particularly in the less well-known parts of the country. It is also important to stress that these studies have been conducted less from the historical viewpoint and more as regional studies set against the geographical conditions which formerly prevailed.

The historical component in contemporary geography

Since the mid-1960s geography in Israel has taken a different direction owing to influences from overseas, particularly Britain and the United States, and the increasing number of geographers and departments of geography in the new Israeli universities. Human geography in Israel has started to concentrate mainly on three elements of research: urban and planning geography; economic and social geography; and continuing research on settlement geography, especially with regard to Arab villages, Beduins, sedentarization and small agricultural settlements. The historical aspect has continued to play a role in all these subjects, but always confined to a preliminary review. In the one case where an attempt was made to include an historical component, the emphasis remained that of urban geography.[15] In the early 1970s several Israeli geographers completed their doctoral dissertations in departments of geography in the United States. Their work emphasized spatial distribution, the diffusion of geographical phenomena and similar subjects. In general, these studies did not deal much with historical matters and those that did failed to tackle them comprehensively. Most of the graduates in question have been absorbed by the new departments of geography in the universities of Haifa and Be'er-Sheva. The emphasis of research completed in Israel during this period shifted towards the contemporary social sciences almost to the exclusion of historical aspects.

The development of specialization in historical geography

Although the historical aspect within research in general geography was in decline, the late 1960s witnessed the emergence of a group of Israeli geographers concerned with the study of historical geography based on primary sources. This group is confined largely to the Hebrew University. The difficulties that the group has encountered in its attempts to take root in the geographical and the general academic community stem from two problems: first, the long and special history of Eretz-Israel (spanning more than 3,000 years and characterized by a lack of national continuity, by a settlement pattern disrupted by wars and by the influx of people varying widely in origin and culture) makes it very difficult for Israeli geographers to penetrate this area of study; secondly, the analytical methods which are required for tackling the data are numerous and varied, and almost beyond the reach of an individual, as they require expertise in archaeology and both ancient and modern oriental and European languages. Israeli historians and archaeologists mostly confine their work to a single period, which means that their knowledge of it is very thorough; the Israeli geographer can only compete with them if he masters, as they do, the sources of the periods in question. However, Israeli historical geography cannot readily confine itself to synchronic geographical studies of successive historical periods. It lacks the requisite manpower. The attempt also seems unjustified given the paucity of the geographical data for many of these periods. Moreover, a student who has gained command of the relevant analytical tools and sources is unlikely to limit himself to geographical studies when he is capable of confronting broader issues and problems. It is similarly the case with the diachronic approaches. The country's history is complicated and such studies risk being attacked as superficial and inaccurate by scholars who have specialized in the various periods. The solution adopted by Israeli historical geographers has been to concentrate mainly on the modern period (the nineteenth and twentieth centuries) and the presentation of the historico-geographical approach to non-geographers.[16]

The concentration of Israeli historical geography on modern times is also justified by the fact that major decisive changes occurred in the country's geography during this period. For many centuries from the time of the Crusades (twelfth century) until the beginning of modern times the country was in a state of almost complete economic stagnation and played a marginal role in the Middle East. At the beginning of the nineteenth century Palestine was a derelict province of the decaying Ottoman Empire with no political importance of its own, a primitive economy, a sparse population with a dismally low standard of living, a few small towns and a neglected road system. In the course of modern times the country went through drastic events which brought a complete change in the country's landscape. The major primary sources of the modern period are written in European languages, beginning with accounts produced by European explorers, scholars, missionaries and travellers who since the beginning of the nineteenth century had constructed the first surveyed maps of the country and left many geographical descriptions of its landscape and people. Western consulates and missions were established at the beginning of that period. Most of their holdings of documentary sources in European languages (especially English, German, French and Russian) can be used today as can books, journals, newspapers and records produced by local inhabitants, particularly since the beginning of Jewish and other European settlement in Eretz-Israel during the second half of the nineteenth century.

Concentration on this period has already yielded some fruitful research,[17] and prompted specialization in historical geography in the Israeli community of geographers. This has also encouraged attempts to expand the scope of systematic historical geography, and even to probe the historical geography of earlier periods.[18] A further obstacle to specialization in historical geography was the objection raised by contemporary geographers to the relevance of and need for such work by geographers. This obstacle has also been removed in recent years by the emphasis on the modern period, the relevance of which to contemporary geography is manifest. In addition one can point to the increasing influence of historical geographers from the American geographic community and elsewhere (Darby, Clark, Meinig, Sopher, Merrens, Mitchell), and the role of the work of the Jerusalem group on academic and scientific circles in Israel. The strengthened position of the historico-geographical group is also evidenced by the fact that other geographers, who hitherto have not engaged in historico-geographical studies, have also begun to take part in historical studies and make an important contribution to their development.[19]

The future of historical geography in Israel

The continued development of research in historical geography seems assured. This research will continue to concentrate on the modern period, though occasionally an effort to study earlier historical periods will doubtless be made by endowing the subject matter with a geographical dimension. The emphasis on the last few centuries will follow the line set in the United States and Canada by the students of Andrew Clark during the last two decades.[20] Five main lines are likely to be pursued in the near future: (a) the analysis of comparatively short periods in depth; (b) the use of primary sources combined with field-work; (c) the application of empirical studies to conservation projects; (d) the development of a general systematic framework from empirical data and its comparison with analogous studies, theories and general models; (e) the exploration of social and cultural subjects.These trends are most evident in theses completed and in preparation.[21] Unlike the first researches in historical geography that were completed by Israeli geographers (and which dealt with historical cartography; geographical relics from the past; relations between physical conditions and human settlements; and settlement surveying based on changes in agricultural land-uses and landscapes) Israeli historical geography is today turning more and more to the cultural and social investigations of historical periods, particularly the modern period, and focuses on the activities of various social groups and the ideas and attitudes behind their activities. Process and behaviour now seem to be at least as important as pattern and location.

Hebrew University,
Jerusalem

Developments in historical geography in Britain in the 1970s

R. A. BUTLIN

Because historical geography is a study of the present about the past, it is necessarily a dynamic discipline wherein the scholar is constantly involved in the reappraisal of both evidence and theory. Since it is written in the present, historical geography can never be purely empirical, while its relationship with the past ensures that it cannot consist in theory alone. No historical work of any calibre can fail to relate evidence to theory, the particular to the general, or the past to the present.[1]

There is no shortage of overviews of trends in historical geography in Britain or of more widely based surveys by British historical geographers,[2] but the time and occasion of an international conference on aspects of historical geography might be deemed appropriate for a review of trends and developments in the subject over a period of nearly ten years in a country where its practitioners (or at least its preachers) appear to be relatively numerous. The review that follows does not necessarily constitute a consensus view – it is an individual appraisal – and is based on the publications in the more obvious journals of both scholarly and substantive articles and also on such historiographically useful sources as conference reports.

Historical geography in the early 1970s

In a sense there were two faces of historical geography in the early 1970s, representing continuity and change. The need for change was seen and expressed very much in the context of the 'new' human geography of the time, that is in terms of the more sophisticated methods of gathering and processing data allied to new computational technology, and of the search for more logical 'scientific' modes of analysis and explanation: the precepts and practices of the locational analysts, the quantitative revolutionaries, the model builders and diffusionists were, to some, the examples to be followed. These notions were articulated in Baker's review of historical geography in Britain in *Progress in Historical Geography*,[3] where he suggested that although progress in this direction had been slow, recently published writings and current research programmes gave grounds for optimism, both in terms of the application of more rigorous statistical analyses and in terms of the application, testing and development of spatial theory. Progress in the use of behavioural and perceptual concepts was, however, felt to be very limited.

The other face of historical geography at the time was the more traditional conventional approach to a series of what were, by and large, tried and largely trusted data sources and landscape features: much painstaking and dedicated work went into the analysis of enclosure maps and awards, the tithe documents, taxation survey, Domesday Book, inventories, crop returns, factory inspectors' reports, village forms, settlement desertion, urban morphology, variations in field systems, and the evolution of various transport systems, for example. Published and unpublished census materials provided a rich quarry for historical geographers. It was appropriate that this emphasis should be reflected in a book entitled *Geographical Interpretations of Historical Sources*, containing a series of essays chosen to illustrate the range of historical source materials that exists, the types of problems that these data present to geographical analysis, and some of the methods that have been employed to overcome these problems.[4] This volume contained some interesting indications of further developments in the postscripts which the authors of the reprinted articles had added to their original articles. One of the principal objectives of the more conventional type of work was the identification and explanation of spatial variations of various features of society, economy and landscape, usually in terms of more overtly geographical factors and in the context of intuitive notions rather than explicitly stated theory. The study of the morphology of landscape was much favoured at all levels, deriving much of its character from Hoskins's seminal book of 1955.[5] The emphasis within British historical geography was on the study of the past geography of *rural* areas: the study group within the Institute of British Geographers most closely identified with historical geography had taken unto itself the title of the Agrarian Landscape Research Group (a vigorous plant which had grown from a seedling planted by the active terminological nurseryman Professor Harold Uhlig of Giessen). The generally rustic predilections of British historical geographers then (and perhaps now) might be explained by the romantic appeal of rural life to the educated mind, the relative lack of quantitative data pertaining to the rural world of the past, and the 'essentially rural' nature of the economy and society of the greater part of Britain up to the eighteenth century. On reflection, one of the more curious aspects of the rural historical geography researched by geographers was, and to some extent still is, the exclusion of the notion of the individual as active actor and contributor to change as opposed to that of the rural dweller as passive respondent to cyclical swings and fluctuations in weather, economic fortune and catastrophe. Virtually no dialogue appeared to take place with rural sociologists and anthropologists, hence, perhaps, the singular lack of concept and theory in rural studies.

The methodological and technical soundings taken tentatively in the early 1970s gathered some momentum in Britain in a relatively short time, and by the mid-1970s had gained a measure of acceptance, particularly in those investigations where rigorous data sampling and testing were involved, yet there was still resistance to these diffusing innovations. In some ways, however, the gathering attractions of the quantitative and methodological revolutions for the traditionally data- or source-orientated historical geographer might be construed as a kind of distraction from other and equally important developments. This point was made by Conzen in 1973:

the sessions amply demonstrated that British historical geographers are keen to experiment with new analytical tools, even if the push seems largely from outside. However, the mechanics of exploiting a data source still seem to command more attention than grand issues of interpretation, a sure sign that the field is still nowhere near maturity.[6]

It was not clear, perhaps, to many historical geographers at the time what the implications of this type of statement were. The attractions of positivist empiricism, of theoretical models and of general systems theory, were obvious, recent and close, as also may have been the distractive though short-lived debates on network analysis and the plight of Zelinsky's wild geese.[7]

The problem of imbalance towards data sources and away from interpretation may have derived from an excessive concentration on the derivation of technical and conceptual ideas from too limited a sphere of the new human geography and from a lack of awareness of important developments in other subjects. Would historical geography have taken a different course in Britain if its practitioners had paid more heed to Piaget's *Structuralism*,[8] to the works of Lévi-Strauss, to Prince's 'imagined and abstract' worlds of the past,[9] to the seminal ideas in Harris's 'Theory and synthesis in historical geography',[10] to the behaviouralists, and to the possibilities of a different kind of human geography offered by the phenomenological, existential and structural perspectives articulated and distilled by Yi-fu Tuan?[11] Such counterfactual speculation may make for interesting debate, but the fact is that even by 1975 there is no evidence of a major shift either towards a more satisfactory mode of explanation or towards a more humanistic bias in British historical geography. In 1973, the year in which David Harvey's *Social Justice and the City* was published, there appeared *A New Historical Geography of England and Wales* edited by H. C. Darby,[12] a notable testament to the traditional synchronic/diachronic approach as evidenced through meticulous scholarship and an attachment to spatial perspective. Other works published in the same year included Baker and Harley's *Man Made the Land*,[13] Baker and Butlin's *Studies of Field Systems in the British Isles*,[14] and Perry's works on nineteenth-century British agriculture;[15] and only one of this group – the field systems book – shows much evidence of a shifting basis of explanation, in the form of an editorial attempt to fit an evolutionary model of field systems to general systems theory. In 1973, 1974 and 1975, while the waves of the new quantitative/neo-classical history became increasingly evident, for example in North and Thomas's *Rise of the Western World* (1973),[16] Floud's *Essays in Quantitative Economic History* (1974)[17] and Parker and Jones's *European Peasants and their Markets* (1975),[18] publications by British historical geographers favoured, on balance, the traditional modes of explanation and such topics as landscape evolution, infield–outfield systems and stage-coach systems. In heightened contrast were Wallerstein's *The Modern World-System* (1974),[19] and Yi-fu Tuan's *Topophilia* (1974)[20] and 'Space and place: humanistic perspective' (1974).[21]

In 1974, however, Gregory sounded a timely warning note of the inadequacy of explanatory structures. Writing of a research conference organized by the now retitled Historical Geography Research Group, he stated that

observers of research conferences in historical geography have been reiterating the same comments for a disconcertingly long time: that a self-conscious imposition and introspection of boundaries of the field is as unbecoming as it is unproductive; that numerate dilettantism is a distraction which results in the framing of explanations within structures which are so narrow that they necessarily appear naive or tangential to other disciplines. Despite so many bugle calls, however, there have been few changes in historical geography.[22]

1975 and after

The lack of response to the bugle calls may have been occasioned by musical deafness or by the overriding and seductive rhythms of the quantitative and positivist schools. However, in 1975 and 1976 there began a change in historical geography in Britain which, though acknowledged by few, was to be of long-term significance. Almost predictably, the stimulus to examine new possibilities for explanatory structures derived from disciplines external to geography; hence the comment by Billinge that

It should no longer surprise the historical geographer to learn that not all the fairies at the bottom of the garden are fellow geographers. Neither is there anything revolutionary or even new in the assertion that geography possesses a number of related and well-endowed neighbours, whose gardens have frequently appeared rather more ordered than our own.[23]

The neighbours he had in mind were the anthropologists, from whom, he suggested, the geographer should be more willing to borrow conceptual tools, and the significant developments, at least for a few historical geographers, for the next few years were those which involved a broadening of interaction with other disciplines. In 1973 Harley had warned of the difficulties of relying on external stimuli without reciprocation: 'An early goal must be that our current rash of plagiarisms – both technical and conceptual – are quickly complemented by a counter flow of ideas and methods generated within historical geography,'[24] and although the initial input to the dialogue which began in the mid-1970s was rather one-sided, at least a dialogue of sorts had begun, and historical geographers were not spending all their time talking to themselves. The most obvious external stimuli were those of sociology and anthropology together with philosophy.

One of the operational difficulties facing historical geographers in this newly developing situation was their training: just as the beneficial effects of the useful statistical techniques of the quantifiers were not felt in historical geography until a new generation of graduate students emerged who had been trained in the new techniques and were able unhesitatingly to apply them in their research, so it was almost certain to be with the newer directions in historical geography. The new 'humanistic' explorations in historical geography involved struggling with the difficult concepts and prose of philosophers, structural anthropologists and sociologists.[25] Yi-fu Tuan, in an article on 'Humanistic Geography', advised that 'It differs from historical geography in emphasizing that people create their own historical myths,' and that 'A humanistic geographer should have training in systematic thought or philosophy. His works serve society essentially by raising its level of consciousness.'[26] This new direction was, however, followed by few: the balance of work published and communicated remained firmly in the positivist mode. In 1975 the new *Journal of Historical Geography* was launched as a vehicle for easier communication among historical geographers, but its articles, with few exceptions, were no more symptomatic of the *avant-garde* than were works published elsewhere: it might even be argued that its appearance merely confirms a view that a safety-in-numbers principle operated for historical geographers, who preferred to publish in convoys in their own journal or multi-author volumes. The state of the art was summarized by Baker in a short book published in 1975,[27] and the way ahead indicated by Gregory in his article 'Rethinking historical geography' published in 1976,[28] but while some historical geographers were looking ahead, while Anne Buttimer was 'grasping the dynamism of life-world'[29] and at a time when Castells's influential *La Question urbaine*[30] was published in its second edition and Raymond Williams's *The Country and the City*[31] was first published, the major books by historical geographers dealt with *The Geography of British Heavy Industry since 1800*,[32] *The Lay Subsidy of 1334*,[33] and *Agrarian Landscape Terms*.[34] Some novelty, at least in technique, was evidenced in the periodical literature, and indicated by the use of computer-processing of Domesday data[35] and work on distance and social interaction in the Victorian City.[36] New perspectives were also provided by Billinge's article 'In search of negativism: phenomenology and historical geography'[37] and by Baker's conference report entitled 'Rhetoric and reality in historical geography'.[38] A closer dialogue with Canadian geographers had proved beneficial, through the first British–Canadian Symposium in Historical Geography, the proceedings of which were published in 1976.[39]

In the last two years, the significance of ideology in historical geography has been an interesting exploration.[40] The notion of a value-free social science of humanity was discarded at least a decade ago by some social scientists, and even longer ago by a handful of Marxist historians, yet historical geographers have tended, albeit unwittingly, to cling to a belief in the sacrosanctity of the objective and scientific study of data. It is this claimed objectivity which has perhaps rendered so uninspiring much of the work of the 'majority' interest in this country, namely rural societies and landscapes, and which heightens the need for alternative procedures and perspectives. Hence, perhaps, the influence of the work of historians like E. P. Thompson[41] and R. H. Hilton,[42] and of anthropologists such as A. Macfarlane.[43] The rapidly growing urban interests of historical geographers in this country may well also in future reflect the influence of urban social historians.[44]

Perhaps the latest phase of interest is in Marxism in which some interest has been belatedly shown by historical geographers in Britain,[45] well behind their British and continental historian counterparts. The appeal of Marxian analysis rests partly in its emphasis on the structure and processes of change and on the lot of the individual in contradistinction to the market allocation principles of the neo-classical economic schools, whose precepts are still adopted by economic historians. It will, however, be some considerable time before there emerges any group of Marxist historical geographers sufficiently well versed in the literature to be able to make any significant contributions to debate.

Conclusion

This selective review has done little more than highlight what for the author have been the significant changes in historical geography in Britain in the last nine years. Stress has been placed on technical, methodological and ideological developments, but the fact remains that as far as the bulk of published work is concerned there is not a great amount of evidence that the new ideas have penetrated very far. Thus, while the attractions of the methods and approaches of social and urban historians, narrative historians such as Richard Cobb, total historians such as Braudel and the members of the French *Annales* school, and of anthropologists and sociologists are frequently advertised and advocated, little of this potential influence has as yet penetrated to the literature. While recent volumes[46] have incorporated the recent work of historical geographers on both rural and, increasingly, on urban and demographic topics, the modes of explanation which they embrace show a lack of consensus. They do indicate that new techniques of data processing have been widely adopted, even though the modes of explanation employed generally show a balance in favour of traditional intuitive and positivist views. The future, however, will almost certainly witness a heavier commitment to the ideological basis of historical geography, to such topics as time and historical geography, urban and industrial societies in the past, and to the continuing investigation of changes in population and community structure, an investigation in which historical geographers in this country have played an important role, noticeably in an interdisciplinary context. New sources must be explored above and beyond the documents, maps and field evidence which have been the mainstays of work in this country. More work and new ideas are badly needed for a clearer picture to emerge of the historical development of Scotland and Wales and, indeed, for many of the regions and regional space-economies of England. Above all, what is badly needed is debate, between geographers and their colleagues from other disciplines and between geographers and geographers, for the literature of British historical geography shows little evidence of passionate debate on critical issues.

Loughborough University of Technology,
England

PART II

Reconstructing Past Geographies

Reconstructing societies in the past: the collective biography of local communities

M. BILLINGE

The underlying premise of this chapter – that the identification and subsequent 'explanation' of spatial order is, in itself, an insufficient permit for the prosecution of historical geography – is scarcely new.[1] Wider familiarity with the rich seams of mainstream historical research, together with a continuing self-education in the fertile language of sociological analysis, has given rise to a refreshingly critical spirit within the sub-discipline which is less easily satisified with the narrowly morphological concerns of ten years ago, or with those expeditious though unexceptional means employed in their achievement.[2] What is perhaps more novel in the current enterprise is the attempt (cursory and inadequate though it doubtless is) to apply these strictures to a particular field of inquiry (urban historical geography), to indicate some of its past preoccupations and finally to offer an alternative prospectus based upon a means of reconstructing historical communities (large or small, spatial or aspatial) which is both more sensitive towards and more reflective of the role of human agency in the skilled accomplishment of historical change. It will be argued, that such an alternative must be capable of revealing in all its complexity and perplexing ambiguity the role of *individuals* and *collectivities* in the purposeful reproduction of the conditions of social life: of recognizing what Giddens[3] terms the *duality of structure* – that position which 'accepts the fundamentally recursive character of social life and expresses the mutual dependence of structure and agency'. For historical geographers of society, this involves at the very least a careful examination of the dialectical relationship between on the one hand the *context* in which historical change occurs (in which social transactions are effected and social resources evaluated and drawn upon) and, on the other hand, the *clientele* whose formulations and actions are most closely associated with the management of those generative practices which have come to be differentially described as either the modernization of urban social structure, or, more accurately, the creation, manifestation and actuation of class

19

consciousness within the city. Since it is the situation and structuration of each which informs and conditions the other, it will be argued that such a *relational* view (of what will be termed *agency* and *structure*) is central to any diacritic theory of urban social change.

Much of the research by historical geographers into communities, classes, institutions and social groupings in the eighteenth- and (more commonly) the nineteenth-century city in Britain has taken as its central concern the identification of residence pattern as evidence of social segregation and by implication community if not class formation.[4] The basis for such differentiation where explicitly examined (it is often tacitly assumed) has normally been ascribed to the tendency of social groups to cluster in areas of particular morphological or locational character and utility, or to the adamantine will of employment groups to identify exclusively with those of their own or similar 'socio-economic' group status, thereby reinforcing within group allegiance through the most basic of geographical mechanisms – residential propinquity. Here, in the splendid isolation of many such locales, each stratum of society offers and experiences the security and mutual support which enclosure reputedly brings by way of the self-sustaining operation of formal, informal and quasi-institutional devices (the pawn shop, credit shop and public house in the case of the working class; the salon, society and *soirée* in the case of the middle and upper strata). Such a view, which accepts the conditioning and proscription of human behaviour by broader and immutable social forces, can of course look to a wide tradition within the canons of social theory, since (circumscribed as it is) its basis is essentially *functionalist* in inspiration, albeit tinged with more than a measure of Parsonian voluntarism.[5]

Even when some sense of the dynamic of urban experience has been evoked, this has on the whole involved little more than a recognition of the breakdown of localized, cellular residence patterns based upon a single factory, a common employer or an institution enjoying spatially restricted patronage (church, chapel, public house, etc.) and the replacement of this detailed mosaic by a broader (and more easily mapped) residential structure painted with the cruder brush of ethnicity, socio-economic rank, decreasing functional heterogeneity, normative marriage paths and the supposedly unimpeachable economic force which unaided by subtler hegemonic mechanisms compels individuals to live (if no longer work) exclusively in the company of others of like mind and common life-style. It is a vague socio-economic vector which impels and predicts each turn of the historical actor, but by all accounts it is an exceptionally powerful and beguiling one.[6] Here the irresistible force ('social change') meets an unexpectedly emasculated moveable object (man as both individual and collective) and the result, if somewhat predictable in these terms, has nevertheless proved of endless fascination to a generation of British urban historical geographers.

The object of such studies and of more recent attempts to calibrate the spatial extent and temporal persistence of particular social areas through concepts as diverse as mean information fields, marriage distances, interaction densities and even rateable values appears to have been, *first*, to establish beyond question the existence of different – mutually repelling – social 'classes' within the city (brought about apparently by the operation of spatial preference factors) and, *secondly*, to trace out changing inter-group relations by recourse to the most immediately apparent though perhaps least satisfactory of mechanisms – spatial rearrangement. Thus the emergence of distinctive classes within the city and the struggle of each to achieve identity, power and legitimacy has been unhappily translated via a series of perilously circular arguments – areas define classes and classes live *de facto* in characteristic social areas – into a tactical analysis of preordained moves on an imaginary urban chessboard upon which square after square is preferentially claimed by one social group or another as the city itself lurches from medieval chaos to modern ecological order. Curiously the authority structures required for even so simplistic a game appear to have been largely unexplored since there seems to have been no commensurate desire on the part of investigators to probe the character and configuration of those 'social rules' the engagement and activation of which necessarily lie at the heart of any putative explanation. On the whole, therefore, the evidence appears to suggest that work conducted within this spirit has remained largely uninformed by articulate theories of social structuration, human agency and class formation, even to the extent that those discussions which addressed themselves specifically to the spread of broad-based socio-economic group relations and the consequent decline of localized community affiliations paid little or no attention to the once burgeoning argument over the implications of the Foster thesis and its charting of working-class politicization, as first local, then revolutionary and finally false sectarian consciousness reputedly moved the aspirations of that sector of nineteenth-century society.

It is of course impossible in a paper of this length to offer a well-rounded and exhaustive critique of recent trends in the writing of urban social geography in Britain. Indeed, the foregoing comments seek merely to highlight one aspect of its less satisfactory development, even at the risk of seeming dismissive of the entire enterprise. However, before passing to other and more constructive issues, one charge against the current 'art' requires forceful expression: above all it has elevated to the level of a problematic the *spatial expression* of class consciousness at the expense of the issues of *class formation* and *class consciousness itself*.

A matter of only three years ago, one author could suggest that: 'Quite when the spatial structure of Victorian cities adjusted to their new class structure is currently the subject of much debate.'[7] It is the contention of the present author that such a statement reflects in microcosm the shortcomings and circumspection of current approaches to the social geography of the city, since it prefers to establish not only the *when* rather than the *how* and the *why*, but equally insists on the primacy of the changing spatial structure (with the class formation implicit or assumed) rather than the centrality of the social dynamic which lay at the heart of the transformation. Such criticisms are not necessarily confined to historical urban geography alone, of course; indeed at least one author has applied similar animadversions in relation to the conduct of urban geographers more generally, arguing that an emphasis on morphological analysis has 'delayed the realisation that towns are inhabited by people' with the consequence that the advent of a distinctly *social* urban geography has been long delayed.[8] Robson subsequently identified the emergence of a newer approach which promised to redress this unfortunate imbalance, at least in part, and which at root comprised a recognition of the importance of three major reorientations: a change in scale from the aggregate to the individual case; a widening of the areas and periods from which the case studies are drawn in order to investigate a greater variety of social conditions; and, more importantly, a conscious incorporation of formal sociological concepts in order to overcome the crudities of geographical theorizing – an observation levelled particularly at the geographers' understanding of class (see below). The opportunities offered by such a programme should not be ignored by those exclusively concerned with the social organization of the city in the past, for the prospectus, like the critique which it implies, deserves the widest recognition. In short, like its broader counterpart, historical urban geography, in maintaining its admirable sensitivity to the morphology of particular places, has failed to be truly social in its investigation of the mechanisms of intentioned social reproduction which underlie the more immediate patterns of perceivable spatial relations. Though the detailed investigation of the latter is by no means inadmissible in itself, as a final object of inquiry it remains circumscribed, and if uninformed by a deep understanding of the former, of dubious explanatory value.

The incorporation of concepts drawn from sociological analysis is not unproblematical, of course, not least because of the need to use the vocabularly and conceptual apparatus involved with due regard for their definitional and contextual integrity. Already in this paper a number of terms of central importance have appeared – class, community, individual, collectivity, institution, action, structure, agency – and their use so far has remained imprecise if not always incorrect. These somewhat inperspicuous terms require more formal treatment if they are to support our endeavour to penetrate fully the continuity of social life in the past and to understand the motivations and outcomes of the historical actor's attempt to rationalize and tranform the society of which he is part, though it would be foolish to attempt such a project here.[9] Certainly the rather casual and infrequent usage of these and similar concepts in the geographical literature to date does not augur well for their future employment.

The term 'class' has had a relatively recent baptism within historical geography, and a serious discussion of the role of both class formation and class struggle in shaping the social accomplishments of the past is long overdue in the sub-discipline.[10] There is much to be learned from E. P. Thompson's insistence that 'Classes do not exist as abstract, platonic categories, but only as men come to *act* in roles determined by class objectives, to *feel* themselves to belong to classes, to define their interests as between themselves and as against other classes' (his emphasis) and that they are emphatically not '. . . heavenly hosts to be marshalled, sent on manoeuvres and marched up and down whole centuries'.[11] Not least there is a need to recognize that classes cannot be uniquely defined, invariably constituted or abstractly conceived either as socio-economic group or as any other context-independent typological category. Class formation, like social structure more generally, does not have independent integrity but exists instead only insofar as agents (knowingly or unknowingly) draw upon it as a set of utilizable resources or procedural practices instantiated in the effectuation of daily life or the accomplishment of specific social actions.[12] Similarly, the class struggle cannot be dismissed simply as a battle for political hegemony impelled by an inalienable *economic* force. More than ever historians are beginning to realize the importance of social and cultural constituents in the creation of the hegemonic and ideological dimensions of class relations – elements not easily reduced to vague geographical notions of neighbourhood type, community infrastructure or area social status. If culture is itself a 'lived hegemony',[13] then the struggle between dominant and subordinate groups necessarily transgresses the boundaries of overt political or economic policy, residing with equal force in the cutural forms of everyday life. In this as in many other senses, then, the characteristics and even the existence of classes and their ideological make-up cannot be assumed or derived from housing type or density surfaces upon a morphological map, any more than they can be defined by the Registrar General's classifications or the guilt by association equations of residential proximity. On the contrary, spatial segregation may have facilitated and perhaps even strengthened the creation of class feeling through the sharp juxtaposition of rich and poor, but the initial forging of group contacts, the establishment of hegemonic and counter-hegemonic forces, the genesis of conflict, the points of orientation and asperity, the formulation of policy through cultural and social as well as economic channels – these require explanation outside the traditional domains of historical geography, where the spatial language has little or no power to speak.

If the concept of class has thus far experienced a brief and somewhat unsatisfactory use within historical geography, then the rather more familiar formulation of *community* (together with that of *institution* which necessarily accompanies it) has scarcely fared better, particularly in urban social research. Without doubt it is the general preoccupation with rural society amongst British historical geographers which has shaped our expectations of the term[14] and led in turn to a remarkably impoverished interpretation of it. The traditional associations of community – as cohesiveness, as naive security, as a small-scale almost familial nexus of supportive emotional relations of the type assumed to dominate the 'unmodernized' rural scene – have generally misled historical geographers in their search for viable units of social organization in the city, suggesting the existence of localized foci which existed *only* to facilitate minor social transactions of largely engendering nature. Such identifiable foci with different degrees and levels of patronage – clubs, societies, churches, institutes – are thus assumed not only to provide the strongest evidence of an area's social character by their style and frequency (that is they are assumed to have *locational* importance) but also to reinforce those characteristics through their routine activities – facilitating marriage contracts, creating the illusion of personal security in the largely unfamiliar and impersonal urban environment, and more generally attending to the routine needs of a narrow-minded depoliticized group which required only diversion and support. Communities through institutions are equally the most immediate point of contact between individuals and their wider social world, though their mediating role at this pivotal juncture is perceived rather narrowly in current geographical formulations as that of administering, directing and even controlling the activities of puppet-like individuals by their efficient transmission of the oppressive strategies generated by 'society' at large.

That such communities and institutions (the importance of which does indeed require emphasis) existed as political instruments designed not simply to maintain the fabric of urban society in its contemporary configuration but often to transform it beyond recognition along those lines espoused by the institution's 'patrons' appears, surprisingly, to have been entirely ignored. Surprisingly, that is, because an investigation into the activities of particular communities in the manner advanced below appears capable of answering the important questions of precisely how local affiliations became transformed into city-wide and even supra-urban *class* consciousness, how individual actors through the medium of collectives change society and, in turn, how and why the spatial structure of the city came to reflect this. An equally surprising shortcoming of current research remains the failure to recognize that some institutions were not the spontaneous invention either of their own clientele, or of the natural 'process' of social evolution, but rather the carefully designed apparatus of other (hegemonic) groups mobilized in an anxious attempt to control and deradicalize the numerous subordinate community factions. Examples of such externally generated institutions are not hard to find, but none demonstrates the ideal or the practice better than that of the mechanics' institute developed by the middle class as a consciously derivative form of their own much-vaunted scientific academy[15] and existing primarily (despite its charitable facade and liberal appeal to self-improvement) to capture first the imagination and subsequently the loyalty of the most articulate and thus potentially most threatening elements of the working class. Here in the mechanics' institutes, with their potentially crucial impact on the artisan elite of Foster's discussions, lay something ideologically far removed from the conventional image of a warm, community-promoting and benign social organism; for if ever an institution was launched with a specific (and perhaps sinister) brief – the political emasculation and social 'rehabilitation' of selected fractions of the working class – then the mechanics' institutes represent such a launching in direct fashion. The tone of the promoters, like the tone of the 'improving' literature they dispensed, is quite unmistakable.

Most communities centred around institutions – whether formal or informal, built or simply 'lived' (see below) – perform functions vital to the continuity not only of the particular social group of which they are the cultural property, but also of society at large. In this way social attitudes, political views, cultural beliefs and the mundane patterns of daily experience – at the same time the lineaments of individuality and the vital cement of community relations – achieve wider recognition and normative *class-based* expression through the power with which cohesive institutionalization endows them. Here the private sensibility of the individual becomes transformed through collectivism into legitimized policy in the public domain, and group ideology itself takes on new meaning as part of the artillery in the struggle for class emancipation: the struggle of subordinates for first counter-hegemonic and eventually hegemonic status.[16] This in turn, married to theories of *action* as well as of *structure*, in the manner advocated by Giddens, provides an important cognitive lead towards the solution of the fundamental problem of how *individuals* in their contributions to the reproduction of specific institutions also change the nature of their (the institutions') personalities and in turn contribute to the reproduction of society more widely. In short, a vital link can be forged between the individual *client* (agency) and the social *context* (structure) in which his actions and transactions take place.

It can now be argued that in addition to those important community sustaining functions already recognized and partly exploited by historical geographers, institutions provide a practical means of relating not only

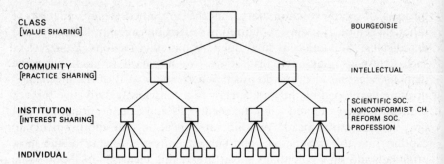

Fig. 1. *Institution, community and social structure: a model for eighteenth-century Britain*

community aspiration to wider class association and *class* aspiration (i.e. they are the focus of power in the class struggle), but also of explaining the mechanisms of class membership recruitment (i.e. they are the foci around which class formation actually takes place). It will be clear that thus far the term 'institution' has enjoyed a double usage, no distinction having been drawn between the *physical* attributes of established institutions (buildings or formalized societies) and the informal attributes – the *constitutive practices* shared by a social group – themselves equally institutional in character. This second sense – institutions as practices, as traditions, customs, conventions, precepts, unwritten rules – though by far the less tangible is by no means the less important. Indeed, in cultural terms, shared convention probably constitutes the strongest motor for social readjustment and change.[17] For the remainder of this essay, however, it is the more formal sense which will be most frequently invoked, simply because this best suits the purposes of the current project, certainly not because it is more important in determining the overall design of social activity.

Thus armed with the triumvirate of concepts briefly outlined – class, community and institution – it is now possible to return formally to the examination of those twin elements of social composition alluded to initially – context and clientele in the eighteenth- and nineteenth-century city (see Fig. 1).

The method of study most appropriate to this type of investigation is that of prosopography, the detailed technicalities of which need not long detain us. According to Laurence Stone, its modern-day advocate, it facilitates 'the investigation of the common background characteristics of a group of actors in history by means of a collective study of their lives', and in employing such a collective biography it becomes possible to establish links between actions and their structural context in a manner somewhat akin to that of the 'multiple career line analysis' of the sociologist.[18] Thus in its ability to establish common patterns within a known interest group it is particularly well suited to the analysis of institutions and the communities which gather around them. Fuller details of an ongoing prosopographical study of the institutions and social milieu of the Manchester community are available elsewhere,[19] and only the broadest indication of the scope of such an investigation will be offered here.

In addition to their contemporary function, institutions provide the historical geographer with a useful *entrée* into the social, cultural and political environment of the past through their membership lists which naturally constitute its *immediate* (though not necessarily complete) clientele. As we shall see, the impact of an institution can be felt (via its members' external social contacts and abilities to instrument institutionally derived policies) outside its elected assembly, though in the initial attempt to cut into patterns of social organization, membership rolls generate the most tangible contact we have with a complete interest group which regularly enjoyed its own company. From the characteristics of such a self-selected and relatively homogeneous group – their occupations, beliefs, connections, policies, resolutions and activities – social reconstruction can begin, first of that community most directly nurtured by the institution itself, and then, through common contact and external relation, of the wider social faction of which the institution's membership is a participant and constituent part. The research issues which can be tackled in this way are numerous, though three of particular interest and utility can be highlighted: the examination of past *social belief*, the characterization of past *social action* and the crucial issue of purposive *social reproduction*.

Though the reconstruction of individual beliefs – social, moral, religious or political – is normally amongst the most difficult (indeed unapproachable) of tasks for the historical geographer, in the case of privatized institutions, the *raisons d'être* of which are either known or discernible, the general difficulties of personal empathism, highlighted by the idealist debate,[20] do not arise. Since contemporaries were equally aware of the credo and liturgy which both underlay and motivated the outward ceremonial of particular institutions, active steps towards membership (as well as continuing membership) can be taken to signify on the one hand an individual's tacit agreement with the views held privately and publicly by the institution and community of which he is member-elect, and on the other hand the individual's own acceptability to other current members. In this way, though only a small and active fraction of any institution's membership may come to our attention other than in name, the public statements, traceable writings, explicit beliefs, constitutional assertions or manifest predilections of the more notable can be taken to represent (on crucial issues at least) the persuasions of the total membership whose fees, attendances or plain silence signify agreement, consent and support. This is of course particularly true of political organizations, though given the nature of all late eighteenth- and early nineteenth-century institutions, most communities, however overtly cultural or dilettante, were deeply political in their divisions over church, state and equity in government.[21] In this way, the beliefs of the passive membership are as known to us as those of the active, and in one such institution – the Manchester Literary and Philosophical Society – its investigable members constitute a sufficiently uniform group in terms of their religious affiliations (Unitarian dissenting); their economic make-up (wealthy manufacturing free-traders); their political colours (Liberal or radical); cultural interest (science, itself a radical call for the rational restructuring of social and political life along meritocratic lines and hence a symbolic structural focus); and immediate fears (the revolution of the working class) for us to be able to define their essential features. Certainly they demarcate themselves easily from the membership of other institutions whose interests lay in diametrically opposed directions; for example the 'aristocratic' faction clustering around the clubs of the metropolis or rural periphery, espousing the cause and legitimacy of wealth, protection, the Old Corruption, Anglicanism, Toryism and the more mannered pursuits of the leisured and perpetually idle.[22] Nor is it merely a case of relying upon public statement to establish private belief – always a dangerous course. Any such connection as societies or their members enjoyed with outside institutions mainly serves to reinforce the picture of a dense web of interconnected, mutually supportive and reciprocally dedicated relationships.

Again, in the case of the Manchester Literary and Philosophical Society, its inauguration in rooms adjacent to the Cross Street Unitarian Chapel and its members' active support and trusteeship of the services, schools and voluntary programmes which dissent spawned stand as testimony to their close association of interests. Indeed the beliefs of the dissenting congregation (similarly opposed to a political system which through the operation of Church and State prevented their active participation in the governance of the nation) not only closely reflect those of the Literary and Philosophical Society's own membership but equally qualify the non-Society Unitarian Chapel members for inclusion in the same class as the electorate of the Philosophical Society itself. Similar ties of a formal and personal kind can be established both with other bourgeois institutions within the city (the Reform Club, Atheneum, Royal Manchester Institution, Statistical Society, etc.) and with ideologically sympathetic institutions outside it (literary and philosophical societies generally, dissenting academies and teaching institutions), as well as with openly Jacobin organizations abroad. In this way a truly national bourgeois class-consciousness was formed (irrespective of 'place') and actively confirmed in its own progressive beliefs as well as in the promotion of social reform along the lines determined by middle-class sensibility. Clearly, therefore, though not every member of one institution was an active member of all others, and though consequently the particular communities generated by each institution frequently overlap but never exactly coincide, the dense network of renewable social contacts within and without societies represented both a utilizable social resource to contemporary political operators, and, from our own point of view, a traceable core-group whose common biographical patterns are sufficiently detailed to allow context-sensitive social reconstruction of a society in active formation. Such information is unrivalled elsewhere, and the position of observation it allows us to adopt is highly privileged by comparison with that of more aggregate documents normally employed in the city-wide reconstruction of social configurations.

Social belief and *social action* are clearly linked in a strong and positive manner. Again, taking the Literary and Philosophical Society as representative of a whole range of investigable institutions, it becomes clear that its corporate membership derived well-defined social policies, the private advocacy of which they were not slow to translate into public activism of a directly purposive kind. Such aspirations included the peaceful overthrow of aristocratic hegemony through financial strength and parliamentary attrition, the promotion of the 'just' (because rational, middle-class and self-made) cause of the stigmatized *nouveaux riches*; the attainment of political power commensurate with economic strength; and the control (social defusing) of the urban proletariat through mechanisms which we have already encountered. In practice actions designed to promote these goals – middle-class advancement and proletarian containment – varied enormously though stealth and subtlety remained the most obvious keynote. In the case of the former task, the social status of the Literary and Philosophical Society membership was steadily increased through a narrowing exclusivity: candidates for national office (the spearhead of middle-class advance) were drilled and tutored via a programme of selection, local sponsorship, regional promotion, metropolitan recognition and maturation in the skills of oratorical technique and political theory. Contemporaneously the prevailing system of oligarchic government was challenged by covertly sponsored national campaigns of a reformist, pamphleteering (and even insurrectionist) stance, and though the Literary and Philosophical Society officially stood apart from such business in a proprietorial sense, its membership, as externally united as it was constitutionally cohesive, unofficially sponsored campaigns designed to bring to fruition the burning middle-class hopes of the day. In the case of the latter – the social and political control of the working class – enormous range and flexibility again characterized the Society's intervention: the foundation of a series of 'containing' intermediate institutions, organizationally a model of the sponsoring body and hierachically determined such that the governing body of a lower institution was always drawn from the most active and trustworthy members of the institution higher up. Such an arrangement ensured both the maximum loyalty of the governors and the most reliable system for telegraphing intelligence to those most able to use it. Equally the system promoted the contrived fragmentation of a growing proletarian consciousness by encouraging petty jealousy, institutional in-fighting and synthetic antagonism between those otherwise tempted by the opportunities of 'combination' and united opposition. Similarly, covert, non-institutional means were employed – the creation of common practices amongst Literary and Philosophical Society members in dealing with the workforce in the factory; schemes to promote self interest and loyalty; to reduce mobility in the hope that long-term employment and indoctrination would counteract the dangerous tendencies displayed by the short-stay operative. Nevertheless it is, yet again, in the coercive institutions that the historical value of such vainglorious bourgeois activity lies, since the creation of an institutional fabric, the rise to prominence of selected members within it (under the much promulgated banner of self-help), and the attempts by renegades to found alternative institutions free from the overbearing influence of artificial middle-class fraternity, afford other and further opportunities for prosopographical analysis in different though equally vital situations. By the second quarter of the nineteenth century, the working class of Gramsci's counter-hegemonic ideal[23] show themselves capable not only of independence, organization and political vision, but also of sculpting the rival architecture of a genuine and indigenous institutional structure. The endurance of these authentic communities has proved vital not only to the contemporary success of organized class struggle but also to the ability of modern-day observers to reconstruct those patterns of belief and action which brought about instrumental change in a period of bewildering complexity.

Yet again the discussion of social action has merely scratched the surface of an exceptionally rich vein, but the point remains that through these and a whole series of similar connections and conjunctions, beliefs either as spoken in debate, recorded in scientific papers, evidenced in membership or simply espoused in routine behaviour, can be closely tied to the subsequent actions expressly designed to bring about their instrumentation. Most importantly it is possible even in so anthropocentric an approach to avoid the normally thorny issues of psychological motivation – of relating generic belief and motivic action – since in the closed ideological community which specific institutions nurture, the presence of one is immediately and unambiguously translatable into the other.

In the question of social reproduction lies perhaps the most problematical issue of the three, and that because it is not merely the reproduction of the individual institution or even its wider though like-minded community which is at stake, but rather the reproduction of society itself, together with the contributions which agents make to the evolution of social forms. It has already been suggested that the relationship between social form and individual action is not a one-way control system reducible to theories of containment or evolutionary adaptation. Rather this essay has tried to argue that any interaction between an individual and his environment is best seen as a dialectical process in which each informs and enables the operation of the other: that is, agents draw upon social structure as a resource, and the actions of agents constitute (though only at moments of instantiation) the structural properties of social organization. These properties may, of course, be different from those subsequently and recursively drawn upon by other agents.[24] As we have seen, in the institutions themselves, continuity and quality of membership was ensured by the election system allied to careful recruitment. The most cursory examination of membership lists (particularly those of the prestigious institutions) will reveal the dominance of particular families both numerically and in the tenure of important directorial offices, so that in the Manchester Literary and Philosophical Society, for example, perhaps fifteen families – themselves linked through intermarriage and outside business or chapel connection – steered the Society through its formative years and bequeathed to subsequent generations its precise social, cultural and political character. These recruitment and marriage programmes were not, however, designed to promote the furtherance of the institution in isolation, nor, as some geographers like to believe, was an institution founded only to ensure intra-class liaison by bringing together (in the manner of a locally franchised Thomas Cook agency) unfortunately remote marriage partners denied a natural courtship by a growing physical mobility. On the contrary, the social reproduction of an institution served primarily to promote the *individual* to prominence, first within its own ranks (the policies of which he could then influence) and, subsequently, with the backing of a peer-group in the politics of society at large. In this way, social institutions whatever their overt purpose provided a means of contact and *entrée* into the organized system of power, whereby individuals could relate first to their own community, next to their own social class, and finally to society generally, in which arena they could with skill and experience understand, manipulate and finally master the art of intentional engagement.

Thus from institutions and communities via social classes to society itself, we can trace the individual and collective life-paths of agents reflexively experiencing the social geography of the urban environment. Of course geographers, with the accumulated expertise of many years, can use such data sources in more traditional ways, plotting the residential patterns of all such institutionally revealed souls. These patterns can themselves be aggregated, analysed and factorially manipulated to reveal social areas, morphological zones and interaction spaces of gripping originality. All this is perfectly feasible and utterly legitimate, but if there is room for such a worthy census-based approach, then there is equally room for a sensitive community-based approach, which recognizing both the dynamics of agency and the duality of social structure, and utilizing (through the techniques of prosopography) the *entrée* afforded by institutions and their generated clienteles, seeks to reconstruct not only the outlines of social pattern but also the lineaments of social reproduction without which no theory of urban change can be even partially fulfilling.

University of Cambridge

Modernization, restoration, preservation: changes in tastes for antique landscapes

H. C. PRINCE

At different periods, people have expressed different attitudes towards old buildings and relict features in the landscape. At times, they have clamoured for modernization, for clearing slums and removing eyesores. At other times, they have appealed for preservation, for saving monuments and protecting so-called 'landscape heritage'. Some people have professed sentimental attachments to the past. The survival of ancient landmarks has given them a sense of security. They have been comforted by the old-fashioned appearance of familiar surroundings. Some people have stated preferences for particular periods. Some have cherished associations with classical antiquity, while others have romanticized gothic, or have spurned all but Middle Pointed Gothic. Some people have valued features as sources of evidence for archaeological and historical study, while others have felt morally bound to pass to future generations all material remains from the past. While some have tried to get rid of past accumulations of grime and rubbish, others have tried sedulously to restore and repair decayed or damaged objects. At different periods, one or two attitudes have been more widely or strongly held than others. People have changed their tastes in modernization, restoration and preservation.

In this essay, I shall illustrate three different attitudes towards historic landscape features in Hertfordshire. Social upheavals preceded all three changes in taste. The Renaissance followed a rise in population, the defeat of feudal lords in the Wars of the Roses, and the confiscation of church property. Tudor statesmen, wealthy lawyers and landed gentry rejected medieval superstitions, revived classical learning and commissioned classical designs for their houses and gardens. After the Civil War and the abolition of divine-right monarchy, a romantic taste for ruins and ancient monuments emerged. Whig aristocrats led the fashion, collecting antiques, patronizing local histories and laying out landscape gardens in a picturesque manner. The industrial revolution and parliamentary reform preceded the dawn of scientific archaeology and the imposition of statutory protection for buildings. The new leaders of taste included university professors, members of parliament, mayors, aldermen and councillors. Those possessing power and wealth set the fashion for others to follow. In all three periods, speculative builders, guided by craftsmen's manuals, copied ornamental details from aristocratic houses. In all three periods, popular tastes in gardening, in sight-seeing, in antiquarianism, in history and in historical biography imitated those of the elite.

Landscapes of the Renaissance, 1540–1680

At the end of the fifteenth century you would have found few venerable landmarks in Hertfordshire. You might have walked the length of the Icknield Way, scrambled over Bronze Age burial mounds, traced the lines of Belgic forts and admired Norman or Early English workmanship in a score of parish churches, but before the sixteenth century none of these relics was cared for or protected as a historic monument. Sacred relics alone were venerated and ecclesiastical buildings alone were magnificently decorated. The grandest secular building constructed in late fifteenth-century Hertfordshire was Bishop Morton's palace at Hatfield. Its hall looks like a barn by contrast with the sumptuous hall in neighbouring Hatfield House, built little more than a century later.

During the sixteenth and seventeenth centuries, a new aristocracy arose. Vested with extensive powers by Tudor monarchs, amassing immense wealth from acquisitions of monastic land, securing privileges through practice in law, they founded estates that were expected to yield incomes to their children and grandchildren, and they designed houses to last for many generations. The new dynasts settled in Middlesex and south Hertfordshire, within half a day's journey from London and Westminster. They also introduced a new style of building. Primitive Hertfordshire vernacular succumbed to the refined accents of reinaissance Italy and the Low Countries. Timber and thatch were banished. Walls were built of brick and faced with stone. Roofs were tiled, gutters were wrought in lead or iron and interiors were lit by large glazed windows. Builders and patrons proclaimed their membership of a civilized elite by decking their houses with classical ornaments.

The new rulers cut their ties with the immediate past. They seized power from feudal lords and demilitarized Norman castles. They took control of the church from Rome and pulled down hundreds of monasteries. They invested newly gained wealth to clear woods, to drain marshes, to reclaim heaths, to sink coal pits, to reorganize iron and woollen cloth manufacturing and to venture into overseas trade. Renaissance scholarship inspired them and opened their minds to useful knowledge. Not only professors, but courtiers, clergymen, and gentry wrote scholarly treatises, used Latin syntax, applied the canons of Greek philosophy to science and politics, observed Euclidean principles in geometry and adhered to classical orders in architecture. Through a deep understanding of classical antiquity they discovered keys to power in the present and means of anticipating the future. A knowledge of history was not only a qualification for entry to the ruling class, it also provided material for popular entertainments and private recreations. Playwrights assumed that their audiences would recognize allusions to Greek and Roman myths and would be familiar with events in ancient history.

Many people, educated in grammar schools and in newly founded colleges at Oxford and Cambridge, began to study and copy antique objects. In the 1540s, Henry VIII's Treasurer, Sir John Cuttes, built Salisbury Hall, a moated manor house near Shenley. The exterior is more traditional than modern, but the hallway is adorned with large medallions of Roman emperors, faithfully imitating Roman low-reliefs.[1] In 1564, Queen Elizabeth's Secretary, Sir William Cecil, built Theobalds near Cheshunt, a palace richly decorated with classical columns, arches and pediments. Four years later, Cecil's brother-in-law, the Lord Keeper, Sir Nicholas Bacon, built Gornhambury near St Albans, a mansion with octagonal turrets at the corners of the main front. A highly ornate classical porch carried Ionic and Tuscan columns, inlaid marble panels and Roman figures in the niches. About 1575, local gentry, the Capels, added to a late medieval gatehouse at Hadham Hall symmetrical brick wings of classical proportions. In the early seventeenth century, Hatfield, Cassiobury and other splendid houses built by successful lawyers and rising gentry were sumptuously furnished with classical ornaments.

Gardens as well as houses were designed on regular, symmetrical lines observing classical rules of proportion. The earliest formal gardens were small. That at Theobalds, laid out in the 1580s, was larger than most, containing nine compartments, a fountain at the centre, canals, a banqueting house, busts of Roman emperors and a labyrinth of Venus.[2] At Hatfield, the Pondyard and Vineyard, laid out around 1610, covered no more than twenty acres. In 1625, Francis Bacon considered thirty acres a proper size for a princely garden. He drew his account of an arbour, a mount and pleached alleys from his own water garden at Gornhambury. In the 1630s, at Little Hadham, Sir Arthur Capel created a miniature Italianate garden embellished with fountains and statuary. Later in the century, Sir William Temple praised the epicurean garden at Moor Park as 'the perfectest Figure of a Garden I ever saw'.[3] He particularly admired the disposition of two terraces cut into the slope of a hill and applauded the arrangement of walks, parterres and grotto. These designs reflected faintly and remotely the magnificent Italian renaissance gardens of the Vatican Belvedere, of the Villa d'Este and of the Pratolino.

Renaissance patrons borrowed liberally from history but from a narrowly selected period of history. Medieval art was despised and neglected. Some welcomed the destruction of monasteries and the dispersal of medieval libraries as a means of purging the country of graven images and erroneous doctrines. Elizabethan scholars cautiously began to acknowledge the value of studying medieval history and began to appreciate the importance of materials that had survived. Long after historians rediscovered the richness and variety of medieval thought, prejudice against medieval art persisted. In 1697, the diarist John Evelyn scorned gothic 'congestions of heavy, dark, melancholy and *Monkish Piles*', with 'slender and misquine *Pillars* . . . ponderous arched Roofs . . . sharp *Angles, Jetties,* narrow *Lights,* lame *Statues, Lace* and other *Cut-Work* and *Crinkle-Crankle*'. Gothic forms were already returning to favour when Evelyn wrote, but echoes of that derogatory attitude were heard as late as 1771, when Smollett's old-fashioned Mr Bramble complained: 'The external appearance of an old cathedral cannot but be displeasing to the eye of every man who has any idea of propriety and proportion.'[4] Renaissance critics not only turned a blind eye towards medieval art, but they showed little respect for wild scenery. Mountains, moors, heaths and marshes were not counted as assets in a tally of Britain's landscape heritage. They wanted discipline and domestication. They cried out loudly for agricultural improvement. Their earlier histories were unedifying and best forgotten.

The dreams of renaissance aristocrats were rudely shattered. Dynasties set up to rule for ever toppled as fast as one monarch succeeded another or as fast as one set of favourites was ousted to make room for others. Even bishops and judges were unseated when doctrine and constitution were amended. When the King himself was beheaded in 1649, the illusion of permanence finally vanished. During the Civil War houses belonging to both sides were demolished. Royalists sacked Ashridge and drove deer out of the park, while Parliamentarians allowed their soldiery to pull down Theobalds and carry away the stones. Thomas Fuller commented that 'from the seat of a monarch it is now become a little commonwealth; so many entire tenements, like splinters, have flown out of the materials thereof. Thus our fathers saw it built, we behold it unbuilt.'[5] At the same time, many fine old trees were chopped down in the park, and great quantities of wood and timber were removed from Enfield Chase. By the end of the seventeenth century, no fewer than 353 out of 395 Hertfordshire manors had passed out of the hands of the families who owned them in 1540. Only 42 manors remained in possession of the same families throughout that turbulent century and a half. The fortunes of families in the sixteenth and seventeenth centuries were every bit as unstable and ephemeral as those of their medieval predecessors.

The dream of reviving a golden age of classical humanism also failed to materialize. Elizabethan and Jacobean mansions were encrusted like wedding cakes with decorative details from classical architecture but plans and elevations of sixteenth-century buildings in Hertfordshire bore no resemblance to Roman buildings, nor even to Italian renaissance buildings. The first British architect to build a correctly proportioned renaissance villa was Inigo Jones who learnt this craft sketching stage sets for royal masques. In 1616 he designed Queen's House at Greenwich, and in 1619 he started work on a Banqueting Hall in Whitehall which was intended to form a part of a full-sized renaissance palace. The Whitehall scheme remained unfinished, and Inigo Jones turned his mind to planning a layout for an arcaded piazza and a Doric temple on the Earl of Bedford's estate at Covent Garden.[6] These efforts made little impact on the appearance of the English landscape. Indeed, the Renaissance was more remarkable for the destruction of historic monuments than for their revival. Apart from wholesale demolition of medieval structures, sections of London's Roman wall were plundered for stone and parliamentarian cannons bombarded Roman masonry in the walls of Colchester castle. Renaissance architects hoped to dispel the darkness of the middle ages by letting in the light of ancient Greece and Rome, declaring that 'light is cheerful and cheerfulness is the disposition of innocence'.[7] But their achievements fell short of their expectations.

While the new elite failed to establish lasting dynasties, heralds, genealogists and local historians succeeded in ramifying aristocratic lineages and tracing the descent of manors. While the new elite failed to impose their ideas of classical order on the landscape, antiquaries, topographers and mapmakers explored and delineated in great detail the geography and antiquities of Britain. Following the appearance in 1540 of John Leland's *Itinerary*, a systematic search for ancient relics began. Leland was guided on his travels by accounts of classical authors and by medieval chroniclers. He overlooked Stonehenge and monuments of prehistory. William Camden's *Britannia* (1586) not only examined prehistoric as well as historic features but investigated coins, inscriptions and place-names in addition to literary evidence. Camden opened a new field of historical inquiry and his work, translated into English and edited by later scholars, held a leading place among topographical studies for over two centuries. But Stuart Piggott reminds us that 'we have to wait until after the Civil War before we really see the beginning of antiquarianism of the kind which was then to persist well into the nineteenth century'.[8] In the second half of the seventeenth century, John Aubrey, Elias Ashmole, Robert Plot and William Dugdale made remarkable discoveries in England while Edward Lhwyd and Robert Sibbald charted Celtic orgins in Wales and Scotland. Anthony Wood, an associate of John Aubrey, complained that the fellows of Merton at Oxford 'Would not let me live in the College for fear that I should pluck it down to search after Antiquities'.[9] Seven-teenth-century antiquaries almost literally opened the eyes of educated people to the history of stones, tracks, burial places and fields around them. It was a great awakening. Sir Henry Chauncy's *History of Hertford-shire* (1700) full of antiquarian finds and renaissance speculation probably made a deeper impact on men's minds than the ostentatious houses and gardens built by Cecils, Bacons and Capels.

Romantic antiquity, 1680–1830

In the middle decades of the seventeenth-century, the material gains of the previous century were lost. Population was stricken by plague and by a succession of deadly epidemics, the Civil War was followed by Dutch wars, two-thirds of London was burned down and market places in provincial towns were less busy than they had been in Elizabethan times. Confidence gradually returned after the restoration of Charles II. A yearning for classical order and prosperity prevailed over medieval chaos and scarcity. Building resumed in the grand manner and extensive agricultural improve-ments were undertaken. Ralph Freeman of Aspenden, son of a London merchant, was acclaimed a shining example among seventeenth-century country gentlemen for having 'made his House neat, his Gardens pleasant, his Groves delicious, his Children chearful, his Servants easie, and kept excellent Order in his Family: He has general insight in Architecture and Husbandry.'[10] Travellers rejoiced at the regularity and, above all, at the luxuriance of the new landscapes. They sang the praises of Ceres, Pomona and Flora for bestowing abundant crops upon well-cultivated fields. On a clear day around 1725, Daniel Defoe accompanied by two foreign visitors looked down from the heights of Bushey into the vale of St Albans. There they observed 'the inclos'd corn fields made one grand parterre, the thick planted Hedgerows, like a Wilderness of Labyrinth divided in Espaliers; the villages interspers'd looked like so many noble seats of gentleman at a distance. In a word, it was all nature and yet look'd all art.'[11] A multitude of settlements and small fields, tended with garden-like neatness, filled the whole length of the vale. In the Chiltern Hills, the fields were less regularly shaped and hedges were deeper. William Ellis, a farmer at Little Gaddes-den in the early years of the eighteenth century, characterized the Chilterns as a wood and pasture district by contrast with the vale of Aylesbury which, at that time, was predominantly arable. The entire county was being partitioned among fat and fertile farms.

Amid scenes of orderly cultivation and plodding industry, a new generation of topographers scanned the countryside for visible reminders of primitive disorder and eye-catching relics. Among the first antiquaries to take a romantic view of ruins was Anthony Wood, who in 1657 at

Eynsham was 'wonderfully strucken with veneration of the stately, yet much lamented ruins of the abbey'. At that spot he 'spent some time with a melancholy delight taking a prospect'. In 1708, the young William Stukeley 'frequently took a walk to sigh over the ruins of Barnwell Abbey . . . lamenting the destruction of so noble monuments of the Piety and Magnificence of our Ancestors'.[12] In the eighteenth century, observers delighted in the decadent allure of crumbling mossy stonework. They wallowed in the sadness of ruins reflected in silent pools, and they thrilled at the sight of broken arches or dark towers outlined against an evening sky. They regarded utilitarian, working landscapes as insipid and disgusting. Romantic scenes held them in suspense and played on their feelings. The Buck brothers, James Thomson, John Dyer, the young Thomas Gray, Elizabeth Montagu, Mrs Delany and a host of others turned topography into poetry, while painters made antiquity picturesque.

The objects of pictorial composition and poetic effusion were now jealously guarded as precious relics. At the site of Roman Verulamium, Stukeley complained that at the beginning of the eighteenth century, diggers hauled away 'hundreds of cartloads of Roman bricks' for road-making, but a few years later the unearthing of a tessellated pavement was greeted as a major discovery. Excavators went on to uncover parts of the outer ditch, wall, towers and gateway of the Roman city. At Braughing, remains of a Roman villa were found, and ancient coins and pottery were collected from many different sites. While few relics were thrown away, many were heavily restored or turned into picturesque objects. The shell of the Norman castle at Hertford was gothicized in 1800, and at Benington Lordship a Neo-Norman fantasy was fabricated to match the keep of Benington Castle.[13] At Berkhamsted, the London and Birmingham railway line was diverted across a marshy valley floor to avoid breaking through the historic ramparts of Berkhamsted castle.

Eighteenth-century architects followed closely the patterns of Palladio and Vitruvius. English Palladian villas were identical with their Italian counterparts. The rules of proportion were strictly observed, but within the rules architects and patrons entered freely into the spirit of classicism.[14] People acted parts in a classical charade. Philosophers engaged in imaginary conversations with Horace and Cicero, guide books propagated largely fictitious accounts of the Roman histories of Bath and Hadrian's Wall. Upon the ashes of a village in Dorset, the Duke of Marlborough conjured a Roman market place named Blandford Forum. Another lord, whose property included part of the site of Roman Verulamium, styled himself 'Verulam'. The promotion of agricultural knowledge was carried out by Georgical Societies and the ancient universities created Senate Houses to deliberate on academic matters. Eighteenth-century Englishmen lived in a partly make-believe classical world.

A taste for ruins kept dozens of learned antiquarians fully occupied, but the demand for picturesque towers and follies far exceeded the supply of genuine antiquities and stretched the powers of imagination of the least scrupulous scholars. Builders and landscape gardeners were called in to make good the deficiencies by contriving sham castles and abbeys and stone circles. At Gobions, Brookmans Park, among features considered by Horace Walpole to 'indicate strongly the dawn of modern taste', is a gothick arch supported by square castellated towers. The house was designed by James Gibb and the grounds were by Charles Bridgeman, either of whom might have planned the arch. At St Pauls Walden Bury a flint pyramid and possibly also a grotto were constructed in the 1760s, and in 1770 at Ware, John Scott, a Quaker poet, dug a many-chambered grotto which displays 'the true morbidity of the less patrician labyrinth builders'.[15] At the end of the century, a Quaker builder ornamented the grounds of his house at Hoddesdon with charming gothick screens, gates, buttery, pergola, bath-house, orangery and grotto. At about the same time, George Thellusson M. P. put together some fragments of a sham gothick ruin which he dubbed Aldenham Abbey. Hertfordshire is without megalithic follies or cast-off ruins removed to parkland resting places, but it received Temple Bar removed from the City of London.

Late eighteenth- and early nineteenth-century architects built in a wide variety of antique styles. At Ashridge, James Wyatt indulged in the most exuberant mock Perpendicular, furnishing the chapel with a fan-vaulted ceiling, an appropriate accompaniment to Humphry Repton's Monks' Garden.[16] Repton's Cassiobury Park, in addition to a Tudor gatehouse, featured a Swiss cottage to house a lock-keeper on the Grand Union Canal. The Mimram valley, exquisitely landscaped by Repton, formed an enchanting sylvan setting for four otherwise unremarkable Regency houses. The most original, Marden Hill, was ennobled by Sir John Soane's graceful Ionic entrance porch. A huge Ionic portico dominated the garden front of Digswell House. Tewin Water House was elegantly Grecian, whilst Panshanger was romantically gothick. Towns exhibited as much architectural diversity as the country. St Albans, for example, possesses some of Hertfordshire's most handsome, brick-built Georgian town houses, a solid, plainly stuccoed Grecian town hall, built in 1829 by George Smith, a gothick almshouse, a colonial-style chapel and, next door to Regency shops, some early nineteenth-century mock Tudor decorations.

Eighteenth-century householders and shopkeepers treated historic buildings in a free and easy manner. They pulled down, restored, converted and adapted old structures to new uses. They altered exterior faces of buildings as architectural fashions changed. Well-to-do tradesmen proudly stuck Georgian brick fronts on sixteenth-century timber-framed houses, and scholarly clergymen did not hesitate to remove medieval screens, choir-stalls, baroque tombs and other impedimenta in order to release a sense of lofty spaciousness, uniting nave and transept. If a belfry were unsound, the tower might be rebuilt in Wyatt's free-style gothick, and if a rustic porch collapsed a stone structure might be put up in its place. The fabric of a historic building would be renewed without embarrassment as long as a feeling for the past remained. Some artfully contrived additions served to heighten the historic atmosphere of a place. An eighteenth-century observer judged a restoration to be in correct taste if it evoked the spirit of the past, no matter how poorly it reproduced the original design or materials. A flight of imagination was nobler than slavish imitation.

The past for its own sake, from 1830

A revolution in taste accompanied the industrial revolution. The actual, measurable present was considered more precious than an insubstantial, imagined past. Realism replaced romance and utility surpassed beauty. The study of history was confined to an examination and verification of material remains from the past. Periods from which few objects or inscriptions had survived were regarded as dark ages. Eighteenth-century inventiveness was condemned as fraudulent.

Dissatisfaction with imaginative reproduction of historic relics and other artifices was first intimated in polite philosophical discussions between landscape gardeners, in William Mason's *An Heroic Epistle to Sir William Chambers* (1773) and in correspondence between Richard Payne Knight, Uvedale Price and Humphry Repton. In *Sense and Sensibility*, Jane Austen allows her heroine gently to chide the arbiters of taste by remarking that 'admiration of landscape scenery has become mere jargon. Everybody pretends to feel and tries to describe it with the taste and elegance of him who first defined what picturesque beauty was.' In 1795, John Carter called for an immediate stop to Wyatt's commissions, so that he might be prevented 'from effacing the still remaining unaltered Trails of our ancient Magnificence which are but faintly to be imitated and perhaps never to be equalled'.[17] Carter protested, in the name of truth, that no substitutes for genuine antiques could be invented. He was the first writer to raise a moral objection to the fabrication of antiquities.

The quest for truth took a different turn in the minds of a group of high Anglicans. The Cambridge Camden Society, founded in 1839 by two undergraduates, John Neale and Benjamin Webb, sought to revive the rituals of medieval worship, separating the priest from congregation by erecting a screen between nave and chancel. They planned to restore the interiors of churches to the pure forms of fourteenth-century Middle Pointed Gothic. In 1845, a Camdenian writing in the *Ecclesiologist* had 'no hesitation in urging the propriety of entirely removing late clerestories and restoring roofs to the form they undoubtedly had when the earlier arcades of the nave were built.'[18] These early Victorian purists claimed the right to convert, restore, and ultimately, to destroy features they disapproved of. They justified their actions by asserting that the Middle Pointed represented the apex of spiritual achievement, that earlier medieval forms were crude and imperfect and that later forms were debased and decadent. In the second half of the nineteenth century, the restorer's licence to alter was revoked.

In 1849, John Ruskin denounced the practice of restoration as 'a Lie from beginning to end'. He decreed that 'it is no question of expediency or feeling whether we shall preserve the buildings of past times or not. *We have no right whatever to touch them*. They are not ours. They belong to those who built them and partly to all the generations of mankind who are to follow us.'[19] Ruskin's call for an end to restoration was endorsed by the Society of Antiquaries. In 1855 the executive committee of the Society recommended that 'no restoration should ever be attempted otherwise than . . . in the sense of preservation from further injuries. . . . Anything beyond this is untrue to Art, unjustifiable in taste, destructive in practice and wholly opposed to the judgement of the best Archaeologists.'[20] Art historians, archaeologists and high church zealots saw the truth from different angles.

During the middle years of Queen Victoria's reign, high churchmen gained power and financial support from middle-class laymen. For nearly a quarter of a century after Ruskin's proclamation, they continued to restore churches in gothic revival style with unabated enthusiasm. On 5 March 1877, a letter to the *Atheneum* from William Morris raised the issue in a sharper manner. Having learned that Tewkesbury Abbey was about to be 'destroyed' by Sir George Gilbert Scott, Morris called for an association 'to keep watch on old monuments, to protect against all "restoration" that means more than keeping out wind and weather, and by all means, literary or other, to awaken a feeling that our ancient buildings are not mere ecclesiastical toys, but sacred monuments of the nation's growth and hope'.[21] Morris borrowed the words Ruskin had used, yet achieved an entirely different result. Otherworldly churchmen were swept away by a rising tide of rationalism, liberalism, materialism and Darwinism. Vestiges of the past gained new value as sources of evidence for evolution and as tokens of mankind's progress. Bourgeois intellectuals responded immediately to Morris's appeal. Within a few days, many influential historians, painters and a few architects joined the newly formed Society for the Protection of Ancient Buildings. Later in the year, J. J. Stevenson carried the attack into the lecture hall of the Royal Institute of British Architects. He declared: 'It is a delusion of restorers that their new work, because it is correctly medieval in style, is of any historical value.'[22] Whilst

Morris was primarily interested in saving medieval buildings, he objected to the destruction of seven of Wren's city churches on the grounds that they formed 'a distinct link in the history of ecclesiastical art of this country'. All medieval buildings were sacrosanct, and in the course of time, official recognition and protection were extended to Tudor, Stuart, Georgian and Regency buildings.

Since 1882, successive Ancient Monuments Protection Acts and Historic Buildings Acts have widened the powers of central and local authorities to survey, purchase and protect ancient monuments. The law now enshrines John Ruskin's and William Morris's principle that the public has an overriding interest in the preservation of historic buildings. Their present occupiers are regarded as 'only trustees for those who come after us'. Listed buildings may be mended and maintained but permission to alter or convert them is difficult to obtain. In practice, an insistence by planning authorities that listed buildings be kept exactly as they are has deterred some owners from carrying out essential repairs and modernizing them.

University College London,
England

Reconstructing Old Prussian landscapes, with special reference to spatial organization

H. JAEGER

Spatial organization by social groups such as tribes, or political institutions such as states, is relevant for the understanding of many historico-geographical functions and processes. A fundamental basis of many spatial organizations is administration, which is often neglected by geographers. In Europe, for want of documents, there are not many landscapes which provide an opportunity to study the development of the political organization of space from prehistoric times to the present. Old Prussia is one of the few regions which might allow such work.

The basis of my essay is the *Historisch-geographischer Atlas des Preußenlandes*,[1] which belongs to a series of great regional atlases of the Federal Republic of Germany. I shall try to illustrate by examples what the maps of that atlas in combination with available sources, books[2] and articles could offer to their users in respect to spatial organization.

The Preußenland comprises the former state of the Knights of the German (or Teutonic) Order, the subsequent Duchy of Prussia and later province of East Prussia, as well as those parts of the former kingdom of Poland that emerged from the state of the German Order (see Fig. 1 and note 16). The documents of the former record office of Koenigsberg, now belonging to the Stiftung Preußischer Kulturbesitz in West Berlin, provide the dates for most of the maps of this atlas. Beginning with the Order's first activities in the thirteenth century, the maps present cross-sectional views of the area at various significant dates. These maps, in connection with and in comparison to a remarkable series of printed records[3] and chronicles,[4] provide us with a valuable basis for further studies. As most of the maps are published on a scale of 1: 300,000 they provide much detailed information, valuable for further research work. An atlas of this type is both a record and an instrument of research.

Studies of landscape history of Old Prussia[5] might be of general interest, because in a region without even the smallest Roman influence there existed until the invasion of the Order in the thirteenth century a tribal society combined with a spatial arrangement which is directly comparable to that found in the regions between the Elbe and Oder in the eighth and tenth centuries and to the land even further westward in pre-Roman times. In those lands west of the Vistula the characteristics of such early landscapes are less well known and documented because in the West the change from prehistory to history happened far earlier, while the Order on the other hand had a developed literacy. Even the spatial organization of Iron Age Britain or Iron Age and early medieval Ireland might be illuminated by comparative Prussian evidence.

In Old Prussia the transition from prehistory to history took place as a result of the conquest of the land by the Knights of the German Order starting in 1231 near the later town of Thorn.[6] As this conquest occurred in an epoch characterized by abundant documentation by the Crusaders, the spatial organization of the prehistoric tribes within ancient Pruzzian society have been brought to light with rare clarity. Pruzze and Pruzzian are names relating to the Baltic tribe which formed the indigenous population of Old Prussia. The Pruzzians in this sense have been akin to the Lithuanians and Letts. As these and some Slavonic territories in their early history had similar features in their territorial organization[7] we may look at Old Prussia as a general example of prehistoric society in Europe.

Spatial organization implies control over territory, and this is not possible without the mental and administrative division of land into different districts, for which purpose one needs names. Therefore we have to deal with names of lands and landscapes. In early times there was a close connection between names of peoples and lands. Nearly all the names of the Old Prussian landscape, which are shown in a map of our atlas,[8] are derived from the names of the tibes who inhabited these areas. Fig. 1 is based on that map. The 'terre Prussie', as it is recorded around 1288/1326 by Peter of Dusburg,[9] consisted of the 'terra Colmensis et Lubovia' and ten tribal 'terrae'; for example in Pomesania there lived the Pomesani, in Pogesania the Pogesani, in Warmia the Warmienses and so on (see Fig. 2). Peter of Dusburg's record is incomplete as a number of additional tribal 'terrae' are known (see Fig. 1). Each tribal 'terra' consisted of a smaller or larger number of 'territoria', sometimes also called 'districtus' in Latin documents and 'Gebiete' in German ones. Each 'territorium' had a castle with a nobleman (occasionally called 'rex'), so that in German research it is called 'Burgherrschaft'.[10] One is reminded of the territorial organization of Ireland in the seventh and eighth centuries, with its at least 150 small local kingdoms.[11] Smaller spatial units in Pruzzia generally had been the 'moter' (Pruzzian word), likewise with a castle and a few settlements, sometimes surrounded by woodland ('Burggau' in German). The smallest units or cells of the Pruzzian landscapes had been the 'campus', in Pruzzian 'lauks', in German 'feld' or 'gefilde'. All 'fields' had some grassland, most had

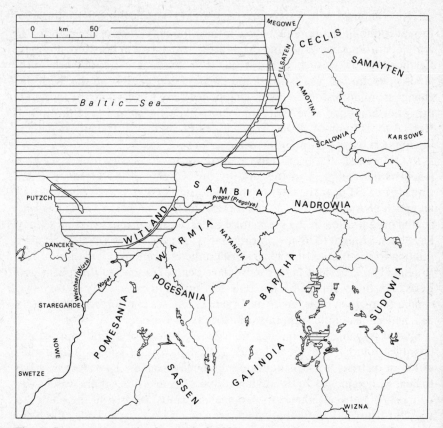

Fig. 1. *Prussian terrae (landscapes), c. 1230*

arable and/or small villages, hamlets or dispersed farmsteads.[12] The scheme of Fig. 2, representing the spatial organization of Old Prussia, can only be a generalization of the former reality which was less systematic. Though by modern standards the geographical terminology of the medieval sources is inexact, nevertheless the chief features of the former territorial organization are revealed by comparing different sources and their context in combination with maps.

From 1231 until 1283 the Knights of the German Order conquered the whole of Pruzzia and established a completely new administrative organization for its sovereignty, offices and types of administrative centres and castles. But in the first phase at least the territorial arrangements of the Order partly followed the older one of the Pruzzians, though with a more structured and systematic administration as well as the laying out of large

Tribal terrae[1] about 1230	Pomesania	Pogesania	Warmia	Nattangia	Sambia	Nadrowia	Scalowia	Sudowia	Galindia	Bartha
					TERRA PRUZZIA					
tribes[1]	Pomesani	Pogesani	Warmienses	Nattangi	Sambite	Nadrowite	Scalowite	Sudowite	Galindite	Barthi

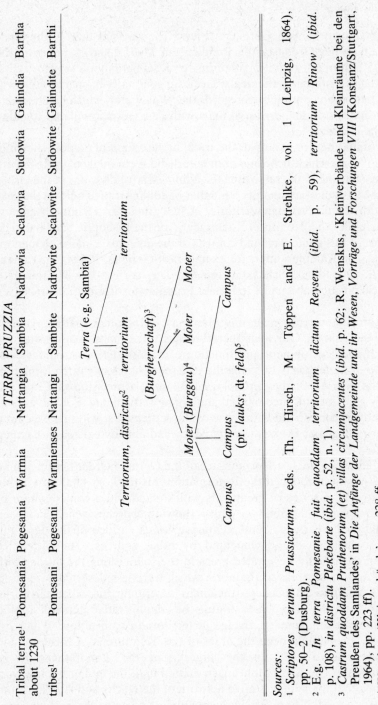

Fig. 2. *Spatial organization of a prehistoric society, exemplified by Old Prussia*

Sources:

[1] *Scriptores rerum Prussicarum*, eds. Th. Hirsch, M. Töppen and E. Strehlke, vol. 1 (Leipzig, 1864), pp. 50–2 (Dusburg).

[2] E.g. *In terra Pomesanie fuit quoddam territorium dictum Reysen (ibid. p. 59), territorium Rinow (ibid. p. 108), in districtu Plekebarte (ibid. p. 52, n. 1).*

[3] *Castrum quoddam Pruthenorum (et) villas circumjacentes (ibid. p. 62;* R. Wenskus, 'Kleinverbände und Kleinräume bei den Preußen des Samlandes' in *Die Anfänge der Landgemeinde und ihr Wesen, Vorträge und Forschungen VIII* (Konstanz/Stuttgart, 1964), pp. 223 ff).

[4] Wenskus, 'Kleinverbände', pp. 228 ff.

[5] *Ibid.* pp. 237 ff.

villages and towns with German settlers. The relevant map in the atlas, 'Verwaltung des Ordenslandes Preußen um 1400,'[13] shows mainly in the older 'Komturein' and the subordinate 'Kammerämter', which at first consisted of Pruzzian settlements, a certain continuity of spatial organization. There is no continuity as regards the 'Waldämter' which had been big forest estates or later territorial units with new German villages founded after the clearance of woodland.

By comparing, for example, the tribal organization of Sambia shown in the map 'vorgeschichtliche und mittelalterliche Wehranlagen' (note 8) with the map showing in the same area the administrative divisions of the Order around 1400[14] one can identify a number of administrative units in the year 1400 with certain Pruzzian territories of 1230; thus 'terra Sambia' had now become either the 'Komturei Koenigsberg' or the Bishopric Samland. The first part of this name Samland consists of the main place-name element of Sambia. The Kammerämter, for example, of Germau, Pobethen, Rudau, Wargen, Quendnau, Schaaken and Waldau, correspond in their geographical position and name to former Pruzzian 'territoria' or districts (see Fig. 3).

In European territories an important part of the older spatial organization is the church. Our atlas therefore has three maps dealing with the distribution, development and function of ecclesiastical institutions.[15] In the map of Lieferung 3, showing the different phases of church formation since the year 1230, the chronology is of such a precision that one can identify areas of old, medium-old and young settlements. For the ages of the churches correspond with those of the settlements, with the exception of many villages of Pruzzian origin which had already existed in heathen times.

In 1525, when the last Hochmeister of the German Order became Duke of Prussia and introduced the Reformation, his territory had been highly devastated by a series of great wars with Poland and a confederation of Prussian towns and nobility. A map showing churches which had been deserted in the early sixteenth century gives us an idea of the desertion process which is also documented by other sources. The difference between the heavily devastated areas in the south along the border with Poland and those areas to the north which were less deserted is remarkable. A comparison between the maps describing the older territorial structure with the map demonstrating the administrative network around 1785 shows a fundamental change in territorial organization. What, for example, in 1400 had been the areas of the 'Komtureien' Christburg and Osterode was in 1785 for the largest part the 'Landrätliche Kreis' Mohrungen.[16] The Kreis Mohrungen existed until the end of the last war, indicating that the administrative network of the Duchy and later kingdom of Prussia persisted to a certain degree almost down to the present time.

Central administration (e.g. in the castle of Marienburg)

Komtureien, independent Vogteien, Pflegämter (partly comprising areas of Pruzzian *terrae* (see Figs. 1, 2)[1]; e.g. Christburg (Pomesania), Elbing (Pogesania), Balga (Warmia), Königsberg (Sambia)

Kammerämter, subordinate Vogteien, Pflegämter, Fischämter, Waldämter (partly in areas of Pruzzian *territoria (Burgherrschaften)*): e.g.: Germau (Girmow), Quednau (Quedenow), Pobethen (Pobeten), Rudau (Rudowe)

Note:
[1] The names in brackets are of the Pruzzian *terrae, territoria* or *districtus.*

Sources:
W. Ziesemer (ed.), *Das Große Ämterbuch des Deutschen Ordens, 1364–1524* (Danzig, 1921); P. G. Thielen (ed.), *Das große Zinsbuch des Deutschen Ritterordens, 1414–1438* (Marburg, 1958); *Historisch-geographischer Atlas des Preußenlandes;* P. G. Thielen, *Die Verwaltung des Ordensstaates Preußen vornehmlich im 15 Jahrhundert,* Ostmitteleuropa in Vergangenheit und Gegenwart, vol. II (Köln/Graz, 1965).

Fig. 3. *Spatial organization of the Order of the German Knights*

I have tried to show, by taking examples from the *Historisch-geographischer Atlas des Preußenlandes*, that there existed an administrative organization of space from prehistoric time to the present. Of course, I consider studies of this kind only one basis for research into the influence of the former administration upon society, settlements, economy and transport. The success of a working group of the Akademie für Raumforschung und Landesplanung dealing with such studies, though relating to the nineteenth century, allows us already to assert that those questions would be promising ones.

University of Würzburg,
West Germany

Soldier settlement in British Columbia, 1915–1930: a synchronic analysis

P. M. KOROSCIL

Canada became an industrial state as a result of the high level of economic growth created by World War I. Canadian leaders realized that the period of pioneer achievement, 1891–1914, was over and that Canada had to abandon her previous expedient methods of placing people on the land and that she now had to recognize the fact that a scientific plan of development, that took account of the individual's economic and social needs, had to be prepared in advance of settlement. With a new philosophy of public policy, Canadian leaders were confident that they could solve the major problems of the 'Reconstruction' period: immigration and land settlement. In relationship to both of these problems, the immediate task before the leaders was the reabsorption of ex-service men into civilian life. The Federal and Provincial governments responded by establishing a national policy for ex-service men. British Columbia, however, played a major role in initiating the national policy and implementing her own soldier settlement programme.

The purpose

The purpose of this essay is to assess the impact of the placement of ex-service men on the British Columbia landscape. Two questions are considered: first, what were the soldier-related land settlement and development policies; secondly, how effective was the implementation of these policies? The analysis will examine the factors of change that created the rise and decline of soldier settlements in British Columbia between 1915 and 1930. The goal of the analysis is not to arrange chronologically the historical events related to soldier settlements but to seek an explanation of this phenomenon. From the analysis the following nineteenth-century theoretical inferences can be raised concerning the settlement process in Western Canada: first, the attack on the land was still the accepted norm of behaviour during the *Reconstruction* period and the aim

51

of public policy was not socialization but development; secondly, the vehicle of the settlement process was still the colonization land company and community settlement, and the image that they promoted was that Western Canada had progressed from the outopia, 'nowhere' or *terra incognita*, to utopia, a 'somewhere' or 'good place' of unlimited progress, enterprise and development.

The approach

Over the past three decades, practitioners of historical geography have used a variety of approaches in seeking explanations to the past. Some of the approaches have achieved greater acceptance than others as historical geographers, particularly in the last ten years, have debated the merits and shortcomings of their usefulness within a positivist or non-positivist philosophical framework.[1]

At one stage in the subject's growth, the reconstruction of past geographies was not only viewed as the essence of the subject but also the approach.[2] The validity of such a viewpoint, particularly as an approach, was brought into question and the majority of the practitioners agreed that the single time period cross-section, which described some or all aspects of an area, did not offer a sufficiently dynamic form of explanation. However, there are situations where period reconstructions are valid if the structure of the approach is changed. If the changes include the incorporation of fact, theory,[3] the actor, observer and the employment of the classical method[4] of analysing documents then the final explanation of man-made landscapes that existed for one period of time will answer questions that go beyond the inventory explanations offered by the traditional *past geographies* approach. The use of this restructured approach is conducive to investigating the phenomena of soldier settlements in British Columbia.

The framework for the restricted time period is 1915 to 1930. Soldier settlements in the province were conceived and established during that time, and did not exist before or after that time frame. Fact(s) and theory relate to the Act(s) established in British Columbia for soldier settlement according to a nineteenth-century theory of settlement growth in Western Canada. The actor is represented by the government through its representatives who make the policy decisions in the settlement process, and the observer is the researcher who interprets the ramifications of the policies. The classical method employed in analysing the soldier settlement documents is in-depth analysis that is subjective in character with a rational basis.

The analysis

Soldier settlement policies

With a philosophy of commitment, the Canadian government organized a meeting in Ottawa in October 1915 at which representatives from the Military Hospital Commission and the Provincial governments discussed the potential problems that the soldiers would face on their return to Canada. It was agreed that Provincial committees would be established to handle the responsibility of finding employment for discharged soldiers in each province. In accordance with this agreement, the British Columbia Returned Soldiers' Aid Commission was organized on 29 November 1915.[5]

The Commission's objectives were basically threefold: first, to establish a Provincial Employment Bureau; secondly to provide education, technical and agricultural training for returned soldiers; and thirdly to devise a land settlement policy that would place returned soldiers on farm lands.[6] The first two objectives were immediately acted upon by the Provincial government; however the third objective was somewhat more complex and it received considerable attention from the Commission.[7] In 1916 the Commission recommended to the Provincial Legislature that a series of cooperative community settlements be established not only for placing soldiers on the land but other settlers desiring to live in such communities. In 1917 the Provincial Legislature had not only to make a decision on this latter recommendation but it also had to deal with speculators who held large amounts of idle agricultural land in the province. To solve both problems the Provincial government passed an Act to Promote Increased Agricultural Production.[8] This Act was known as the Land Settlement and Development Act. A Land Settlement Board in the Department of Agriculture was created to administer the Act.

The Provincial government felt that it had made a considerable amount of progress in establishing aid programmes and a land settlement policy for discharged soldiers. However, the Provincial government believed that the Federal government should contribute to part of the costs of the Provincial aid programmes and that the Dominion as a whole should be involved in an overall land settlement policy.

In September 1917, with political pressure from British Columbia, the Federal government passed the Soldier Settlement Act.[9] It was described as an Act to Assist Returned Soldiers in Settling upon the Land and to Increase Agricultural Production. The Act established a Soldier Settlement Board composed of three commissioners to administer the provisions of the Act. Some of the provisions included the granting of loans to the maximum of $2,500 for returned soldiers to be used for such purposes as stock. The loans were to be offered at 5 per cent interest over a period of twenty years and could be applied to holdings already owned or leased by returned soldiers or to assist them in settling free Dominion lands. In this latter case, the Act authorized the reservation of any available Dominion lands for the purposes of the Act, and provided for the granting of a free entry for 64 hectares of Dominion lands in addition to the ordinary homestead right of 64 hectares or settlement conditions similar to homestead duties.

On 20 January 1918 the Soldier Settlement Board of Canada began the task of implementing the Act. While the Board was reasonably successful in granting loans to returned soldiers it was not as successful in allocating free Dominion lands. The Board felt that there was not enough available land to satisfy the large number of applications. With the seemingly endless flow of soldiers returning to Canada and clamouring for work and land the Dominion government again found itself in an uncomfortable dilemma.

During this period of indecision, John Oliver, the Premier of British Columbia, proposed that the nationwide problem was by no means insoluble and that Prime Minister Borden should call a national conference to discuss possible amendments to the Soldier Settlement Act. Borden willingly assented to Oliver's suggestion and a conference was convened in November 1918 where a number of amendments to the Federal Act were adopted.[10]

Some of the most significant amendments pertained to land reclamation, land expropriation and agricultural training of soldiers. It was also agreed that the provinces would be provided with Federal funds to purchase lands for soldier settlement purposes. All of the amendments were incorporated in the revised Federal Soldiers' Settlement Act which became effective on 7 July 1919.[11] However, Oliver did not wait for the legislation to be passed. In 1918 he decided to implement the agreed national policy by passing an Act to Provide Lands for the Use and Benefit of Returned Soldiers[12] which was referred to as the Soldiers' Land Act for British Columbia veterans. The Act provided for the Lieutenant-Governor in Council to purchase lands for returned soldiers out of a consolidated Revenue Fund provided that the aggregate of such payments did not exceed $500,000. Oliver appointed a Superintendent of British Columbia Soldier Settlement under the Department of Lands to administer the Soldiers' Land Act. Oliver and the government were now in a position to control totally land development and the settlement of returned soldiers and bona fide settlers under the Soldiers' Land Act and the Land Settlement and Development Act. It was under the latter Act that veterans had a direct impact upon the British Columbia landscape.

The impact of the Land Settlement and Development Act

In British Columbia, Oliver was confronted by the problem of securing attractive land for settlement as most of the reasonable agricultural land was held by speculators. To resolve this problem, Oliver decided to use Section 46 of the Land Settlement and Development Act which provided for the establishment of 'Settlement Areas' on undeveloped agricultural land under the control of the Land Settlement Board. Prior to designating the Settlement Areas, the Board had to choose the site and its situation and determine how to acquire properties within the site. It was agreed that the Settlement Areas should be located near transportation facilities on land that would require very little improvement to bring it into production to support permanent settlements.[13] Once the Board had designated a Settlement Area the owners of the various parcels of unimproved land were to bring that land up to Board standards of active agricultural production within a specified time. If owners failed in this obligation a tax of 5 per cent of the appraised value would be levied in addition to all other taxes, or they had the option of surrendering the land to the Board at the appraised value to sell to bona fide settlers.[14]

On 2 July 1918 the Land Settlement Board designated the Bulkley and Nechako Valleys as the first two Settlement Areas.[15] By the end of 1919 the Board had designated fourteen Settlement Areas. Thirteen of the areas were located in the Central Interior mainly on or near the Grand Trunk Pacific or the Pacific Great Eastern Railways. The other area was located in the Kootenays at Fernie (Fig. 1).

By 1920 in nine selected areas the Board had designated 48,456.4 hectares of which 18,658.0 were purchased by the Board for a cost of $210,642.29, and 7,662 hectares were resold to bona fide settlers. Almost all of the acquired land in Area No. 1 and more than half of the lands available in Area No. 2 were sold to bona fide settlers. In Area No. 5, 1,664 out of 4,640.4 hectares were sold to twenty-six settlers while 416 hectares were improved privately to escape the penalty tax (Table 1).

The Board's settlement area policy had both a positive and a negative effect on the province's landscape. In the former case the policy induced private owners to improve their land to escape the penalty tax. In Areas 1 and 2, for example, during 1919–20 a total of 4,370.8 hectares were improved. Combined with the Board's settlers, a total of 14,986.4 hectares were improved as against 5,940 hectares before the two areas were established.[16] The effect of the settlement policy on actually peopling the landscape was rather negative. In 1920 there were approximately 120 settlers in the Settlement Areas. Only fifty-three returned British Columbia soldiers, each of whom was allowed the statutory rebate of $500 on the

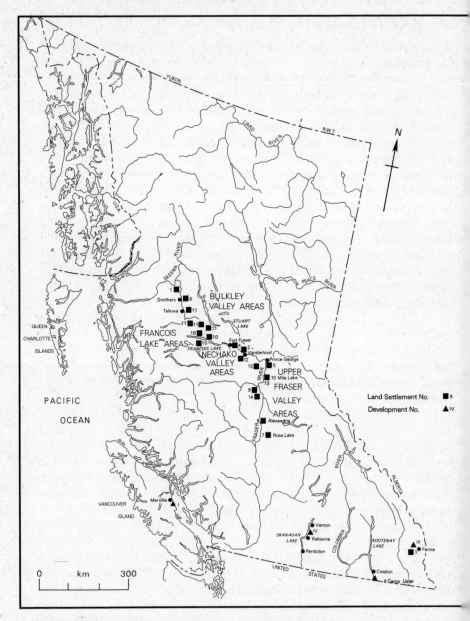

Fig. 1. *Land Settlement Areas in British Columbia in 1919*

Table 1. *Nine selected Settlement Areas in British Columbia, 1920*

Area	Location	District	Purchase price $	Development costs $	Total hectares	Acquired	Sold	Available for sale
1	Bulkley Valley	Telkwa	30,200.60	3,240.32	6,885.6	2,193.6	1,887.6	306.0
2	Nechako Valley	Vanderhoof	72,672.07	7,815.23	14,143.2	5,492.0	2,788.0	2,704.0
4	Nechako Valley	Marten Lake	16,735.17	1,450.06	5,707.2	1,548.0	646.8	902.0
5	Upper Fraser Valley	Prince George	55,643.21	2,602.61	7,465.2	4,640.4	1,664.0	2,976.4
6	Bulkley Valley	Smithers	5,318.40	1,042.25	2,124.0	547.2	186.4	360.8
7	Upper Fraser Valley	Rose Lake	23.01	890.41	2,608.4	632.8	—	632.8
8	Upper Fraser Valley	Alexandria	1,448.88	576.03	1,324.4	650.0	—	650.0
9	Upper Fraser Valley	10-Mile Lake	14,100.65	539.66	1,950.0	1,623.2		1,623.2
10	Francois Lake	Francois Lake	14,482.30	2,950.31	6,248.4	1,330.8	489.2	841.6
Total	9 areas		$210,624.29	$21,106.88	48,456.4	18,658.0	7,662.0	10,996.8

Source: British Columbia, *Sessional Papers*, Land Settlement Board, 1921, T5, T12.

purchase price of lands that they selected,[17] took advantage of the 7,662 hectares that were sold by the Board.[18] By the end of 1922 the number of applications for land declined and the Board reported that its work was continuing 'on a modified scale'.[19] Despite the fact that the number of settlers had risen to 194 and the total land occupied in Settlement Areas was 11,730.8 hectares, not more than eighty of the settlers were veterans (Table 2).

A partial explanation of the lack of success in attracting settlers lies in the Board's choice of the site and situation of each of the Settlement Areas. 'Most of the settled areas in the Central Interior suffered from low soil productivity, marginal climate, and lack of established markets.'[20]

Disappointed with the failure of the settlement area policy to attract bona fide settlers, particularly veterans, to the land, Oliver made the decision to pursue the concept of settlement by communities of soldiers as recommended by the British Columbia Returned Soldiers' Aid Commission in 1915 and the 'Empress of Asia Plan of Community Settlements' proposed in January 1919 by 300 returned soldiers.[21] To try out his experiment Oliver used his Land Settlement and Development Act.

Since there was a considerable amount of idle forest and logged-off land in the province, Oliver decided that these areas would be most suitable to convert into productive agricultural land. Oliver instructed the Land Settlement Board to purchase these lands and designate them as 'Development Areas' under the Act and to institute his cooperative plan[22] for soldier settlements. Under Oliver's plan, each Development Area would be surveyed in large units. Only soldiers who wanted to work cooperatively and acquire farms would be chosen to clear the land. For their labour in clearing the land together, the veterans would receive four dollars per day per man. The object of the low wage was to keep down the soldier's costs when he purchased his land, the price of which would be based on the original sum paid by the Board for the land, plus the clearing costs.

Work camps, which would contain temporary buildings and a cooperative general store, would be established within each unit. After the areas had been cleared lots would be subdivided and the workers would clear and fence a five-acre plot of each of the subdivided lots, a plan intended to place as many settlers as quickly as possible on their own land. As soon as the veterans attained their land, which would be allocated by lot, they could erect their permanent buildings. After enough soldiers had settled on their lots, the Board would transfer the management of the store and other institutional buildings to the community. To oversee the entire plan, the Land Settlement Board would appoint a superintendent for each Development Area. If complaints arose, a soldier committee could confer with representatives of the Board.

Early in 1919 the Board purchased the first Development Area, compris-

Table 2. *Thirteen selected Settlement Areas in British Columbia, 1922*

Area	Location	Total hectares in Areas	Hectares to which Board had title	Hectares under option	Hectares sold	No. of settlers	Hectares improved under Act	Total penalty tax assessed against un-improved land
1, 6, 11	Bulkley Valley	16,702.4	3,778.8	930.0	2,493.6	44	4,106.6	$10,236.20
2, 4, 12	Nechako Valley	32,472.8	8,745.2	1,057.2	4,657.6	75	5,198.8	28,918.90
10	Francois Lake	6,248.4	2,127.6	—	933.2	15	1,267.2	2,691.26
5, 7, 8, 9, 13, 14	Upper Fraser Valley	21,832.0	9,292.0	910.0	3,646.4	60	2,400.4	6,827.78
Total	13 areas	77,255.6	23,943.6	2,897.2	11,730.8	194	12,972.0	$48,674.14

Source: British Columbia, *Sessional Papers*, Land Settlement Board, 1923, Z6.

ing 5,464.03 hectares of logged-off land, from the Comox Logging Company. The area was situated 'about six miles from Courtenay, in the Comox Valley, on the east coast of Vancouver Island, and extended from the Strait of Georgia on the east to and beyond the Tsolum River on the west'.[23] The area was connected to Courtenay, the business centre of the Comox Valley, by the Island Highway as well as by several well-maintained side roads. Other transportation links in the area included the Comox Logging Railway and numerous abandoned logging roads. Prior to the Land Settlement Board acquiring the area, H. Nelems, Chairman of the Board, indicated that the site had been logged and burned over, 'leaving the land fairly clear of everything but stumps and logs'.[24] From his observation of the soils in the area, he concluded 'that at least fifty per cent of the land offered will prove suitable for agriculture and the balance for pastural purposes'.[25] Later a technical soil report, prepared for the Board, indicated that only two of the three types of soil found in the area could be brought up to agricultural standards.[26]

Despite the rather bleak agricultural potential offered by the site, the Board designated 3,200 of the 5,464.03 hectares for development. In April 1919 the Board implemented Oliver's plan. The Merville Development Area was surveyed into seven units. Two work camps were established and seventy veterans were chosen to begin the procedure of rough clearing. In May the *Victoria Daily Colonist* reported 'that the returned soldiers were doing excellent work in clearing the land and establishing their quarters and . . . they were enthusiastic and confident that they would make a success of their venture'.[27] On completion of the rough clearing operations the units were surveyed into farm lots ranging from four to forty-eight hectares. The lots were not surveyed on a standard grid plan but seemed to conform to the abandoned logging roads (Fig. 2).

By the beginning of 1920 there were forty-five farms available for settlers, the average being twenty hectares, with '180 hectares ready for the plough'.[28] These farms were selected by lot as planned, and it was reported to the Board that the draw 'had gone off in a most satisfactory manner with each man getting what he wanted'.[29] However, there were a number of soldiers who were displeased with the costs of their farms and other decisions made by the Board. In May 1920 the split between the soldiers and the Board widened when the Board decided to abandon the original idea of trying to make development and land settlement complementary. The Board indicated that it wished to concentrate on development and that it was not feasible to promote the two functions under the same Board without sacrificing efficiency.[30]

As of 1 June 1920 development operations were terminated, 'following which allotment was made of all lands sub-divided, totalling 126 farm units, averaging, exclusive of small allotments, between 20 and 24 hectares

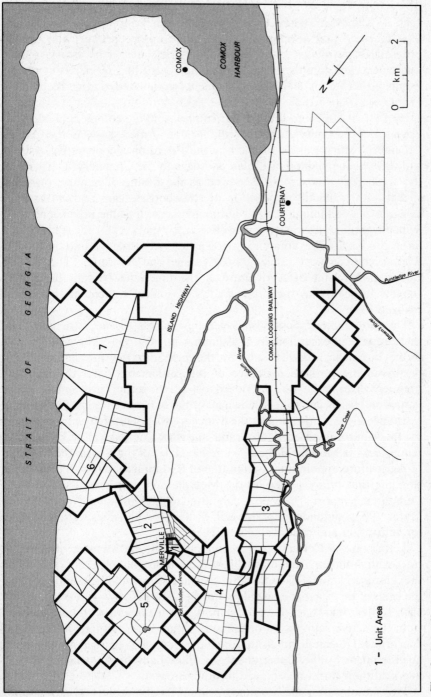

Fig. 2. *Merville Development Area number one*

1 – Unit Area

each'.[31] The Board's new policy, which affected approximately 400 settlers, specified that development work was to proceed under a system of progressive payments, by which each settler could, if necessary, secure assistance each month to an amount not exceeding 60 per cent of the estimated value of actual improvements completed during the month (Table 3).

By 1922, it appeared that the agricultural soldier settlement at Merville was a success. Ninety of the Merville farmers owned shares in the Comox Creamery, which was established by the Board on a cooperative system, with fifty of them shipping cream and eggs to the Creamery. Dairying at the settlement was successful as well as the raising of poultry, pigs and sheep, with a healthy production of strawberries, eggs and clover hay. Logging and coal mining camps in the area as well as the urban centres of Vancouver and Victoria were viewed as ready markets for the settlement's farm products. The community townsite had developed to include a school, church, post office, store, garage and tea-room. The British Columbia Minister of Agriculture at the time, the Honourable E. D. Barrow, argued that the original idea of soldier settlements had been realized.[32]

The Government's optimism over the success of the settlement was shattered by an exceptionally dry summer in 1922. On 5 July a forest fire broke out near Merville, and by the next day the fire had virtually destroyed the physical existence of the settlement. After the disaster, Premier Oliver authorized the Board to assist the settlers in rebuilding their homes and barns and to seed down all of the burnt-over lands. Despite the assistance given by the Board, the Minister of Agriculture was approached by the Courtenay Board of Trade and the Comox Valley farmers to reappraise the Merville project.[33] On the advice of the Board, the Minister of Agriculture appointed a Committee of Reappraisement with the understanding that future policy on the Merville area would be based on the Committee's report. The report, submitted to the Minister of Agriculture in March 1923, contended that one-half of the Merville lands were worthless for cultivation and of no value whatever.[34]

Acting on the Committee's recommendation, the Minister of Agriculture, with authority from Oliver, indicated to the soldier settlers that all of the improved lands sold to them on special terms would be reappraised on the basis of their actual cash value. Further, the Board would grant title to each settler, take back long-term mortgage loans and withdraw entirely from the active supervision of the area so far as the settlers' affairs were concerned. Dejected and disillusioned by what they regarded as their open abandonment by the Government, by 1929 many of the original settlers had sold their farms and moved to other areas.

Two months after the beginning of the Merville project, Oliver had in-

Table 3. *Development Areas in British Columbia, 1920*

Area	Location	Soldier settlement	Purchase price $	Development costs $	Total hectares	Soldier settlement population (estimate)
1	Vancouver Island	Merville	69,699.91	437,231.89	5,464.03	400
2	Kootenay District	Camp Lister	187,431.46	286,185.81	2,374.42	70
3	Kootenay District	Fernie	10,256.65	24,572.57	477.20	0
4	Okanagan Valley	Kelowna, Christian Ranch	33,070.50	24,665.95	176.00	0
Total	4 areas		$300,458.52	$772,656.22	8,491.65	470

Source: British Columbia, *Sessional Papers*, Land Settlement Board, 1921, T12. British Columbia Journals of Legislative Assembly, 1921, 11 Geo. 5, 77.

structed the Board to purchase from the Canyon City Lumber Company a second Development Area, comprising 2,374.42 hectares, for the Camp Lister soldier settlement (Table 3). It was a partially logged-off area located south-east of the town of Creston, Kootenay District, and extended to the international boundary.

This tract of land was situated in the heart of a prosperous fruit growing and mixed farming area in the Creston Valley. The nearby town of Creston, with a population of 600, acted as the principal business and distribution point of the district. Since the town was located on the Crow's Nest branch of the Canadian Pacific Railway produce from the valley could be placed on the markets of the prairies twenty-four hours sooner than from any other fruit shipping district of British Columbia.

Before the Land Settlement Board purchased the area, its chairman M. H. Nelems, stated that: 'The Creston lands are the best I have inspected in this section of the Province. . . . The district has sufficient rainfall for fruit growing and agricultural purposes. On none of the lands is irrigation necessary.'[35] After purchasing the site the Board found that the area was on a level bench about 121 metres above the Goat River. The soil in the area contained a large percentage of clay and sand, and water would have to be obtained by wells three to twenty-five metres in depth.[36]

Despite these constraints on the development of an orchard industry, the Board adopted almost the same policy to establish Camp Lister, as had been followed in Merville. The area was surveyed into four units with work camps established for clearing operations. The only change in procedure related to the payroll system. Although most of the veterans chosen to work in clearing land were placed on the payroll system, some were offered individual contracts.

After the initial clearing of the units the land was subdivided to meet the requirements of orchard farming. Each area was surveyed on a north–south grid pattern with a community townsite in the middle. Wherever possible south of the community townsite the land was divided into '8 hectare fruit farms with half a section dividing into 16 units with four lots facing each way of the compass'.[37] North of the townsite half sections were subdivided into four-hectare farms (Fig. 3).

In 1920, seventy settlers were engaged in clearing two-hectare plots on the ninety lots of eight hectares each in the first surveyed unit of approximately 800 hectares. By the end of the year the soldiers had cleared 114.2 hectares, partially cleared 15.2 hectares, completed the construction of eighteen permanent farm houses and were engaged in constructing an additional fifteen homes. By the end of 1921, 146 hectares had been ploughed in the settlement and twenty-eight of the two-hectare plots had been planted in apple trees by the Board.[38]

Despite the progress made in the settlement during 1921 relations

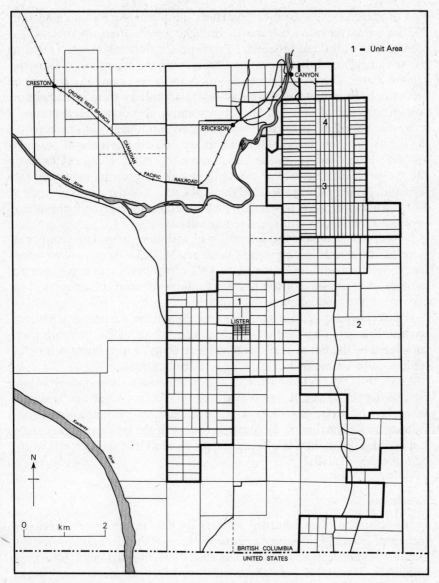

Fig. 3. *Camp Lister Development Area number two*

between the soldiers and the Board were strained because the working of the payroll system, four dollars per day pay allotment, in the clearing phase were not adequate to sustain the soldier settler and his family. In addition, the financial returns from their orchards did not help many of the settlers because only a fraction of orchards were planted on well-drained hillsides that produced quality fruit. The settlers' problems were compounded in 1921–2 when the area suffered a drought which dried up their wells. Confronted with these problems, development work ceased and some of the settlers ignored their farms and found work in mines and mills in the United States. Others attempted to switch to livestock and the growing of alfalfa but found that their twenty-hectare allotments were inadequate to sustain this type of farming. Still others simply abandoned their farms.

By the spring of 1926 many settlers were no longer able to keep up payments on their farms. On 1 February 1926 the arrears of payment amounted to $4,508.93. In the face of mounting public consternation over the Government's neglect of the settlers and the growing debt they had incurred, Premier Oliver decided to cut the prices of the soldiers' farms in half. 'While this gave new heart to the people to carry on, the major problem of irrigation still remained unsolved.'[39]

In order to examine the feasibility of installing irrigation facilities in Camp Lister and adjoining areas Oliver established a committee to report on economic conditions in the area. This committee's report contained a number of examples[40] of the harsh conditions experienced by settlers on account of the inadequate water supply.

The Premier reacted favourably to the committee's report and ordered the installation of an irrigation facility at a cost of $50,000. The project was completed by the fall of 1929 but it had arrived too late as only twenty-one soldier settlers remained in the Camp Lister Settlement.

Apart from Merville and Camp Lister two other Development Areas were acquired by the Board for soldier settlement: 477.2 hectares near Fernie in the Kootenay District and 176 hectares near Kelowna in the Okanagan Valley (Figure 1). After investing in the two areas, the Board stopped development work because they realized that the projects would be too costly (Table 3).

Conclusion

In his efforts to place returned soldiers on the land Premier Oliver was successful not only in influencing the policies of the Federal government but he was also decisive in establishing a settlement programme for British Columbia. Under his Land Settlement and Development Act arrangements were made for individual returned soldiers, communities of soldiers and new settlers to take up British Columbian lands. However, the decisions made by Oliver and the Land Settlement Board in implementing the Act contributed to the failure of soldier settlement in British Columbia.

The most crucial decision under the Act was the choice of sites. Prior scientific studies to determine the agricultural potential of the sites were never undertaken or commissioned by Oliver and the Board before they made their decision to purchase the areas. They took account of the agricultural potential of the site only after purchase of the areas. The situation factor was the major criterion used by Oliver and the Board in their decision to purchase the areas. Their decision proved to be economically unsound in the Settlement Areas because of the lack of established markets in or near the areas. In the Development Areas their decision was sound, but the type of agricultural production that could be carried on in the areas was totally restricted by the site constraints. Another critical decision made by Oliver and the Board in establishing the Settlement Areas was the fact that they assumed that the majority of the settlers who would take up these lands would be soldiers rather than other settlers. After this failure the decision was made to settle only soldiers on the land under the Development Areas of the Act.

In theory Oliver viewed his designed plan of cooperative community soldier settlements as a joint decision-making venture between the government and the soliders. However, the Board, with Oliver's approval, had the final decision-making power. For example, in 1920 and 1922 the Board made the decision, without consulting the soldiers, to drop the payroll system for a new progressive-loan system of land clearing in Merville and Camp Lister respectively. The result of this decision left the soldiers without sufficient funds to support themselves, and in many cases they had reached a position of insolvency where they found it impossible to pay off their loans from the products of their land.

Oliver's failure to place more returned soldiers permanently on the land basically reflects an extension of a nineteenth-century theory of settlement expansion in Western Canada that concentrated on developing the agricultural base. The necessary population to develop these lands was not only the available soldiers but any bona fide settlers who wished to become producing farmers. Despite the new philosophical planning rhetoric[41] promoted by the Dominion government to include a greater social concern for the 'agricultural class, the mainstay of the nation'[42] in the settlement process, there was, for example, no scientific plan of settlement development that took account of the socialization of the future farmer in Oliver's Settlement Areas. The only concern was to bring idle agricultural land into production to serve the established markets. The farmer was on his own to take care of his own social needs.

In Oliver's Development Areas the social concerns of the soldier settlers were initially taken into account in the plan to establish cooperative community settlements. However, when the decision was made to concentrate on development the social aspect of the plan failed and the settlement began to decline. The cooperative community plan was not an innovation in Western Canadian settlement.[43] In the nineteenth century it was one of the vehicles by which the prairies were settled. This vehicle was extended into British Columbia in the early 1900s, for example, by the Kalevan Kansan Colonization Association which attempted to establish the settlement of Sojntula on Malcolm Island.[44] In part, Oliver's plan reflected the Finnish model, except in establishing Merville and Camp Lister where the British Columbia government replaced the private colonization company. In summary, Oliver and the Board, by their careless decisions, were responsible for the failure of soldier settlement in British Columbia.

Simon Fraser University,
Canada

PART III

The Identification and Interpretation of Geographical Change

Geographical analysis of imperial expansion

D. W. MEINIG

The aggressive encroachment of one people upon the territory of another, resulting in the subjugation of the latter people to alien rule, is one of the great processes of history. Timeless and ubiquitous, evident somewhere in every era, affecting at some time every area, it has given shape to the world we live in.

What we commonly categorize as 'modern history' commences with the predatory spread of Europeans upon the lands of non-Europeans, and what we have commonly called 'modernization' refers to the relentless outward spread into world-wide dominance of a European-derived cultural system. However, it must be emphasized that imperialism is not an invention of Europeans, nor is modern aggressive expansion peculiar to European peoples. It is far older than that and it is also endemic in the non-European world, as is apparent in the news day by day. In this essay I wish to consider imperialism first of all as a generic phenomenon, not as any specific historical movement.

To speak of imperialism as one of the great 'processes of history' is to gloss over the fact that such 'processes' can be painful experiences for the people caught in them. It is therefore a kind of history, and especially in its more recent manifestations, that tends to engage our emotions and thereby become enmeshed in polemics and coloured by political controversy. Nevertheless, as scholars we must try to cut through current ideological connotations of such heavily loaded terms as 'imperialism' and 'colonialism' and seek first of all to understand as clearly and dispassionately as possible *what has happened*: to describe results before we search for cause and, if we wish, assign blame.

Imperialism defined

As geographers we may translate 'what has happened?' to mean: 'how have areas been changed?' as the result of the encroachment of one people upon the territory of another. We need to identify the *essential geographical features* of imperialism as a set of processes and patterns.

Imperialism defined in this very general and basic sense would seem necessarily to involve the following:

1. The exercise of ultimate *political* authority by the invader over the invaded. This subordination requires the presence of agents (governor, commandant, lesser officials) supported by coercive power (police, military forces) as extensions of the central instruments of the imperial state.

Geographically this is expressed in the positioning of such agents at strategic points within the area to be controlled, a network of routes linking these points, and a trunk line connecting this network of the subordinated area to the capital and core of the imperial state. The routine movements of personnel, goods, information and directives within this network exhibit how the two areas are bound together in a spatial system.

2. This exercise of political authority requires direct contact between agents of the two peoples, and the inequality of the political relationship imposes an inequality in *social* relationships so as to create a new social stratification in which the agents of the conquerors assume a dominant position. They form a new ethnic aristocracy. Sustained imperialism will lead to a broadening of the forms of contact and the emergence of many kinds of social intermediaries (servants, lawyers, teachers, missionaries, translators, prostitutes, bankers, brokers, traders, transporters).

Geographically such contacts take place at specific points and times, and in the localities of these contacts the two peoples are likely to live in some degree segregated from one another. There is thereby created a new social geography which can be described in terms of bi-cultural localities, separate residential areas, and social interaction patterns between the two peoples. Wherever imperialism involves the encounter of two markedly different racial groups, sustained contact will result in some amount of *miscegenation* creating a visibly distinct third people (Eurasian, mestizo, mulatto). Such persons will likely be ascribed to specific places in the social stratification and in the social geography of the area.

These statements describe only the most minimal changes. Sustained imperialism may bring about widespread alterations of social geography as a result of killings, expulsions, relocations, colonizations, recruitment of labour, and many kinds of voluntary movement. Furthermore, these new social realtionships may be diffused directly into the home area of the imperial state through the migration (forced or voluntary) of some of the conquered peoples (prisoners, labourers, servants, students, traders), forming minorities and new bi-cultural social areas and thus altering the internal geography of the imperial state as well.

3. This sustained contact between two peoples will result in *culture* change in both. Such encounters between cultures are always asymmetric and the resulting acculturation is always selective in content, uneven in diffusion, and unbalanced in its effect upon the two groups. Ordinarily the greater pressures for change will be upon the invaded people. Some of these pressures may come from explicit instruments of the invader (schools, churches, law courts), but much of it will simply develop from the routines of ordinary life. Change will take place to some

degree regardless of intent, and it can never be exactly managed through specific programmes.

Geographically such change begins at points of intense interaction and spreads outwardly. Such diffusion will likely be complex: partly contagious, and declining with distance from the centres of contact; partly hierarchical, concordant with social and geopolitical structures; always most rapid among those who regard culture change as a means of personal gain within the bi-cultural society. Imperial control of the main specific institutions can be mapped, but the evidence of change must be sought in diagnostic features, such as language, dress, intermarriage, shifts from traditional to new activities and modes of behaviour.

4. Imperial expansion is basically predatory. Although motives may vary among specific cases, agents of the imperial power will seek to extract wealth from the conquered territory, creating new *economic* relationships. These may take many forms, the most obvious being direct taxation of the conquered population, the confiscation of existing facilities and resources, and the initiation of new economic activities. But there may well be many more subtle forms of control and change, such as indirect forms of taxation, penetration of businesses by imperial agents, manipulation of regulations so as to alter capital flows, reinterpretation of property laws and tenure relationships. As with culture change, the impact is not uni-directional. Wealth also flows into the conquered area in the form of direct wages, purchases of supplies and services, and investments. Thus the conquered area becomes an integral part of a larger economic system (it may have been so before, but less directly, firmly, comprehensively).

Geographically the locations of facilities and resources seized and new activities initiated can be mapped, and the creation or augmentation of transportation links and the more obvious circuits of economic interaction between the two areas can be identified. There will likely be much that cannot be readily discerned in the often subtle, intricate and indirect net of economic relationships. One might hope at least to identify where basic decisions are made with reference to major programmes of investment and employment. We must strive for better descriptions of economic interactions in spatial systems terms than we have yet achieved.

5. In order to continue their domination at minimum cost and trouble, imperial rulers seek the allegiance of the conquered people. This requires some shift in *psychological* focus and involves the manipulation of symbols of authority, power and prestige so as to invoke respect, fear and admiration.

Geographically this involves the management of landscape in order to give visible display of the imperial presence. This is done by the adornment of carefully selected sites, such as those of important political or cultural significance to the conquered people (capitals, shrines), or prominent landmarks of strategic signifi-cance (gateways, junctions, regional centres), with an architecture of authority. This refers to the building of headquarters, fortresses, official residences and other major facilities on a scale and in a style which physically attest to the power of the imperial state. In addition to such conscious symbolic manipulations there may be the routine display of differences in culture and wealth in the contrasting architecture and form, and in the physical demarcation (walls, gates, open space) of the residential (and perhaps business) areas of the two people ('native and European quarters', 'old town–new town' pairs).

Thus I have made use of five common categorizations of different aspects of human life – political, social, cultural, economic, psychological – as a framework within which to define a distinctly geographical approach to the study of imperialism. I have tried to extract imperialism from any specific ideological meaning and recognize it as a generic phenomenon, a type of relationship between two peoples, recognizable in some form throughout the record of human history. I have defined imperialism as first of all a *political* phenomenon, for it refers to an unequal *power* relationship. Aside from that no ranking of importance is intended by the sequence of discussion of social, cultural, economic and psychological phenomena. Nor, of course, are these five categories at all sharply distinct, they are merely conventional ways of focusing upon different aspects of a whole. It would be hard to think of any individual feature, such as a governor's house, a business establishment, an army base, a railway, a school, or any of the transactions taking place within them, which does not have multiple connotations in these terms. (I am also aware that to speak of 'conventional ways' cannot refer to universal ways, for the use of these basic terms differs among various national and intellectual traditions.) These five categories are used therefore as a convenient strategy for description and analysis. They have the further advantage of linking our geographical studies directly with those of the major social sciences (political science, sociology, anthropology, economics and social psychology) on which we are necessarily dependent for much of our understanding of processes and behaviour. (And, again, I recognize that this list of fields does not exactly fit all of our academic structures, but it approximates most of them.)

Within each of these five categories I have noted some specifically *geographic* manifestations. These may be grouped into several basic kinds of geographical phenomena:

1. *spatial systems:* network and circulation which serve to bind the two areas, that of the conquered and that of the conqueror, together.
2. *locational distributions:* areal patterns of elements and complexes diagnostic of the imperial presence and impact.
3. *man–land relationships:* imperial intrusion and disturbance of older ecological, tenurial and resource patterns.
4. *social ecologies:* intimate areal and environmental relationships between two peoples brought together by imperialism.
5. *cultural landscapes:* the visible scene and its symbolic imperial content.

These, too, are somewhat arbitrary categories selected as a convenient strategy for thinking geographically about an area.

As individual geographers we may choose to select any one of these and work on the comparative analysis of different imperial examples; or we may attempt to synthesize them all for a particular imperial case. As a field we need the vigorous cultivation of both kinds of work. The first leads us toward the development of a basic set of terms, concepts and axioms: toward a basic grammar of the geography of imperialism. The second leads us toward an orderly regional geography of imperialism and the interpretation of consequence and significance of particular cases. Both may be connected to and informed by broader theory.

To speak of analysis and synthesis in these terms may suggest an essentially static view, the study of an area at a particular time. It need not, but we must make more explicit what an historical geography of imperialism implies. I suggested at the beginning that our most basic question is: 'how have areas been changed as a result of the encroachment of one people upon the territory of another?' This common English phrasing contains an ambiguity that can be put to good use. 'How have areas been changed?' can be taken to mean: 'how do areas under imperial control differ from what they were like before they were brought under such control?' This leads us directly to the comparative cross-section approach, the study of the same area at different times. Such an historical geography would examine the degree of concordance between the superimposed alien pattern and that of the indigenous pattern, and assess the consequences. It would also examine variations in the intensity of that superimposed imperial surface, the gradations of the alien pressure and power. Imperial rulers usually control less than they might wish or claim, and it should be axiomatic that coercive power can never be exerted simultaneously with equal effect upon any broad area. Together these lead toward what might well be called a geographical morphology of imperialism, and we may wish to create a sequence of such views in order to define important changes from era to era for a particular area. By such means we can begin to identify the most critical points, zones or areas of change, and of resistance to change. This kind of sequential approach represents the study of imperialism in terms of *changing geographies*.

On the other hand, we may interpret the question: 'how have areas been changed?' as asking: 'by what means have areas been changed as a result of imperialism?' This leads us directly to the study of imperialism as a set of processes, each with significant geographical results. Such an historical geography would focus upon strategies of imperial conquest and control which involve perceptions and evaluations of areas in connection with specific motivations, and the attempts to carry out the policies emanating therefrom. Such study must give special attention to movements and diffusion stemming from the interaction of the two peoples, as well as the resistances and reactions of the invaded peoples to imperial programmes. The focus upon processes means that our analysis depends upon our understanding of the way instruments and institutions (bureaucracies, financial systems, corporations, missions) actualy function. To the extent that we can trace the links between policies and behaviour on the one hand and their impact upon areas over a period of time, we would be addressing imperialism as a *geographical study of change*.

I believe that these two kinds of historico-geographical study are inherent in the most venerable conceptions of geography. They are open to many adaptations and specializations within these general frameworks. They are equally valid, complementary and interdependent, and ideally might be combined so as to give a more complete description of change.

Commentary

So far I have referred to imperialism in its clearest form. It is important to realize that imperialism may endure in some of its aspects long after blatant political coercion has eased. It may persist in a form of cultural dominance that Hector has called *internal colonialism*.[1] The concept refers to the pressures felt by a 'minority people' upon their continued ethno-territorial identity within the body of a large state. We have increasingly come to realize that such ethnic groups are not simply dwindling residues doomed to eventual assimilation, but represent forms of consciousness which are open to manipulation and may wax as well as wane depending upon changing conditions and stimuli. This outline for the geography of imperialism is readily adaptable to the study of such critical internal features: of the pressures of the English upon the Welsh, the French upon the Bretons, Castilians upon Catalans, Russians upon Latvians, Yankees upon Southerners, and many, many analogous cases.

The concept of *neocolonialism* refers to another form of imperial legacy, with emphasis upon continued economic dependency and exploitation. It has been most commonly applied to former overseas imperial holdings whose people now have the technical trappings of full sovereignty and are not under the same assimilative pressures as minorities within a state. Where there is a strong consciousness of a differentiation within the country of that which is directly part of the imperial heritage (neocolonial) and that which is not (indigenous), and where such differentiation generates important internal socio-political divisions and tensions, this geographic analysis of imperialism remains pertinent. The current agents of that imperial legacy need not be ethnically different from the rest of the population, but key elements (corporations, churches, schools, social clubs, political parties, newspapers) must be recognizably distinct and understood as being at least symbolic, if not a direct continuation, of the former imperial relationship.

Galtung's 'structural theory' offers a framework within which to consider such imperial connections, whether these be politically explicit or not.[2] He sees imperialism in *core–periphery* terms, the critical relationship being that between the centre of the centre (dominant) nation and a centre ('beachhead') created within the periphery (subordinate) nation. Imperialism thrives when there is a strong mutual interest between the two, where the actors in both of these centres are enriched by the continuing inequality between the two geographical parts of the imperial system. Galtung's centre and periphery must be defined first of all in socio-political terms. They may not always have simple locational identities but they perforce have geographical dimensions and should be amenable to much of the analysis I have suggested.

The most obvious category of Galtung's beachheads is the *colonial city*. Earle's schematic table of the 'colonization process' offers a useful guide for work on these centres of the periphery.[3] Although restricted in scope, the focus upon such intensive points of encounter may provide the most effective entryway into the immense complexities of imperialism.

The broad topic of national expansion (in a geographic sense) has been usually treated in two bodies of literature which, though intersecting in various ways, have been quite separate in theme, example and method. On the one hand are studies of imperialism (or colonialism) which have been mainly concerned with the spread of European political and economic dominance over non-European peoples, and the reactions of the latter to such aggression and subordination leading to the eventual dissolution of such empires. On the other, is a huge literature on *the frontier*, focused mainly on the permanent migration of European peoples into relatively thinly populated non-European lands, the spread of 'civilization' into the 'wilderness', and the growth, divergence and eventual independence of such offspring from their mother country. I think it is time that, in the broadest view, the topic of the frontier be subsumed under that of imperialism. We must face the fact that there were *no empty lands* (though some may have seemed so to invaders at times), that every frontier represented an encroachment of one people upon territory claimed and used (however lightly) by another. Even where areas were opened through negotiations rather than bloodshed, the negotiation itself was an imperial encounter. The moment we re-examine familiar frontier areas from such a point of view we will likely discover a very different history, as Jennings has vividly shown.[4]

Osborne and Rogerson have argued for the advantage of the dialectical, exploitative *world-system* approach of Wallerstein over the diffusionist, integrative, basically progressive emphasis of the Turnerian frontier process.[5] I agree that Wallerstein's geographical structure and hypothesis provides a more satisfying context for the consideration of many aspects of the 'modern world'. However, it would be unfortunate if geographers simply accepted his theory and devoted most of their imperial studies to its explication. Of course we must perforce work with some notion, however vague, of imperialism as a kind of system, and we must welcome attempts to make that system much more vivid and comprehensible. So, too, Blaut's assertion that most Western studies of imperialism should be regarded as a species of 'ethno-science', deeply grounded and laced through with cultural and ideological bias, is useful and persuasive, but his 'Third World model', though valuable as a counterview, is no less biased and is not the only alternative.[6] It would be naive to think that we can ever be free of some such bias, but it is not unworthy to try to minimize such influences upon scholarship. I believe we might do so by greater emphasis at this stage in our work upon detailed descriptions of local areas. That is not a call to search for an objective reality, but only for a common focus, using whatever lens we may prefer, upon the basic elements of a special kind of geographic area: where unequal peoples are locked together in an imperial context. The best example I know of this kind of study is *Cycles of Conquest*, by the anthropologist Edward Spicer, a meticulous examination of policies, impacts and responses through a succession of imperial systems upon a wide variety of peoples within one broad region.[7]

The word 'imperialism' – despite its intimidating load of emotional connotations – has the virtue of forcing us to think in terms of unequal power relationships between peoples and demands that we as geographers examine such relationships in our own ways. Effective comparative and theoretical work requires a far larger body of reasonably consistent studies which describe and interpret imperialism in its local and regional settings. Nor does description need to be justified only as a servant of theory, as a lower order of professional work. Good description is difficult, and therefore rare, and at its best can be powerful and evocative. Even at its mildest imperialism is a form of stress, a chronic pressure with explosive potential. And even in its harsher forms it involves negotiations, accommodations and acculturation. By focusing directly upon such bi-cultural areas, describing to the best of our abilities the context of issues and feelings that smoulder deeply and of those surficial daily encounters that alter subtly, we might contribute significantly to a greater understanding and appreciation. That would be making description a servant of humanity – unexciting, perhaps, but not an unworthy objective for professional work.

University of Syracuse,
USA

Agricultural improvement in late-colonial tropical America: sources and issues

J. H. GALLOWAY

The agricultural revolution in Europe has proved a lively subject of debate among scholars. Though traditionally it has been associated with the eighteenth century, opinions now differ on when between the 1600s and the 1800s the revolution took place and on whether 'revolution' is the correct word to apply to what increasingly appears to have been a gradual process of change accumulating its effects over many years. The European interest in agriculture had its counterpart in tropical America where in late colonial times planters, doctors, clergy and administrators became aware of the advances being made in agricultural practices in Europe. Many members of this intelligentsia had indeed been educated there and knew of the Physiocrats, Adam Smith and agricultural writers such as Arthur Young. In their turn, they wrote critical accounts of the Caribbean islands, Brazil and Spanish America in the tradition of the English 'improvers' and the French 'agronomes'. Absentee West Indian landlords and travellers to the Americas added to this literature. The possibility of making colonial agriculture more productive not surprisingly attracted the attention of the metropolitan governments. The writings of these men and the support they received from governments raise the question of whether tropical America, like Europe, experienced if not an agricultural revolution at least an 'age of the improver'.

My purpose in this essay is to explore this question. The colonial improvers and their ideas are part of the intellectual history of tropical America, but the more they succeeded in translating their ideas into action, thereby bringing about changes in agriculture, the more significant they become to historical geographers. It is therefore important that we should know what they accomplished. To begin the discussion we can note the criticisms the improvers made of colonial agriculture and the innovations they advocated. The next steps are to discover where, when, how and with what results the improvements were made. We require also explanations for any regional variation in the adoption of improvements. The interpretation of the record should reveal not only the process of agricultural change in late-colonial tropical America, but the attitudes of the various interest groups, including governments, towards change. An appreciation of the improvers' work can come from viewing their achievements in the perspective of the long-term trends in tropical American agriculture between that new beginning of the years immediately following 1492 and the development plans of the present day. This programme reveals a field of research which contains many issues subsidiary to the central question. Here, I will briefly review the sources for the study of the colonial improvers, put forward some preliminary conclusions and suggest further lines of inquiry.

The sources

The most evident testimony to this interest in colonial agriculture and the most accessible source of information on the criticism and recommendations of the improvers are the books, pamphlets and agricultural manuals the improvers wrote. This literature is extensive, varied and includes some of the best-known books written about tropical America in the late eighteenth century.

The books are difficult to classify, being in part histories, in part travel accounts and economic reports: discussion of agriculture shares the pages with descriptions of landscapes and lifestyles, with trade statistics and narratives of the doings of colonial governors. Most parts of tropical America are described in greater or lesser detail in one or another of these books. Prominent English examples of this writing are the anonymous *American Husbandry*,[1] *The History, Civil and Commercial of The British Colonies in The West Indies* by Bryan Edwards[2] and William Beckford's *A Descriptive Account of The Island of Jamaica*.[3] A comparable French work is Moreau de St Méry's *Description topographique, physique et historique de la partie française de L'Isle de Saint-Dominique*.[4] Alexander von Humboldt drew on his travels in the early nineteenth century to write outstanding accounts of the life and economy of Cuba and Central America.[5] Southey includes much geographical information about late colonial times in his *History of Brazil*.[6] Inevitably such works are of unequal value to students of land use and agricultural change, but they do constitute a source of major importance.

The agricultural manuals are much more specialized works. Some offer advice on estate management while others deal with the techniques of cultivating and processing particular export crops. Samuel Martin's manual on sugar plantations, *An Essay Upon Plantership*,[7] passed through seven editions during the years 1754–1802. Also interesting for their recommendations on improving the efficiency of sugar plantations are the reports of Dutrône La Couture[8] and Citizen Avalle,[9] published during the French Revolution. In Spanish America, in addition to manuals such as those of Arango y Parreño,[10] the debates and publications of the economic societies of Havana, Bogota, Guatemala and other cities reveal the interest in and ideas about agricultural improvement of the colonial elite.[11] Lisbon became a modest centre for the diffusion of agricultural knowledge. Papers on agricultural topics appeared in the *Mémorias* of the Royal Academy of Sciences[12] and the government encouraged research and the publication of reports on various crops.[13] A Brazilian priest resident in Lisbon, Fr Veloso, undertook a programme of translating into Portuguese selections from the works of foreign writers for distribution among the landowners of Brazil.[14]

Government archives provide evidence of the extent of official interest in agriculture and of government policies towards the reforms the improvers recommended. Assessing the effectiveness of these policies is a more difficult task than describing them. Trade statistics and tax returns tell part of the story, revealing the increase – or decline – in exports and any diversification in the crops produced by a colony. Estate muniment rooms, the records of botanical gardens and even industrial archaeology can provide information on the adoption of innovations by landowners and the effects these innovations had on the productivity of agriculture. These various sources have already been tapped in part with interesting results.

Improvers' criticisms and government policies

The agricultural geography of late-colonial tropical America presented the improvers with a very varied scene. On the Caribbean islands and along some stretches of the mainland coast between south-central Brazil and Mexico plantations worked by slaves produced crops for export to Europe and North America. Landowners without easy access to the Atlantic stream of commerce, such as those of interior Mexico or coastal Peru, produced for local markets. On the margins of the estates, squatters and smallholders eked out a precarious existence. Throughout a vast hinterland semi-feral herds of cattle roamed, supporting a trade in hides, tallow and dried beef. In many regions indigenous forms of land use still survived. The density and composition of the population varied from island to island, from Vera Cruz to Rio, according to historical and geographical circumstance.

The improvers concentrated their attention overwhelmingly on only one aspect of colonial agriculture: the development of the plantation economy. The manuals, the government reports, the agricultural sections of the books discuss the problems of improving the efficiency of the plantations but give in comparison scant attention to the agriculture of those groups who were not contributing to exports. This emphasis helps account for the lack of concern shown by most of the writers in the potential of the grazing lands in contrast to the contemporary European interest in breeding livestock. Investment in new breeds of cattle would not have improved the existing trade in hides and tallow and, without rapid, refrigerated, sea transport, the export of high quality beef could not be contemplated. Though some of the writers did express a concern for the welfare of the population, a concern which came to the fore most insistently in the criticism of slavery, the main thrust of the movement to improve the agriculture of colonial America was in the direction of increasing the supply of tropical crops for the temperate world.

The longest established, the most widely cultivated and still the most important of all the cash crops was sugar. Understandably, the sugar industry was the focus of the attention of the improvers. Their aim was to reduce costs and improve productivity in what was a highly competitive industry. All aspects of the industry, from the planting of cane to the final manufacture of sugar, came under scrutiny. Efforts to improve the yield of cane and maintain the fertility of the soil led to pages of discussion of the properties of the different types of soil and the virtues of the different methods of manuring. This interest was particularly strong among French and English writers whose experience was of small, intensively cultivated islands. In St Domingue, the French began to irrigate the canefields, and Citizen Avalle, drawing on his investigations in the colony, proposed an ideal layout for a plantation's canefields which would facilitate, among other matters, the movement of the cane from field to mill, the control of fire and the supervision of the work force. Labour was a major item in the cost of production. Traditionally, gangs of slaves wielding hoes prepared the fields for cultivation, but some writers thought that the introduction of ploughing, being less labour-intensive, would reduce costs. They reported on the experiments. Planters also sought cheap and reliable sources of food for the slaves and plantation livestock – sources which might also be economical in the use of land and so permit planters to convert some of the acreage in pasture and provision grounds to sugar. The possibility that breadfruit might be a useful component of slave diet prompted Captain Bligh's famous voyage to the South Seas. In the second aspect of the sugar industry, the manufacture of sugar from cane juice, the planters strove for technological improvements in their mills, furnaces and boiling houses.

Improvers and governments recognized the risks inherent in mono-culture and hence wished to diversify the agriculture of their colonies. They urged landowners to experiment with a range of crops. To this end, numerous descriptions appeared on the methods of cultivating cocoa, coffee, indigo, cotton and tobacco. The Portuguese government revived its interest in the possibility of developing a Brazil-based spice trade and sent advice, seeds and even Asian experts to the colony. In Spanish America, the economic societies debated the prospects of finding overseas markets for native American crops not as yet on the export lists. The improvers saw botanical gardens as playing an important role in advancing the colonial economies. Such gardens, they considered, could serve as centres of experimentation where botanists would cultivate exotic plants and new varieties of familiar ones, assess their potential for enriching the local agriculture, and distribute samples accordingly to landowners.

Criticism was muted of plantation society. The few improvers who made recommendations for social change usually supported their position with arguments that the reforms would bring benefits to the state such as an extension in the area under cultivation or a reduction in production costs to the plantations. At least one writer argued that reform would lead to an increase in population. A main target of the criticism was slavery. Slaves were inefficient workers, the critics claimed. Moreover, the close association between slavery and agricultural labour made such labour demeaning to free men, so discouraging them from participating in the work force. Abolition of slavery would not only be a humanitarian measure but would release the reserves of labour in the free population. The critics also cast around for alternate sources of labour, in Chinese or Indian immigrants. The fact that planters continued to resist abolition suggests that the criticisms of slavery on economic grounds may not have been well-founded. Another focus of criticism was the colonial pattern of land tenure in which large, only partially exploited estates were predominant. In eighteenth-century Spain, reformers commented on the harmful effects of such estates on the nation's economy and on the inherent injustice of a situation in which good land lay uncultivated while many of the rural poor had no work to do. Not surprisingly, these discussions found an echo in the debates of the Spanish American economic societies. Von Humboldt, too, criticized the estates,[15] but perhaps the most vigorous colonial expression of dissatisfaction came from Luís dos Santos Vilhena, a professor of Greek, in Salvador, Brazil.[16] Vilhena was shocked that even after more than two hundred years of colonization only a meagre extent of land was cultivated in Brazil and that the inhabitants were not only few in numbers, but in good part unemployed and underfed. He blamed the pattern of land tenure as well as landowners who neglected food crops in favour of exports. In Vilhena's mind, landownership, stable family life, the increase in population and prosperity were closely and causally linked. To remedy the defects of Brazilian agriculture and society, he proposed an 'agrarian law' in which he argued that the government should exercise a strong measure of control over land use to ensure that sufficient food was grown. He also considered the government should distribute the unused portions of the estates in small plots to those with the ability to cultivate them. The implementation by the government of Vilhena's 'law' would have switched land and labour resources from the export sector to production for domestic consumption, changing thereby the course of Brazilian development.

Some of the recommendations of the improvers were translated into action. The sources clearly reveal that cotton and coffee, for instance, as well as several more new crops became prominent items in many a colonial export list. In other words, the landowners responded to market demands and were amenable to suggestion. The sugar industry benefited from the introduction of a new variety of cane. In the late eighteenth century, the British and French, separately, brought Otaheiti cane from the Pacific to their Caribbean colonies. It gave higher yields than Creole cane, the variety which had been cultivated in the Americas since the beginning of colonial times, and within thirty years had replaced Creole cane in the major sugar-growing regions. Guinea grass, a chance introduction from Africa, proved an important fodder for plantation oxen. Breadfruit and rice, the latter ultimately the more significant of the two as a source of food, began to spread through the American tropics. Many a governor or town council founded a botanical garden, a few of which did fulfil their intended role as disseminators of plants of economic significance. But the record also shows that governments were uninterested in social reform though, with the passage of time, as the eighteenth century turned into the nineteenth, the campaign to abolish slavery provides increasingly an exception to this remark. During these years, in the only colony where the traditional structure of plantation society was destroyed, St Domingue, the change came violently, through revolution. Rather than attempt to redress the balance between rich and poor, *fazendeiro* and labourer, governments designed their policies to increase the flow of tropical produce to the home countries.

These government priorities were shared by the colonial landowners who stood to benefit from any increase in the production of export crops on their estates. They welcomed government support in obtaining new varieties of plants, in organizing agricultural experiments, in building roads and bridges which would help them get their crops to the docks; but they resented any government infringement of their freedom of action in managing their estates and criticized what they considered to be undue regulation of trade, even invoking the newly fashionable name of Adam Smith to give weight to their protests. To the extent that the policy of boosting the export economy was successful, the 'age of the improver' in tropical America led to a strengthening of the plantation system and to a tightening of the bonds of economic dependence which linked colony to metropolitan power.

Unresolved issues

We are, therefore, as the preceding paragraphs show, in a position to make general statements about the evolution of land use in late-colonial tropical America and even to reach the significant conclusion that the movement to improve agriculture was chanelled into a very conservative direction, but the sources and state of research still leave many aspects of the changes in agriculture unclear.

Two lines of questioning seem particularly worth exploring if we are to unravel the full measure of the improvements taking place during these years. One is to try to establish, and the more precisely the better, the contribution of particular innovations to increases in such indices of production as the intensification in land use, higher crop yields per unit area or output per man employed. The introduction of Otaheiti cane is illustrative of our unsatisfactory state of knowledge in this sphere. It was a better variety of cane than the Creole – its rapid diffusion attests to this – and von Humboldt's comments[17] that it raised yields by more than one third in Mexico and by a quarter in Cuba gives us an idea of how much better it was, but accurate figures are hard to come by on the yields of the two varieties and on what difference Otaheiti cane made to the profitability of plantations in the various regions of tropical America. Answers to this type of question may lie in the account books and records of individual plantations. Ward Barrett's study of *The Sugar Hacienda of the Marquesas del Valle*[18] points to the achievements and the difficulties of the research. He was able to show very significant increases in the yields of cane in terms of Kg/ha and Kg/worker but was unable to be precise about the comparative importance of the various improvements over the period from 1600 to 1800.

The second approach is to try to understand why some seemingly important innovations were adopted slowly, attaining only a restricted distribution by the early nineteenth century. Irrigation is a case in point. Well known in parts of central and Andean America before European times, irrigation was rare in the Caribbean. During the eighteenth century, the French built networks of canals to extend sugar cultivation into the drier valleys of St Domingue where they subsequently obtained yields nearly two-thirds higher than those Jamaican planters obtained from their unirrigated land.[19] This comparison suggests that the use of irrigation to supplement natural rainfall would have been an advantage to planters in many regions. Studies of the cost benefits of investing in irrigation might explain why indeed irrigation was not more common. The evidence of the rather slow diffusion of the fuel-saving furnace known as the Jamaica train, of the use of steam power in sugar mills and of the new saw gins for ginning cotton in comparison to the rapid diffusion of Otaheiti cane or even of breadfruit, suggests that landowners found the integration of new plants into their agriculture easier than improvements in technology.

New technology of course required capital and 'know-how'. Part, therefore, of the growing regional variation in agricultural practices and rates of change is no doubt attributable to the presence or absence of mechanics in a colony's population, as well as to ease of access to capital and markets and to the inequalities in the resource base from one part of tropical America to another – the abundance of land and fuel in Brazil, their scarcity in Barbados, for example. Confirmation of these surmises could come from the analysis of estate records and the discovery of the rewards particular innovations could bring to landowners working in different geographic and economic circumstances.

Conclusion

A full assessment of the achievements of the improvers of the late-colonial period will have to wait until answers to some of the above questions are forthcoming, but the outlines of that assessment are already emerging. The improvers introduced a spirit of scientific inquiry into colonial agriculture and succeeded in increasing the productivity of the export economy. They did not transform agriculture by introducing new types of land tenure or new social structures as when the first European colonists dispossessed the Indians to establish ranches, plantations and to experiment with the unfamiliar environments; nor, probably, did they achieve advances in productivity comparable to those which came later in the nineteenth century with new means of transportation, the development of plant genetics and technological advances which permitted economies of scale as represented by *usinas* in the sugar industry. The 'age of the improver' in tropical America, as in Europe, was one of gradual rather than revolutionary change.

University of Toronto,
Canada

Relating structure to process in historical population analysis: case studies from eighteenth-century Spanish America

D. J. ROBINSON

Discussions of the relationships between patterns and processes have long been debated by historical geographers, as have the merits and defects of cross-sectional and longitudinal analysis. The principal questions concerned with either methodological mode are not difficult to identify, even if providing suitable answers is considerably more so. First, there exists the morass of inference; when process is to be. seen through pattern indeterminacy, inertia, equifinality and multi-causality enter the scene.[1] Secondly, there still remain several questions concerning the extent to which comparative statics can be used in interpretative situations when data can be used at the micro-scale, and in short temporal phases. When one penetrates far into the thickets of defining so-called 'process', one can see blurred boundaries between cause and effect. Thirdly, it should also not be forgotten that there still remain many patterns that derive from social processes that have yet to be constructed by historical geographers. Here kinship and ritual kinship are offered as examples. Their analysis, it is argued, is enhanced by a combination of synchronic and diachronic methods, for each reveals distinctive aspects of phenomena, and raises further questions.

This paper considers some of the implications of such issues within the framework of two specific problem areas at present under investigation. Both relate to socio-demographic issues, are concerned with the key question of the most appropriate scale of analysis and are grounded in Latin American data, which will hopefully not reduce their general relevance.

Population patterns and change in urban areas

The use of population density maps is commonplace among historical geographers. They usefully summarize for specific dates the distribution of

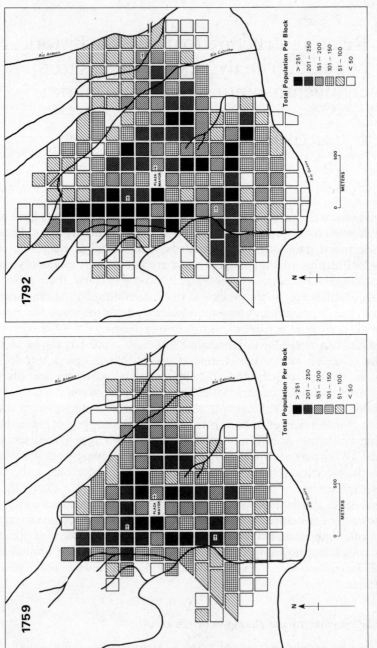

Fig. 1. *Population distribution in Caracas, 1759 and 1792*

a population, or some isolated structural features. In the present case the maps of Caracas (Fig. 1) capture the changing distribution of population in the middle and at the end of the eighteenth century.[2] Each map is constructed from census data originally at the level of individuals within households, which have been aggregated to their respective blocks.[3] In 1759 a differentiated pattern was already discernible; extensions of high density population extended out in distinctive directions from the main square (*plaza mayor*). By 1792 a further fifty-six blocks had been added to the urban frame, and population had been considerably resorted. Of the 1759 blocks some 53 per cent had gained population, with twenty-one losing population and the remainder showing no change. An intensification of density in a north–south band, west of the square, is apparent, as well as the appearance of several new secondary concentrations, especially in the south and east. That growth had taken place there can be little doubt, but exactly what the relations were between different parts of the city is less easily identified.

If one examines not the spatial patterns, but the temporal sequence of population change (Fig. 2), it becomes readily evident that Caracas grew in an episodic fashion during the period 1750–1820.[4] Two downturns mark its demographic progress, one coming in the 1760s and the other after 1810. The first was triggered by a measles epidemic that swept into the capital from Coro in 1763, killing a thousand persons within a year.[5] In spite of out-migration of population into surrounding rural parishes, which can be traced through the extant censuses, the effects of the epidemic were felt for a decade. The second period of loss was related to the impact of the wars of independence as well as the calamity of the 1812 earthquake. Between 1809 and 1815 Caracas lost over a third of its inhabitants.[6]

What the graph of the city's change does not demonstrate is the rapidity and almost continual fluctuation of population within the several urban parishes. This patterning speaks of continual migration to and from the surrounding countryside, as well as a shift of population from one urban parish to another. However, such complications cannot be identified adequately from simple and widely spaced cross-sectional analyses. Only after one has been able to establish the significance of temporal patterning can further spatial analysis become rewarding, and then at a distinctive scale, and by tracing individuals or cohorts through time. If a sample street section of the city is examined between 1768 and 1776, during the latter stage of the first urban crisis, a remarkable pattern of population change is evident (Fig. 3). At the level of individual households population was fluctuating rapidly.[7] Stable households were the exception, and of the individuals listed in the 1768 census, only 70 per cent could be found in 1770, a mere 52 per cent in 1772, 48 per cent in 1773 and 36 per cent in 1776. Not only do a bewildering number of persons rent or occupy the

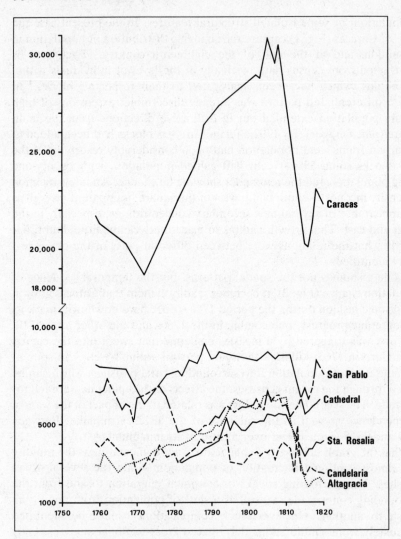

Fig. 2. *Population changes in Caracas, 1750–1820*

houses but, as has been shown elsewhere, the housing units themselves were undergoing rapid morphological change.[8] In Caracas in the eighteenth century people were on the move, and such movement makes analysis extremely complicated.[9]

Significant changes were also underway in the overall family and household structure within the city (Table 1). As is being identified for an

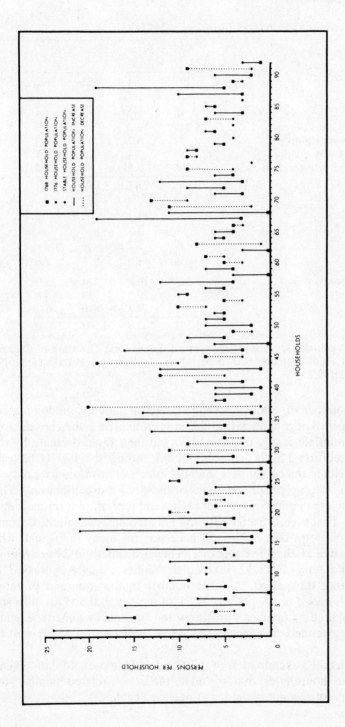

Fig. 3. *Household population change in Agonia Street, Caracas, 1768–1776*

Table 1. *Household structure, Caracas, 1759–1792*

Types	1759 N	1759 %	1792 N	1792 %
Solitaries	191	7.4	185	5.2
Nuclear				
–Couples	50	1.9	58	1.6
–Couples with children	344	13.2	385	10.7
–Widows with children	19	0.7	141	3.9
–Widowers with children	89	3.4	28	0.7
–Unmarried with children	66	2.5	81	2.2
	568	21.7	693	19.1
Extended				
–Lateral	186	7.1	–	–
–Lineal	96	3.7	–	–
–Complex	57	2.2	–	–
	339	13.0	275	7.6
Non-kin extended	513	19.8	1,274	35.0
Multiple family	532	20.5	354	9.8
No family	448	17.3	816	22.7
TOTAL	2,591	100.0	3,597	100.0

Source: K. Waldron, 'A Social History of a Primate City: The Case of Caracas, 1750–1810' (unpublished dissertation, University of Indiana, 1977), pp. 110–22.

increasing number of colonial localities, nuclear families predominated, mostly composed of couples with children.[10] Of interest is the considerable number of multiple family units in 1759, and their rapid decrease by the end of the century. This is explicable by the chronic shortage of housing units in the city at the earlier date, and the effects of town council policy in the 1770s to open up peripheral zones of the city for urban housing. This meant that a large number of resident kin could hive off to form their own households. That such housing could still not accommodate all the demand is clear if one notes that it was still necessary for many individuals who were not related at all to live together. They accounted for 22 per cent of all household types by 1792. Extended families actually decreased in number during the period. A large number of the thousand or more housing units added to the physical stock of the city in the 1770s must still have been shared by families with slaves and servants of some type, since the non-kin extended class increased sharply to amount to 35 per cent by 1792.[11]

A more detailed examination of the Candelaria household data reveals that even in households that included other non-related families the principal type of secondary units was nuclear (Table 2).

Table 2. *Family structure in Candelaria Parish, Caracas, 1761–1768*

Type	Primary family N	Primary family %	Secondary families N	Secondary families %	Total N	Total %
			1761			
Solitaries	88	30.0	46	17.6	134	20.2
Co-resident						
siblings	7	1.7	–	–	7	1.0
Nuclear	257	64.1	204	78.4	461	69.7
Extended						
–lineal	17	4.2	4	1.5	21	3.1
–lateral	30	7.5	5	1.9	35	5.3
Complex	2	0.5	1	0.4	3	0.5
TOTAL	401	100	260	100	661	100
			1768			
Solitaries	110	24.0	–	–	110	17.2
Co-resident						
siblings	15	3.3	9	4.9	24	3.7
Nuclear	239	52.2	165	90.6	404	63.2
Extended						
–lineal	29	6.3	8	4.3	37	5.8
–lateral	60	13.1	–	–	60	9.4
Complex	4	0.8	–	–	4	0.6
TOTAL	457	100	182	100	639	100

Source: Archivo Arquidiocesano de Caracas, Matrículas de la Parroquia de Candelaria, 1761–1768.

What is very evident from this abundance of data is that individuals were behaving in complex interacting processes of household formation and modification, controlled by the socio-economic norms of the period. Almost all were affected by familial ties of kinship, god-kinship, or patron–client relations. To live in the city meant that one had to gain access to land resources that were controlled by a relatively small but powerful urban elite, which itself was bound together by the bonds of kinship and mutually profitable reciprocal relationships. As elsewhere in Spanish America and beyond such social linkages, the patterns of marriage and family/linkage formation were of critical importance. Only recently, however, have the spatial dimensions and consequences of such phenomena been outlined.[12] The space–time location of each and every individual (some far more than others due to their positions of power) in Caracas radically affected the overall population patterns that emerge in cross-sectional analyses. The cohort of temporary out-migrants of the 1760s produced in turn, on their return in the 1770s, a rise in specific parish population densities. Several of those who returned had moved on to another stage in their life-course or family cycle, returning as single adults, married spouses or in many cases widows. Their 'choice' of residential location was more a concern with the changed circumstances of the urban elite and their primary social contacts than it was to any national freedom of action at the individual or family level. An increasingly well-defined caste (*casta*) system articulated the social and spatial patterning of society.[13]

Spatial dimensions of kinship and *compadrinazgo*

For a variety of reasons it has not been possible, as yet, to reconstruct the ties of kinship and ritual kinship (*compadrinazgo*) that prevailed during the eighteenth century in Caracas. To do so would require the merging of census and parish register data at a scale beyond that which could be processed manually.[14] Instead, an analysis has been made of the kin linkages within the Argentine city of Córdoba, which had a population in excess of 7,000 by the 1780s. It was thus roughly the same size as that of Caracas' Cathedral parish. Previous studies of racial, status and household and family patterns in Córdoba had produced interesting results that demonstrated quite clear residential zoning strongly influenced by differential access to the urban land market, as well as the cumulative effects of episodic vital rates of change.[15] However, it became clear that in attempting to explain the distribution of solitaries or nuclear families one was, in the synchronic patterns of censuses, artificially severing the social and biological bonds that tied individuals and households together. To be solitary in a residential sense was not to be socially alone in the city; or so it was assumed. Equally, it was argued that separate nuclear families might be but spatially separated extended family networks.[16] The relative simplicity of the data portrayed on Fig. 4 belies the difficulty of its compilation. A combination of census, parish register and notarial records was required to generate a list of identifiable individuals whose kin linkage was established beyond that of their sharing the same family name.[17] For each of the 924 households in the 1779 census of the city a search was made for kin relations of any persons who were still resident in the city at that date, together with their specific residential location. Some 113 links were positively established (Table 3). More than a third of those linked lived either on the same block-front, or across the street, providing further evidence of the significance of family and clan compound structure in the colonial city of the late Empire. As had been hypothesized previously, the linkages within blocks (*manzanas*) did not appear to have been as significant as those along or across facing-blocks.[18] Only the very rich could obtain enough adjacent property to dominate an entire city block.

It is not suggested, of course, that such patterns in any way provide

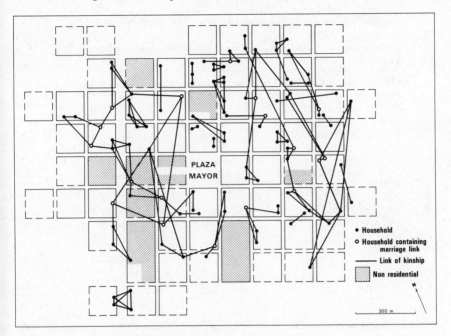

Fig. 4. *Identifiable kin linkages in Córdoba, Argentina, 1779*

surrogates for the emotional bonds that tied individuals or families together; on the contrary, it may well be that as in other contexts sufficient social distance from relatives of specific types was appreciated. However, the fact of life for most newly wedded couples or established families was residence with or close by one's parents and in-laws for a period of time. Just as homes often contained workplaces, so wives were also often the daughters of employers. Marriage was a social strategy more than an affair of the heart.[19]

Distances separating kin are included in Table 3, and compared to European samples appear to be not unusual.[20] Only when other Latin American urban and rural patterns have been derived will it be possible to isolate perhaps the effects of occupational grouping or racial segregation and the modification of such structures with the progression through the various phases of family time.[21]

For the Latin American colonial social world another form of social linkage was common: that of *compadrinazgo*. By a process of selection individuals (and their kin families) were spiritually and socially linked together.[22] The most important of the many god-parents and co-parents that were selected were identified at an individual's baptism and marriage, and other types will not be considered here. Essentially what this process

Table 3. *Location of non-resident kin in Córdoba, Argentina, 1779*

Location	N	%
On the same block-front (*media cuadra*)	21	18.6
Across the street (*cuadra*)	19	16.8
On the same street (*calle*)	17	15.0
In the same block (*manzana*)	8	7.1
Elsewhere in the city	48	42.5
	113	100
Link lengths (in street metres)	N	%
< 100	60	45.1
101–300	32	24.1
301–450	27	20.3
451–600	10	7.5
601–750	2	1.5
> 750	2	1.5
	133	100

accomplished was an increase in the density of the web of socio-economic, moral, political and other ties binding people together. It could provide a supportive cushion or an extended network of opportunity and liability as the occasion demanded.[23] Surprisingly, given the spatial implications of the process of sponsor choice, little rigorous attention has been paid to the subject in the past, either by historians or historical geographers. The reason would appear to be that although its significance is well known, and usually clear from the records, to establish exactly who the sponsors were, and, more important here, where they lived, is much more complex. To undertake a complete analysis would require the tracing of god-children (*ahijados*), god-parents (*padrinos*), and co-parents (*compadres*), from their place of residence at the baptism of the child to its death – clearly a formidable reconstruction. Though such extended treatment is not presented here, it is worth noting that *compadrinazgo* had (as it still does) important demographic consequences, for such bonds normally proscribed marriage relationships among all of the persons concerned. Spiritual bonding may thus have required an extension of search for a spouse.[24]

For Córdoba an analysis was made of all baptisms and marriages for the decade before the civil census of 1779. For each ceremony the names of god-parents were extracted and a search was made in the 1779 file for the names of all persons who were still resident within the city's single parish (Table 4). Over half of the baptismal sponsors for the decade were chosen from within the single parish of the city, with less than an additional 5 per cent from contiguous parishes.[25] Of the 392 who were baptised with city

Table 4. *Padrinazgo links in Córdoba, Argentina, 1769–1779*

| | Baptism | | Marriage | |
	N	%	N	%
Inside the city				
With kin	12	14.4	16	25.8
With non-kin	71	85.6	46	74.2
Within household	9	10.8	8	12.9
Within *cuadra*	15	18.0	18	29.0
Elsewhere in parish	59	71.0	36	58.0
Total identifiable in 1779 census	83	100.0	62	100.0
Total for city	392	57.4	95	38.4
Outside the city				
In contiguous parish	48	7.0	30	12.1
In non-contiguous nearest parish	32	4.7	7	2.8
Other parishes	14	2.0	25	10.0
Residence of *padrinos* not given	196	28.7	90	36.4
TOTALS	682	100	247	100

Source: Archivo de la Curia Eclesiástica de Córdoba, Libros de Bautismos y Matrimonios de la Catedral, 1769–1779.

padrinos, some 83 (21 per cent) can be identified in the 1779 census. Of that group a large proportion was selected from kin relations, thus intensifying social relationships. Only 29 per cent were selected, however, from within the same household or households on the same block-fronts (*cuadras*). Most were sponsors who lived elsewhere in the city, probably distant enough to reduce the potential strain on the ritual and formalized relationship of day-to-day contact. The majority of those who selected sponsors from within their households chose non-kin residents who were probably absent from the city on the numerous occasions that commercial trading demanded, or were of such status to make their selection worth the risk of conflict and the sacrifice of rank.[26]

Marriage sponsors were selected with the active participation of the prospective god-children, and it is of interest to note that fewer links were established with persons resident in the city proper (38 per cent). The fact that more dispersed localities supplied the sponsors may speak of an actual or potential wider field of socio-economic activity. To have a sponsor from another town – or better still the vice-regal capital – could be a great advantage.[27] Within the city more sponsors were chosen from nearby locations than in the baptismal pattern, which may hint at the desire to cement mutually advantageous bonds with well-known individuals. By the age of marriage the potential risks and benefits for all parties concerned were becoming clearly established: careers were underway, dowries allocated and wills prepared.

In colonial Córdoba, as in other Latin American contexts, it can be demonstrated that kin and *compadrinazgo* links forged significant social relations, and provide the researcher with potential means of measuring the interdependence of settlements and populations when all others are absent. Further work may demonstrate that at the regional and imperial scale the role of kinship and *compadrinazgo* was of vital significance in the formation of business enterprises and in the manipulation of regionally specialized economic systems. This is one means by which one can measure a sense of belonging in a colonial world of vast distances, of major social cleavages, and continual tension between metropolis and empire, and regional capital and hinterland.[28]

Conclusions

Both of the above brief studies have involved the components basic to historical population research: births, marriages, migration and death. Each has demonstrated in a distinctive manner the means by which it is possible to deepen our understanding of the social fabric of the past. In Caracas widely spaced cross-sections or data at the city level can mask important processes operating at lower levels. In Córdoba the distribution of kin and god-kin suggests socio-economic structuring that facilitates the interpretation of household and family change, and population migration between and within the settlement.

Yet both studies also demonstrate that whether one approaches the task of interpretation from a synchronic or diachronic point of view, both modes of analysis will be required for a full interpretation. To study individual life-cycles, or family cycles, or generational patterning, or specific cohorts, involves their abstraction from the aggregate populations within which they operated.[29] And such a combination of data from one mode of analysis with those from another also poses serious difficulties. As soon as one moves into the evidence of population one becomes aware of the problem of defining the communities to which people belonged, since they were often in an unsteady state of flux. It seems likely, at least for the immediate future, that those who attempt to reveal the complexities of the past and to probe the relationships between populations of individuals will have to adopt a methodology which blends the advantages of synchronic and diachronic and yet permits the fullest use of the extant sources.

University of Syracuse,
USA

Questions of scale in the study of population in nineteenth-century Britain

R. LAWTON

Introduction

Scale is important in several ways in population studies of nineteenth-century Britain.

Time scale

The minimum time-scale of study is, ideally, the individual's life-span, but studies of process demand information on the experience of family and household over several generations.[1] Such cohort studies pose problems of continuity and consistency of data and the various scales at which they are available. Processes shaping population trends at national, regional and local levels are not easily defined in terms of a single time-span over which the modernization process and its associated demographic transition extends.

Recent studies have tended to focus on the mid-nineteenth century for which more abundant population and socio-economic data are available.[2] Yet many changes can be understood only in the context of a longer period from the mid-eighteenth century to the 1920s, the time-span of the British demographic transition,[3] over which evidence varies greatly in character and reliability.[4]

Areal scale

Information at different scales, over relatively lengthy time periods, covering a wide range of demographic, economic, social and environmental data is not easily integrated within a single spatial framework. Changes in the structure of English local government during the nineteenth century led to changes in administrative areas for registration of vital events, census-taking, health and sanitary control, and other social and economic legislation.[5] Hence, it is impossible to study population within a single administrative framework. The early nineteenth-century structure of parish, hundred and shire[6] was modified by early Victorian administrative reforms which also created many new, *ad hoc* administrative areas – Poor Law Unions, Population Registration Districts, Sanitary Districts and the like – which differed in structure and extent. This problem was only partly resolved by the Local Government Acts of 1888 and 1894 which created an all-purpose two-tier structure of Administrative County and County Borough, and of Municipal Boroughs, Urban and Rural Districts.[7]

Levels of explanation

Levels of explanation of population behaviour require study at several scales. General models of population development such as the demographic transition model, which describes vital trends resulting from complex socio-economic causes, is based on large-scale statistical aggregations. Its applicability to different regions or social groups demands a wider range of explanations[8] – genetic, ecological, environmental, economic and social – at larger scales. However, complex relationships between variables are difficult to integrate at various scales. Moreover, explanations at one level of study are not always applicable at others. Thus, micro-scale populations are unstable, vary widely in structure from one population to another and are not easily compared with larger population groups.[9] The findings from micro- and sample studies must therefore be applied with caution at other scales.

Population development in nineteenth-century Britain at various scales

Evidence

The first and most basic question is the availability of evidence from which to generate hypotheses at various levels of explanation. Comparable census and registration data are not easily available at the succession of scales required in geographical analysis. Published census tabulations discard information collected for individuals, and laborious reconstitution from the original records is needed to cross-link population characteristics at scales from the micro to the national: for example, there is no cross-tabulation of occupations by birthplace in British census reports, though the information is recorded in the original schedules.

Explanatory relationships

Explanation of population trends involves both establishing precise relationships between vital trends, mobility and population structure at levels from the individual family to the national population, and linking these with a wide range of environmental, economic, social and behavioural factors. Environmental factors such as water supply and sanitation, housing and working conditions, and levels of nutrition, are basic to an understanding of variations in mortality between social groups and from one area to another. Yet evidence is scattered among a variety of local and national records, many of which are not directly comparable or which have been incompletely preserved, so that individual studies are often not comparable.

Economic forces are crucial in relation to population growth, first because in combination with social attitudes they underlie variations in fertility, and secondly, as a key factor on mobility. Yet there are no nineteenth-century statistics relating directly to employment, unemployment or industrial output. Detailed comparison of fertility is difficult before the 1911 census analysis of marital fertility.[10] Worker mobility has to be painstakingly assembled from individual entries on occupation and birthplace in the census enumerators' books. Indeed, despite considerable information on population structure, family and household structure, occupation and birthplace in censuses from 1841 and on social and economic matters in Reports of Royal Commissions and Select Committees, the influence of socio-economic factors on population cannot be fully tested because of incompleteness and incompatibility of information and the limited range of cross-classifications and the areas for which they are given.

Modes of analysis

Different approaches to the study of population behaviour at different scales require different modes of analysis. For the individual and family we need longitudinal information on demographic events, socio-economic data on life-style and environment at various stages in the life cycle, and information on decisions leading to changes in demographic or social status. At higher levels of generalization and larger scales of study, the emphasis changes: for example, the impact of general economic factors on regional population trends is often evident in migration, while national changes in mortality may reflect general environmental improvements which increase life expectation. In each case, however, local trends may differ owing to specific local factors.

At all levels of study, however, two types of data linkage are essential: first, between the wide range of factors involved in explanations of population phenomena; secondly, the ability to integrate such information at a variety of scales.

Data availability

Such requirements raise many problems of data availability which are basic to population studies of nineteenth-century Britain at all scales.

Demographic data: early nineteenth century

Population totals are enumerated in the decennial censuses from 1801 for individual townships, but they are not universally available prior to that, although parish listings and local urban censuses are more frequent than was once thought.[11] From 1841, census schedules identify individuals and families with considerable precision in relation to household, street and place of residence: from 1851 the enumerators' books placed them both within an administrative hierarchy of parish, ecclesiastical district, town or village, city or borough, and under registration sub-districts and districts. Nevertheless areas of enumeration change over time, while discrepancies between the areas for which different types of census information are categorized make studies at different scales and over different time periods difficult (Fig. 1).[12]

Age and sex structure, essential for detailed analysis of vital trends and a useful indicator of population history, is difficult to reconstruct before their first full enumeration in the 1841 census.[13] Family reconstitution from parish registers may help to remedy this deficiency at local level but care has to be taken in applying findings based on local data at the regional and national level.

Prior to civil registration from 1837, information on baptisms, burials and marriages from parish registers provides material for aggregative and family reconstitution studies.[14] Parochial registers can be matched with population totals in the early nineteenth-century censuses and, where bills of mortality and local enumerators' schedules from the censuses of 1801–31 are available, it may be possible to make a detailed analysis of population trends.[15] Moreover, street directories and other local surveys often permit some study of contrasts between different residential districts.[16]

From 1837, there is a vast amount of information in individual birth, marriage and death certificates, but little attempt to use these in detailed cohort studies. Thus, while aggregate studies provide a good picture of the components of population growth at regional and sub-regional levels, there have been fewer analyses of local and family population history than for the eighteenth and early nineteenth centuries.

Early nineteenth-century evidence for population migration is meagre and largely indirect, though in listings and parish registers the large-scale disappearance of individuals from parish registers and listings over relatively short time-spans point to considerable mobility. Poor law settle-

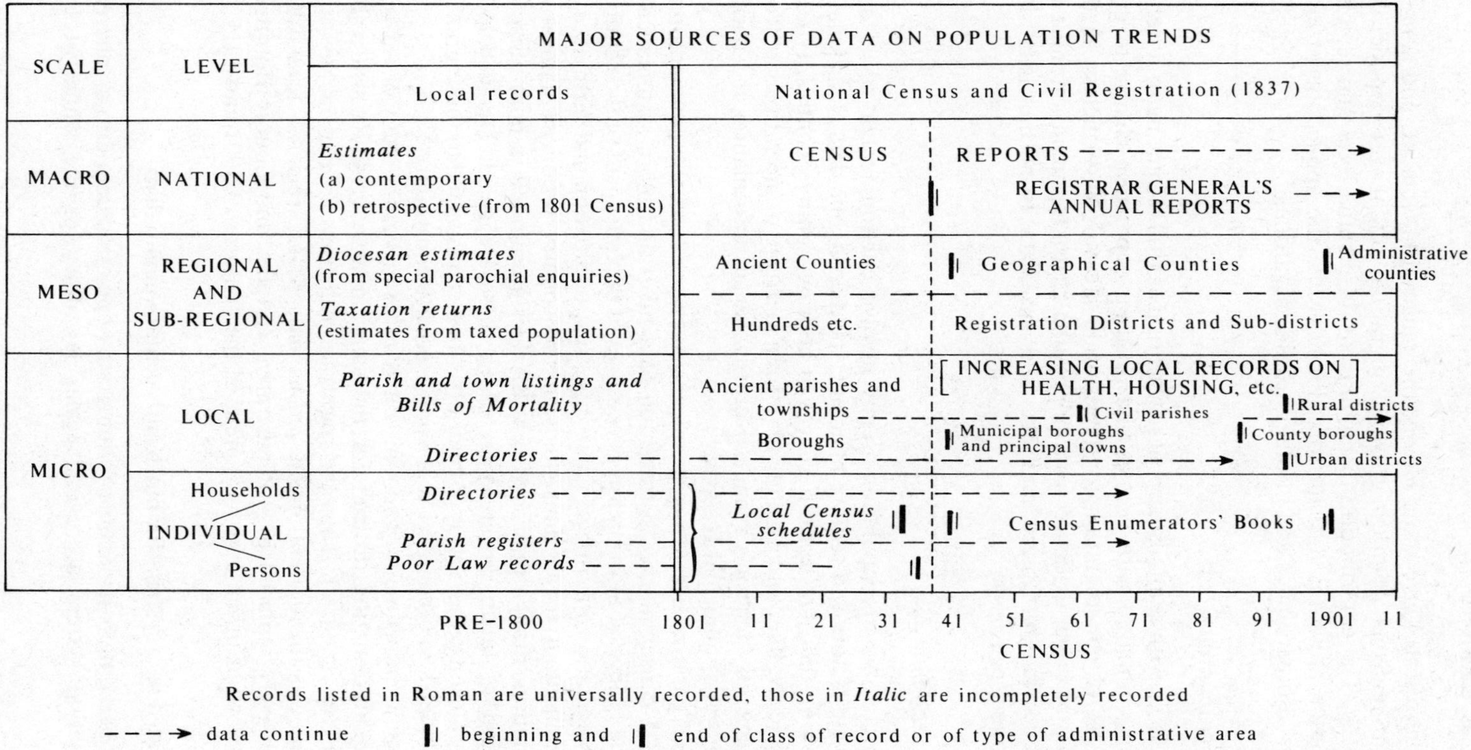

MAJOR SOURCES OF DATA ON POPULATION TRENDS

SCALE	LEVEL	Local records	National Census and Civil Registration (1837)
MACRO	NATIONAL	*Estimates* (a) contemporary (b) retrospective (from 1801 Census)	REPORTS — REGISTRAR GENERAL'S ANNUAL REPORTS →
MESO	REGIONAL AND SUB-REGIONAL	*Diocesan estimates* (from special parochial enquiries) *Taxation returns* (estimates from taxed population)	CENSUS — Ancient Counties / Geographical Counties / Administrative counties — Hundreds etc. / Registration Districts and Sub-districts
LOCAL	LOCAL	*Parish and town listings and Bills of Mortality* — *Directories* —	Ancient parishes and townships — Boroughs / Municipal boroughs and principal towns / Civil parishes — INCREASING LOCAL RECORDS ON HEALTH, HOUSING, etc. — Rural districts / County boroughs / Urban districts
MICRO	INDIVIDUAL (Households → Persons)	*Directories* — *Parish registers* — *Poor Law records* —	*Local Census schedules* — Census Enumerators' Books

Time axis: PRE-1800 | 1801 | 11 | 21 | 31 | 41 | 51 | 61 | 71 | 81 | 91 | 1901 | 11

CENSUS

Records listed in Roman are universally recorded, those in *Italic* are incompletely recorded

- - - → data continue
‖ beginning and ‖ end of class of record or of type of administrative area

Fig. 1. *Schematic diagram of demographic data at various scales for England and Wales in the eighteenth and nineteenth centuries*

ment certificates give some idea of the range of movement, and apprenticeship registers point to growing migration, often over considerable distances. The contribution of mobility to differential local and regional population growth is difficult to estimate, while the application of local studies at other scales and in other areas is hazardous.[17]

Demographic data, 1837–1900

From 1837, with compulsory civil registration of vital events, natural trends may be compared with census data on total population change to give estimates of net migration for registration areas.[18] Nevertheless, in the absence of direct evidence from population registers, migration must be inferred from birthplace and age and sex data from the 1841 and subsequent censuses.

Socio-economic data

Interpretations of population trends involve environmental, social and economic factors and require matching socio-economic data. Local variations in mortality reflect differences in housing, sanitary control, type of work and the like, and its study requires a marriage of mortality data from the Registrar General's Annual Returns, census information and parliamentary and municipal records.

While early nineteenth-century censuses were basically enumerations, the 1841 census marked a transition to a fuller and more systematically classified range of information in censuses of the latter half of the century. The systematic gathering of name, age, sex, occupation and birthplace of each inhabitant in all households in the country produced a mass of information, though published census tables are limited in both range of information and in the areas for which these are given. Detailed local studies must use the census enumerators' books, restricted to those prior to 1881 under a one-hundred-year confidentiality constraint.

Frequent adjustment of administrative areas makes the study of any one class of information difficult for the same areas over any considerable period (see Table 1). Thus the registration districts created in 1837 and used in classification of much census data at sub-regional level were progressively replaced by administrative counties and County Boroughs and lower-tier urban and rural areas in the censuses of 1901 and 1911.

Integrated data systems for nineteenth-century populations

At no one time is it possible to integrate population data into a coherent information system at several scales let alone for the whole of the nineteenth century. The coordination of the data raise several major problems: first, the development of a data matrix from published sources, mainly at a meso- and macro-scale; secondly, the development of more comparable local and micro-scale studies based on information for individuals or families and using standard linkage and sampling procedures: thirdly, the developing of a standard spatial framework capable of use in studies at a variety of scales.

A data matrix

The integration of data from a variety of sources at several scales of study cannot be satisfactorily achieved from published statistics. Changes in areas of enumeration, in classification of data and in details of tabulation often preclude direct comparability between censuses and, occasionally, between one scale of classification and another. But a range of demographic and socio-economic variables can be assembled within a number of spatial frameworks. Many, for example, age and sex data, have standardized and comparable classifications. But much work has had to be done to develop standard classifications of occupational data and socio-economic class, owing to inconsistent census definitions.[19]

Linking vital data to census variables for registration districts and sub-districts would allow comparison of regional and sub-regional trends with national trends in morbidity and mortality.[20] Much more information and greater comparability on population migration could be derived from birthplace data by standardized calculations of inter-censal migration[21] and classifications of the distance and type of mobility.[22]

While such integration of data for standard areal units (such as the registration district and the county) would provide a basis for comparative analyses, to develop a coherent framework of study at a variety of scales one must go back to the original sources and build up from the individual. Computerized data systems permit both fuller use of original data than in published tabulations and a wider range of information on family and household structure, on shared attributes of individuals within households and communities and, by cross-tabulation, age, birthplace and occupation.

Micro-scale studies

Nominal record linkage using individual information on vital and other events is possible from parish registers for a high proportion of the population by the early nineteenth century and for virtually all from vital registration certificates from 1838 and census enumerators' books from 1841. These may be combined with an increasing range of information from directories, ratebooks, school records and the like to provide much

Table 1. Principal areas of England and Wales for which tabulations are given in Census Reports, 1801–1911

	1801	1811	1821	1831	1841	1851	1861	1871	1881	1891	1901	1911
I Population totals and other characteristics[a]												
1. Ancient or geographical counties	×	×	×	×	×	×	×	×	×	×	×	—
2. Hundreds, Wapentakes, etc.	×	×	×	×	×	×	×	×	×	—	—	—
3. Ancient Parishes	×	×	×	×	×	×	×	×	×	—	×	—
4. Townships, etc.	×	×	×	×	×	×	×	—	—	—	—	—
5. Boroughs, Cities and Principal Towns	×	×	×	×	×	—	—	—	—	—	—	—
6. Registration Districts	—	—	—	—	×	×	×	×	×	×	×	×
7. Registration Sub-districts	—	—	—	—	—	×	×	×	×	×	×	×
8. Registration Counties and Divisions	—	—	—	—	—	×	×	×	×	×	×	×
9. Boroughs and Principal Towns	—	—	—	—	—	×	×	×	×	×	×	×
10. Administrative Counties	—	—	—	—	—	—	—	—	—	×	×	×
11. County Boroughs	—	—	—	—	—	—	—	—	—	×	×	×
12. Metropolitan Boroughs	—	—	—	—	—	—	—	—	—	×	×	×
13. Municipal Boroughs	—	—	—	—	—	—	—	—	—	—	×	×
14. Urban and Rural Districts	—	—	—	—	—	—	—	—	×	×	×	×

II Population totals only[b]

15. *Parliamentary Boroughs*	—	—	—	—	×	×	×	×	×	×	×
16. *Parliamentary Counties*	—	—	—	—	×	×	×	×	×	×	×
17. *Parliamentary County Divisions*	—	—	—	—	—	×	×	×	×	×	×
18. *Parliamentary Borough Divisions*	—	—	—	—	—	—	—	×	×	×	×
19. *Ecclesiastical Provinces*	—	—	—	×	×	×	×	×	×	×	×
20. *Ecclesiastical Dioceses*	—	×	—	×	×	×	×	×	×	×	×
21. *Ecclesiastical Parishes, Districts*	—	—	—	×	×	×	×	×	×	×	×
22. *Poor Law Unions*	—	—	—	×	×	×	×	×	—	×	×
23. *Lieutenancy Sub-divisions*	—	—	—	×	—	—	—	×	—	—	—
24. *Petty Sessional Divisions*	—	—	—	—	—	—	—	×	—	×	×
25. *Quarter Session Boroughs*	—	—	—	—	—	—	—	—	×	×	×
26. *County Court Districts*	—	—	—	—	—	—	—	—	—	×	—
27. *Non-Borough Towns over 2000 popn.*	—	—	—	×	×	—	—	—	—	—	—
28. *Wards (Municipal Boroughs)*	—	—	—	—	—	×	×	×	×	×	×
29. *Wards (Metropolitan Boroughs)*	—	—	—	—	—	—	—	×	—	×	×
30. *Civil Parishes*	—	—	—	—	×	×	×	×	×	×	×

Notes: (a) The censuses fall into three main groups: first, the 1801–31 enumerations were limited in range and were organized locally for historic administrative areas; secondly, from 1841 censuses were organized nationally by the Registrar General and processed a wider range of information for registration areas and various urban areas; thirdly, the 1911 census gathered much more data which was tabulated principally for administrative areas resulting from the Local Government Acts of 1888 and 1894.

(b) Population totals only were processed for a large variety of areas at several scales which reflect changing administrative needs and structures.

Source: based on Table 6.5.1, *Guide to Census reports, Great Britain, 1801–1966* (H.M.S.O., 1977).

detail of individual life histories. However, in addition to problems of confidentiality, nominal linkage raises considerable technical problems.[23] British records lack the single spatial and conceptual framework of, say, modern Swedish databanks, and it is often difficult to link different types of information: for example, mobility with vital events or social with demographic data.

In such studies, evidence from several sources is usually filed separately and subsequently brought together.[24] Computer-based systems now permit linkage of individual and family data, which are then aggregated to various spatial levels. One such system – ROBOT – uses transposed data files in an efficient storage and search procedure which permits input and validation of individual information and easy internal cross-referencing and extraction of sub-sets. Nevertheless, despite computer-based systems, the problems of bringing together very large data sets are considerable and they have yet to be applied on a large scale to nineteenth-century Britain, though a number of studies of individual towns have been completed.[25]

Sampling

Because of the size of the data sets, such studies are usually based on samples which impose a variety of problems. Pre-census studies have imposed samples, being restricted to those places for which there are good parish registers. It is often difficult to apply their findings regionally, though collectively they yield valid generalizations on national demographic trends.[26] From the mid-nineteenth century abundant vital and census data, together with environmental data from local sources, provide comparable and wide-ranging spatial information for all areas of the country, which requires sampling to be manageable.

Early sample studies were subjective, selecting case studies in which all available information was processed,[27] but their conclusions are often not of general application and their methodology often does not follow standard procedures for classifying and analysing data. Much effort has recently been expended in the development of standard classifications of census data[28] though, for example, in the analysis of household and family structure and of birthplace, this process has some distance to go. While sample studies must have some flexibility to adapt general classifications to local needs – for example, to encode greater detail on agricultural occupations and status in rural areas or on cotton workers in textile districts – such systematization helps in standard coding for computer analysis, cutting down work and reducing the margin of individual classification error.

There is a need for national samples such as that for the 1851 census of

Great Britain by Michael Anderson which will provide a national data archive on population and social structure from a stratified 2 per cent clustered sample of 945 places (totally 415,000 people), including complete communities (places under 2,000 population) and particular areas within towns.[29] It will provide a unique basis for studies of specific aspects of population at regional and national level, a yardstick against which local studies may be judged.

In local sample studies the choice of sampling unit must satisfy two criteria: first, the individual information must be as wide-ranging as possible; secondly, information must be capable of aggregation to successively larger scales within a coherent spatial framework. The best sampling unit is the household into which information on individuals can be fitted and to which census and other data can be accurately related, although there are difficulties with purely nominal information. Moreover, household units can be sampled randomly (by assigning numbers to each household) or systematically (which is preferred in many topographically based studies)[30] or in clustered samples. Moreover, if studies are to be applied at a variety of scales, the basic sampling unit must be sensitive to areal differences.

Spatial frameworks for sample studies

Interchangeability of studies at different scales, necessary for a fuller understanding of spatial aspects of population and social change in nineteenth-century Britain, demands a flexible spatial framework of analysis. For the nineteenth century detailed areal studies must be built up from the census enumerators' books. The nature of the appropriate areal unit will vary: in a small town contrasts within a street or a part of a street may be significant; in a large city quite large areas may be relatively homogeneous. Where considerable detail of cross-tabulation is required the size and reliability of sub-samples will determine the size of a valid sample population and, in turn, influence the areal framework: areas of sparse population require full-scale investigation and large units of study; areas with a range of population density may require a varying sample fraction or very uneven areas of analysis.

There are three main types of framework suitable for small-area studies. First, individual referencing linked to unique topographic coordinates in a geo-coding system requires high quality data and a very precise and detailed topographic base but it can be aggregated to many levels and is readily comparable over time: unfortunately few areas in the nineteenth century have the necessary consistency of individual and topographic information for such a data bank. Secondly, topographic areas such as streets or census enumeration districts are easily related to individual

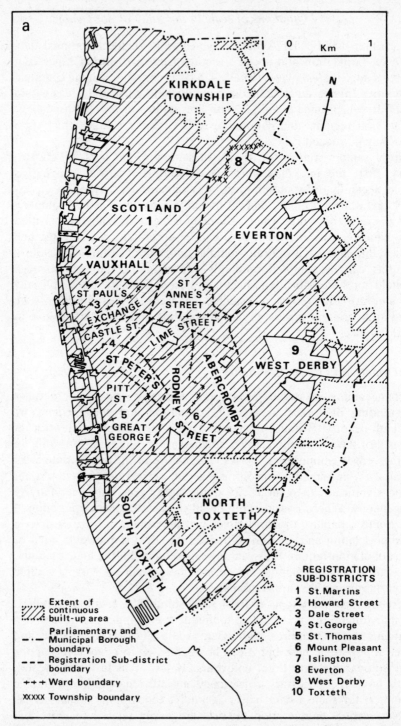

a

0   Km   1

N

KIRKDALE
TOWNSHIP

xxxxxx
8
xxx

SCOTLAND
1

EVERTON

2
VAUXHALL

ST PAUL'S

3

EXCHANGE

CASTLE ST.

4

ST PETER'S

ST
ANNE'S
STREET

7

STREET

LIME

RODNEY

STREET

ABERCROMBY

9
WEST DERBY

PITT
ST

5

GREAT
GEORGE

6

SOUTH TOXTETH

NORTH
TOXTETH

10

REGISTRATION
SUB-DISTRICTS

1   St. Martins
2   Howard Street
3   Dale Street
4   St. George
5   St. Thomas
6   Mount Pleasant
7   Islington
8   Everton
9   West Derby
10   Toxteth

Extent of
continuous
built-up area

Parliamentary and
Municipal Borough
boundary

Registration Sub-district
boundary

+++ Ward boundary

xxxxx Township boundary

Fig. 2. *(a) Administrative areas and revised enumeration districts in Liverpool Borough, 1871*

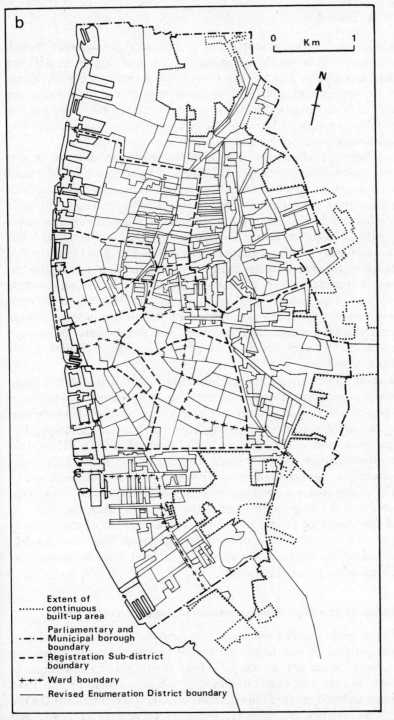

b

0   Km   1

N

Extent of
.... continuous
built-up area

Parliamentary and
-·-·- Municipal borough
boundary

Registration Sub-district
boundary

+++ Ward boundary

——— Revised Enumeration District boundary

*(b) The revised enumeration districts were based on 512 census enumerators' districts
used in gathering the 1871 census.* Note: *In the revision, used for sampling purposes,
boundary irregularities (for example, split enumeration districts) were removed and
very small districts amalgamated. Source: R. Lawton and C. J. Pooley,* The Social
Geography of Merseyside in the Nineteenth Century *(Department of Geography,
U.C.W. Aberystwyth, 1978)*

households and to areal units used in published tabulations, though changes over time may make comparability difficult. Thirdly, an arbitrary standard topographic grid remains constant over time and is early aggregated to any level of study but demands very precise information on location of households within the topographic grid: while objective and comparable over time and from one scale to another, sampling errors may be high in moderately populated areas.[31]

Most British studies have used either enumeration districts or grid squares, the choice depending on the type of area being studied, the need for total as against sample information, and the range and quality of both population and topographic information. For small populations, full-scale analysis related to grid squares has advantages: constancy of areas over time; ease of aggregation to sub-regional level; greater detail and less internal variability than enumeration districts.[32] For large towns or densely populated areas, sample studies using topographic areas of varying size can be used, but more uniform populations are preferable and such sample studies may miss 'within area' contrasts greater than those between districts. Streets or street-blocks offer an appropriate compromise, though even at this scale contrasts between 'street' and 'court' houses or between tenements on different floors in the same house (as in Scotland) may constitute a problem.

Whatever framework is adopted, other than a standard grid, it is likely that some generalization will have to be made to remove anomalies of area, population size or pattern and, if direct comparison between one census to another is needed, to reshape the areas accordingly. For example, in a study of the social areas of Liverpool in 1871, 512 original enumeration districts, which ranged from 78 to 696 households, were reorganized into 394 revised districts with a mean sample household size of 29.1 (143.2 persons) and a minimum of 20 households, thereby preserving the validity of the 10 per cent sample (Fig. 2).[33] Moreover, the choice of spatial framework of large-scale sample studies influences the resulting patterns and the conclusions drawn: the findings of large-scale sample studies cannot be automatically applied at all levels, nor do they necessarily explain the processes at work.

Conclusion: scale and levels of explanation of population behaviour

Population geographers have tended to focus on meso-scale studies of regional patterns of population distribution, emphasizing environmental explanations. In the last decade there have been considerable changes in approach. On the one hand, studies over substantial time periods have attempted to build up macro-models of population development. On the other hand, studies of individual responses to general economic and environmental factors, and of personal motivations and behaviour are attempting to improve understanding of process of change. Both types of study involve micro-level investigation of the experience of individuals to illuminate conclusions based on aggregated data: it is at the micro-level that 'the realities of the human existence' are revealed.[34]

This topic is too large to examine here: a single brief reference to population mobility must suffice.[35] Much of the regional variation in population growth in nineteenth-century Britain is due to local and inter-regional responses to economic factors through population mobility. Many of the suggested relationships are inferential; a fuller understanding of the processes at work requires aggregation of information based on occupation, life-cycle stage, family and household structure, and other characteristics of individual movers. In mid-Victorian Liverpool there were marked contrasts in the occupations of different migrant groups: for example, the Irish were mainly in unskilled, labouring jobs, the Welsh were important in the building trade, the Scots in shipbuilding, and West Midlanders in the metal industries.[36]

Internal mobility within the city, a vital factor in shaping its distinctive social patterns, varied between social classes and their job status, work-places, family-cycle stage and housing. These may be inferred from a study of residential mobility based on directories and census enumerators' books. But there were also a great many personal reasons for movement which we can only partly appreciate from very limited evidence from diaries or other biographical information.[37] Underlying inter-regional population movement are complex histories, the analysis of which demand studies of different data and different modes of analysis at a variety of scales even in explanation of movement over an individual's life-span.

Spatial studies at one scale or a single point of time cannot explain such complex dynamic and multi-causal problems. Better understanding of historic population processes requires studies at a variety of scales, using comparable methods. Explanation must also involve theories appropriate to each level of analysis, for our understanding of processes cannot be advanced on the basis of empirical studies alone.

University of Liverpool,
England

Geographical changes in cities following disaster

M. J. BOWDEN

'Some valuable information could be gathered by studying the rebuilding of cities after catastrophe in a scientific, objective manner,' wrote Helmut Landsberg in *Man's Role in Changing the Face of the Earth*. He continued: 'what patterns did reconstruction take? . . . what improvements were made? Did people make "choices"? were there notable differences in different nations?'[1] In this essay I draw on the Clark University hazard group's studies of urban reconstruction following major natural disasters. This consists of four intensive studies – San Francisco (1906), Anchorage (1964), Managua (1972) and Rapid City (1972) – and work on five cities using secondary material. Such a group makes it possible to offer some answers to Landsberg's queries for cities in mixed and capitalist economies.

Research methods

The research methods were developed in studying San Francisco in the early 1960s. A complete economic-geographic cross-section of the city was reconstructed on the eve of disaster (1905–6), using city and business directories to locate economic activities by building and floor. The detailed map of buildings and addresses was based on city block books, fire insurance maps of the Sanborn Map Company, illustrated directories and photographs of the city taken during the fire that consumed it. Data were aggregated for grid blocks that divided the average city block into six equal parts.[2] For the ten years before and after the disaster economic activities, selected by stratified random sample, were followed on a year-by-year basis in their paths of locational change, stabilization and failure.[3] In order to reconstruct the social-residential structure of San Francisco, Roboff and Gelman drew a sample of one in fifty (2,100 heads of household) from the 1905 city directory. They recorded for each: residential address; business address; socio-economic class (based on a modified version of socio-

114

economic categories derived from occupational data by U.S. census statistician Adna Edwards in the 1930s); and ethnic identity (based primarily on the individual's surname). For every year (1905 and 1907–15) each individual was assigned to a single cell within the 87 by 107 grid which covered the city.[4] Output from the computer program consisted of maps of residential population, space–time analysis for each individual showing path and cumulated distance of post-disaster movement, journey-to-work data for various groups, extent of socio-economic mobility, measures of group location (orthogonal medians) and of segregation, and of persistence and attrition within the city and the Bay Area.

Recent as the other disasters were, it proved necessary to use these historico-geographical methods to reconstruct sections of each city on the eve of disaster because of the obliteration of all visible clues to the form and function of the past by both the disaster event and post-disaster bulldozing and levelling. The problem was compounded in Managua by the government's unwillingness to allow us to consult the landholding records and plot maps of the 450-block area totally levelled in the city centre.

Various business and telephone directories and census materials were used for Managua to establish the city's commercial and industrial structures. We were forced to supplement our findings with materials drawn from aerial photographs, government maps, field surveys and interviews with businessmen. In the absence of comprehensive directory data on the location of Managua's householders we reconstructed the pre-disaster residential structure by drawing a random sample of householders in Managua in April/May 1973, and establishing the address and other particulars of each on the night of the disaster. This evidence was supplemented by data aggregated at the district level and derived from the Nicaraguan planning ministries, housing bank and census.[5]

For Anchorage and Rapid City the names of all householders and businesses directly displaced by the disaster were collected and made available to us by U.S. Government agencies. These data were supplemented by materials drawn from city directories and Sanborn maps. The absence of disaggregated data from the U.S. census of population in this century, and the known omission by city directories of people from the very lowest economic strata and the 'outcast' ethnic groups (Chinese in San Francisco, 1905), forced us to seek out representatives of these groups for intensive study in Rapid City and Managua. For San Francisco we were fortunate to have, as part of the San Francisco Relief Survey, aggregated data on 800 households of this type, for 1906–13.[6]

Process and pattern of reconstruction

There are some clear regularities in the process and pattern of the reconstruction. The dominant temporal process of reconstruction is the return of residential groups and economic activities in a regular sequence; the dominant spatial processes are segregation, centralization and decentralization, and areal expansion. Ongoing before the catastrophe, these processes accelerate rapidly after it – changes often occurring in one-third to one-half the time needed in the pre-disaster period.

Sequence of return in the inner city

For any large disaster some dislocation is inevitable. A chain reaction of relocation, displacement and further relocation is initiated in the inner city by commercial activities and in the outer city by residents able to pay the highest rents and house prices. This evolutionary pattern is accelerated by the need to return to normal and by the removal of the inertia endemic in the built city. Many businesses fail, land suddenly becomes available, and fresh capital is injected in the form of insurance settlements and in recent cases by government financing. Ordered structural changes characterized as the *sequence of return* collapse into a few years the *normal sequence of reaction* recognized in climactic growth periods in fast-growing cities.[7]

In the central zone, for example San Francisco after 1906, this sequence of return is measured in the chronology of decisions and acts of rebuilding recorded in monthly real estate circulars, newspapers and business magazines (Fig. 1). Districts have priority according to the ability of activities to bid for land and pay rent. Rents result from different demands for proximity, both to the area of maximum accessibility in the central area and to similar activities within a particular district. At the top of the ranking of districts is the financial district, followed by the apparel shopping district. The critical reconstruction decisions in the latter district were made in San Francisco by the department stores as soon as the decisions of the large banks and stock exchanges had made clear the outline of the financial district.

In the next year medium-sized apparel specialty stores established the bounds of the apparel district and etched the outlines of the three subdistricts, just as the minor banks, insurance companies, stock companies and major real estate companies each filled out the financial district and split it into four subdistricts. The hotel district, third in rank, was prevented from return to its pre-disaster location by the expansion of the financial district. Within two years of the disaster, however, large hotels had established a new hotel district, filled out by medium-sized and small hotels by 1911.[8] Critical theatre, garment, office and household furnishing establishments then established the core and bounds of these districts in the central zone in the third year after the earthquake (Fig. 1). Banks, department stores and hotels were critical in re-establishing downtown

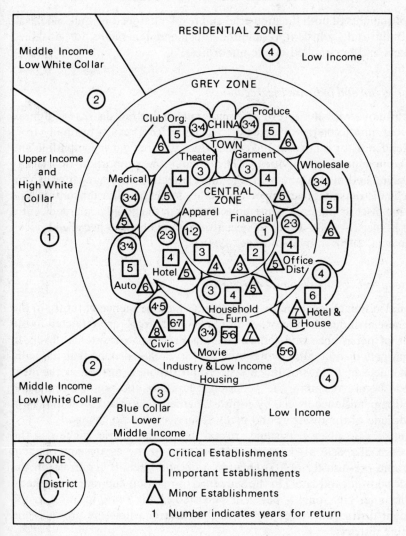

RESIDENTIAL ZONE

Middle Income
Low White Collar

④ Low Income

GREY ZONE

Produce

Club Org. CHINA

Theater TOWN Garment

Medical

CENTRAL ZONE

Apparel Financial

Wholesale

Hotel

Auto

Office Dist

Household Furn

Hotel & B House

Civic

Movie

Industry & Low Income Housing

Middle Income
Low White Collar

Upper Income
and
High White
Collar

Blue Collar
Lower
Middle Income

Low Income

ZONE

District

○ Critical Establishments
□ Important Establishments
△ Minor Establishments
1 Number indicates years for return

Fig. 1. *Sequences of return in the residential and commercial zones, San Francisco, 1906–1915*

Anchorage, while banks and the department-style stores established the new commercial centres on the periphery of Managua.[9]

Between the districts of the central zone and the housing sectors of the outer city is a grey zone of post-disaster indecision. Within this zone the peripheral districts, for example, civic centre, wholesale produce and printing districts were outlined four to five years after the disaster. The remaining land in the grey zone was thrown open to the lowest ranked establishments of both the industrial and residential sectors: bulk wholesaling, industrial, transient residential uses, and tenements for unskilled workers and low-ranked ethnic minorities.

Commercial and industrial segregation

Synchronous with the return of commercial–industrial districts is a more efficient and accelerated segregation. The process results normally from the tendency for related or linked activities to force out incompatible and non-complementary activities.[10] The greater the proportion of the city destroyed and inertia removed, the more effective the segregation. Commercial districts that overlapped each other in the pre-disaster central zone became discrete either as contiguous districts in the greatly enlarged centre (San Francisco, 1906–15) or as decentralized and highly specialized nuclei (Managua, 1970s and Anchorage, 1960s).

Consequences of the sequence of return

The indecision of location for those lowest in the sequence of return in the commercial–industrial sector, and the resultant stress, are reflected in the levels of persistence and failure. In San Francisco persistence levels in the garment district, after being stable for forty years, dropped substantially in the decade following the disaster, and declined further in the next decade before resuming the persistence levels of the pre-disaster years. Banking persistence levels, by contrast, actually increased substantially in the decade of the disaster, and medical services saw no change.[11]

Statistics on place persistence reveal that in the district highest in the sequence of reaction – banking – 34 per cent of the establishments held the same pre-disaster (1905) location a decade later. By contrast, in the districts lower (and later) in the sequence of reaction and more peripheral in the inner city, only 4 per cent persisted in the same location in the garment district and none did so in the theatre, wholesale produce and printing districts.

Printing and garment-clothing industries are particularly impacted by central-area disasters. In San Francisco 61 per cent of clothing industries present in 1905 had failed by 1915. In the printing industry, whereas 45 per cent of activities failed in the normal decade, 1897–1906, 66 per cent failed in San Francisco in the disaster decade, 1906–15 (7 per cent went to the East Bay), and of the printers who persisted (1897–1906), only one-third changed location, whereas all who survived the disaster of 1906 were forced to change locations in the period 1906–15. These two industries were also hit hardest by failures in Managua. Whereas other manufacturing industries (mainly located away from the central destroyed area) saw employment losses of no more than one-third, printing and publishing, and the manufacturing of clothing and footwear (both localized in the centre but low in the sequence of return) lost respectively 85 and 63 per cent of their jobs.

Manufacturing of most types is of the lowest priority in the sequence of return in the central area. Consequently in San Francisco there were 450 fewer manufacturing jobs three years after the disaster than there were before it. By contrast, employment in office, administration, finance and retailing occupations in districts high in the sequence of reaction and quickly re-established after the disaster increased relatively and absolutely in the same period.[12]

Other losers from disasters affecting central areas are the wholesale and manufacturing concerns heavily dependent upon the *low rents of old and amortized loft buildings* in near-central locations, close to the external economies that come from the concentration of hundreds of linked activities in a tightly circumscribed area. These activities – generally small, marginal, often innovative and experimental – are sizeable employers in the city. The districts that house them, called incubators, in that activities within them may eventually be hatched into big employers barring a disaster, are lost. But as in San Francisco after 1906, Managua after 1972, and the many man-induced urban renewal disasters in central areas in the last twenty years in the U.S.A., incubator activities can find no comparable situational niches in the city because low-cost, speculative loft-type buildings stand low in the priority of landowners and builders, and are rarely built in the five-year aftermath of a major disaster.

Social-residential segregation and the sequence of return

A process similar to that operating in the districts of the central commercial area also operates in the residential area. Steepening of rent gradients, resulting from excess demand and lack of housing supply, produces a fiercely competitive selection process that removes incompatible and marginal occupants, establishes a queueing process, and produces purer districts according to socio-economic class, as well as a well-defined sequence of return.

Displacement of large numbers of San Franciscans and Managuans from the predominantly mixed cores, and the subsequent increase in demand for housing in what remained of the pre-disaster high-income housing, sent rents soaring in San Francisco to levels a hundred per cent above those of the pre-disaster years.

Evictions of renters were common throughout the non-damaged area. Low white-collar and blue-collar owner-occupiers who found themselves in districts sought by groups above them in socio-economic spectrum sold houses at high prices and bid for housing elsewhere. With prices of new houses at highly inflated levels, landowners and builders turned first to building high-income housing mainly on undeveloped land west of and contiguous with the undamaged high-income area and later to low white-collar housing to the north and south of the high white-collar sector (Fig. 1). They completed 8,000 units in the first eighteen months, mostly for the white-collar groups. In the next four years, after house prices had begun to drop, they completed 12,000 units mainly for low-income people. High white-collar, low white-collar, blue-collar and unskilled residential areas crystallized in that order for a six-year period.[13]

Managua, residentially mixed before the disaster, became thoroughly segregated after it. The wealthy were quickly rehoused within eighteen months and the middle class within three years. Large numbers of the lower classes are still waiting in cramped quarters for promised housing.[14] In Rapid City the wealthy displaced from the flood plain bid up house prices and occupied homes in a neighbouring district, and were stabilized within six months. Many of those at the lower end of the economic spectrum – minorities and the elderly, formerly in their own houses – were in government-supplied trailers or renting apartments two years after the disaster, with little prospect of being homeowners again.[15]

Social consequences of the sequence of return

In the wake of disaster above-normal stress is placed on the social classes lowest in the sequence of return. They are dislocated for the longest period and many are forced by the indecision in the grey zone to move to locations peripheral to the city or permanently outside it.

The San Francisco statistics on *attrition* demonstrate that stress is so great on the lower income groups in a major disaster that most are forced to emigrate. A large proportion of the 300,000 who left both San Francisco and Managua in the two weeks after the disaster were of the lower socio-economic classes. Three-quarters of the unskilled sampled in 1905 had failed to return to San Francisco or the Bay Area by 1907, and all but one-eighth of the unskilled were gone from the Bay Area by 1911 (compared to just over half of the high white-collar workers sampled in 1905) (Fig. 2).

The results of social workers in San Francisco for 1908–9 dramatically confirm our findings. Some 40 per cent of their sample of refugee families, many of whom were too poor to have been included in the city directories, disappeared in that year. Of the 680 families who remained – mostly female-headed, recent minority migrants or both – most could not have emigrated if they had wanted to do so.[16]

Clearly, all groups resident in the damaged area were greatly affected by

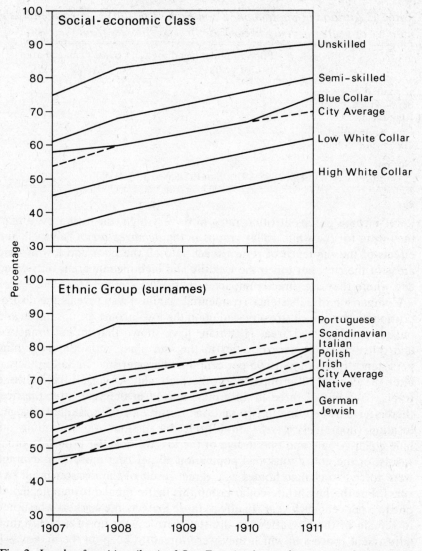

Fig. 2. *Levels of attrition (loss) of San Francisco's pre-disaster population, 1907–1911, by socio-economic class and ethnicity*

the catastrophe (the poor slightly more than the rich). But the proof of the operation of the sequence of return in the housing sector is seen in the class-related differences in the level of attrition of those dwelling in the *undamaged area* on the eve of the earthquake (1906). In San Francisco's undamaged area attrition rates were *normal* for the high white-collar group and only moderately increased for the low white-collar group, but for the

Table 1. *Attrition of population in San Francisco, 1905–7, measured by the number of years normally needed to effect such losses from the city*

	Popn in undamaged area No. of years	Popn in damaged area No. of years
Unskilled	15	24
Semi-skilled	14	23
Blue collar	14	18
Low white collar	3.5	11
High white collar	2	8
Normal	2	2

Control cases: Omaha 1895–1910; San Francisco 1890–1900

lower-income groups attrition rates were very high, far higher even than they were for the white-collar groups in the *damaged area* (Table 1). The effects of the sequence of return reach into all the poor and low-income areas of the city, but touch the wealthy and high-income areas only when and where they are directly impacted by the disaster event.

Comparison of persistence (residential stability) also reveals the disproportionate amount of stress placed upon the low-income groups inside and outside the damaged area. Historians have shown that in San Francisco and other North American cities in the late nineteenth century annual persistence levels of 88 to 95 per cent are characteristic. In San Francisco after the disaster all groups except the high white-collar fell below these levels. Two out of three in all groups moved in the year after the fire; thereafter between one in two and one in three of the unskilled changed location (home) *every year* until 1911; one in four did so among the blue-collar people and one in five of the low white-collar group. In other words, of the entire unskilled population 30 per cent more than average were forced to change homes as a direct result of the disaster in all five years. For the high white-collar group this figure ranged from a negligible one to 3 per cent each year. In effect, those low-income workers who opted to remain in the city after the disaster were caught up in a highly fluid adjustment process in which they were forced to keep on the move, as it were, until 1910–11, after which time low-income housing became more readily available. Dealing with a much smaller disaster in Topeka, Russell found that persistence levels for the upper classes were re-established after two years, the middle classes after four years, and the lower classes after six years.[17]

Another measure of disruption is the journey-to-work (and to a lesser extent the journey-to-shop). In Managua re-establishment of one central market for the poor, with no peripheral commercial centres (such as those provided for the wealthier groups), meant one- and two-hour journeys for thousands displaced to the periphery from the completely destroyed centre. The cost of goods in small local stores was much higher than in the central market. Similarly, the destruction of central-area jobs and the re-establishment of wholesaling and manufacturing industries far from the centre saw massive increases in the journey-to-work of most Managuans fortunate to get employment in the aftermath of disaster. In San Francisco, distance travelled to work by the unskilled and blue-collar workers increased dramatically as many left the refugee camps in 1907 and 1908: respectively, by 76 and 73 per cent. For these groups, it was not until 1910–11 that some readjustment and stabilization began to occur.

Centralization and decentralization

Centralization and decentralization are superimposed as macro-level processes on the micro-level process of segregation. They are also greatly accelerated by the disaster. In the four study cities disaster was to accelerate the rate of decentralization of activities that had begun to leave the centre, for example wholesaling and industry. At the same time, there was increased centralization of the establishments in activity groups striving for proximity to the centre, for example, financial and legal.

Disaster-induced areal expansion

In major urban disasters the operation of the sequences of return and the process of segregation ensure that each district expands and returns at a lower density than before the disaster, and this produces cumulative waves of areal expansion at the residential edges of the city. In addition, indecision in the grey zone forces many of the low-priority activities located there before the disaster to go to the edge of the city. The result is an expansion of the city's building area that often doubles and sometimes triples the area originally destroyed (Fig. 3). A major population redistribution occurs. Five years after San Francisco's disaster, when population had risen to pre-disaster levels, the number of San Franciscans living in the old destroyed area dropped by 135,000. The loss from the centre was matched by a population increase of 50 per cent in the next zone and by a gain of 100 per cent in the outermost zone (Zone 4, Table 2).[18] All socio-economic groups were part of this exodus and areal expansion in Managua and San Francisco.

In Managua the problem of areal expansion was compounded by the authorities' indecision and later decision to prevent an early return or hope of return to the 450-block destroyed central area and by the sale to the U.S. by a few wealthy landowners of land for emergency housing for the poor well beyond the city's pre-disaster bounds.[19] Massive areal expansion

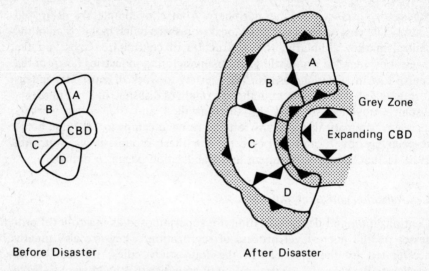

Before Disaster   After Disaster

Fig. 3. *Forces and extent of areal expansion after disaster*

and a population under severe economic, social and political stress resulted, as recent headlines of massive unrest reveal. Few were displaced from Anchorage and Rapid City, but the freezing of land formerly occupied by the wealthy contributed to building booms and unexpected increases in the white-collar population in the outlying zones of both places.[20]

Conclusion

Reconstruction following natural disasters compresses in time and exaggerates in process, but does not basically change the growth and evolution of cities. In most cities in countries with capitalist and mixed economies following disaster the main objective of reconstruction is a return to normal as quickly as possible. This is often paired with a desire on the part of the business community to take advantage of the disaster to improve their own position and the city's economic efficiency. The result of both in the capitalist city is to give free rein to the market mechanism, and to initiate a predictable succession of locational changes and areal extensions of districts. This pattern of change serves as a model for the spatial evolution of cities in the process of reconstruction. Despite governmental constraints it appears to be applicable to all cities in market or mixed economies in the wake of natural disasters. The critical locational decisions are generally made by businessmen backed by insurance settlements and local capital long before the government acts.

Table 2. *Location of sampled population (1905) by socio-economic class and zone, 1905 and 1911 (%)*

	Zone 1 0.1 – 1.49	Zone 2 1.5 – 2.99	Zone 3 3 – 4.49	Zone 4 more than 4.5
		Miles from centre		
Unskilled				
1905	48	31	11	10
1911	12	36	32	20
Semi-skilled				
1905	40	24	23	13
1911	10	21	34	35
Blue collar skilled				
1905	37	32	17	14
1911	10	30	32	18
Low white collar				
1905	32	36	23	9
1911	17	36	31	16
High white collar				
1905	29	38	25	8
1911	6	36	38	20
City as a whole				
1905	36	32	21	11
1911	12	33	33	22

Sequences of return in the residential and commercial–industrial sectors of the city recapitulate the normal sequences of reaction recognized in fast-growing cities. There is a rapid acceleration in the locational changes underway before the disaster but slowed down previously by fact of the permanent, finished city. At the same time businesses and people low in the economic and social hierarchies lose their normal protection from the ruthless efficiency of the market mechanism and the freely operating sequence of reaction. The city's normal inertia is removed and gradual growth is replaced by a locational revolution. The result is a chronic increase in stress and social disruption for people and businesses low in the sequences of reaction/return.

The value of catastrophe as ecological and historical source is that it provides a priceless outdoor laboratory in which to watch the creation on bare gound of an entire society. A commercial–industrial city is built from scratch in five years. One can measure accurately the transport and communication fields of the place, the mass of technology, capital and labour needed to build it, and the efficiency of the market mechanism when least constrained by the inertia of the past. Most important we can point to inefficiencies, misplaced priorities and social inequities, and strive to rectify some of them next time.

Clark University,
USA

Applied historical geography and geographies of the past: historico-geographical change and regional processes in history

D. DENECKE

It might seem paradoxical to stress that historical geography has a present dimension and might even deal with planning the future. However, the events of history pass while the shape of the cultural landscape and the processes of its change are vivid, present history. In this sense the heritage of the past is an object of modern geography and so of planning. We have not only to reconstruct and explain landscapes of the past but we have also to make understandable the historical dimension of the contemporary visible past. We have to engage in planning the past for its continuation into the future. Planning continuity in our landscape is an important contribution of historical geography to activities of public interest. If historical geography has any meaning in the everyday life of the public it has to be applied in town and landscape planning and it has to help to make understandable the past as an experience.

Historical geographers should endeavour to project their studies more to preserve our historical environment and to make it understandable through individual, social and political activity and decisions. There is a growing engagement of historical geographers, historians and archaeologists in planning the past but there is yet no theoretical approach, no concept, no strategy. This also becomes evident when analysing the terminology touching the field of an applied historical geography used in publications of different countries and in different languages.[1]

The application of a historico-geographical regional survey (*historisch-geographische Landesaufnahme*)[2] and an inventory of a rural as well as an urban landscape heritage for the purpose of planning usually has to proceed from the present situation of the cultural landscape and the visible remains of the past. For the purpose of application in planning and conservation, historico-geographical research has to be concentrated on the archaeological potential, on the features of past human occupation or the heritage of landscapes, on features of past human activity, and on an environment built during historic periods. These features may have their historic structure or function preserved, they may have changed their functions over time, or they may remain as relics in the field, ancient and anachronistic.

The historico-geographical and archaeological regional survey as an inventory of historico-archaeological potential

The historico-geographical regional survey is a large-scale and as far as possible comprehensive mapping and recording (inventory) of all relics in the terrain of a limited area that result from human activity and settlement during historic periods,[3] and a reconstruction of the topography of past cultural landscapes or historic features on the base of systematic fieldwork (field survey) and an evaluation of all documentary and cartographic source material (documentary survey) which indicate features of past human occupation.

The historico-geographical regional surveys, based on systematic field work and documentary evidence, as well as the archaeological survey, were initially developed for research purposes. The primary aim was a reconstruction of the development of the cultural landscape as a base for a history of settlement (making of the landscape, *Kulturlandschaft-sentwicklung*).[4]

The archaeological potential of fossil sites indicated in a scatter of potsherds on ploughed topsoil has to be surveyed as a marker and indication of the need to protect these sites of former human occupation. As most of the archaeological sites in Central Europe are under the plough a strategy and method has to be developed to protect the patterns of soil-marks and human activity *in situ* underground for future archaeological investigation.[5]

Intensive arable cultivation and the use of modern machinery cannot be prohibited, but there are many ways of restricting or adapting cultivation and tilling to the needs of protecting the remains in the subsoil. Farmers have to be advised how sites of fossil archaeological remains might best be farmed and how cultivation techniques could be minimized.[6] Before any measures are taken in this direction an exhaustive field survey of cultural relics has to be undertaken together with a classification of the sites according to their archaeological importance.

A survey and immediate measures are urgently needed in those areas where former woodland is to be cleared or where grassland that has long remained untilled is broken up and turned to arable cultivation, as for example recently in several parts of southern Bavaria or in Norfolk. In most of the cases there was no such programme developed.

The regional survey and inventory should be as complete as possible, since it should not only serve for planning and conservation purposes but also for an academic interpretation and reconstruction of the development of the cultural landscape and the regional history of settlement. The degree of completeness depends on the amount of soil erosion or accumulation, on the methods and intensity of field work employed, and also on the standard of previous research. The methodological problem of achieving completeness has been rarely discussed and has not been considered thoroughly enough.[7]

Examples of regional surveys so far published are very different in scale, aim, topic, and underlying methods as well as sources, giving a great variety of different types of regional surveys or inventories. For example, a general historico-geographical survey has been made for the area between the Solling and Harz Mountains in southern Lower Saxony,[8] archaeological regional surveys have been completed for Schleswig-Holstein and some other counties in Germany, for Denmark and for Hungary,[9] many regional inventories of deserted medieval settlements have been published by archaeologists, historians or geographers for different parts of Germany with general maps and additional catalogues.[10] A comparison of these inventories and maps, however, shows that their standard is very different, using parameters of scale, completeness, sources or accuracy of location.[11]

A specific survey of mining and smelting sites of the medieval period for the Harz Mountains is an example of a special survey concentrated on selected types of sites.[12] The survey, published in a map of a scale 1:100,000, results from casual field observations and does not entirely cover the area of the Oberharz (Westharz). A similar map was compiled for the sites of glass-making from the twelfth century to 1900 for the area of southern Lower Saxony and northern Hessia.[13] There are also surveys of mills, mounds (*Wurten*) and old fields, but most of them were published as small-scale outline maps. These specific surveys are especially valuable to compile a picture of the distribution pattern of a special feature and to give an impression of a possible uniqueness or concentration of single features.

The application of academic inventories for planning, for the Ordnance Survey, or for touristic purposes was propagated, but a theoretical outline or an organized programme is still missing.[14] An institutionalized historico-geographical survey, which is urgently needed, has never been organized in Germany. On the other hand, the departments for the protection of monuments and archaeological sites (*Bodendenkmalpflege*) and the departments for the protection of monuments and historic buildings (*Baudenkmalpflege*) at the ministries of the *Länder* work separately on inventories of archaeological and architectural monuments. These official catalogues were continued, rearranged, revised or even initiated when new laws for the protection of monuments (*Denkmalschutzgesetze*) were enacted.[15] Archaeological, architectural and historico-geographical regional surveys are indeed the most useful base for any official listings of monuments. Until recently there was often no connection between the surveys made for research and the public inventories, but now the departments of monuments have begun to integrate the already published surveys into the official records and inventories.

There are a number of public files of monuments in Germany, different in their legal background, their organization and arrangement and also in their extent and purpose. There is a catalogue of listed monuments protected by law (*Denkmalbuch, Denkmalliste*), a catalogue of proposed listed monuments (*vorläufige Denkmalliste*), a selective inventory of historic buildings, urban and rural (*Denkmalkartei*), and an inventory of all reported historic and archaeologic monuments, sites and finds (*Fundkartei, Fundortkartei*). These inventories of the *Länder* and their departments have very different standards. Most of them are not up to date, but recently great efforts were made to revise and to enlarge them extensively.

A serious problem, especially of interest to historical geography, that has not yet been solved adequately, even by the newly enacted preservation laws, is the needed protection of field monuments or larger areas comprising historic monuments, features, relics and sites in their natural setting (old fields, relics of mining activities, old road tracks, ditches, marked boundaries, etc.). A model for the discussion of this problem is the comprehensive British Parliamentary Report of the Fields Monuments Committee.[16] In Germany, for example, a controversy about the protection of large-scale relics of industrial activities (*technische Baudenkmale*) came up about the protection of the old waterflows and reservoirs of the mining era in the Harz Mountains.[17]

The potential of monuments and sites recorded in maps (1:50,000 or 1:25,000) as a result of a historico-geographical regional survey should also be selectively transferred to the official topographic maps (*Amtliche Topographische Kartenwerke*). The regulations (*Musterblatt*)[18] of the German topographical map 1:25,000 (TK 25), for example, require that all significant ruined buildings (churches, castles, etc.), fortifications, sites where court was held, burial mounds and deserted villages (at least by name) must be included and supplemented in new or revised editions. Comparisons of historico-geographical surveys with corresponding topographic sheets of selected test areas in Lower Saxony and Hessia showed that in the topographic sheets only about 10 to 30 per cent of the actually identified historic objects or sites were recorded.[19] Supplements were added infrequently in new editions, according to the information of recent publications. Additions are usually based on casual reports. In the offices of the provincial surveys (*Landesvermessungsämter*) in the Federal Republic of Germany there is no one assigned to work on the historico-geographical information of the topographical surveys so that there is nothing comparable with the Ordnance Survey Archaeological Data Collection of Britain, recorded since 1791.[20]

Historical treasures very often function as tourist and leisure attractions. Many historic sites and monuments are already opened up and arranged, reconstructed, or even designed or constructed for educational and touristic use.[21] A great number of features and places are still hidden and away from the main tracks of tourism. Most of the less attractive features or fossil sites, however, are only known by local residents or specialists. A systematic survey and record of the surviving landscape features of past historic periods may also be taken as an inventory of the potential of historical objects and sites for recreational use. To apply this inventory for touristic planning it is necessary to evaluate the objects as tourist attractions. This quantification and qualification of attractions in the countryside and in towns has to be based on the statistics of visitors, on the results of questionnaires, and on a detailed catalogue of criteria of tourist demands for representatives of our heritage.

To date there are in Germany just a few pilot studies of this kind that show that an objective evaluation – one that might be measured – is very difficult to achieve.[22] There is also no elaborate typology of historic landscape features, historic sites, parks or open air museums as educative or recreational attractions. This, however, seems to be necessary to create a planning strategy and to improve a modern didactic or an educational use of the historical–cultural landscape and its relics. The study, preservation and reconstruction of past and historic landscapes only makes sense to the public when we teach and learn to enjoy the past, when we try to interpret our heritage, and when we help to mediate a sense of living in past periods.

The survey, investigation, conservation, and preservation of ancient landscape reserves

Large-scale and exhaustive surveys of micromorphologically well-preserved visible relics above ground in selected, defined areas often result in quite comprehensive plans of preserved period landscapes, though the remains usually are vanishing relics. Surveys of this kind have been undertaken to date mainly within the context of historico-geographical regional studies.

Often very well preserved are the relics of mining activities, such as pits, tip heaps, broken-down shafts or adits, remains of ditches, waterflows, water reservoirs, platforms as former sites of machinery, etc. There are representative examples of large-scale surveys for different parts of Germany.[23]

These 'ensembles' of ancient field monuments should be legally bounded and defined as ancient landscapes or historic landscape reserves (*Atlandschaftsgebiet, historisches Landschaftsgebiet*) with a legal status similar to that of nature reserves. Defined ancient landscape reserves, completely surveyed and researched carefully, should be integrated into strategic landscape plans.[24] The strategic landscape plan (*Landschaftsrahmen Plan*), as it was elaborated in the Federal Republic of Germany for several counties in recent years, is a statement of objectives and of measures for the conservation of landscapes, the preservation of nature, and the protection of natural and cultural resources.

Whereas a survey of the Lerbach mining district in the Harz Mountains was made as a pilot study for a regional field survey of the Harz and a test for an investigation and delineation of a past mining district reserve,[25] the investigation of Altenburg, a deserted medieval mining settlement and iron mine in Westphalia, resulted in the establishment of a well-managed mining reserve and tourist attraction.[26] Thus a large area of a complete period landscape (outdoor historic site) was developed in a manner similar to an open-air museum, although this ancient landscape reserve has to be markedly distinguished from the usual open-air museum where ancient structures are brought together or transplanted from a wide area into an artificial settlement.

In Germany the establishment of ancient landscape reserves is just beginning. Some experiments have been made, ideas about management, conservation, and reconstruction have been proposed and legal measures are being discussed; but this is not yet sufficient.

Ancient landscape reserves as field examples give a lively visual representation of former settlement, farming, mining, and other human activities in historic periods. They help to stimulate a sense of historic dimensions and may also be exploited by recreational and educational activities.[27] The reserves of ancient relics and patterns are even more attractive when on some sites remnants of buildings, machinery, or other structures are reconstructed or still preserved.

Surveys of scatters of artefacts on sites of former human occupation or activity

The range of the sites of deserted places of human occupation and activity in the field must be exactly delineated if we want to consider areas of fossil relics in land-use planning or as legally protected historical and archaeological monuments. For this purpose it is necessary to have a detailed large-scale field survey of the scatter of the artefacts on the archaeological site of a totally vanished settlement.[28]

The interpretation of surveys of scatters has to be based on long fieldwork experience. Tests and methodological experiments have shown that the changes of the topsoil by erosion or accumulation have important influences on the results of the survey.[29] Experiences gained by field walking also led to the conclusion that on fields that were used over a long period as ploughland, nearly always a thin 'veil' of potsherds covers the surface as a result of farming and manuring activities. Concentrations of adobe or mortar often indicate the location of half-timbered buildings or churches, concentrated potsherds suggest the proximity of a house, slagheaps the location of smithing or smelting. So the pattern of distribution of finds has to be analysed with care. These experiences are mainly important for Central Europe as most of the deserted places of past landscapes have become arable land today.

Together with the survey of potsherds should also go a large-scale aero-topographic inventory of the soil- and crop-marks of the site. To prove the interpretation of the survey of artefacts or the aero-topographic survey, additional networks of drillings should be made to locate the sites of dwellings and to reconstruct the pattern of the settlement.[30]

A large-scale survey results in a detailed plan of an archaeological site that has to be integrated into land-use plans and lists of protected areas. The survey may also serve as a most important orientation and base-line for archaeological excavations. On this kind of site, arable farming should be restricted or at least be controlled under experienced advice.

The historico-geographical buildings' survey

The historico-geographical survey of buildings is a complete inventory of the surviving structures in old centres of towns or villages according to the age of the building, to its primary function as recognizable in construction, and to later changes. These historico-geographical town plans based on comprehensive field work and on the evaluation of sources are the base-line for overall concepts of planning preservation and conservation of historic buildings in old town and village centres. In contrast to the usually selective inventories compiled by departments of conservationists, mainly to keep up the catalogue of listed buildings, these historico-geographical town maps represent complete surveys of the whole town or village. Nearly all the surveys done to date were undertaken in the frame of academic studies as research in historical urban geography.[31]

In some cases federal or local departments are concerned with buildings surveys, mainly from the viewpoint of a history of architecture and building[32] or with the aim of compiling a catalogue of listed buildings, groups of buildings or historic districts.[33] Many national or local projects were started in all parts of the world to rescue parts of the old building fabric and to conserve historic districts in developing and renewing cities, towns, and villages.[34] Conservation in the countryside (*Dorferneuerung*) has become a kind of crusade in Germany.[35] Historical geographers should step in and apply their research methods and the experience of traditional academic settlement geography.

Recently, local planning authorities and private planning companies have compiled local buildings' surveys in Germany within the framework of structural analysis (*Strukturuntersuchungen*) of old inner cities and of situation analysis (*Situationsanalysen*) for planning, redevelopment and restoration purposes. The urban renewal and town development act (*Städtebauförderungsgesetz*) of the Federal Republic of Germany, enacted in 1972, requires these preparatory studies and inventories for renewal or conservation projects.[36]

In connection with the redevelopment of destroyed cities after the war in Germany, and even more with the urban renewal projects since about 1965, archaeological research, surveys, and inventories in historic town centres began to develop.[37] The work was initiated and carried on mainly by archaeologists for pure research purposes, by planning departments with the help of trained specialists, but unfortunately controversy between professionals, the public and local policy also developed.

The historico-geographical buildings' surveys and inventories should not only find their application in urban planning and conservation projects. As the buildings of an old town illustrate our past to us, these town plans should also have a widespread distribution to the public and to visitors as information and as a guide through the visible past manifested in buildings that represent human activity and thought from the past. The buildings of a historic town 'keep the past in the present'[38] and 'express in a tangible way the evolution of a civilization that we seek to conserve as symbols of the continuity of human purposes and institutions'.[39]

Description and measurement of single structures and their remains

With full-scale measurement, investigation and perhaps even reconstruction of the remains of single structures in the field, historical geography touches on the activities of architects, conservationists and institutions protecting monuments. These inventories of single buildings or structures nevertheless should be undertaken by historical geographers when the objects are integrated parts of ancient landscapes (for example, an old church on the site of a deserted medieval village). Research on past landscapes and vanished places of former human occupation then becomes an obligation of landscape conservation and of preservation and restoration of field monuments.

Many descriptions, sketches, measurements or investigations in the field has been completed already, mainly in connection with local studies by specialists or volunteers. All this published and unpublished information has to be compiled systematically and be arranged and added to for planning and conservation purposes.

Geographical Institute,
University of Göttingen, West Germany

The interface of physical and historical geography: the analysis of farming decisions in response to drought hazards on the margins of the Great Plains

D. A. McQUILLAN

In the last twenty years the interests of historical geographers in the English-speaking world have proliferated as their numbers increased and as their contacts strengthened with other scholars in the social sciences and humanities. The result of this expansion has been the adoption of paradigms, analytical techniques and philosophical underpinnings from cognate disciplines. These methodologies generated excitement by opening new research fields, but they also presented a danger that some basic skills and traditional geographical concerns, such as the study of human responses to environmental challenges, will be neglected.

While many historical geographers have been advancing social theory, physical geographers have provided new and detailed information on environmental history. For example, recent research in physical geography has begun to delineate climatic fluctuations, and rates of soil erosion within the historic past.[1] The environment is no longer taken as a constant, it is a continuously changing condition. Not only is there an opportunity for increased cooperation among researchers in the two sub-disciplines, there is also an opportunity to re-emphasize one of the distinctive characteristics of historical geography, namely, its ability to draw together research in the physical and social sciences. This essay is a plea to put more physical geography back into historical geography without giving up the concern for advancing social theory. I propose, as an example, that a study of immigrant adaptation to a new environment in North America provides insight into the process of Americanization and the development of American agriculture.

When the agricultural frontier moved from the Mississippi lowlands to the margins of the Great Plains during the last quarter of the nineteenth century, pioneer farmers faced numerous environmental challenges, some of which were not new. Problems of wheat rust and cinch bugs continued to

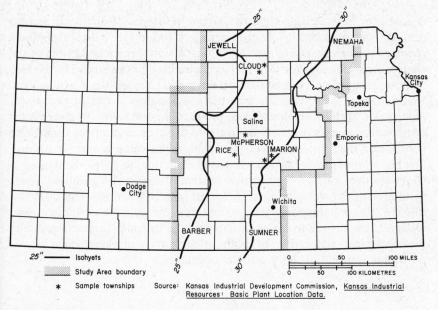

Fig. 1. *Location of the study area in central Kansas*

bedevil the frontier farmer. The incidence of grasshopper plagues seemed to increase as the frontier moved westward. Severe winter weather produced winterkill of fall-sown grains, and the length of the frost-free season fluctuated with late spring and early fall frosts. Summer hailstorms wreaked havoc on the crops. The most unrelenting challenge, however, was the unreliability of the moisture supply. On the one hand, major droughts could occur at any time; on the other hand, less subtle changes in the moisture supply were not readily discernible. Farmers from Illinois, Iowa and Wisconsin who took up land in central Kansas and Nebraska often did not realize the significance of a small decline in the rainfall supply as they moved westward. In a general way they knew that rainfall was abundant in the Mississippi lowlands and that it was scarce on the Plains. But in the transitional zone of central Kansas, despite great annual variability in rainfall, good years or months within years caused farmers to gamble on planting those crops that had been grown farther east. The uncertainty of the drought hazard produced a transitional climatic zone in which the farmers' responses to imperfectly perceived drought hazards may be analysed.[2]

This study compares the farming strategies of three immigrant groups with the strategies of American-born farmers between 1875 and 1925. The three immigrant groups are Swedes, Mennonites and French-Canadians. Data about the immigrant and American farmers were drawn from six sample townships in central Kansas (see Fig. 1).[3] Each farmer had to decide how he would allocate the labour resources of his farm, and his decision was reflected in the crop acreages and in the livestock numbers reported to the census enumerator. Consequently, the manuscripts of the Kansas state censuses furnish the basic data used in this study. In the face of both drought hazards and uncertain market prices, the newly arrived Kansas farmer had to decide whether to specialize in one or two major enterprises, such as wheat and corn production, or whether to diversify his farm operation with a variety of crop and livestock enterprises. In making his decision the farmer revealed something of his value system. In a word, one has an opportunity to see what made him tick, to judge the degree to which his decision was conservative or that of a high-risk gambler. Then, by analysing the changing distribution of high-risk and low-risk decisions for the three immigrant groups and for the American farmers one observes: the degree to which the immigrants became Americanized, and the ecological adaptation of both immigrants and Americans to this particular segment of the American ecumene.

Estimating risk in farming

The first step in the analysis of farming decisions is to summarize the strategy for each individual farm. Crop acreages and livestock numbers reported in the census manuscripts are converted to labour units. The number of man-hours required per acre of crop/per head of livestock are derived from estimates of farm labour developed by the United States Department of Agriculture.[4] By use of labour units, it is possible to determine the percentage of total farm labour which was expended on each farm enterprise, for example wheat growing, dairying or corn production. Finally, it is possible to distinguish the really important farm enterprises from the minor enterprises by application of a modified version of Weaver's crop combination method.[5] The summary of the farming strategy thus obtained permits an examination of each farming decision in terms of the *number* of major enterprises and of the *combination* of enterprises.

The next step in the analysis of farming decisions is to estimate the degree of risk in the various combinations of crop and livestock enterprises. Individual crops reacted differently to the variable nature of the annual precipitation cycle. In some years the wheat harvest was excellent when the corn crop failed; in other years the opposite was true. Thus a method of analysis is required that combines the *variance* of crop yields with the *correlation* among crop yields. The desired coefficient of variability is obtained for two enterprises, x and y, in the following manner:[6]

$$V_{x+y} = \sqrt{\frac{v_x + v_y + 2\,r\,s_x\,s_y}{\bar{x} + \bar{y}}} \times \frac{100}{1}$$

v = variance
s = standard deviation
r = correlation coefficient

It is possible to include fluctuating market prices, a second major source of variability in farm income, by estimating the dollar-return-per-man-hour of labour for each acre of crop and for each head of livestock. With data from local Kansas records on crop yields and market prices the dollar-return-per-man-hour is obtained with the following equations:

$$\frac{\$\ \text{return}}{\text{for crops}} = \frac{A \times B(D)}{E} \qquad \frac{\$\ \text{return}}{\text{for livestock}} = \frac{C(D)}{F}$$

where A = crop yield in bushels per acre
       B = market value per bushel
       C = market value per head of livestock
       D = wholesale price index divided by 100
       E = man-hours required per acre per year
       F = man-hours required per head of livestock per year

Several important points emerge from this analysis of farm strategies. The greater the number of enterprises in a combination, that is the more diversified the farm strategy, the lower the variability of farm income will be. The inclusion of livestock farming, especially dairying and hog raising, in the farm combination often reduces the degree of risk in farm income. During the entire fifty-year period, corn proved the most variable and consequently was the riskiest of all crops; barley and millet were the least variable crops. Furthermore, the addition of other small grains, such as oats, rye and barley, to a farm strategy that already included wheat did not greatly reduce the variability of farm income.

Farming decisions over fifty years

In 1875 agriculture was in the pioneer stage in central Kansas where much of the prairie was still being converted to farmland. By 1885, however, after a decade of farming and several years of favourable harvests in succession, the farming communities began to assume a mature image. Many of the Swedish and Mennonite farmers broadened their farming activities and developed three-enterprise farm operations that included corn growing, dairying and wheat production. In sharp contrast the American and French-Canadian farmers showed a distinct tendency toward farm specialization; the number of single- and two-enterprise operations increased after 1875, and most of their effort went into corn production. The French-Canadian and American farm strategies indicated a higher level of risk than the Swedish or the Mennonite farm strategies.

The full dimensions of the drought hazard were not recognized by the farmers in central Kansas during the 1880s. Although there were a few minor setbacks harvests were generally good. By 1895, however, the severity of the drought hazard had become apparent. Not only had a disastrous and prolonged drought started in 1893, but also a major economic recession sent the prices of farm produce in the United States plummeting. It was a serious reversal for everyone, although less serious for the farmers who had not specialized, particularly the Swedes and the Mennonites. In the years between 1885 and 1895 Mennonite farmers were reducing the risk level in their farming strategy by giving more attention to dairying and wheat production than to corn. Their basically conservative approach to agriculture protected them in the harsh years of drought and depression. French-Canadian and American farmers, however, did not achieve the same degree of diversification. Among them were many more single- and two-enterprise farms than could be found among the Swedish or Mennonite farms. Furthermore, the French-Canadian and American farmers continued to emphasize corn production in their farming strategy. Farmers who gambled on that high-risk crop might do well in years of good harvests and high prices, but in years of drought and depression those farmers paid dearly. During the difficult decade of the 1890s French-Canadian and American farmers suffered a much higher rate of mortgage preclosure than Mennonites or even Swedes.

The decade between the census of 1895 and that of 1905 was one of slow recovery from the depressed market conditions and disastrous droughts of 1893–6. The annual moisture supply was generally adequate to produce good harvests although the drought danger did not completely disappear. Each farming group responded differently to the recovery. On the one hand, the Swedish, French-Canadian and American farmers diversified their operations; the tendency was greatest among the Swedes and least among the Americans. On the other hand, the Mennonites, who had developed the least risky strategies in the 1890s, organized fewer of the four- and five-enterprise operations and increased the number of two- and three-enterprise strategies. The crops and the livestock included in the Mennonite and Swedish strategies, however, remained essentially unchanged between 1895 and 1905. The most popular farming pattern on Mennonite farms was a dairy–wheat–corn combination and on Swedish farms corn was primary with a secondary emphasis on wheat and dairying. Despite some reduction in the emphasis given to corn on French-Canadian and American farms after the disaster of the early 1890s, the crop retained top position in a corn–dairy–oats/wheat combination.

By the time the next state census was taken in the spring of 1915, war had started in Europe and the prices for farm produce, especially for wheat, were rising rapidly. Although no major droughts occurred during the decade, farmers were keenly aware of the importance of moisture changes from month to month. For example, a short severe drought in August 1913 accompanied by hot desiccating winds seriously reduced the corn harvest. But this was the only serious drought of the decade. In general, conditions were ideal for those farmers who gambled and specialized their farm operations. Surprisingly, there was no significant increase in the number of two- and three-enterprise farms. The trend toward four- and five-enterprise operations, begun in 1895, continued through 1915, even among American farmers. One discernible change was an increase in wheat growing. It is difficult to ascertain with any certainty if the dramatic increase in wheat prices had been too recent to affect crop sowing decisions in the spring of 1915, but Mennonite, French-Canadian and American farmers did increase their wheat production sharply above levels of a decade earlier and continued to de-emphasize corn-growing. Only on Swedish farms did corn retain a dominant position in the farming combination.

The euphoria of the wartime boom had disappeared by 1925 and the market for agricultural produce slumped with the onset of a postwar depression in 1919. There were no severe droughts in the early 1920s to remind farmers to diversify their farming activities. The harvest record was mixed; moderate harvest years alternated with years of poor crop yields. Consequently, many farmers must have felt the pressure to specialize farm production in order to maintain their incomes as the prices for farm produce sagged. Among the Swedish, the American, and especially the French-Canadian farmers, the trend was a reduction in the number of four- and five-enterprise strategies and an increase in the number of two- and three-enterprise operations. The exceptional group was the Mennonites, among whom there was evidence of further diversification above the levels that existed in 1915. Furthermore, the Mennonites continued to de-emphasize corn production and to increase the attention given to dairying and wheat growing. The Americans followed a similar trend. Swedish farmers introduced only the smallest changes in their crop and livestock combination. Registering the most dramatic changes of all, French-Canadians turned away from wheat farming and returned to corn growing. In 1925 there was a higher degree of risk in French-Canadian farming than in Swedish farming. Mennonites, on the other hand, continued to develop a conservative, low-risk farming strategy.

Americanization of immigrants

One of the aims of this research is to investigate the degree to which the

Table 1. *Values of the D^2 statistic for differences between the ethnic and American farming systems, 1875–1925*

Groups	1875	1885	1895	1905	1915	1925
Swedes/Americans	14.86	17.49	7.35	6.59	4.89	3.19
Mennonites/Americans	4.95	6.30	12.00	4.98	4.33	4.77
French-Canadians/ Americans	5.18	1.58	5.63	5.53	3.74	2.72

immigrants became Americanized. A discriminant analysis test is performed on the farming strategies of the immigrant groups in each census year to determine the degree to which they become similar to their American neighbours. The D^2 statistic derived from this test indicates how closely each group approximated the farming strategies of their American neighbours; the lower the value of the statistic the closer the farming strategies of the two samples.

Throughout the first half century of farming in central Kansas the French-Canadians were always more similar to Americans than either Swedes or Mennonites in farming strategies. Once the most dissimilar group, Swedes also had become very similar to Americans by 1925. The Mennonites were exceptional. Although the differences between Mennonite and American farming strategies were diminishing in the later decades, the differences were greatest in 1895, a period of acute stress for all farmers in central Kansas.

The Mennonites are a key to understanding the process of ecological adjustment because their farming strategy often involved the lowest degree of risk of all groups considered here. It is possible to suggest that Mennonites, as immigrants from southern Russia, were better prepared for the special environmental conditions in Kansas than Swedes, French-Canadians, or even Americans, who had farmed in Illinois before coming out to Kansas. Southern Russia is an area where droughts are a recurring agricultural hazard and where the variability of the moisture regime is similar to that of Kansas. The Mennonites, however, had to learn by experience the full range of moisture variability in Kansas, as everyone else did. It is easy to overemphasize the extent to which Mennonites duplicated their Russian farming strategies in Kansas.[7] The successful ecological adaptation of Mennonites is also attributable to their value system which emphasized community cooperation in times of stress and caution in terms of spreading risks. Furthermore, changes in the Mennonite farming strategies occurred much more gradually than in any other group. There is not, for example, the wild fluctuation from one strategy to another, from one decade to the next, that is found among the French-Canadians. Consequently, the Mennonites, the least similar to Americans of the immigrant groups by 1925, had achieved a greater degree of ecological adaptation than the other farmers, including the Americans.

It is clear that the process of Americanization cannot be equated with successful ecological adaptation without some modification. The process of Americanization has often been described in terms of the transition from European peasant to American commercial farmer. The European immigrant would eventually free himself from the constraints of community, of limited access to land and capital, and of production for a local market. He would adopt the characteristics of the American farmer who was mobile, had access to relatively cheap land, could borrow capital for the development of his land, and produced goods for distant markets – an individualistic, capitalistic entrepreneur whose goal was profit maximization. This stereotyped process implies a reordering of the immigrants' value system until it approached that of farmers whose families had lived in North America for several generations. However, the flow of information and influence was not a one-way stream. The new immigrants' impact on those who preceded them across the Atlantic has often been underestimated. I have shown elsewhere that the Mennonites were financially successful farmers who became capitalistic and surprisingly mobile farmers.[8] The results of the present investigation indicate that they were more successful in their ecological adaptation than other groups. A strong argument can be made that the influence of the Mennonites might have been greater on American farming strategies than vice versa. The evidence here suggests that American farmers abandoned farming strategies which were very risky and maximized profits in the short term, in favour of the Mennonite approach which produced lower risks and lower profts but which assured a good income in the long run. In the development of this segment of the American ecumene the immigrant contribution was paramount.

Conclusion

This review of farming decisions by American and immigrant farmers reveals one way in which financially successful and socially conservative rural communities came to terms with the uncertainties of moisture supply on the margins of the Great Plains. Analysis of the farming decisions over fifty years would not have been possible without the work of meteorologists and climatologists, who have worked on problems of drought frequency and intensity, crop yields and climatic change in the breadbasket of the American Mid-west.

There are many physical geographers today who are deeply concerned with the issues of environmental history. Geomorphologists, climatologists and biogeographers are keenly interested in determining stream flow, flood levels and soil erosion, in plotting climatic fluctuation, and in reconstructing biotic patterns from the pollen record over the last millennium.[9] Many of these physical geographers have been drawn to an historical perspective in their research in order to explain recurring world food shortages, to understand the nature of ecosystem evolution and to find ways of utilizing our natural resources efficiently while preserving the natural environment. The reconstruction of climates of the past, to select one example, requires careful analysis of documentary evidence. Climatologists are interested in what we can tell them about the interpretation of the sources, and historical geographers have much to learn from the results of their work.[10] The opportunities for cooperation between the two sub-disciplines are very great, and a central theme in geography will be reasserted in historical geography.

University of Toronto,
Canada

Individualistic features in a communal landscape: some comments on the spatial organization of a rural society

U. SPORRONG

This essay will consider a number of features characteristic of early medieval society in central Sweden. Its main purpose will be to determine the age and function of the ancient traces of cultivation and settlement to be found in the area, as well as to investigate the nature of that society which produced them.[1] The main method used is that of comparing field evidence with the known land-use patterns of the past as revealed in surviving contemporary maps.

The typical form of settlement in the region is a small 'irregular' hamlet consisting of perhaps two farms. This structure of settlement appears to have been stable over a long period of time, and the basic pattern has probably changed very little since the earliest part of the Middle Ages. The explanation for this remarkable permanency appears to lie jointly in the concept of individual land ownership (which was characteristic of that time) and in the particular field system of the area which was one of strip fields under a two-course rotation. On the basis of field evidence we can confirm the suggestion that this system was first established during the later part of the Viking Age (A.D. 900),[2] though according to current knowledge the strip fields themselves are somewhat younger than this. What caused the change over from prehistoric farming methods to the relatively well-known medieval system of a two-course rotation and why had this reorganization taken place in some areas as early as the Middle Ages?

In addition to different forms of tenancy, a system of freehold farming also existed in central parts of eastern Sweden, and in general the best land (in the plains around Lake Mälar and in the river valleys) was owned by such freehold farmers. Larger landowners (noblemen) were concentrated around these central areas, including those districts where there had been shore-movements during the period investigated. Looking first at the structure of settlement it becomes clear that there is a reasonable degree of correspondence between the physical resources of an area and the size of

145

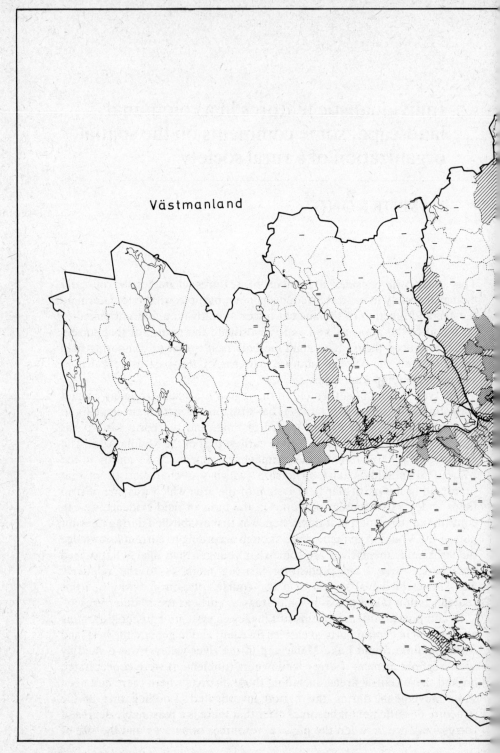

Fig. 1. *Village sizes in the Mälar area*

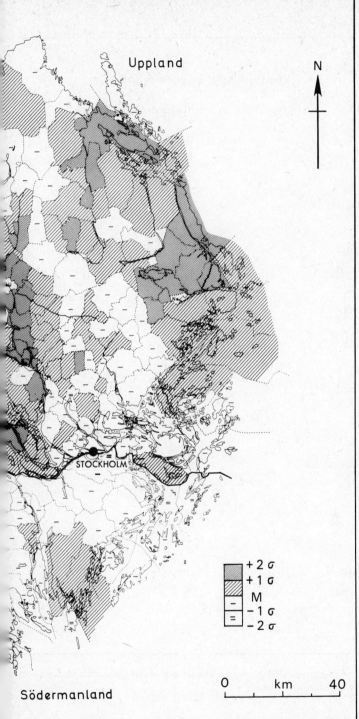

Uppland

N

STOCKHOLM

+2 σ
+1 σ
M
— -1 σ
= -2 σ

Södermanland

0   km   40

Fig. 2. *The regulated settlement units of the Mälar area recorded on seven*
and eighteenth-century maps

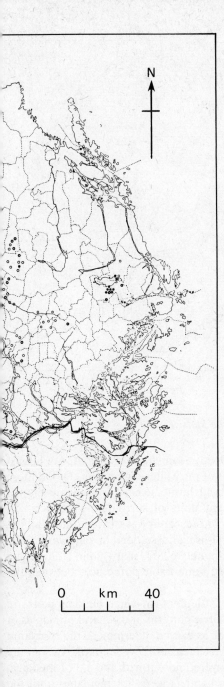

N

0   km   40

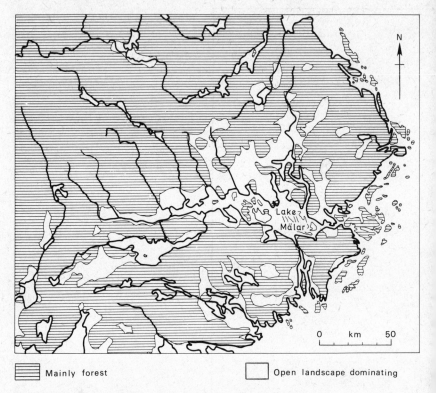

Mainly forest   Open landscape dominating

Fig. 3. *The physical characteristics of the Mälar region*

the settlement units it sustains. Indeed, as might be expected, the largest
hamlets are to be found in the plains of the Mälar region (Fig. 1). Do these
hamlets, often dominated by freehold farmers, have a more developed
land-use pattern than the settlement units of surrounding districts? In
order to test such a hypothesis detailed research was carried out on all the
maps of the area showing the land-use and settlement patterns of the
hamlets of eastern Sweden (approximately 60,000 maps), and from such a
study it is clear that there are indeed remarkable differences between the
Mälar region and other areas.

In the plains a regulated form of settlement (in which building plots are
drawn up according to certain geometric patterns and general principles of
measurement) is often found. As far as can be determined, the transition
towards regularity in settlement forms in eastern Sweden took place in the
early Middle Ages.[3] Building plots were laid out with the aid of medieval
length and square measures. Many hamlets were not regulated until the
seventeenth or eighteenth centuries, although these later reorganizations
are easily distinguished since at this later time surveyors used 'modern'

ell-lengths and 'modern' square measures ('tunnland'). Figs. 2 and 3 show that there is a fair spatial correspondence between the areas of early regulated settlement and the physical conditions of the area. Regulated villages are to be found in the plains to the north of Lake Mälar, around Uppsala, along the Temnar River (to the north) and in the area around Eskilstuna (to the south of the lake).

In the rest of the province of Södermanland there is little regulation since (in the southern part of the region particularly) the hamlets are extremely small (see Fig. 1). Similar characteristics are evident in eastern Uppland, though a small area of regulated hamlets can be found here. These regulated hamlets are situated in an open-plain landscape dominated by moraine-clay deposits and are therefore a reflection of these special circumstances.

In general there appears to be a clear spatial correspondence between the shape and organization of the settlement units and the physical conditions of the surrounding landscape over the whole of eastern Sweden. More specifically, five 'physical' variables are crucial in determining this relationship. These are outlined below and also incorporated into Fig. 4.

(1) *Open landscape without forest:* a square grid two and a half by two and a half kilometres was placed over a topographical map and every square with more than 50 per cent 'open-space' was marked on a matrix. (2) *Agro-geological characteristics:* those areas containing more than 50 per cent light-sandy or clay soils were marked. The data were extracted from the geological map of Sweden. (3) *Topography:* all the 'closed' contour-lines on the topographic map were counted. If less than forty 'hills' were found in any one square, this was recorded on the matrix. (4) *Relief:* differences of less than fifty metres between the lowest and the highest points were registered. (5) *Actual water-area:* if the water-area was greater than 1 per cent of the total area, there was to be no registration of that area in the matrix. Figure 4 shows all those squares of the matrix wherein all the above conditions were satisfied.

If we now compare Figs. 2 and 3 with Fig. 4, it becomes clear that the regulated villages occur only in a landscape with the following characteristics: openness, sandy or clayish soils, favourable (undulating) land surface and moderate relief. Few lakes in the area are associated with regulated settlement. Clearly there is no *direct* causal connection between the shape of a settlement and the landscape in which it stands, so that the nature of the relationship between them needs to be explained more subtly. The probable explanation appears to be as follows.

The physical landscape varies in terms of its resource base. This variation is apparent over the entire study area. We know very little about the nature of the settlement pattern in prehistoric times, but the cultivated area seems to have been expanding all over the region for a long period of

RESTRICTIONS

				PER CENT OF THE TOTAL NUMBER OF SQUARES
OPEN LAND %	50	= X	= 100	10.65
SOIL CONDITION %	50	= X	= 100	10.70
NUMBER OF "HILLS"	0	= X	= 40	49.79
WATER AREA %	0	= X	= 1	39.83
RELIEF (METER)	0	= X	= 50	81.29

ALL THESE CONDITIONS ARE FULLFILLED
IN 4.5% OF THE MATRIX SQUARES

■ TOWN

■ MATRIX SQUARE OF .2.5 KM × 2.5 KM

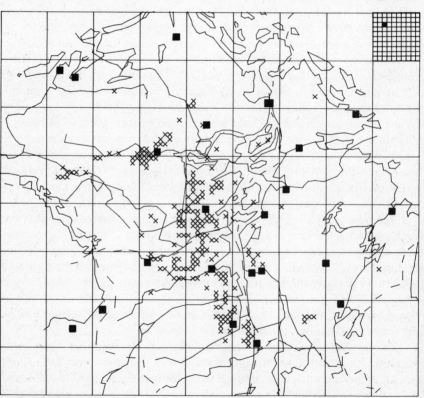

Fig. 4. The spatial coverrespondence between five physical variables

time, particularly in the period A.D. 600–900.[4] Towards the end of that period, according to several radiocarbon datings, we find the oldest surviving traces of structures which were to become well known in the Middle Ages. Thus it seems that by about A.D. 900, a system of fields and the means of communication (for example, roads and cattle paths) were established within the boundaries of farms and hamlets. It also appears to have been a relatively easy task to carry out such improvements since in the Mälar region generally, every settlement unit exhibits the same structure. The rationale behind such improvements was most probably a need to intensify corn production. A little later, at the beginning of the Middle Ages (A.D. 1000–1100), the land was divided into privately owned strips following the practices prescribed by medieval law, and this resulted in the strip-cultivated landscape typical of almost every farm around Lake Mälar. Because of the physical characteristics of the area, the average farm could not be enlarged after this land-division and consequently a stable pattern of small hamlets and strip-fields emerged. Newcomers were thus forced to settle outside the existing hamlets – probably in the more peripheral areas of eastern Sweden.

Elsewhere, however, a rather different type of evolution occurred. Here the area of cultivated land was greatly expandable, and evidently new units could be introduced into the system so that there was a need for further reorganization later in the Middle Ages. This reorganization not only affected single farms in certain hamlets, but was more broadly influential, often transforming border hamlets into the regulated village form which are to be found in certain plains areas. Again the rationale behind the change was almost certainly the need to increase corn production in order to supply the urban districts of the Mälar region.[5]

Who carried out these improvements? The ideas behind the reorganization certainly originated outside Sweden, somewhere in Western Europe, as did the rules and techniques of regulation.[6] It is the author's contention, however, that in eastern Sweden it was the farmers themselves who promoted the new ideas and also at a later stage innovated them. If we look at the spatial structure then it is clear that the most developed settlement units of the region occur in the central areas. These units are often larger than the unregulated hamlets which are so typical of the rest of the region. In the central districts the freehold farmers probably played an important role through their own acceptance of the new ideas.

In conclusion it can be said that the spatial distribution and ownership patterns described above make it probable that the evolution of and changes in spatial organization in eastern Sweden depended mainly upon a relationship between the available resources and the need to increase corn production. Studies of the great land division in Sweden during the eighteenth and nineteenth centuries (*storskifte* and *lagaskifte*) confirm the fact that great changes in field systems and other forms of spatial reorganization in an agrarian society must be acceptable to freehold farmers before they can be successfully accomplished.

University of Stockholm,
Sweden

Land use and settlement patterns in the Mälar area of Sweden before the foundation of villages

U. GÖRANSON

In Sweden the enclosure movement in the nineteenth century resulted in the disappearance of many hamlets and the emergence of settlements consisting of single farmsteads. Yet hamlets are still regarded as the 'normal' form of settlement in the Swedish countryside. Thus it is understandable that in discussions of early settlement patterns in Sweden the crucial question concerns 'foundations of villages' or *bybildning* in Swedish. An attempt to translate the Swedish word *bybildning* impels the realization that it is a very complicated concept and that the very word has influenced our attitudes to the evolution of settlement. *Bybildning* incorporates both the agglomeration of farms, and the occurrence of cooperation between the farmsteads. The very existence of the word *bybildning* provokes the belief that villages came into being as a result of an agrarian revolution wherein the landscape was totally changed, which implies discontinuity. *Bybildning* also conveys an impression of action – a village was actually created.

Evolution before A.D. 1050

Studies in human geography during the late 1960s and 1970s concerning Swedish society during the first millennium A.D. envisaged the evolution of settlement in general terms.[1] Findings from these investigations can be compiled into a model starting with a *landnam* (colonization of land) which was in progress during the first century A.D. The concept of a *landnam* with a single farmstead clearing new land is now doubted by some, but this is still the general interpretation of events at this time. It is assumed that the number of units increased either because the first single farms were divided or because new farmsteads were established. The most striking feature of studies of the next phase of settlement is the lack both of data and of researchers. We find further information about settlement when hamlets

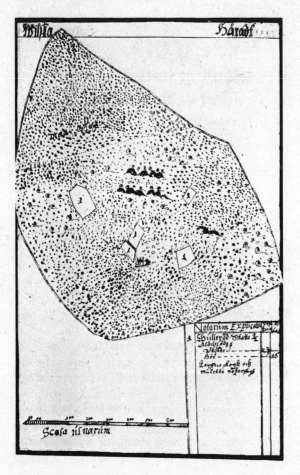

Fig. 1. *Gullered (Västergötland)*

were founded but little evidence is available from the preceding stage. In the absence of hard facts, certain deductions have been made about settlement partly from comparison with later sources.

Evolution as technical development

Sweden possesses some remarkable sources because a large proportion of its hamlets were mapped c. 1650. There are thousands of large-scale cadastral maps of settlements varying from single farmsteads to scattered hamlets, large and densely populated hamlets, and hamlets with buildings in a long, neat row; the cultivated lands range from irregular parcels to strict sun-divisions or complex systems of fields divided into strips.

Understandably enough this was interpreted as a process in which single farmsteads with scattered parcels of fields seemed to be the most primitive form (Fig. 1). This kind of hamlet was most common in the areas which were colonized in the Middle Ages, which suggests the conclusion that this was the form of settlement in which the *landnam* appeared also in antiquity. More advanced forms are represented by single farmsteads where some kind of cooperation existed between the units, and other hamlets with loosely clustered farmsteads and mixed strips of land (Fig. 2). Indeed, settlements sometimes large enough to be called villages found in highly developed agricultural areas possessed a compact core of houses, sometimes on a regular *toft*, and the accompanying strips are mixed with regard to both arable and meadow land (Fig. 3). This of course presents a kind of evolutionary process – technical evolution, primarily the technique of land division. But to conclude from this that a row of single farms with one-field systems cannot yet be called a hamlet,[2] or that in a hamlet with a 'primitive division of land into parcels much work remained before attainment of a division as elegant as in . . .'[3] also means that hamlets in the most developed stages presumably proceeded through these primitive phases.

The strips and parcels of land are very important in the discussion of *bybildning* since the theory is that this division of fields presupposes village cooperation. Remains of fields showing that the land was divided into strips allegedly prove that a village existed, and if the remains can be dated, for example, through C_{14} dating of carbon beneath their boundary stones, these results can also be used to fix the time of the *bybildning*. Explanations of the *bybildning* therefore tend to be connected with the reason for the division of the land into strips. This state of affairs was interpreted as evidence that when several farms had to share one field the need arose to ensure an equitable distribution.[4]

Individualization or collectivization

It is never explicitly stated but these interpretations of *bybildning* intimate an ideological change in the society from individual to collective cultivation, something which we, with our ideas about individual freedom, would hardly call development today. This explanation of development in settlement and cultivation therefore seems implausible. Free peasants could not be expected voluntarily to choose to change to cooperative cultivation. The division of land in connection with the *bybildning* was, it is suggested, a demonstration of private property rights and an indication that land was hitherto owned by a group of people entitled to farm within the bounds of the village. From c. A.D. 1000 arable land and meadow land were owned by families. Enclosure in the nineteenth century brought the

Fig. 2. *Påverås (Västergötland)*

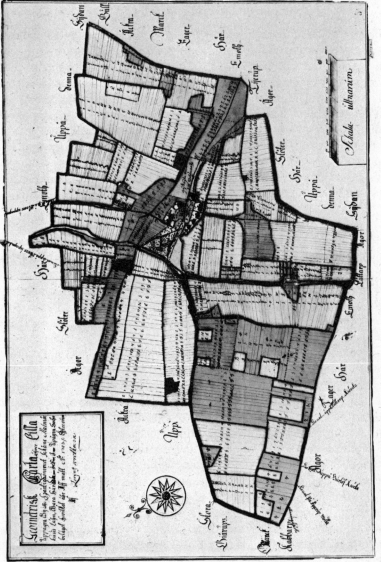

Fig. 3. *Lilla Uppåkra (Skåne)*

residue of the village land, mostly forest and pasture, into private hands. The point at issue is therefore whether the society was more collective before the *bybildning*.

Two ways to interpret three different materials

I shall try to illustrate the use of different sources to construct the picture of the prehistoric agrarian evolution which we now envisage, and the way in which the same material can be adduced to support the theory that the *bybildning* represents a change from collective to individual and private cultivation. At present I can only make a few suggestions as to how the problem can be tackled. There is an obvious lack of data in support of my assumptions, and much more research is needed. For example, more traces of settlement from the late Iron Age must be found, but we cannot assume that this will happen by coincidence. Speculation on what remains could have survived and where, creates a better chance of finding them. In this essay I will only deal with material from, and conditions in, the Mälar area.

Settlement

Clusters of settlements seem to appear in the Mälar area c. A.D. 1000. Very few remains of settlement have been dated to the preceding phase and the finds are limited in extent. The remains usually consist of hearths with carbon which can be dated by C_{14}, post-holes and a layer of seared stones and sooty soil. Crude artefacts occasionally come to light. Real house-foundations are rarely found.[5]

The limited extent of the settled area provoked the assumption that the remains derive from a single farmstead. The cultivated area of these dwellings has not been found. The interpretation of these finds is probably affected by the seventeenth-century maps which show small, separate units with primitive cultivation that seem to resemble these remains. These late Iron Age dwellings are often accompanied by small burial grounds from the same period, which reinforces the impression of a single unit. Some remains of late Iron Age dwellings within the area of one farm are interpreted as implying that their occupation was not constant at this time,[6] which explains the vague nature of the remains. This interpretation adds little to our knowledge of *bybildning*, since this unit never comprised more than one farm but, on the other hand, a larger settlement of short duration would also leave fairly indistinct traces, particularly if the migration was voluntary and everything was collected before departure. When the traces of habitation are more distinct and numerous artefacts are found, there is often also evidence of fire showing that the house was burnt down, which might have happened by mistake.

Settlement prior to the *bybildning* perhaps consisted of few houses but many huts which were moved around from time to time. Remains of this type of habitation were found in southern Sweden,[7] but not so far in the Mälar area. Nevertheless, this could produce the remains which we have found, so that we need not assume that settlement consisted of single farmsteads. In fact, on some late Iron Age sites up to 70 hearths were discovered, indicating a concentration of activities. Real house-foundations are often accompanied by ovens, slag and crucibles, indicating smithing. Houses with stone foundations were perhaps used only as workshops while huts were used for habitation.

The few remains of late Iron Age settlement do not suffice as proof that the settlement consisted of several simple huts which were moved from place to place, but can hardly be used to rebut this theory. However, a thorough search must be made for further remains of settlement.

Place-names

In the history of settlement place-names are generally adduced in support of interpretations made by archaeologists or geographers. Place-names as such are rarely used to construct a picture of events. Names of settlements may provide information of earlier physical conditions or they can be used for dating a settlement, but it rarely happens that this can be based on purely philological grounds. As a rule, a group of names has been dated from burial grounds, which dating was then accepted as valid for all names which can be assigned to the same group. Two groups of names in central Sweden can be dated with comparative certainty.[8] Place-names ending in *-inge*, *-unge*, *-ling*, etc., belong to the oldest naming system which was no longer used in the Viking period. Names ending in *-sta* and *-by*, which are of somewhat later date, form another group which is dominant in central Sweden.

These datings were used for the following interpretation of the evolution of settlement. During the early Iron Age, settlement units covered larger areas and bear names ending in *-inge*, etc. Some time in the late Iron Age these settlements were divided into smaller units with names ending in *-sta* or *-by*. These units are the cores of the later villages or hamlets. The explanation of these place-names supports the theory of a single farmstead preceding a hamlet, but the same two groups of names can be used in a different way. Names are not given fortuitously. Both the name *per se* and the subject are somehow selected. A place which acquires a name must have a role to play in the society. Closer scrutiny of place-names in the aforesaid groups reveals a difference. Names in *-inge*, etc. refer to *people*. Kävlinge, for instance, means 'those who live by the bridge' (kavle = bridge). The group of people was important and are therefore named. Names in *-sta* and *-by* refer to an *area of land*. The exact meaning of the syllables *-sta* and *-by* is not yet clear. One interpretation suggests that *-sta* denotes parts of the terrain privately or co-operatively owned and cleared for cultivation. The *-by* names are no longer considered to carry the same meaning as the later *by* (= village). The reason is not yet agreed but every hypothesis so far proposed for *-by* refers to land. This gives us another kind of information about the society. In an earlier phase the principal character of society was a *group of people* (not individuals, a group). Land was a resource but was not sufficiently important to dictate the name. The settlement was not defined by the property of its inhabitants. Later on land and probably ownership of land was essential, and a new type of place-name emerges. This interpretation can be used to support the belief in an evolution from a collective society to one based on individuals.

Population

The assumption that hamlets were preceded by single farmsteads must be confirmed by evidence that the population was growing when hamlets were founded. The only Swedish material available for estimations of prehistoric population is the burial grounds. There are more burial grounds in Sweden from Viking times than from the preceding period. It therefore seems reasonable to assume that more people were buried during the Viking period than earlier, which would support the assumption of population growth. But then of course the question must be asked whether more people were buried because more people died or whether there was some other reason.

To give a general picture of burial grounds from A.D. 1 to the end of antiquity (A.D. 1050), we use three periodic divisions: early Iron Age (A.D. 0–400), middle Iron Age (A.D. 400–700) and late Iron Age (A.D. 700–1000). During the early Iron Age, burial grounds were large and boasted a wide variety of grave-forms. From the middle Iron Age there are fewer, fairly small, burial grounds but the gifts are richer (this period is sometimes called Sweden's Golden Age). From the late Iron Age there are many, but often small, burial grounds and the graves are very similar, with a simple form and few gifts. The youngest graves have no marks above ground and lack gifts, thereby closely resembling Christian graves.

The evidence could be interpreted as signifying that the earliest burial grounds were intended for a larger group of people with a closer relationship within the community. In the second phase perhaps a representative of the group, a village leader or chief, was buried at which time the whole group shared in the honour of a costly funeral ceremony because the group was the important unit in the society. During the Viking period, on the other hand, a more 'democratic' society evolved in that everyone was entitled to burial. If this is correct, the increasing number of graves from the Viking Age is not a result of population growth, and therefore cannot be used to support the assumption that an increasing number of settlement units created the hamlets.

Ideological changes around A.D. 1050

With these three short examples I have tried to show that our sources from the period when hamlets were founded allow the conclusion that hamlets meant either a more collective way of life or more private ownership. Now we need to know something of the ideology of the contemporary society to see if there is any change in that respect too. No doubt major changes were in progress in Sweden c. A.D. 1050, one of the most obvious being the conversion from paganism to Christianity. The earliest Christian missionary visited Sweden in A.D. 830, and in A.D. 1008 King Olof Skötkonung was christened. The oldest churches can be dated to the twelfth century, and were probably preceded by wooden buildings, so the introduction of Christianity in Sweden must have progressed during the ninth to eleventh centuries.

Such a revolutionary event as conversion to another religion must have affected and been affected by other ideological changes in the society, such as political and legal innovations. Naturally there is very little evidences of this kind of change, but the mere fact that written material is slowly evolving in the twelfth century shows that a new society which could afford educated people then existed.

As I suggested previously, the society seems to have become more 'democratic', if every member had the right to be buried. Moreover, the rich graves for chiefs disappeared but the rulers did not. The administrative regions grew and the leaders probably aspired to higher posts. The graves only disappeared from the rural burial grounds.

An individual ownership of land, on the other hand, would change the society in a more 'undemocratic' direction. In the first generation it would be possible to give every production unit, probably a family, a parcel of land, but if every member of the next generation had the same right to inherit the pieces would soon become too small to provide a living. In the Mälar area the size of the farmsteads was fixed soon after the hamlets were founded. Afterwards some people owned land and could build up capital, and some did not, and had to accept poverty. The Christian tenet that it is easier for the pauper than the rich man to enter heaven could have helped to support a change in privately owned land. Moreover the equality of status implied by the universal right to burial could be used to compensate those forced to remain poor, particularly when life after death is regarded as more important than life on earth.

University of Stockholm,
Sweden

The significance of time for rural settlement patterns

I. EGERBLADH

Research on rural settlement has a long tradition and is conducted within a variety of methodological frameworks, each focusing upon different aspects of settlement. With regard to the spatial arrangement of settlement units – especially the logic behind it – one main difference in the approaches is based upon whether locations are viewed as unique or general, which implies a mainly idiographical or nomothetical mode of explanation. The former has been dominant in the sense that patterns and their development over time have to a large degree been given specific explanations based upon a multitude of factors influencing detailed location in a certain region. The latter, on the other hand, has produced static and dynamic models implying certain patterns with regard to a restricted number of general factors.[1] Presupposing that locations are both general and unique these approaches are complementary, since the models may also be of help in judging the impact of local or unique factors on location. Thus the relevance and accuracy of the patterns implied by the models become of great importance.

In dealing with patterns the impact of time is essential, and this has been stressed in, for example, theories of central places.[2] The focus of this essay is thus the evolution of rural settlement patterns over time as conceptualized in models by Bylund and Lindquist, and in Hudson's theory,[3] in which the processes imply specific patterns assuming a homogeneous physical surface. However, in judging the relevance of these implied patterns, the author's present research indicates that the significance of time has not been considered sufficiently. It is suggested here that the velocity of the processes in conjunction with the date of the initial foundations of settlement ought also to be taken into account. Besides having an impact on patterns itself, this also offers scope for the prediction of hierarchical structures in settlement units measured in terms of the number of farms.

164

Models of rural settlement evolution over time

The development of rural settlement units is generally divided into processes or phases of colonization and spread, though, in Hudson's theory, a third process of competition is incorporated. Each process generates specific patterns, but the first two need not be sequential: they may run parallel in time. In the colonization process (meaning long-distance migration to a hitherto unoccupied area), the initial location of units is seen as random, though the final distribution is supposed to be dispersed. However, in Lindquist's model, it is also assumed that the colonist units at the end of this process occupy or lay claim to all the area which is then subdivided between them by boundaries.[4] The second process, here termed spread,[5] is characterized by a short-distance migration from the colonist units, caused by regeneration. Views on the mechanisms whereby this is achieved and of their spatial consequences differ between Bylund/Hudson and Lindquist.

In the former case the process is one of infilling in areas between the colonists in a way that creates clusters and thus an agglomerated distribution.[6] However, if this process continues until no space is available for new units, then the pattern ought to be dispersed since an implicit assumption is that the units are of equal areal size. The creation of agglomerations is clearly shown in Bylund's models, based upon the assumption that new settlements are located successively further away from the origin units.[7] A random element is included through the incorporation of alternative locations at the same distance from the origin unit, but the detailed location within the chosen place is seen as being governed by physical prerequisites. These models, together with diffusion and ecological plant distribution theories, also form the bases for the process of spread in Hudson's theory.

In Lindquist's process of spread, both his assumption of delimitation in the prior phase and his definition of settlement units are crucial. The units, *bebyggelseenheter*, might by definition[8] mean both a single farm and a place (for example a hamlet or village), but the postulated mechanisms refer only to the latter. The growth of farms is restricted to the delimited areas of the colonist units, and their locations are considered only if they create or function as new units/places with their own domains arising from the subdivision of land belonging to the colonist units. Thus socio-economic and legislative changes in land-holding systems are implicitly considered. These new secondary or 'satellite' units are supposed to be located either peripherally to or in the vicinity of the original units, and the total spatial effect implies a random pattern.

Limited space for expansion is also a condition of the third, 'competition', phase in Hudson's theory. This process starts when the farmers seek

to increase their holdings or domains, and implies that successful competition for land ultimately leads to a decreased number of farms and hence a
lower overall density. However, only if the remaining farms have equal-
sized domains will the pattern change from the earlier agglomerated
distribution to a dispersed one.[9]

The different character of the processes before and after colonization
could be explained partly by the definitions of the settlement units involved
but, as for instance in the case of spread, empirical tests on rural places[10]
support the emergence of both agglomerated and random patterns.
Apparent contradictions in these two spread processes might equally be
explained by the time factor in both an absolute and relative sense – a
factor which also implies a varying degree of deviation from the expected
patterns.

The significance of time

As the evolution of pattern occurs in both time and space, time is treated
here as a functional factor in mechanisms or processes which create
changes in spatial distributions. In one of the models outlined above the
time factor refers to regeneration – that is, the internal growth of population – in the spread processes. The impact of time upon the areal bases for
rural activities, and thus on the domains of the units, is somewhat
neglected, however, even though it is implicitly regarded as a cause for
both competition in Hudson's theory and spread in Lindquist's model. But
given that the domain sizes can be expected to reflect general economic
factors at the time of the foundation of the units – for example, the
resource base and the technology for extracting the resources – the
domains may then be expressed as a function of time, that is, their stage of
economic development.

Clearly, the relationship between domain size and economic level will
depend on many factors, but some general trends in changes over time may
be outlined. Thus in a long-term perspective the size of the domain for a
farm settlement unit can be expected to decrease continuously in a
traditional society, owing to the change in subsistence base from a high
degree of dependence upon fishing, hunting and stock-raising to an
increasing reliance upon cultivation, within which technology rapidly
evolved, particularly during recent centuries; or more generally, owing to
the successive change from an extensive to an intensive form of subsistence. But with a general increase in living standard and the economies of
scale associated with the emergence of industrial and especially post-
industrial societies, the domain required to maintain a farming household
at a comparable level is likely to increase. Thus, in the case of a traditional
society, if a settlement unit at its foundation occupies an area sufficient to

sustain one household, its domain size at a later time will necessarily exceed contemporary needs. According to the process of spread advocated by Hudson/Byland, a location near the parent unit is most attractive. Hence, when the domain of this unit makes it possible to sustain more than one household, new farms will be located at first within that domain. The number of farms or households that one domain can support will therefore increase over time in proportion to the diminishing domain size required for each household. This development suggests that the definition of a settlement should be treated as a function of time, because a unit initially sustaining only one farm may later become a rural place (hamlet or village) sustaining several. However, when all the area is occupied and demand for larger domains arises, an enlargement of any individual domain can then be achieved only at the expense of other farms.

These outlined changes in domain size suggest that the two processes conditioning limited space for expansion (Lindquist's process of spread and Hudson's process of competition) are relevant, but mainly during different time periods. In a traditional society it is the subdivisions of early founded units into several farms which is most likely to occur – indeed, there is a wealth of evidence to support this. The process of competition, on the other hand, is largely applicable to more recent times and the conditions which prevail in rural society today.

Further tentative conclusions can be drawn about the implications of the time factor for the processes of colonization and spread in a traditional society, based upon evidence of regeneration and domain size. If we take a settlement unit to be a rural place consisting initially of only one farm with a domain size appropriate to its needs (cultivated area, pastures, woodland, etc.) at the time of its foundation, then a rapid creation of such units implies a large immigration and a high rate of regeneration. The occupation of land over a short period of the time also implies a low probability of decreases in domain sizes occurring. Thus, almost every farm will immediately constitute a rural place, and no significant deviation from the patterns predicted by Hudson/Byland is to be expected. Furthermore, the preconditions of the kind of spread suggested in Lindquist's model will not be realized.

However, colonization and spread usually take place over a time period within which there are changes in subsistence base and/or in technology. The longer the time period, the greater the expected decrease in domain sizes becomes, which suggests that the difference in size of domains of rural places founded at the beginning and the end of a period is very great. In this context the number of colonists and the rate of regeneration are important.

However, with a comparatively small number of colonists, the rate of regeneration will govern the growth of new rural places. A low rate means that a large proportion of new farms will be located within existing rural places, and the growth of new rural places will thus be very slow. The faster the rate in relation to the decrease in required domain sizes, the smaller will be the proportion of generated farms with their needs satisfied from within the domains of existing rural places, and hence the growth of new rural places will be more rapid.

Under these conditions a hierarchical structure of rural places will be developed. In general, it can be expected that the earlier the foundation of a rural place, the more farms it will support. The range of the number of farms within the places will depend upon the rate of decrease and regeneration. The faster the decrease, the larger the range. But the faster the regeneration in conjunction with a given rate of decrease, the smaller will be the range, as the area will be occupied over a shorter time, that is the speed of the processes will be greater. Deviations from this ideal may occur however, as subdivisions of rural places are, according to Lindquist's model, now possible.

As the size of the domains of rural places which emerge in the process of spread is inversely related to their distance from the colonist units, deviations from the pattern predicted by the models and the theory will arise. The degree of deviation is dependent upon the relationship between rates of regeneration and decrease, and also upon the part in the processes at which the pattern is measured. At the beginning of the process of spread the pattern should become agglomerated, but as less space becomes available, randomness should increase. This tendency should also increase if subdivisions occur.

Examples

The significance of time will be illustrated assuming simplified conditions of regeneration and decrease in domain sizes. Case I refers to a decrease from one to one down to one to thirteen during a time period expressed as fifteen generations, while in case II a larger decrease is assumed for the same period. In both cases the decrease is discontinuous, as indicated by empirical findings. In relation to the rate of regeneration, the growth of farms is assumed to be proportional to the increase in population. Two different rates per generation are modelled: one constant (50 per cent), and the other a successively increased rate (25–50 per cent), according to the first phases of the demographic cycle. If a generation represents about twenty-five to thirty years, these rates are not overestimates since, for instance, the rate of 50 per cent means that each farm generates only half a farm per generation. The total number of farms generated by one colonist and his descendants will thus be 291 or 71, assuming the constant or varied rate.

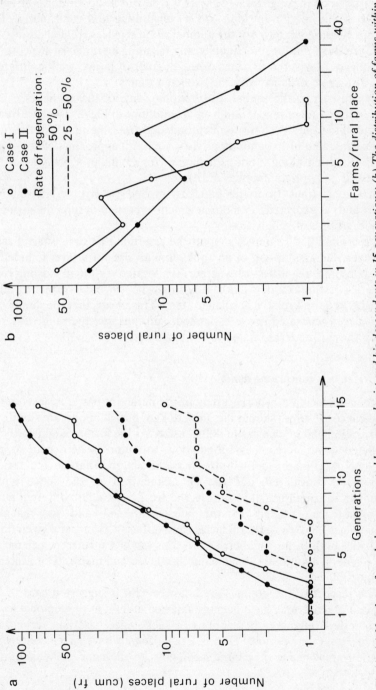

Fig. 1. (a) Number of rural places generated by one colonist and his descendants in 15 generations; (b) The distribution of farms within these places

Owing to the different rates of decrease and regeneration, different proportions of these generated farms will have the opportunity of being located within the parent units, or of constituting new rural places. The effects, measured in terms of the number of rural places created during this time, are shown in Fig. 1a. Equally, the resulting hierarchical structure of rural places, measured in terms of the number of farms, will be different (Fig. 1b), in accordance with the expected trends.

With respect to the spatial distributions, some of the results of case I with a varied rate of regeneration are exemplified in Fig. 2. The occurrence of randomly located colonist units founded at the same time and the rural places generated in 15 generations gives a pattern approximately as in (a), but if attraction along a line is assumed (for example, a main road) the result will be approximately as in (b).

Thus, deviations from the patterns implied by Bylund/Hudson will occur, and, as expected, a random element is present despite the assumed non-occurrence of subdivision.

These simplified examples support the assertion that time is significant. However, the assumption of an equal domain size for a farm founded at the same time, regardless of whether it is located within an existing rural place or constitutes a new place, is not realistic, since the former location probably required relatively smaller areas. This means that the number of rural places generated is overestimated, and thus that the range of farms within these is underestimated in the examples.

Empirical tests concerning domain sizes

In order to elucidate hypotheses about the nature of patterns, tests of the significance of time should be undertaken based upon rates both of regeneration and of changes in domain size. As the former might easily be estimated from increases in population, attention is here paid to the problems of estimating domain sizes in traditional societies. Several factors need to be considered, and can be summarized as: the actual types, quantities and qualities, of resources; the areas required for different kinds of subsistence, related to the aforementioned and to changing technologies; and also cultural factors and diffusion. Thus, at a given time, disparities both within and between regions can be expected, which means that a general hypothesis about actual size levels and their rate of decrease is impossible.

With respect to the domain sizes, however, it is suggested here that a common practice may have been established at least at the regional level, which reflects changing perceptions of subsistence base and technology during certain time periods. Hence, a practice may have arisen concerning the total areal needs of a farm, analogous to the concept of *mansus*,[11]

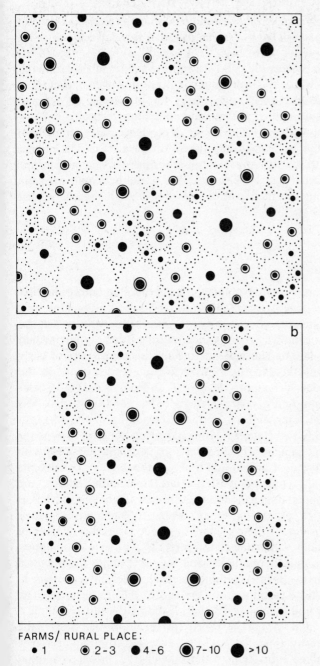

FARMS/ RURAL PLACE:
● 1　◉ 2-3　⬤ 4-6　◉ 7-10　⬤ >10

Fig. 2. *Patterns of spread of colonist units (a) randomly located and (b) presupposing the attraction of a road*

which refers primarily to cultivated/arable land. Such practices also mean that the changes in size will be discontinuous rather than continuous owing to a time-lag in adaptation to reality.

Indications of such practices may be drawn from studies in a coastal area in northern Sweden, where the process of colonization started in prehistorical, probably medieval,[12] times, and where the process of spread had virtually ceased by the end of the nineteenth century. Throughout this period, agriculture, together with a varying dependence upon supplementary areal-based activities, constituted the subsistence base. The area is therefore deemed to be appropriate for studying early stages in the development of agrarian society. Examples are presented from two main periods of expansion, the medieval colonization and the spread of the nineteenth century.

Medieval settlement units

Our knowledge of settlement development is very limited before the first fiscal record, *jordeboken*, from 1543. Colonization of this area was stimulated by the State at the beginning of the fourteenth century, but the effects of this are not known. A royal decree stated that settlers should obey the provincial law of Hälsingland, the northernmost part of early medieval Sweden, and this law, in contrast to contemporary laws in the other provinces, which were more developed and organized in a socio-economic sense, supposedly reflects much older conditions and was probably valid in this area at least until the beginning of the fifteenth century. In it, there are two clauses relating to private holdings as opposed to common land, which might provide a basis for deducing an appropriate domain size for a settlement unit at that time. As the domains of the units were not, in general, regulated until the late eighteenth century, the domains of units founded under the terms of this law might be expected to be of this deduced size, preventing the occurrence of subdivisions.

The specific provisions of these clauses have encouraged a number of different interpretations, since one clause refers to a general delimitation in relation to topographical conditions, and the other states the maximal distance (in time/energy terms) within which a settler was allowed to occupy land in certain directions from the site of the settlement.[13] The interpretation explicated here suggests that, if the unit is situated along a line beyond which land cannot be taken (for example the coast), the maximal domain size for this unit would be expected to be an area of a half-circle with a radius equivalent to the time/energy distance of about seven to eight kilometres. If, however, the possibility exists for expansion in all directions, then questions of areal equality are supposedly of importance and result in a circular area with a radius of about five kilometres.

The resulting area is large (about 80 sq. km), and suggests a very extensive exploitation of resources. In this context, archaeological research by Selinge in another part of the judicial area of this law is of interest. He suggests an adaptive innovatory model, instead of the diffusionist one, to explain shifting systems of subsistence in prehistoric times.[14] Thus, large domains might be regarded as features left over from the conditions of an earlier non-agrarian culture. However, the exploited areas in societies with subsistence based upon hunting and gathering activities are normally larger than that deduced. A common action-space seems to have been within a radius of about ten kilometres of the settlement, or, in time-distance, within one to two hours of transportation.[15] This can be compared with a more recent phenomenon, the Lapp taxation units, *lappskatteland*, based on the raising of reindeer. Throughout the nineteenth century these units were still areas with circle-radii of mainly five to eight kilometres, despite the possibility of earlier subdivisions.[16] However, with the introduction of domestic stock-raising and cultivation, areal needs are expected to decrease. Indications from historical time still support the occurrence of exploitation over large areas in regions where cultivation could not form the primary subsistence base because of physical restrictions. Thus in Lappland, for instance, the rural settlers during the eighteenth century were legally allowed to hunt and use grazing land up to five kilometres from the sites of their settlement.[17]

The predicted domain thus seems to be realistic in size, when considering primitive cultivation and stock-raising supplemented by fishing and hunting activities. Some notions from the seventeenth and eighteenth centuries also tend to support the prevalence of the expected radii for domains of earlier foundations, for example, prohibitions for hamlets to claim woodland more than five kilometres from the site of settlement.[18] On the other hand, according to Chisholm, in a society with a primarily agrarian subsistence base, the maximal distance of grain fields from the farmsteads is three to four kilometres, owing to costs of cultivation; however, the decline in net return is already considerable only one to two kilometres away.[19] Consequently, the domain size deduced is at least twice that calculated for a purely agrarian society, but about half the area for a hunting society.

The theoretical domain has been tested against the actual domains of the settlement units registered in three parishes in the first fiscal record from 1543. Their domain sizes at about this time are reconstructed from description and maps in the official papers dealing with *avvittringen* – the regulations of private domains versus the land of the state from the late eighteenth century.

Results and discussion

The areas of the reconstructed domains have been converted to radii in half-circles, since theoretically this is the ideal shape, and according to the distribution of frequencies a grouping into three classes was made. The expected radius was seven to eight kilometres, but only 20 per cent of the units reached that level. Nevertheless, within a margin of one kilometre, a minor proportion can be seen to support the deduced size (Table 1).

Table 1. *Radii (km) of half-circles for reconstructed domain sizes of settlement units ($\bar{x}$, sd)*

Parish	Radius > 6.0 km			Radius 4.5–6.0 km			Radius < 4.5 km			
	$\bar{x}$	sd	n %	$\bar{x}$	sd	n %	$\bar{x}$	sd	n %	N
Kalix	8.1	1.50	27	5.1	0.34	46	3.9	0.62	27	26
Luleå	7.8	1.62	33	5.1	0.39	43	3.8	0.43	24	42
Piteå	7.2	1.22	39	5.3	0.44	21	3.5	0.71	40	28

Presupposing the non-occurrence of unit subdivision, one conclusion to be drawn is that this proportion alone was founded whilst the law was still in operation. Because of their smaller domains, the other classes seem to belong to later periods – supposedly after the beginning of the fifteenth century. Since reconversion of average radii to areas shows that the unit in one class claim about half the area of units in the next higher-order class, a stepwise reduction is indicated owing to great changes in subsistence up to this time. In a spatial sense (Fig. 3), the small domains are mainly located in the coastal zone where the most favourable arable land is found; and this, in turn, implies an increased emphasis upon agriculture, especially cultivation, which is accompanied by a decrease in domain sizes. Furthermore, the process of land accretion (about one metre per century) had made new land available for cultivation. Thus the locations of units with these smaller domains probably imply a later stage of foundation.[20]

But we must ask: are all these smaller domains merely the result of later stages of foundation, or have some of them emerged through subdivision according to Lindquist's model? With respect to the registered units from 1543, it was observed that two or more units could be located within a joint domain. This indicates an occurrence of secondary settlements, even though a formal division of land had not yet been undertaken; an indication supported by the fact that formal subdivision was often performed later. One plausible reason for this was the primitive nature of cultivation together with restricted supplies of arable land, which might well limit the growth of farms within the core area of settlement. Thus, an earlier subdivision of other units is not improbable.

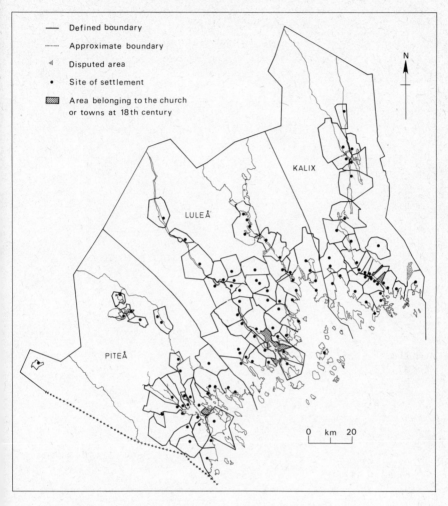

Fig. 3. *Empirical domains of settlement units registered in 1543*

An attempt to estimate the likelihood of earlier subdivision in the registered units was made theoretically. The shape of the derived domain was either a half-circle or, if no barriers existed, a circle, and both of these were used to estimate the maximum number of actual settlement units with the expected domain size. In order to minimize the occurrence of several settlement units within one theoretical domain, the choice of shape and of the site of settlement within it has been governed by empirical conditions. The result (Fig. 4) suggests that only about half of the units derived from theoretical analysis had empirical equivalents in the class with the largest

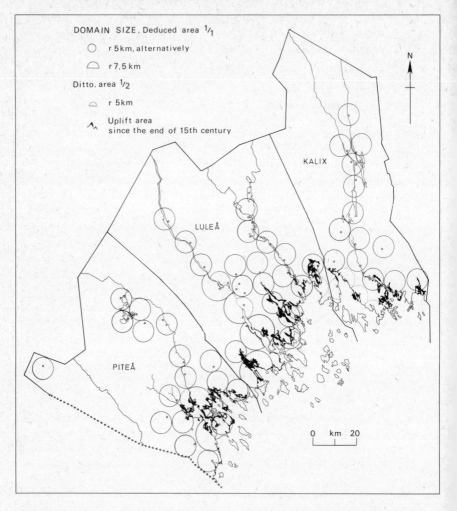

Fig. 4. *The maximal number of theoretical domains for the settlement units registered in 1543*

radii, though on the other hand, almost every unit within this class was represented among these. The lack of correspondence amongst the remaining part (3 per cent) is obviously a result of the difference between the theoretical and empirical domain configurations (especially in Piteå parish). Topographical conditions offer a possible explanation, but this also suggests that, in reality, size was more significant than shape.

However, the occurrence of more than one actual unit within a theoretical domain was much more frequent than that observed within empirical domains, particularly in the coastal area. As evidence of close connections exists in some cases between such units within a theoretical domain,[21] it appears likely that subdivisions have been carried out. But it is difficult to advocate firm conclusions about the extent of this.

Settlement units in the nineteenth century

In order to illustrate the domain sizes at the end of the process of spread, the units founded during the expansion period in the middle of the nineteenth century were investigated. From the late eighteenth century onwards the domain sizes were to a certain degree regulated by taxation instructions, which stated the area of fertile land that a rural settler should contain.[22] Its extent (described in circle-radii) was in the order of 0.5–1.5 km in 1780, and, in a somewhat later instruction (1824), this distance was extended to two kilometres. The range itself referred to both possible taxation levels and varying degrees of fertility of land, and the extension was due to the fact that the land available for new settlers was less fertile. In general, a settler was to be compensated for poor arable land by larger allotments of woodland, and owing to the heterogeneous character of land these stipulated domains were of a minimal size.

However, some understanding of the maximum domain size may have existed, as in the former case, since a later edict (1894) suggested general sizes dependent on the number of farms.[23] This edict referred to areas in which settlement was previously prohibited, but it might have been based on tradition. Here, a unit consisting of one to two farms should have a maximum area equivalent to a circle-radius of 1.3 km, while units with more than sixteen farms, for instance, could obtain land within a distance of 5.3 km. This latter area equals the deduced domain size in medieval times. Thus, the area now proposed for one farm was only one-sixteenth of the older domain area. The large decrease since the sixteenth century reflects the impact of technological change within agriculture in the area.[24]

In the case of fertile land, the expected domain size for a unit founded during the period in question is based upon the instruction of 1824 for the lowest taxation level suggested for subsistence.[25] The proportion of infertile land is assumed to be one-third of the total domain, which is somewhat higher than the average for earlier founded units. On the basis of these assumptions, the domain size will be equivalent to a circle-radius of 1.2 km, and hence comparable with the one suggested in the later edict.

As the number of founded units is rather high (213 or 25 per cent of all units in the area), the calculations are based upon contemporary parishes with the exception of one coastal parish, Nederluleå, within which no new settlement units were possible. This also enables assessments on the effects of varying physical background on the domain sizes.

Table 2. *Radii of circles for domain sizes of settlement units founded 1840–1870 ($\bar{x}$, sd)*

Parishes		Radius(km)		
		$\bar{x}$	sd	N
Coastal	Piteå	1.1	0.31	46
	Nederkalix	1.3	0.32	12
Coastal/Inland	Råneå	1.2	0.57	36
Inland	Älvsbyn	1.2	0.33	45
	Överluleå	1.5	0.41	37
	Överkalix	1.5	0.44	37

The empirical domain sizes of those units, converted to circle-radii, were about the expected size of 1.2 km. Somewhat higher values were also obtained, particularly in inland parishes in the northern part of the area, within which the preconditions for agriculture in general are less favourable. But the deviations could not be explained merely by physical factors, as the empirical proportions of infertile land only exceeded the assumed one in two parishes, Nederkalix and Överkalix. A possible explanation is therefore that the settlers claimed more arable land than was required for the lowest level of taxation, which was thought to be enough for sustenance and which was probably the size envisaged in the proposals of the edict.

Conclusion

Empirical findings support the prevalence of decreasing domain sizes over time in traditional society. The idea that rules or practices existed to determine the total domain size, and hence that a discontinuous decrease should be evident, is also suggested by the results from two different periods. The large domain size, deduced for medieval colonist units and indicating very extensive agricultural exploitation supplemented by hunting, was confirmed insofar as this domain size was apparent in the empirically reconstructed domains for the units registered in the first fiscal record from 1543. At this time, however, the majority of units were about half or a quarter of this size, and this was seen mainly as the result of an increased emphasis on agriculture. Thus, with regard to their smaller domains, these units were probably founded after the terms of the law from which the deduction was made; and some of them originated through subdivisions of primary units. Three centuries later, at the end of the process of spread, the required areal needs had decreased to about one-sixteenth of the medieval size, which still appeared relevant at least in a judicial sense for units of sixteen or more farms. The great decrease since the sixteenth century is interpreted primarily as a function of changes in agricultural technology.

These results confirm the significance of time. Because of the great decrease in domain sizes in conjunction with a successively increased rate of population growth, the expected hierarchical structure evolved. As the rate of regeneration was relatively slow up to the beginning of the eighteenth century, most of the farms could be located within the units founded up to the sixteenth century, but the rapid rate thereafter meant a fast increase of new settlement units as rural places; thus the range in number of farms within the units became very large. This development indicates a rather high degree of deviation from the patterns generated by the models and the theory, and this was supported by empirical tests. However, as many local factors also imply a random pattern, the effects of these simplified processes are difficult to distinguish.

University of Umea,
Sweden

Cotton production in Japan before industrialization

T. UKITA

Graphic representation of old documents

Historical documents which provide us with basic data would be more useful to geographers if we could represent them in graphic form or in maps. It is often the case that we are able to clarify or to discover some significance in written records only through graphic representation of the primary data. For some rural communities in Japan, for example, detailed documentary and cartographic evidence of the Edo era (1600–1868) survives, such as cadasters, cadastral maps and documents which record the various crops in each strip. The reconstruction of large-scale maps based upon these data allows a clear picture of contemporary land-use characteristics to emerge. In order to show the significance of such large-scale mapping of old documents, this essay considers cotton production in Japan.

Cotton was one of the most important crops in south-western Japan from the seventeenth to the nineteenth centuries, although its production declined after about 1890 when faced with the competitive pressure of low-priced imported cotton of good quality. Fig. 1 shows the distribution of cotton production in Japan in 1877 classified by the *kuni*, the traditional regional units. The map is based on the earliest modern statistical data compiled in 1877 on the nationwide distribution of agricultural crops classified by kind.[1] It may be assumed that the distributional characteristics would have been roughly the same during the eighteenth century when cotton production had reached its peak.[2] According to Fig. 1, it is clear that cotton production at that time was distributed mainly in the Kinai district (Osaka, Kyoto, Nara and their environs), Nobi district (Nagoya and its neighbourhood) and Setouchi district (on both sides of the Seto Inland Sea). Agriculture had been highly developed from ancient times in those districts, and as it had developed beyond the subsistence level by the Edo era, commercial agriculture was a common practice.

In terms of the landscape, cotton cultivation generally was concentrated

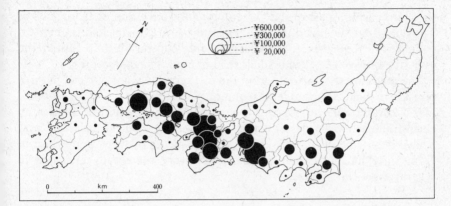

Fig. 1. *The value of cotton production in Japan in 1877*

in sandy upland fields, especially old sandbars and reclaimed land. However, in the Kinai district there was a special type of land use for cotton cultivation. In this area cotton was planted not only in upland fields but also in paddy fields alternately with rice every other year. Such a practice has been well known among historians, for the *Jikata–Ochiboshu*, or *Jikata–Hanreiroku*, manuals for the administration of rural communities, published during the Edo era, recorded it.

It is commonly accepted that the reason why farmers planted cotton instead of rice in the paddy fields where rice would normally be cultivated is that cotton commanded higher prices than rice. Although the cultivation of industrial crops such as cotton, tobacco and indigo in paddy fields was prohibited officially, farmers in the Kinai district, who were generally wealthy, disregarded the official restriction and preferred to grow the economically advantageous crops. The feudal lords would also give tacit approval of the practice as long as tax was paid as specified. Tax was generally paid in cash in this area, unlike in less economically developed districts where it was paid in kind. Farmers, on the other hand, rationalized their illicit practice by insisting that it would be difficult to plant rice in all the paddy fields owing to the lack of irrigation water in the Nara basin or in the southern part of the Osaka plain.

Such is the extent to which historians have been able to clarify the cotton cultivation in the Kinai district. However, concrete details as to how cotton was cultivated in the area have remained largely unknown.

Cotton cultivation in Iwoi in the Nara basin: an example

I have found old records concerning cotton cultivation kept by a family of a former village head in a village called Iwoi, located in the western part of the Nara basin, a part of the present administrative unit of Ikaruga Cho. The documents included the 1679 cadaster, several maps and twenty-two volumes of *Kemi-cho*, or tax assessment ledgers which recorded the assessment of yield per individual strip of land for tax purposes.

The maps are not accurate from the cartographic point of view, but it is possible to make accurate representations by referring to modern cadastral maps. Furthermore, although it is generally extremely difficult to identify each strip listed in a cadaster with a corresponding strip in a cadastral map, I have been able to identify corresponding pieces of strips in the case of Iwoi, since locations of individual strips were specifically indicated in several *Kemi-cho* ledgers.[3]

Different conditions of arable land in Iwoi

Fig. 2 shows the arrangement of arable land based on the descriptions of the 1679 cadaster. Arable land belonging to the village of Iwoi consists of three groups: Part A, located in the north-east surrounding the settlement, and Parts B and C situated at a little distance away from the settlement. About one-half of the land belonging to Part A, developed on a diluvial upland, was used as dry fields, although the improvement in irrigation facilities has since turned most of the upland fields into paddy fields. In contrast, Part C is located in a low-lying and poorly drained alluvial plain, the soil of which is clay. Part B, situated between the diluvial upland and the alluvial plain, forms a transitional zone. In the Edo era, paddy fields were classified into three grades: superior, regular and inferior. The cadaster recorded grades for individual strips, and Fig. 2 shows the grading. While paddy fields in Part A and Part B were designated as superior for the most part, those in Part C are classified mostly as either regular or inferior.

Another document classified paddy fields between those where multiple-cropping was possible and those with only single-cropping. When the information has been transfered to a map, we discover that multiple-cropping was possible in Part A, and the eastern half of Part B, whereas the western half of Part B and Part C could grow only one crop per annum. Field investigation has revealed quite clearly that the former is relatively dry. It would be possible to support a winter crop, barley, after a harvest of rice until early June of the following year. However, poor drainage made it impossible for the latter to support a winter crop, although drainage was improved, and multiple-cropping became possible in the twentieth century. Further, another document reveals sources of irrigation water for the paddy fields. According to that document, the paddy fields in Part A made use of water from the irrigation pond located to the north of the settlement. Those in Part B held water rights to a small irrigation channel

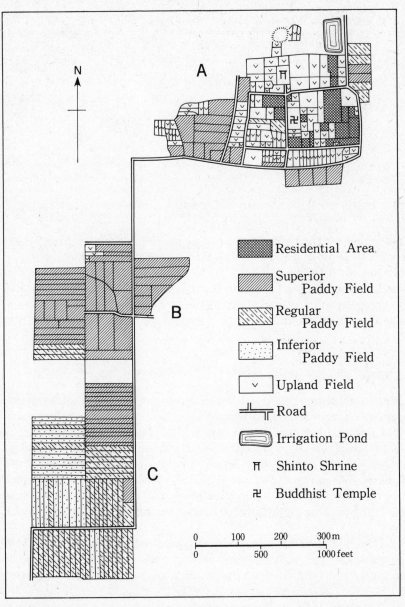

Fig. 2. *The village of Iwoi in the later Edo era, 1679*

which branched off from the river. In contrast, paddy fields in Part C were irrigated by water naturally collected rather than by such artificial means. In times of water shortage, water was obtained from wells. Moreover, one of the maps contained a record of natural hazards most likely to occur for

Table 1. *Arable land in Iwoi village, Nara basin, 1679*

	Part A	Part B	Part C
Grade of paddy field	Superior	Superior	Regular or inferior
Multiple-cropping	Possible	Partly possible	Not possible
Source of irrigation water	Irrigation pond	Small irrigation channel	Natural waterpool or well
Natural hazards	Drought	Drought	Flooding

each of the three field groups. According to the information, paddy fields in Part A and Part B were most subject to drought, whereas those in Part C were prone to flooding.

Marked differences in the quality and characteristics of the arable land in the community are summarized in Table 1. It may be safe to assume that such differentiation continued to exist throughout the latter half of the Edo era.

Cultivation of cotton and rice

As mentioned earlier, there are extant twenty-two volumes of *Kemi-cho* ledgers which recorded yield assessment for each of the entire field strips in Iwoi. The oldest was dated 1697, and the most recent was for 1868. The dates of the volumes were discontinuous for the most part, but fortunately the dates of two volumes were found to be consecutive – 1697 and 1698. Making use of the two consecutive volumes I have compiled Fig. 3, which shows the crops in individual strips for both 1697 and 1698. We may discover the following points through this comparative graphic representation:

(1) Generally speaking, those strips where cotton was grown in 1697 were put under rice in 1698. Conversely, those in rice in 1697 were in cotton in 1698. Those strips where cotton was planted in both years were very few; they were exceptions rather than the rule.

(2) Cotton was grown in either of the two years almost exclusively in those strips graded as superior for both Part A and Part B. No cotton was grown in either regular or inferior fields in Part C during those two years.

(3) The rotation of cotton and rice was practised regularly, and although each strip in a group was owned by a different farmer, alternate planting of rice or cotton was done *en bloc*.

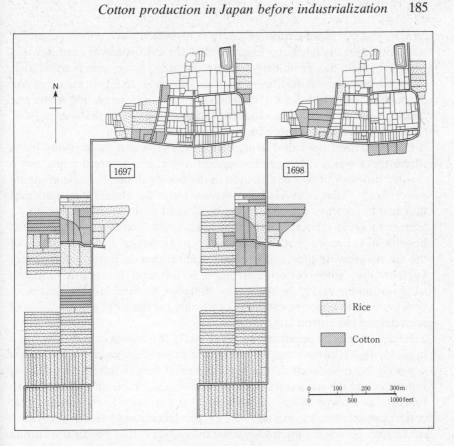

Fig. 3. *Cotton and rice production in Iwoi in 1697 and 1698*

From the foregoing findings obtained through the graphic representation of data documented in the *Kemi-cho* assessment ledgers, certain conclusions may be drawn concerning cotton production in Iwoi during the Edo era.

Characteristics of cotton production

First, it must be noted that cotton was grown only in paddy fields graded superior. We also discover, through records of trial harvesting (*tsubogari*) from 1833 to 1837, that the yield of rice per hectare was 1,962 kg for superior paddy fields, 1,670 kg for regular paddy fields and 1,494 kg for inferior paddy fields. Obviously, the yield from superior fields was the greatest. It may be clear, then, that farmers chose to plant cotton in the most productive paddy fields which were best suited for rice cultivation;

farmers did not plant cotton in paddy fields which were poorly suited for rice cultivation. It has been assumed that the cultivation of cotton would greatly benefit the producing farmers. Besides, since cotton cultivation required commercial fertilizers such as oil meal and fish meal, cotton production has served as a convenient index for measuring economic development in rural areas. Indeed, judging from these findings in Iwoi, cotton production was more lucrative than rice cultivation.

Next, we must note that while cotton was grown in those paddy fields where there was a shortage of irrigation water, and where drought was a chronic problem, it was not planted in the poorly drained, single-cropping paddy fields. That is, it has been assumed that the claim by farmers that they had to resort to cotton growing because of water shortages was only a pretext to avoid accusations by their feudal ruler and to grow as much as possible of the more profitable cotton crop. However, the examination of the cotton-growing practices in Iwoi indicates that such was not the case. Furthermore, since cotton cultivation is unsuited for poorly drained, single-cropping paddy fields, it is erroneous to measure the stages of development of a money economy using only the basis of the proportion of area devoted to cotton cultivation.

Finally, it may be important to note that, in the case of cotton cultivation in paddy fields, cotton was limited by the existence of water rights. It has generally been believed that in Japanese rural society the matter of water rights exerted the strongest constraint in a village, determining its ability to function as a corporate body. Moreover, it has often been assumed that cotton production, as opposed to rice production, was free from such a constraint. However, my findings seem to suggest that cotton production could not escape from the constraint of water rights. As we have observed in Iwoi, the yearly rotation of rice and cotton was done *en bloc*. Thus, there seems to have been some agreement or community regulation restricting the individual farmer's choice as to whether he would plant cotton or rice in each paddy strip.

Kyoto University,
Japan

PART IV

Behavioural Approaches to the Study of Geographical Change

Historical geography and Collingwood's theory of historical knowing

L. GUELKE

The way in which a historical investigation is approached cannot be separated from an individual's underlying philosophical ideas, whether these are formally expressed or not. Many of the philosophical ideas widely accepted by historical geographers have been derived directly or indirectly from the natural sciences. This scientific or positivistic influence has been detrimental to the development of an appropriate methodology of historical inquiry in historical geography. The theory of historical knowing of R. G. Collingwood provides an explicitly historical basis on which a stronger, historical, historical geography can be built.[1] Collingwood made a crucial distinction between the past of nature and the historic past of human societies. In defining history as an independent field of inquiry Collingwood established a criterion of historical meaning which is of basic importance for all disciplines concerned with historical changes in human society.

Collingwood's concept of history

The theory of historical knowing of Collingwood is based on the idea that the study of the human past demands an entirely different approach from that of the natural sciences.[2] In the world of nature 'historical' inquiry is concerned with the reconstruction and understanding of material processes. This objective is approached by using physical and chemical laws to make inferences about the past. In such studies the present is the key to the past, because the laws of the present (which are assumed to be universal) are the basis on which the past is reconstructed. This procedure, however, is not adequate when it comes to human societies. Although a historian might commence his work by seeking to reconstruct the material aspects of a historical situation (in Collingwood's terminology, its outside) his work cannot end there.[3] The primary interest of a historian is not the external manifestations of human activity, but rather the internal thought expressed

189

in these activities. A historian is able to understand human activity from the inside by rethinking the thoughts of historical agents using a procedure that is quite different from that of the natural scientist. Vico has provided the crucial insight here in his *verum factum* principle; as humans we can know our past in a way that we can never know nature precisely because it is a human creation.[4] People have created their own institutions; they have made their own history. In rethinking the thoughts of the past, the historian recreates the past in the present. The human past, therefore, unlike the geological past, which is dead, is a living past.[5]

The method of rethinking the thoughts of historical agents should not be confused with mind reading. The historian is not concerned with recreating in his own mind all the thoughts of those he is studying, but with understanding their objectives and strategies in concrete historical situations.[6] In other words, in rethinking an investigator seeks to uncover the human purpose behind an action. There is danger here. A historian might impute his own thoughts to historical agents or wrongly accept testimony on its face value. A good interpretation needs someone with imagination and a critical attitude to evidence. The acceptance of an interpretation, however, will not depend on the qualities of an investigator as such, but on the logical soundness of the conclusions that are drawn and the reliability of the evidence on which they are based.

An example of Collingwood's approach is provided in his own work on Roman Britain. The problem posed to Collingwood was a continuous earthwork (the Vallum) that archaeologists discovered immediately to the south of Hadrian's wall.[7] Collingwood rejected the idea that the Vallum had any defensive value and argued that it was probably created to avoid confusion arising between the jurisdictions of the military and civilian authorities on the frontier. The wall itself, Collingwood maintained, might well have served both purposes, but would have left in doubt the undisputed authority of the commandant in military matters. An additional barrier was therefore constructed, on the instructions of the Emperor Hadrian, where the financial matters of frontier administration could be transacted. Collingwood noted that there was no proof that his explanation was correct, but that it 'fits the facts.' Whether this explanation is correct or not, however, is less important than the clear illustration it provides of what 'rethinking' entails in a concrete situation.

The essence of Collingwood's approach has been well summarized by Goldstein:

If Collingwood's solution to the Vallum problem is correct, there is a clear sense in which he has rethought the thoughts of Hadrian in all of their historically-relevant character. The essential considerations which presumably passed through Hadrian's mind as he came to the decision to have the Vallum built have passed through Collingwood's as well. There is no suggestion of his having entered fully into the existential experience of the historical actor in the sense of reproducing the feelings, emotions, and other appurtenances of existing-and-experiencing-here-and-now in the way that an historical novelist might seek to do. Here, it seems, is the central feature of what Collingwood thinks history is: it is rethinking thought on the basis of evidence without ever becoming psychology. As rethinking thought, its object is what can be detached from the original context of historical inquiry, hence its object is universal and not existential.[8]

A widespread criticism of Collingwood is that he ignores the non-rational and emotional aspects of human life. Collingwood, however, was not unaware that human behaviour had a biological and psychological component, but he deliberately placed the main emphasis on thought. The issue is not whether human behaviour is propelled by psychological and biological factors, but rather deciding whether these factors have any historical significance. Collingwood argued that the non-rational aspects of human behaviour, although real enough, lie outside history which is concerned with the world humans have made for themselves.[9] For example, the historian is not concerned with a phenomenon like human sexuality as such, but he is interested in the different ways people have interpreted the phenomenon and the institutions and conventions that have been created around it. The human being is a conceptualizing, theoretical animal and it is precisely this element that differentiates him from the world of nature and, indeed, that makes historical existence possible.

The historian is not concerned to offer explanations of events along the lines of the natural scientist. His concern is not to provide a causal explanation of an event (in the sense of listing all necessary and sufficient conditions for its occurrence), but rather to elucidate its historical meaning or significance. This elucidation must be done in relation to thought. For example, the historical significance of the mass-suicide at Jonestown or the nuclear accident at Three Mile Island ultimately will be decided by the meaning people attach to these events. The 'real' events (which, in any case, can never be known or reconstructed as they actually happened) are only of importance insofar as they are endowed with human meanings. These meanings will vary in relation to the ideas and cultural backgrounds of those who are able to form an opinion on them. The task of the historian is basically that of elucidating what the world has meant to various people and how it has changed as people have responded to the events around them and the changing circumstances of their lives.

'All history', in Collingwood's words, 'is the history of thought.'[10] This statement simply reaffirms the intellectual foundation of historical change. The human mind is not capable of apprehending an event as it really happened in all its physical and emotional aspects.[11] The legacy of the past is, therefore, a legacy of ideas about events and the meanings attached to them. It is this legacy which is handed down, modified and extended from one generation to the next. An event, to qualify as a historical event, must change or have the potential to change the way people construe each other and the world around them. The mere repetition of events would not be history.[12] In Collingwood's position the study of the past as such is not history, and all past events are not historical events. The insistence that an event must have an impact on the human mind to be considered a historical event establishes a crucially important criterion of historical significance.

The nature of historical change is dialectical.[13] The world is always interpreted from a specific point of view, which at any given moment is a legacy of the past. The reality of the present is a creation of the historical past, because this past provides the ideas on which the world is interpreted. If we wish to understand the twentieth century we must understand the societies of the nineteenth century from which modern society developed. The nineteenth century must, in turn, be understood in relation to the historical legacy of the period preceding it and so on backwards through time. The objective of history is to understand historical change, but such change never takes place in a vacuum of ideas. Indeed, the impossibility of understanding contemporary ideas except historically makes the study of history important in all fields of human endeavour.

Collingwood and historical geography

There is no logical basis for differentiating historical geography from history. Although historians have tended to concern themselves with political and social questions, geographers with human settlement and the use of the land, these differences, to the extent that they are empirically valid, are of no philosophical importance. The fact that many historical geographers (that is, scholars doing historical geography) are found within departments of geography is justified, if at all, on pragmatic grounds. A historical geographer with a background in, for example, climatology, plant geography and soils is probably in a better position to evaluate and understand human activity on the land than someone without such knowledge, although the researcher in historical geography must be careful not to assume the people he investigates have the same knowledge as he does.

The idea that the word 'historical' is a synonym for 'the past' is a major misconception of many historical geographers. All geography is not historical geography and the use of data from the past does not make a study historical. Neither does the passage of time make a contemporary geographical study historical – it merely creates old geography.[14] A historical study is, by definition, concerned with change. The geographical study of a past period is, therefore, not necessarily historical, even if archival and manuscript sources are used. Although Ralph Brown's study, *Mirror for Americans*, is in many respects an excellent example of an idealist approach to geography, it would, on the criteria advanced here, be classified as contemporary regional geography rather than historical geography, because the study is not directly concerned with historical changes of geographical significance. The use of historical sources is not considered by itself to qualify otherwise conventional human and regional geography as historical geography. Such studies might be termed 'historical regional geography' or 'historical human geography' to differentiate them from historical geography proper.

A concern with past change is a necessary element in a historical study, but such a concern on its own does not make a study historical. A central place theorist might, for example, be interested in testing theoretical propositions about changes in a central place system using data from nineteenth-century France. The theoretical objectives of this type of study are not given a historical purpose simply because somewhat older data than is usual in this field might have been employed. The study of central place systems would, however, become of historical importance in the hands of a scholar who was concerned to elucidate the historical meaning of changes in the character of central places for the inhabitants of the areas in which they were located.

If all history is the history of thought, all historical geography is the history of thought with a bearing on human activity on the land. The historical geographer no less than the historian is concerned to understand the meaning of the human actions of interest to him. However, in historical geography the events of interest are those related to the human activity on the earth. This activity is dependent, in the first instance, on understanding the physical environment in terms of the human meanings it has. These meanings have changed as the human condition has changed and as knowledge of the environment has expanded. The environment must, therefore, be understood by rethinking the thoughts of those who are seeking a living within it. However, the full elucidation of human activity on the earth will involve a consideration of a wide range of political, economic and social ideas, because environmental decisions are not taken solely in relation to the resource potential of the environment.

Although the basic goal of the historical geographer is considered to be the elucidation of the historical meaning of human activity on the earth, many studies properly begin with reconstruction. The careful reconstruction of economic conditions and demographic characteristics can provide a solid empirical foundation for historical geographical study. In Collingwood's terminology such reconstruction would be concerned with the 'outside' of a historical situation. If a historical study may begin with the outsides of events it can never end there. The historical significance of past events is not a question that can be resolved by the statistical analysis of their external attributes. Similar data will have different historical meanings depending on the historical context. For example, discrepancies in wealth among a people might, depending on the context, be a factor in a revolution or be associated with a stable political order.

In the absence of general theories and laws of human behaviour, the notion of rethinking thought provides historical geography with a crucially important criterion of historical meaning. A fact or event becomes significant to historical geography in terms of its actual or potential importance in changing the way people construe their situations. This criterion of meaning is sufficiently flexible to allow that practically any kind of occurrence or event be considered of potential historical importance depending only on its impact (or potential impact) on the human mind. The application of the proposed criterion of meaning will likely lead to considerable disagreements among various scholars. Such disagreements on what constitute historically significant events are to be welcomed, because they are likely to focus attention on specific elements of a situation and encourage further research on them. This kind of disagreement, however, is only likely to be productive if all participants accept the same idea of what constitutes an historical event.

The concept of historical geography presented above has implications for empirical research in this field. The emphasis will be on the study of individual, unique cases. This emphasis is not to deny that similar factors are often present in different areas, but rather to insist that the meaning of such factors be evaluated in the unique historical context of which they are part. The underlying idea is that a landscape is the creation of the historical mind – which is a product of the unique historical experiences of the inhabitants of the earth's regions. To insist that each area of the world be treated as a unique entity is not to deny the importance of comparative studies. However, if such studies are to have empirical validity they must be built upon a foundation of detailed case studies of historical changes in specific situations.

The dangers inherent in an empirical approach are that it becomes a detailed description and catalogue of the attributes of a particular area. This danger is most acute where empiricism is in harness with an implicit or explicit scientific approach which emphasizes description and classification as first steps towards theory-building. For example, the sequent occupance studies, which enjoyed popularity at one time, presented a spectacle of change but generally failed to clarify what the spectacle meant. The problem related to empirical research based on the acceptance of natural scientific or positivistic ideas can be avoided by emphasizing that it is the inside of an event rather than its outside that holds the key to understanding its historical meaning.

Even if well-confirmed theories of human behaviour were available, such theories would not necessarily be of help to historians or historical geographers. It might, for example, be possible to explain (and predict) certain types of unruly or riotous behaviour using theories from social psychology. Such knowledge would not, however, tell us anything about the historical meaning of a specific riot, because the historical significance of a riot or other event is related to the way in which it is construed by others. An event would only qualify as a historical event if it could be shown that it was some measure responsible for a change in the way people thought and acted. Thus the Pennsylvania 'gas' riots of spring, 1979 would be included in a historical geography of energy only if it could be shown that they had affected the energy ideas and activities of the people of the United States in some way, but not otherwise. It is not the cause of an event that is of ultimate interest to historians or historical geographers but rather its historical ramifications.

The positivist conception of history, which equates explanation and prediction, lacks a workable criterion of historical significance. Although the application of formal theories to geographical situations can provide a basis for differentiating 'significant' facts from others, such facts will not necessarily be 'historically significant' in the sense that the term is used here. In other words, there is not necessarily a correspondence between historically and theoretically significant facts. Where such correspondence is claimed, historical research often becomes an illustration of the theory rather than an empirical testing of it. This basic error was at the centre of environmental determinism, but it is present wherever theories of questionable empirical status are used to interpret evidence. The problem is particularly acute in human studies which lack testable or verified theories on which a truly theoretical history might be developed.

The central importance of theory in the natural and social sciences has led many to question whether an intellectually worthwhile study which is avowedly anti-theoretical (using the term 'theory' in a rigorous scientific or logical positivist sense) can have much value. This objection to non-theoretical approaches in the human studies, however, overlooks the fact that human beings are themselves theoretical animals who behave in the world in terms of their theoretical understanding of it.[15] The vital role played by theory in the natural sciences in separating the significant from the insignificant is rendered superfluous, because the applicable theory behind historical action is to be discovered in the thoughts of the actors rather than being imposed upon them by the investigator. In seeking to discover what those thoughts were a historian will put forward hypotheses and interpretations, but these mental constructs (although sometimes referred to as theory) are used to understand individual cases and are quite different from the general or universal theories of natural science. However, hypotheses and interpretations in historical geography could be considered scientific in the broad sense that they must be based on logical argument and supported with empirical evidence before their acceptance can be entertained.

Conclusion

The practice and methods of historical geography still reflect the strong, if implicit, influence of natural science. This essay has sought to put forward an alternative model of empirical inquiry solidly based upon the recognition of a fundamental distinction between the natural sciences and history. Collingwood's idea that history is concerned with the thought behind action is applicable to historical geography. Historical geography is concerned with changes in ideas which are reflected in human activity on and use of the earth's surface. Such an emphasis makes possible an empirical approach to historical geography which, on the one hand, avoids the 'mere description' of extreme scientific empiricism and, on the other hand, the non-historical aims of theoretical approaches. A concern with thought permits the historical geographer to explore the meanings of geographical activities in their unique historical settings. This exploration holds out the promise of providing us with valuable insight into the evolution of human society without need of the formal theory that is indispensable in studies of natural phenomena.

University of Waterloo,
Canada

Images, acts and consequences: a critical review of historical geosophy

R. W. CHAMBERS

Recently some geographers have begun to look at the perceptions people have of the world in which they live.[1] In historical geography such an interest is often called geosophy.[2] Most substantive studies in historical geosophy begin something like this: the images people have of the environment determine (or influence, or guide) their decisions and their behaviour; if we are to understand people's actions we must know how they perceived the environment.[3] This fine hypothesis has unfortunately become a platitude; a way to tell the reader, 'this is going to be geosophy', and little more.

Some years ago Yi-fu Tuan wrote: 'The history of environmental ideas . . . has been pursued as an academic discipline largely in detachment from the question how – if at all – these ideas guide the course of action, or how they arise out of it.'[4] This is still true today. Many have intended to find the connections between images and acts, but for a variety of reasons few have actually done so. The geosophical hypothesis, instead of guiding and focusing research, has become a bromide: many historical geosophers disregard the actual behaviour of people in the past. The influence of environment on behaviour and the unintended consequences of behaviour have also been widely ignored. In addition, the 'image' is a faulty model of mental processes and has been used with little regard for the sociology of knowledge.[5] For these reasons many geosophical studies are catalogues of images: capes and bays geographies of the mind. This essay explores some of the common failings of research in historical geosophy, suggests remedies for these persistent problems, and proposes a role for geosophy within (but not apart from) historical geography.

Whose images?

Substantive historical geosophy begins with the premise that people in the past had different impressions of the environment from people today; that

197

is, knowledge is *historically* distributed. Yet it is often forgotten that ideas are also *socially* and *geographically* distributed. The debate over the images that stalled the farming frontier west of the Mississippi River in the mid-nineteenth century reveals the problem clearly. It should be obvious that we need the images of farmers in that vicinity, but instead we have the images of fur traders, gold miners, explorers, surveyors, promoters and missionaries. It is not surprising that the debate continues: we have been using the wrong images.[6]

The problem, of course, is that farmers did not usually write. Since we must make do with available records there are several options: we can try to find the sources of the farmers' images (perhaps schoolbooks or promoters' pamphlets); we can turn to the farmers' newspapers expecting that they reflect farmers' attitudes; we can look for the images of other common-folk in the area and use them as surrogates for the farmers' perceptions; and in some cases we must own up to the fact that without proper records some of the past cannot be explained geosophically. Historical geosophers have shown a preference for using surrogate images, and I will focus upon this option.

Martyn Bowden offers the perceptions of land surveyors in Nebraska in the 1850s as surrogates for settlers' images. He chooses them because they left detailed field-notebooks and because they were 'frontiersmen reflecting popular western values'.[7] But Bowden never demonstrates that surveyors were representative. In fact, John Tyman's study of a portion of the Canadian prairies shows that settlers and surveyors appraised land quality very differently.[8] This does not refute Bowden's findings, but it should make us sceptical.

Three other papers offer surrogates for the perceptions of Great Plains' pioneer farmers, though this is not explicitly stated. David Wishart tells us what fur traders on the Missouri River during the nineteenth century thought of the agricultural potential of the Plains. He is not concerned with the traders' images of fur resources, and he admits that it is unlikely that the experiences of the fur traders ever became widely known, that is, the traders were not sources of environmental images.[9] We can only assume that he offers them as being typical of frontiersmen. But, like Bowden, Wishart makes no attempt to show that they were typical and so their perceptions tell us nothing about the problem at hand: why the farming frontier stalled. Similarly, Merlin Lawson has detailed the images that the 1849 gold miners had of the Great Plains, and Richard Jackson has investigated the Mormons' trip to Utah.[10] Again, these groups never publicized their images and so it is likely that they had no influence on potential settlers. Were their perceptions representative? Hardly. They did not appraise the Great Plains as settlers; they were passing through on their way to other places. Their goals and circumstances were not the farmers', and it seems unlikely that their impressions were the same.

If we are to use surrogate images to supplant scanty records then we must justify our choices by showing that one group's images were held by another group, or at least that geographical knowledge passed between them.[11] We must begin by doubting that their images were similar or shared, not by assuming that they were.

Some historical geographers have wrongly assumed that all frontiersmen had similar images of the environment, and others have attributed patently elite images and values to common-folk. J. M. Powell, for example, insists that North American farmers held agrarian ideals and were 'spiritually attached' to their land.[12] G. Malcolm Lewis seems sure that the Great American Desert was a dominant and influential image among sod-busters.[13] Martyn Bowden, however, has been working for some time to separate elite and popular images of the Plains, and he asserts that the image of a Great American Desert was strongest in the parlours of New England literati and may never have left the East Coast.[14] Bowden has examined the contemporary schoolbooks in an attempt to show that frontier farmers could not have learned of the Desert from this source. But he does not show how many copies of each text were sold, who read them, or if people believed or remembered what they read. In fact, Malcolm Lewis writes that schoolbooks (presumably the same ones Bowden used) were highly *successful* in spreading the Desert image.[15] Bowden's task may be hopeless since it is far more difficult to show that farmers did not believe in an image than it is to show they did: one mention of a desert in one farmer's letter would be substantial positive evidence, whereas one letter without such a reference would be only slight evidence to the contrary. Nevertheless, it is difficult to see why any student of the past ever assumed that pioneers held an image of the Great American Desert. There is certainly no hard evidence that they did. To use it as an *ad hoc* hypothesis to explain why the farming frontier stalled is simply irresponsible. Educated New Englanders and Great Plains' pioneers were separated socially and geographically; we need proof before we can accept that they shared an image of a Great American Desert.

Acts without images

All historical inquiries have the problem of incomplete records, but this can be particularly stifling for geosophy because the questions it asks are best answered by the subjective impressions found in letters and diaries. Lacking such written records can we derive images and attitudes from other artefacts? There can be little doubt that landscapes and land rents express images and values.[16] The question is: can we accurately *interpret* the complexities of such records?[17]

R. L. Heathcote, for example, uses the rent paid for Australian ranch land as a summary of ranchers' appraisals of land quality.[18] This seems reasonable, but rent is a synopsis of many factors and we must be sure that the important components of rent, when considered separately, are attributes of land *quality*. Land supply, for example, is not a measure of land quality and yet it could greatly influence rents. In addition, only if rents were determined in a free market could we say that rent reflected demand and that demand reflected some composite image of land quality. In Australia, however, the government determined both the supply of land and the rents. Land rents reflected the appraisals of government officials, not ranchers.[19]

There is yet another problem encountered when deriving images from acts – it is difficult to distinguish between the intended and unintended consequences of acts.[20] If we cannot tell an intended result from an unintended one then we risk attributing values, attitudes, images or intentions where none existed in the first place. To interpret the meaning of acts we need *independent* evidence of attitudes: we cannot reliably derive images from acts and results of acts alone.[21]

This fact is often disregarded by historical geosophers because the method of geosophy implies a model of people as conscious decision-makers.[22] The tendency is to interpret history and geography largely as the outcome of intentional acts, and to play down the importance of unintended and unforeseen consequences and practically ignore the influence of the environment. But this is a mistake: people are not free to create the world narcissistically as they see it.[23] Conscious *decisions* can be made on the basis of perceptions of the world, but *actions* are played out in the real world. There will be unintended consequences whenever there is a discrepancy between the world as perceived (and acted on) and the world as it is. This is not some abstract principle, it is simply the observation that faulty or incomplete knowledge leads to mistakes and surprises; since our knowledge of the world is never perfect our acts *always* have unintended consequences.

Geosophy typically ignores unintended results even though it is precisely here that the historical geographer knows more about past events than did the people of the time. To understand the *reasons* for people acting as they did (geosophy's *forte*) it is sufficient to know their intentions and images. But to understand the unintended *consequences* of their acts we need to know that their beliefs were not quite right. The world has been created as much by mistake as by intent, and it is for this reason that to understand the past we need images, acts *and* consequences.

Images of environment?

Historical geosophy has concentrated on images of the physical environment to the virtual exclusion of other images. One reason may be that images of environment seem geographical. For example, J. M. Powell tells us that it is impossible to understand settlement change without knowing the central processes of image-making, which he says is *environmental evaluation*.[24] But this is an article of faith, not a statement of fact. It is wishful thinking to assume that the images that seem geographical to us were also considered essential by the people we study. Non-environmental images clearly influenced migrations, for example, but among geosophers there has been the tacit assumption that soil quality, healthfulness, terrain, vegetation and climate were the crucial images.

Roy Merren's study of colonial South Carolina is an example of how an allegiance to environmental images can lead to dubious conclusions. There is some evidence that during the earliest stages of settlement in South Carolina farmers were interested in soil quality. Merrens writes that later, 'such simplistic evaluations were abandoned as the settlers, presumably by a process of trial and error, began to appreciate more subtle distinctions in land use capabilities'.[25] But he presents no evidence that this happened. It seems just as likely that farmers abandoned distinctions when they realized that differences in soil quality were relatively unimportant in a region of good soils, or when compared to the importance of obtaining good seed, a new plough or a second horse. Merrens, following the geosophical articles of faith, has decided that soil quality became increasingly important in spite of the reticence of the farmers on the subject. Which conjecture (if either) is closer to the truth can only be determined by examining the records more closely.

This is not to say that environmental images were never influential, only that we should not assume that they were always important. Perceived economic opportunity was probably important, and the lure of living in a secure community with people who spoke your language, practised your religion or grew your crops may have been strong.[26] Also, immigrants considered the availability and price of land and access to markets when choosing where to settle.[27] Finally, timing and chance often played a large role. Whether the content of the image was environmental or not is unimportant. It is the geographical fact of people coming to a new place that interests historical geographers. Images that influenced people's use of the earth are important no matter what their content.

Images or concepts?

To say that people have images of the world and that they decide what to do on the basis of those images is to use 'image' as an analogy, or model, for a portion of the complex mental processes we may, in shorthand, call experience. So far I have examined some limitations on using images to understand past events, and I have questioned whether the content of influential images was always (or even usually) the physical environment. In this section I will raise some doubts about the accuracy of the image as a model of mental processes.

Historical geosophers have assumed that people have a specific, visual image in their mind's eye. Others have questioned whether images are visual; to be examined here is whether images are correctly considered *specific*.[28] Many immigrants who came to the New World, for instance, assumed that it was a land of great fertility and numerous opportunities. This is certainly an image of environmental quality, but it is not specific and critical, it is general and undiscriminating. Images became specific only after people were settled for a time; that is, image-making may be a way of adapting to a novel environment.[29] Evidence of this comes from Bowden's work with farmers in Nebraska during the mid-nineteenth century. He identifies two ways in which farmers adapted to the environment of Nebraska. Though he does not characterize them as such, the first strategy was simple, undiscriminating and applicative; the second was complex, discriminating and evaluative. The first sort was typical of frontier farming before the capabilities and limits of the environment were known. Farmers specialized in a single crop and moved to new lands as the frontier of that crop expanded. In this way waves of cattle, wheat and then corn passed through Nebraska. Later, as experience with the environment (and especially its extremes) grew the second strategy was common: farmers grew wheat during dry periods, and the same farmers would raise corn in the wet years.[30] The farmers' image of the Plains environment became specific as they learned to evaluate, or analyse, the climate each year.

This same evolution of strategies can be identified in other cases. Heathcote found that Australian ranchers gradually learned to evaluate climate anew each year.[31] Similarly, James Allen has found that explorers, such as Lewis and Clark, succeeded in their missions not by applying specific and critical images formed prior to their travels, but by adapting, modifying and making specific their general preconceptions. On many occasions their survival depended upon readjusting their concepts to fit the circumstances. That is, explorers replaced concepts (really just notions, ideas or hypotheses) with images. They did not replace one set of images with another set.[32]

Generalizing, then, specific images form when general concepts must be adapted to fit experience. More simply, people learn from experience and especially from mistakes. Lewis and Clark believed that continents had pyramidal watersheds until they traversed North America.[33] Farmers thought that rain would follow their ploughs until their topsoil blew away during droughts. This is what Kenneth Boulding means when he writes: 'Messages from nature have an urgency, an insistence, and an authority in and of themselves which are not possessed by messages that come from people.'[34] Success in exploring and farming alike comes from adapting to the environment and coping with novelty; more from testing concepts than applying images.[35] Rationality is an enterprise, not a logic: it is the procedure for discovery, learning and conceptual change.[36] Using a model of specific, visual images hinders geosophy, especially because a dominant interest is how people adapted to novel environments. Here the value of conception (as opposed to perception) and of conceptual change will become clear.[37]

Conclusion

Substantive historical geosophy has been disappointing because of its errors and omissions. There have been persistent errors in the practice of geosophy: the sociology of knowledge has been virtually ignored. Ideas are assumed to travel effortlessly through society and be naively accepted everywhere; surrogate perceptions are used without due caution; images have been derived from acts under questionable circumstances. Secondly, there have been deficiencies in the *scope* of geosophy. It has become image-geography and has forgotten its goal to connect images and acts. Geosophy has restricted itself to images of the physical environment, a grave shortcoming because there is no good reason to assume that 'geographical' behaviour (such as migration) is caused by environmental images. Further, the image as a model of conscious decision-making is inadequate because it cannot explain conceptual change. Just as images must be seen in the context of the acts they inspire, acts too have their context – the consequences that follow from them and the environment in which they occur. People may be able to decide what to do, but they cannot decide what will happen. F. A. Hayek writes:

If social phenomena showed no order except so far as they were consciously designed, there would be . . . only problems of psychology. It is only so far as some sort of order arises as a result of individual action but without being designed by any individual that a problem is raised which demands a theoretical explanation.[38]

Every past event, such as the stalling of the farming frontier on the Great Plains, is a complex combination of images, concepts and acts, intended and unintended consequences, and the environment. To remove images from this context and use them alone to explain an event simply ignores too much of the evidence available to us. In effect it makes our task as historical geographers more difficult by restricting the facts we can rally to support our case.

In short, geosophy has little value when removed from historical geography. Yet it is the most *human* level on which we can know the past – attitudes, values and concepts are its data. Because of this geosophy could have a moderating and humanizing effect on historical geography. But to have this effect it must be integrated within, not kept separate from, historical geography.

Acknowledgement

The author is indebted to Professor Cole Harris for the many hours of discussion that made this paper possible.

University of Minnesota,
USA

The image of France and Paris in modern times: a historico-geographical problem

P. CLAVAL

Contemporary geography is breaking away from the positivism which for a long time has dominated the social sciences. Its object is not constituted any longer of materialistic things, artefacts and the development of the landscape. It is diversified and embraces subjective elements. Geography exists in the mind as well as in the environment. During the last twenty years, a whole series of steps has been established to specify the perceptions and the representations people make of space. Such studies proceed through interviews: they evaluate in so doing the tastes and the aspirations of each interviewee. Historical geography follows this trend with difficulty: it does not dispose of the data on which research on action-space and on lived-in space is generally based. Is it condemned not to tackle these questions? No, but it is obliged to make use of indirect evidence – such as literary texts.

Since the beginning of this century, French geographers have been aware of the interest which exists in gathering popular names of places: they provide much evidence about the general perception of space. French geography, in so doing, gave more room to the subjective elements than did others. But the method has its weaknesses. The evidence of the names of the country, for instance, is very often misleading: Lucien Gallois showed that the limits are very often fluctuating and that the collective perception changes too quickly to be invoked as evidence of the stability of territorial organizations.[1] Names of places are suitable to circumscribe the stability of spaces divided in homogeneous regions or in clearly polarized areas. They do not tell us anything about the perception of territorial hierarchies or about the way large territorial entities are inhabited. Which documents to explore, which evidence to invoke to catch the genesis of these images? This question will be explored in relation to the image of France and Paris in modern times.

The image of France

There had been, during the whole Middle Ages, one image of France resulting from the partition of the Empire of Charlemagne at the Verdun treaty: the Kingdom stretches out from Flanders to Roussillon and goes in the east to the 'four rivers', the Rhône, the Saône, the Meuse and the Scheldt.[2] Locally, the memory of that border has stayed alive. People still talked about the boundaries of the Empire in the last century and about the boundary of the Kingdom in a part of the Rhône valley. At the end of the Middle Ages, the feeling of belonging to the Kingdom was so much alive in Flanders that nobility spoke French. Charles V had been educated in Ghent, but in French. We witness, however, a progressive decline of the awareness of this boundary from the fourteenth century. The presence of the French sovereign on the other side of the four rivers asserts itself progressively – in the south-east the Dauphiné, and later Provence, come under his control. The Franche-Comté is annexed and lost by Louis XI. Charles-le Téméraire's adventures show a will to build, astride the pluri-secular border of the Empire and of the Kingdom, an original political formation. Pierre Chaunu makes the remark that on the other side of the Kingdom exists a band of territories different in population, but, at the period of the Renaissance, very much marked by the French language and culture: from Flanders to north Italy, passing through Lorraine and Switzerland the merchant heart of Europe stretches itself out; that is the zone where wealth is accumulated and where artistic creation is concentrated – but from a political point of view, this band seems depressed without a modern state to give it a synthesized structure.[3]

In the sixteenth century, the French expansion of this zone is asserted – by the annexation of three dioceses in Lorraine, for instance – while the unity of the more western regions is confirmed. This seems natural to us. But in reality it did not come about so easily. At the time that particularisms were eating up Italy and Germany, one could have imagined a similar evolution for France. The crisis of the Reformation could have provoked a rupture. It never seems menacing, however, even at the moment when the civil riots are at their worst. Modern regional studies underline the fact that in the sixteenth century originality and local sentiment were manifest in many provinces, in the Midi and in Brittany, for example. But, at that time, there was no question of movements and reactions of a really separatist character. In order to explain the surprising resistance of royalty and the Kingdom in the ordeals they had to go through at the end of the sixteenth century, one has to admit that they found a deep support and assent in public opinion. The sentiment of attachment to the dynasty is sufficient to explain the faithfulness of the major part of the country, but that cannot be the case for the peripheral regions and those which escaped the traditional *mouvance* of the sovereign. The events of the second half of the sixteenth century were, incidentally, of such a nature as to sap the strongest bonds of faithfulness. The Huguenots could not accept with the same loyalty as the Catholics the kings who persecuted their religion – and the situation was inverted with the accession of Henry IV. The monarchists were, moreover, the first to cast doubts on the legitimacy of the prince as of divine right, in the most troubled decades of the end of the century. In that atmosphere of irreverence a rebellious intellectual movement could have erupted. One does not find any trace of it. Those who represent the thinking elite appropriated the idea that they were French, even when they did not agree with the government which embodied the country.

The emergence of national feeling can already be detected in the fifteenth century, at the time of the conflict with England – but it is easy to show that the nation of Jeanne d'Arc is different from ours today. The riots and tensions which develop in the sixteenth century create a new consciousness in that respect: the rise of Spanish power, the encirclement from which France felt itself a victim when Charles V assembles in addition to the Iberian peninsula his traditional possessions of Flanders and the Franche-Comté. The captivity of the king after Pavia, the conflict between France and the Imperials and the Spaniards in Italy mobilized public opinion. Rabelais' nationalism was not feigned: it corresponded with popular feeling – a feeling the elite shared and to which it was going to give a new appearance in the second half of the century, during Henry II's reign and in the years after his disappearance. Georges Huppert has written the history of this forgotten intellectual movement, which is one of 'perfect history'.[4] It allows a better understanding of the climate which was prevailing at a time when the ordeals were being multiplied around the Kingdom. The intellectuals of that era tried to give to the nation the instruments which were missing to justify its configuration and to specify its being and its vocation. In modern terms, they felt that the old feudal mythologies were not sufficient to cement the territorial construction in which they lived; they were looking for indispensable ideologies to unite the country. They probed history. It is because they wanted to use its lessons to justify their point of view that they felt the need to make it as objective as possible, to make it perfect: an ideology which is transparent for those who use it is not efficient. Authority, which founds it, has to be unquestionable and unquestioned, if it wants to play its part. The movement of 'perfect history' is the earliest known example of using science to found an ideology.

The intellectual groups which kept themselves busy with that national work were shaped by classic culture. Contrary to the first decades of the sixteenth century they did not take the Italian society of their days as an example; humanism had progressed sufficiently in France that everybody did his utmost to find his inspiration in Latin and Greek texts. From the point of view of the makers of ideologies, antiquity offers two things: first, the image of a discipline which has already come to maturity and which one can use for the justification of the French reality – it here concerns history, without doubt, the most developed of all traditional social sciences; secondly, the image of what foreshadowed France, that is, Gaul.

It would have been possible to see research underline medieval France's diversity, together with its regional and cultural oppositions. But it is not this which intellectuals wanted to evoke. The prejudices of the period required examples to be sought further away, in the Roman era. Perfect history taught the French in a perfectly natural way to think of their country in the framework of the territory which was not that of their own era nor that of the Middle Ages: what appears to constitute the natural borders of the nation were the borders of that Gaul from which France was derived. The makers of epic, like Ronsard, could easily give a considerable place to medieval realities – one has to explain France's birth – but their model is antique. Ronsard obtained his inspiration from the Aeneid. The 'Franciade' is better described in the frame of antique cuttings than in the history of the feudal world. Through that, as through all the texts which formed the habit of thinking of France as the heir of Gaul, the ethnic and cultural diversity which the Middle Ages had created, found themselves erased. The people felt French because they referred to an era where unity did not seem problematic.

Historians have written much about the idea of natural frontiers. Should we or should we not use it as an unchangeable factor in French foreign policy from Richelieu to the Convention? Modern research rightly underlines the absence of an explicit model, of a conformity to a pretended will of Richelieu which had never existed. But they pass in silence a prime source: the ideology transmitted by the idea of perfect history had been so perfectly accepted by French elites that it marked the national consciousness indelibly. Indeed, for the quasi-totality of French of the classic age, the natural borders of France are at the Rhine and the Alps. The image of ancient Gaul taught by the Jesuits or the Oratorians, who shaped the leaders of the country, weighed heavier than that of the actual borders of the Kingdom and explains the ease with which public opinion accepted expansion towards the east. After the failures of the wars with Italy, in Henry II's era, it was appropriate for making the French masses understand the shrinking of French power to what was going to become the hexagon, and to show the conformity of the royal policy to the deep vocation of the nation to its natural frontiers. The policy was remarkably successful. For two centuries at least it has legitimized French expansion. It has prevented linguistic and cultural diversities from instigating deep tensions.

But the victory of another conception of civilization was necessary in order to change this point of view. The classical model lost its prestige when the dignity of popular cultures was discovered. This movement, first developed in Germany although it owed a part of its justification to Rousseau of the 'Vicaire savoyard', only touched France much later. The modern rise of the regional movements is correlative with the obliteration of a certain way of conceiving at the same time civilization, France and history. The unitarian model that the Renaissance had taken from ancient political geography and from the belief in a triumphant reason was replaced by a solicitude for diversity wherein could be seen the token of authenticity. Medieval history is validated – it is in the slaughter of Béziers or in the Breton wars that the Occitans or the Breton autonomy movements find their inspiration. History as told by Michelet is dead: the Middle Ages which he related were still inspired by the national idea; what he wanted to kindle was the formation of a population and the progressive union beyond feudal agitations or dispersion, of popular masses and royalty in the same design. It is that vision, still marked by the presuppositions of a perfect history, which has been erased in recent years. We have left the era behind us wherein the young French followed Lavisse and, unknowingly, Pasquier, when told that our ancestors were the Gauls.

The image of Paris

During the period when modernity asserted itself, in the sixteenth century, the role of Paris was already decisive in numerous fields. In spite of the difficulties during the period of conflicts with England, the city was the most populated of the West; its university was less prestigious than in the thirteenth and fourteenth centuries, but it was there that Ignatius de Loyola came to learn philosophy and theology; its artistic prestige was waning at a time, after an auspicious period, when international Gothic found its inspiration; the kings were sometimes sulky with it, since Charles VII had been condemned to settle on the bank of the Loire. But the progress of the royal administration reinforced its pre-eminence on the country: the competence of Parliament was gigantic, covering more than half of the Kingdom, which prohibited the majority of the cities of northern France from acquiring social diversity and from attracting the elites who commanded the great destinies.[5] The pre-eminence of Paris was already decisive at the beginning of the sixteenth century.

The image which the French had of Paris was, however, very different from what it would be later on. The capital was not yet the only place where it was possible to participate in the ups and downs of history, for Lyon played the part of an economic metropolis and held the first place in this respect until the second half of the sixteenth century. Literary life followed the court, and settled there where lived the patrons of art –

Marguerite de Navarre surrounded herself with the best minds – or in other words thrived in Lyon, whose rich upper middle class was cultivated – did not Maurice Scève and Louis Labé take part in it? With regard to the language was it coming from the centre which contributed more strongly to the distribution in all the circles than the Geneva of Calvin?

The sixteenth century does not yet offer us the face of a state dominated by one single metropolis. Yet it is a question of real organization – in the economic and cultural fields, activity flourished everywhere; it is perhaps more a question of perception. The differences in level of equipment and functioning are not interpreted in terms of differences of prestige. Norbert Elias wrote fascinating studies of the birth of court society.[6] The phenomenon does involve the whole of Western Europe, but in France it was in its purest form – that is where Elias studied it. He shows very well how the climate of competition which was characteristic of feudal society was basically changed by the disappearance of the great direct confrontations between territorial units. The struggle for prestige and power did not disappear, but took the acquisition of royal favours as a pretext. Without that there were only few families who could survive. It is from this that the process of civilization is derived, and of which Elias has also given an account as a historian.[7]

The aristocratic society which organized itself in that way was strongly hierarchical, but not in relation to regions. In the literature of the fifteenth and sixteenth centuries, there is no question of oppositions founded on the fact of belonging to a certain region or of *snobisme* related to regional accent and manners. The sort of life the aristocracy led limited the differences in this field; moreover, the precepts of education and upbringing were the same everywhere in the Kingdom. Very often the good families were happy to place their children as pages at court, which gave them the opportunity to participate in a delocalized society and gave them morals which made the well-born man. So, it is not directly from the stratification of the court society that the feeling of a general pre-eminence of Paris was born – but the evolution of the conception of the sort of life emanating from it.

In the same way as the aristocracy was structured by the hierarchy necessarily related to court life, so does one see more numerous sections of the population admit the idea of a general hierarchy of prestige. The latter was not restricted only to birth and acquired status. In the dynamism of the court society and of the civilization of morals, it resulted from the ability to follow the fashion and to conform to the manners and fancies of those who were best situated. Court society called for a society of fashion which became the court's popular image among an increasingly large part of the population. As long as there remained a fraction which escaped competition or which could not adapt to the habits of the beautiful world, the process could continue. The middle class found, in this competition, the means to distinguish themselves from the people, and the people from the masses of farmers. But fashionable society differed from the court society in that its hierarchies were territorial. The noble people had their land in this or that province, but it became imperative for their functions and their habits to be mobile – almost nomads – even in the sixteenth century, while they were forever touring from estate to estate to consummate the product of the local rights. In order to participate in the hierarchy of prestige of the fashionable society, conditions were completely different: the social groups who entered into competition were sedentary. Their chances to follow the development of morals and tastes were not equal. One had to live near the source of it all in order to profit from the advantages of life.

The change which made Paris the pole of all French social life was related to the social transformation which made all the sections of the population reach out for the court model. The changes were gradual. They took place mainly at the end of the sixteenth century and at the beginning of the seventeenth. At that time Parisian French definitely prevailed over other dialects. In Paris during the first half of the seventeenth century, the process of the civilization of morals was nowhere better expressed than in the salons of the *précieuses*. Madame de Rambouillet, educated in the habits and distinguished atmosphere of the pontifical court, tried to impose the model of the most exquisite refinement on a still badly polished society. She succeeded beyond hope. Molière may well ridicule the *précieuses* who lost their mind and their commonsense; he led a lost battle in a world which from then on was taken over by new ways of life. The transformation which preceded the civilization of morals did not take place completely in court: it was found mainly at the level of the upper middle class in town. That these people felt they had a privileged position in comparison with the rest of the country, what is more natural? His pride and conceit and the reverence with which the Parisian was held in the eyes of the provincial, imposed themselves at the same moment, at the dawn of classicism. Molière gives evidence of this, when he ridicules Monsieur de Pourceaugnac, the gentleman from Limousin who has not learned to equip himself with the new morals. Boileau is more direct when he says:

'Only a Parisian has the gift of the gab.'

The study of global images of the organization of space in the past is certainly delicate. For lack of evidence to explore, one is reduced to exploring the literary texts which must be set in the context of the history of ideas, of morals and of social organizations.

University of Paris – Sorbonne,
France

Perceived space in ancient Japan

M. SENDA

One way to understand how space was perceived in ancient Japan is to look at how space was symbolically expressed at that time. This essay examines certain semantic problems concerning geographical territory and location: what territorial units or spaces meant to the ancient people and how the people expressed them. Two examples concerning the perception of space in fifth- to ninth-century Japan are elucidated below.

The shape and meaning of the territory

In ancient East Asia, including Japan, space was symbolically conceived through circle and square images: a circle represented heaven while a square represented the firmament. These patterns permeate the mandala or Shri-yantra designs of ancient India where one kind of mandala is understood to be a map of the world, 'Imago Mundi' (Fig. 1). In ancient China the mandala patterns were depicted on the back of mirrors which functioned in religious ceremony. A mirror design of Taoism in China shows a mountain in the centre and a square watercourse surrounding it. The former means the centre of the world, and the latter the sea around the world. A model which may reveal how the ancient people perceived territorial space is found also in ancient China.

This is called *Gofuku* and was brought to European attention by Dr Joseph Needham.[1] The model consists of nested regular tetragons, with the capital city at the centre. The domains were apparently perceived as being located according to the degree of Sinicization. The nested territories are, from the centre: the *Denfuku* (the royal territory), the *Kokufu* (the territory of the tributary vassals), the *Suifuku* (the conquered territory), the *Yofuku* (the territory of the allied barbarians), and the *Kofuku* (the territory of barbarians).

This tetragon shape means that the ancient Chinese tried to represent territorial space in terms of four cardinal directions. In relation to the

212

Fig. 1. *Shri-yantra*

shape, they imagined that land was surrounded by four seas like the mirror design. The figure 'four' had important meanings in East Asia. For example, 'four seas' was a synonym for the world, and 'the master of four seas' meant the emperor of the state.

In the case of Japan, which was influenced by Chinese culture, we find that an account of the fifth year of the reign of Emperor Seimu in the *Nihonshoki* described the directions north and south as *hinoyoko*, or the 'sun's width', and east and west as *hinotate*, or the 'sun's length'. The north slope of a mountain was termed *Sotomo* or the 'shadow side', and the south slope of a mountain was *Kagemo*, or the 'sunny side'. We also find that the largest of the administrative divisions of the *Ritsuryo* era, the *do*, were named according to the four cardinal directions: north was represented by the Hokuriku-*do*; south by the Nankai-*do*; east by the Takai-*do* and the Tozan-*do*; west by the Saikai-*do*. The Sanyo-*do* and the Sanin-*do* meant respectively the 'sunny side' and 'shadow side' of the mountain.

The ancient capitals were also constructed on a square plan as in the model of microcosm. For instance, there is an account in the *Shoku Nihongi*, dated the first year of *Wado* (A.D. 708), stating that the location of Heijo-*kyo* (an ancient capital city which was constructed on what is present-day Nara *Shi*) satisfied the directional requirements. That

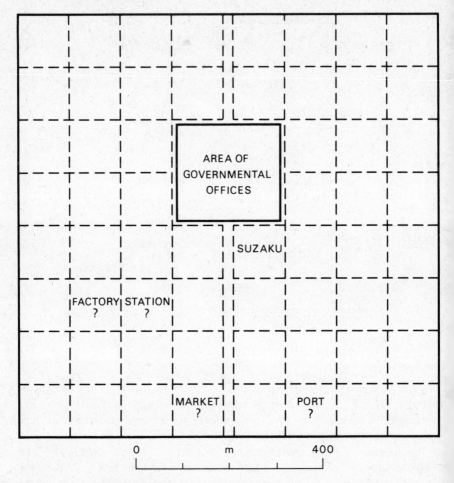

Fig. 2. *Plan of* Kokufu (*Suho*)
Source: *after K. Fujioka*, Kokufu (*Tokyo, 1969*)

is, the location of the capital city had four topographical features which represented the four animals believed to be guarding the four cardinal directions of the capital city. The guardian animals assigned were: north – the black turtle; south – the red sparrow; east – the blue dragon; and west – the white tiger. We may also note the symbolic colour assigned to each direction. In the location of the capitals, the symbol of four animals embodied the geographical objects: black turtle – mountain; red sparrow – pond; blue dragon – river; white tiger – wide road.

Recently two straight courses of old rivers were reconstructed on the outside of Heian-*kyo* in Kyoto *Shi*, which was the capital constructed in

794.[2] There is a possibility that those rivers were imagined as seas surrounding the world.

The same idea was represented in the space of an ancient tomb called Takamatsu-zuka, in the Nara prefecture. In the stone chamber, the guardian animals (except the red sparrow) were drawn on the wall, and on the ceiling is depicted a heavenly constellation, at the centre of which the Pole Star is situated. Clearly, therefore, the narrow chamber was the world of the dead.

The tetragonal capital city planning, in turn, provided a model for the planning of the *Kokufu* (administrative centres of the provinces away from the capital area). Reconstruction of the *Kokufu*, a sort of prototype city, has been successfully carried out by historical geographers (Fig. 2).[3] According to their findings, the shape was commonly a regular tetragon – an example from the *Kokufu* in Sanuki (Kagawa prefecture) will clarify and illustrate this. It has been discovered that streets perpendicular to each other and forming a north–south and an east–west axis at the centre of the city divided it into four equal quadrants.[4] A place-name *Seiryu* (Blue Dragon) remains in the north-eastern quarter of the old *Kokufu* plan. Another example is *Suzaku* (Red Sparrow), a place-name which exists within the limits of the ancient *Suho Kokufu* (Yamaguchi prefecture). Its location has been found to lie roughly in the centre of the reconstructed ancient city plan. Furthermore, although few place-names may be traceable to the four guardian gods, at least the grid plan streets of both *Kokufu* of Izumo and Ohmi embodying the due north–south and east–west directions may be taken as examples of the four-directional world view. This square plan was also adopted in the building of ancient temples, in that their main buildings such as *Kondo* (main hall), *Kodo* (lecture hall) and pagoda were surrounded by cloisters. It is believed that such temple arrangements represent the embodiment of the mandala pattern.

The combination of square and circle expressing heaven and earth can also be seen in the shape of some tomb mounds belonging to the early state elite. Two mounds, one circular and one rectangular, were built adjacent to each other, the latter as if projecting from the former. Viewed from the air, their combined shape resembles an old-fashioned keyhole. The shape of this mound can be regarded as implying the image of the world. Another version is for a square mound to serve as a platform for a round mound built on top of it.

Semantic aspects of centrality

Modern geography suggests that a central place may be defined as a settlement with certain service functions. However, it is doubtful whether ancient people regarded central places, such as the capital cities, the ancient market place and the local administrative centres, as having service functions. Their perceived centrality stemmed from their position at the centre of the inner world, which was often symbolized by trees.

In the chronicles of ancient Japan there are several documented examples of trees which were revered as symbols of the 'central-placedness' of the palace or market where they were growing. For example, in Asuka, Yamato province (Nara Prefecture), the home of the ancient state, there was a Zelkova tree around which various functions of the state were carried out, such as important political assemblies and the reception of emissaries from the frontier areas. In the neighbourhood of a Zelkova tree, a stone object called *Sumisen-zo* was excavated. In Buddhism *Sumisen* (Mount Meru) means the mountain which rises in the centre of the world. A Zelkova tree may be interpreted therefore as the symbol of a central place in the world. Furthermore, it must be noted that *Sumisen-zo* was located along the principal road called *Nakatsu-michi* (middle road), so that it is believed that the city plan of Asuka was founded on the site of the creation of the Buddhistic world.

In relation to market places, the following documents are pertinent (Fig. 3). *Tsuba-ichi*, an ancient market place located in the southern part of the Nara basin, appears in old documents as being located east of present-day Sakurai *Shi*. The market was situated in a transitional topographical zone where the plain gives rise to hills. Thus, the location of the market place may be explained as an example of a central place which came to exist on the boundary of two dissimilar ecological zones. In old records we note that the market place was variously expressed as a crossroad, a traffic station or a palace. The location of this market was plotted at the nodal point of the Hase River and *Kamitsu-michi* (upper road). *Tsuba-ichi* was also cited in the *Manyoshu* (an ancient collection of poems compiled at the end of the eighth century) as a place where a kind of social gathering (the *utagaki*) was regularly held, at which young men and women exchanged poems and danced together. Obviously, *Tsuba-ichi* enjoyed a variety of functions, and could be considered a place of high rank in the hierarchy of central places.

However, we may note that a name of a tree, *Tsubaki* (Camellia), was used to designate the place. What might be the relationship of a tree to a place which had central functions? There are numerous examples of tree-related market places, and some general relations between a tree and a central place seem to have existed in ancient Japan.

From the *Manyoshu*, we learn that in Karu-no-ichi, which is thought to have been located in the south-west of Fujihara-*kyo*, which preceded Heijo-*kyo* as the capital, in the vicinity of Ohkaru in Kashihara *Shi*, Nara prefecture, there was a Zelkova tree which was a landmark of the market. Ega-no-*ichi* is assumed to have been located near Fujiidera *Shi* in Osaka prefecture, and there again, we learn in the *Nihonshoki* that a *Tachibana*

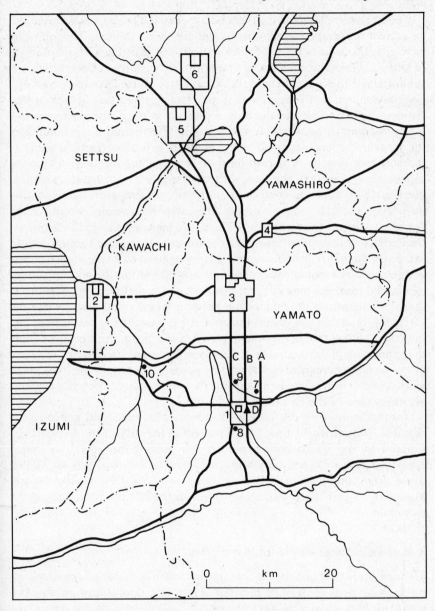

Fig. 3. *Sites of ancient capital and markets in the Nara basin*

(a kind of wild citrus tree) was growing in the market place. Further, a part
of the name, Ato-no-kuwa-no-*ichi* – whether designating a place in
Kawachi (Osaka prefecture) or in the vicinity of Tawaramoto *Cho* in
Yamato (Nara prefecture) – may be defined as a Mulberry tree.

Another example involving trees is discussed in *Hitachi-no-kuni Fudoki*, an ancient regional geography written in the eighth century. The following passage is taken from it: 'A large Zelkova tree is growing at the south gate of *Gunga*.' *Gunga* was the ancient administrative centre of *Gun*, which was subordinated to *Kuni* province. Why was a tree chosen as the symbol of a place which had many functions? It may be suggested that because a tree grows straight and pierces the holy heavens, the place where a tree grows may consequently be considered holy ground. Furthermore, the holiness of the area directly encompassed by the branches extending from the trunk of the holy tree may be projected onto the surrounding location. As for the supernatural powers of the tree, we may cite other evidence from ancient literature. In a poem composed in praise of Emperor Yuryaku and included in the *Manyoshu*, a Zelkova tree was symbolically described: the upper branches of the tree covered the entire heavens, the middle branches the entire sovereign territories, and the lower branches the countryside. In the myth, *Sakaki (Cleyera ochnacea)* is recognized as a tree via which the gods come down from heaven, and it is now offered to the gods in shrines as a sacred tree. We may intepret this as implying that the straight trunk of the tree symbolized the connection between heaven and earth, while the spreading branches suggested the spatial expanse of the territories, and thus the Zelkova tree in the Asuka area can also be interpreted as not only the expression of the centrality of the place, but more strongly as the centre of the world as perceived by the ancient people. Thus, both the trees in the market places introduced earlier and the Zelkova trees described above are suggestive of the so-called 'World Tree'.

Another symbol of centrality is a mountain as suggested above in the *Sumisen*. Mount Kaguyama, which was often the subject of old poems, is situated in the south-east corner of the Nara basin. As it is called *Ame-no-Kaguyama* (heavenly Kaguyama) and is described as having fallen down from the heaven, Mt Kaguyama is recognized as the 'World Mountain'. Significantly also, *Nakatsu-michi* (middle road) runs across the mountain.

A semiological approach to the new horizon

The mainstream of historical geography in Japan has long placed emphasis on the empirical analysis of the past. However, doubt must persist with regard to how accurately any 'reconstruction' of the past can mirror the spatial perspective of ancient people if that reconstruction is based solely on modern topographical sheets, which reflect, for example, the assumptions of modern scientific cartography. Although the mechanical imposition of modern *a priori* assumptions in reconstructing the past is the common practice of historical geographers generally, it is the author's belief that we must exercise caution in applying modern theories to any analysis of the past. The peculiar nature of perceptions of space characterizing each stage of history not only deserves serious recognition but ought to become of fundamental concern to all historical geographers. We can specify only a few signs, such as square, line and point in the maps of ancient Japan. It may be argued that the simple nature of this analysis stems from the paucity of the historical records. More important, however, is the fact that the map reflects 'the age of the landscape composed of signs'. It is possible therefore to analyse the morphological aspects of the ancient landscape by the method of semiology. According to this method, the aim of historical geography has to be seen as that of understanding the messages inherent in the signs. When such an analysis was undertaken of the ancient Japanese landscape a set of binary oppositions was revealed; palace (vertical)/capital area, outer area of the capital (horizontal) – capital area (inner world)/outer area of the capital (outer world).[5] This analysis was subsequently presented to the congress of the Human Geographical Society of Japan in 1979, and a basic syntagma of landscape morphology was proposed.[6] In particular an oppositional relationship of 'marked landscape/unmarked landscape' was elucidated in which 'marked landscape' suggests a landscape in which the fundamental set of morphological signs is present. Geographical space can be understood as the dialectical relationship between the marked and unmarked.

Nara Women's University,
Japan

Problems of interpreting the symbolism of past landscapes

D. E. COSGROVE

Understanding the meaning of past human landscapes demands a theory of collective behaviour or culture appropriate to their context. Historical and cultural geography have traditionally been weak in producing such theory, adopting a 'laissez-faire' attitude to the concept of culture. Even Carl Sauer, who regarded historical geography as a part of cultural history, failed to specify exactly what he understood by 'culture'.[1] More recently behavioural and methodological debate in historical geography has raised precisely the issue of theorizing culture.[2]

Derek Gregory, for example, has made a plea for theorizing spatial structures as 'implicated in' social structures, and for spelling out the constitutive elements of social communication or intersubjectivity: its constitution as 'meaningful'; its constitution as a moral order; and its constitution as relations of power.[3] A humanistic 'revival' in human geography has reminded us of the need to interpret the specific geographical event in its own context, but a purely idiographic approach disallows discourse: theory remains a necessity. Such theory must be dialectically constituted: between individual subjectivity and culture, and between social and spatial structure.[4]

Social order and symbolic order

Paul Wheatley has stressed that in the Chinese urban landscape spatial structure 'afforded a ritual paradigm of the ordering of social interaction at the same time as it disseminated the values and inculcated the attitudes necessary to sustain it'.[5] But this formulation is not fully reciprocal, for the cultural and symbolic landscape remains a secondary expression, and the social order theoretically pre-exists its constitution as a symbolic order. Too easily the claimed dialectic of social order and symbolic order becomes subsumed in practice under a more powerful linear logic wherein the symbolic is the outcome of an existing social structure. This tendency is observed in the base–superstructure model of Marxist cultural theory and in the deep and surface structure model of linguistic structuralism.[6] In both, the dialectical autonomy of the symbolic constitution of the world within a social formation gives way to a version of what Marshall Sahlins has called 'practical reason'.[7]

Sahlins urges us to recognize that any notion of a productive base is a social concept: conscious human beings produce. The tendency to reify the economic or practical order is culturally specific to capitalist society where, uniquely, the production of material goods provides the primary site of symbolic production also.[8] Because we conflate these two orders, historical materialism, which originated in Marx's early writings as a cultural thesis, rapidly became grounded in work, and specifically in material work. The theory was thus robbed of its cultural properties, and the symbolic order was eliminated from production to reappear as 'sublimates of the material life process'. Once the symbolic becomes superstructural to an economic or productive base the symbolic character of the system itself is lost, and the dialectical unity of cultural and practical reason, nature and consciousness, the 'real' and the symbolic is eliminated. Any mode of production is a 'mode of life', a *genre de vie*, constituted by men and symbolic *ab initio*. To this extent all human landscapes are symbolic because they are the geographical expression of a mode of life to which, dialectically, they give rise and which itself comprises the reciprocal unity of nature and culture at specific locations.

To regard praxis as symbolically constituted is not to adopt an idealist stance, for material forces and constraints are dialectically necessary to the existence of the cultural order. The point, however, is that the effects cannot simply be read off in a linear fashion from the operation of these forces and constraints, for they depend equally upon their cultural encompassment.

Symbolic production and symbolic power

The argument developed above emphasizes that the characteristic of bourgeois capitalist society lies in its locating the primary site of symbolic production in the economy as a producer of goods, and thus regarding behaviour as a species of practical reason by ignoring the symbolic constitution of the economy itself.[9] It is a similar position to that of substantivist anthropology, following Karl Polanyi's distinguishing Western market societies from reciprocal and redistributive economies where economic integration is 'embedded' in social integration.[10] The difference lies in the fact that Polanyi simply inverts the linear logic of base and superstructure for non-market economies while Sahlins maintains the stress upon dialectical interpenetration of economic and social categories, but differentiates market societies in terms of the primary site of symbolic production being in the production of goods. Because this is true of our own society we fail to recognize the symbolic constitution of our world, for us it is the world of practical reason. In historical, non-market societies it is at once easier to identify and more difficult to give credence to the symbolic. This is one of the difficulties associated with the application of *Verstehen* as a methodology for understanding the past and penetrating the meaning of historical landscapes. For unless we recognize and examine the symbolic constitution of our own assumptions in the light of the past we fall into the trap of assuming that the 'thought behind the action' of creating and changing human landscapes is symbolically constituted in a structurally similar way to our own. We underestimate the power of alternative symbolic systems to provide rational grounds for action and obviate the very humanistic and subjective hermeneutic we claim.[11]

The precise structural location of the primary site of symbolic production in a non- or pre-capitalist society is a matter for specific empirical study, but Polanyi's classification still provides an initial and suggestive set of ideal types. In a redistributive economy, for example, in a centric form of social integration, the site of symbolic production would appear to lie not in the production of goods, but in the social production of the sacred. This both structures and is structured by a ranked society whose emergence is itself symbolically promoted and legitimated. The means of symbolic production are appropriated by the dominant group which institutionalizes the sacred into a religious system and conjointly centralizes the appropriation and redistribution of the material surplus. Symbolic production here becomes symbolic power, the key ideological weapon for structural maintenance. Pierre Bourdieu has emphasized that symbolic power is at once a structured and structuring instrument of imposition or legitimation of class dominance. While the formulation is congruent with Marx's thinking on ideology insofar as it recognizes the class use of culture and symbolism, it does not thereby necessarily locate symbolic production in the economy as material production, but argues for a homology between social structure and ideological or symbolic structure: a homology which hides their specific relationship because 'the truly ideological consists precisely in the imposition of political classification systems under the legitimate appearances of philosophical, juridical and religious taxonomies'.[12]

To summarize, social order and symbolic order are dialectically unified, and they cannot be read off from a notion of practical reason which underlies theories of economic base or universal structures. Dialectically related to material forces and constraints and to each other, they produce a 'mode of life' structuring and structured by symbolic production whose prime location is not necessarily in material production. All human landscapes may thus be regarded as symbolic. In class society, culturally constituted and reproduced, symbolic production is appropriated by the dominant class, either through its control of the means of material production in capitalist society, or of sacred production in redistributive society. As symbolic power it is structured and structuring ideology homologous with class organization.

We are aware from Wheatley's work of the degree to which a centric redistributive society gave rise in China to a particular ordering of the symbolic landscape around an urban focus and may indeed be a primary basis for urban origins.[13] But a crucial question for historical geographers is that of change from one mode of life to another as it is expressed in and underpinned by landscape change. They have recently involved themselves in the debate over the European transition from feudalism to capitalism: from a dominantly redistributive and centric to a market-economy mode of social and economic integration. This long transition implied a radical shift in the location of the primary site of symbolic production and requires that we examine it as much from the perspective of struggles over symbolic production and power as of struggles over material production. The second part of this essay provides a tentative demonstration, with reference to one landscape type from the period of the transition, of how the theory outlined here may assist our understanding of the meaning of past landscapes.

The Renaissance ideal city

For more than one hundred years from the mid-fifteenth century nearly every major Italian architectural writer produced designs for the building of an ideal city. Space does not permit detailed examination of individual plans, nor of the specific distinctions between them and the few full, and many partial, realizations of such plans on the ground.[14] Rather the ideal city is treated as a theoretical form, regarded by its designers as a practical programme of urban construction. It is significant because it represents a major break in the European tradition of urban design and because, as a spatial expression of Renaissance humanism, it provides an *entrée* for historical geographers into an important cultural dimension of the feudalism–capitalism transition, a dimension which they have been slow to draw upon.

The form and structure of the Renaissance ideal city, despite variations in specific designs, may be generalized as follows: a circular or polygonal, closed urban space of fixed dimensions is centralized upon an open *piazza* – a civic and sacred precinct – itself of ordered proportions. From this square radiate roads lined with monumental buildings whose own proportions both in plan and elevation conform to the mathematical regularity of the city as a whole. Minor open spaces, monuments, gates and so on are symmetrically arranged around the city to give an overall plan of perfect regularity, symmetry and proportion (Fig. 1). The specific architectural plans for the ideal city have received detailed descriptive attention, but in accounting for the Renaissance ideal city three approaches immediately offer themselves. These are summarized below.

The appeal to innate spatial structures

The form of the Renaissance ideal city has obvious similarities to that of other urban plans in time and space, especially to those developed under centric-redistributive social formations in China, Egypt, Mesoamerica and in Japan (as evidenced by Minoru Senda in the immediately preceding essay). Ultimately it may be related to the structure of sacred geometry theorized by Mircea Eliade.[15] Some of the implications of this are explored by Yi-fu Tuan who links the common properties of such plans in symmetry, centrality and axiality to common psychological structures which derive ultimately from human physiology and biology.[16] While this proposal in part may account for the cross-cultural regularity of the form it does not explain its specific historical occurrence, its cultural constitution in centrically organized societies, nor why it should achieve such explicit realization at an important juncture of northern Italian history when centric redistribution was far weaker than it had been at the high point of European feudalism.

The appeal to a Renaissance Weltanschauung

Studies of Renaissance cosmology and humanist philosophy have a strong bearing on the ideal city, suggesting that it was the architectural and geographical manifestation of a new conception of man and cosmos promoted particularly in early fourteenth-century Florence and rapidly diffused throughout northern and central Italy. In questioning the central theological problem of Aristotelian scholasticism, that of the possibility of man's having knowledge of the spiritual world, neo-platonic philosophers developed a theory of man as a microcosm of God, containing within the body the divine and universal proportions (Fig. 2) and capable by exercise of mathematical reason of understanding the laws of symmetry and proportion whereby the world had been created.[17] This allowed for the development of a new world view, expressed and developed in humanist philosophy, painting, architecture and literature and, supremely, in the ideal city as itself a microcosm of the created universe and of a perfect society.

Such an interpretation is superficially attractive because it locates the

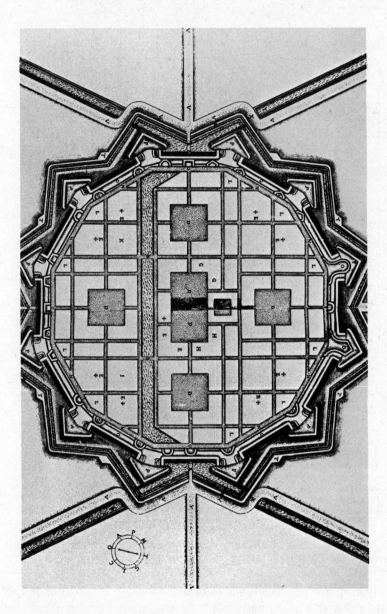

Fig. 1. *Ideal city plan.* Source: *V. Scamozzi, L'Idea dello Architettvra Universale, 1615*

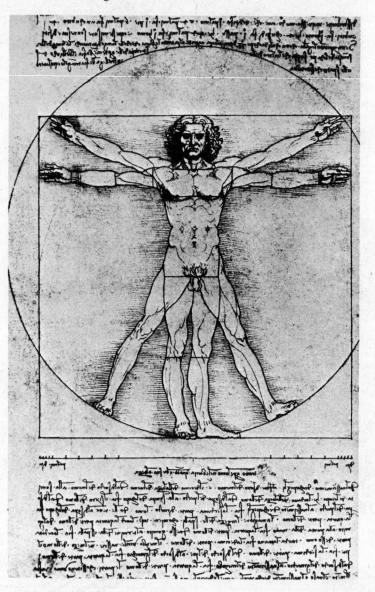

Fig. 2. *Ideal proportions of the human body (Leonardo da Vinci, Galleria dell' Academia, Venice)*

ideal city in an historically specific cultural movement, but it depends upon an assumption that ideas and beliefs develop autonomously from their social and material context, and fails to account for the emergence of such ideas in the particular historical and geographical moment, lapsing into the Hegelian idealism which has characterized so much cultural history.

The appeal to historical materialism

A materialist interpretation of the ideal city locates it as a superstructural expression of the particular material circumstances obtaining in Italy during this period of transition. The social formation of feudal northern and central Italy displayed certain unique characteristics.[18] The 'ancient' mode of production had dominated the synthesis between itself and the 'germanic' mode which produced the feudal mode of production. Municipal urban life, the precocious revival of commerce and industry and a consciousness of civic and legal traditions from the Empire all served to mark this part of Italy off from other European feudal states. The manorial organization of production was weak and short-lived, and indeed a unitary feudal state never emerged here, where the politico-legal role of feudal landlord was seized by competing urban communes over their surrounding rural areas (*contadi*). Conflict within the cities between different factors produced a series of changes in political authority, most significantly between urban merchants and artisans on the one hand and landed *feudatories* on the other. The significance of merchant capital and trade, the economic and social interpenetration between the two factions, the tradition of the *vita civile*, the weakness of the Imperial crown and the maintenance of quiritary property meant that even the landowning class were urban dwellers.

Political struggle within the communes led in the late thirteenth and fourteenth centuries to the domination of the city states by *signori* whose emergence represented the victory of landed power.[19] The economic significance of landownership was then reinforced by both internal and external structural changes. Control by the seigneurial class led to technical and entrepreneurial inertia in the Italian cities. A fully capitalist separation of the artisan from his tools was blocked by guild restrictions; mercantile and military innovations lagged behind those of more unified northern and western European states. The emerging world economic order promoted by these latter was shifting the core area of European economic activity to the North Sea, leaving Italy in a semi-peripheral position, a position politically reinforced by Spanish hegemony from the early sixteenth century and aggravated by Turkish penetration of the eastern Mediterranean. Wealth was increasingly diverted into land and agrarian development, strengthening the power of landowners. The pattern of labour exploitation in the *contadi* through share-cropping leases (*mezzadria*), formerly a net advance over feudal rural relations of production, bringing them in line with urban artisanal and merchant relations, now became regressive rather than revolutionary. Terms of leases were tightened and labour mobility restricted throughout the sixteenth century as the countryside underwent a process of 'refeudalization'.[20]

Landowning nobles had traditionally involved themselves in urban mercantile activities and many merchant families had joined their ranks by purchasing land. Now, however, the group began to close its ranks by excluding new members and by seeking to legitimate its dominance through identification as an hereditary caste.[21] Feudal legal and political forms had no legitimacy in the cities which still held hegemony over their *contadi*. Lacking the legitimacy of ancestry and continuity, the dominant group seized upon urban civil authority, classical learning and humanist notions of *virtù* and *ragione* to produce a complex ideology of rural refeudalization and domination of the cities.

The ideal city expressed and communicated this ideology in the urban landscape. There was no return to a rural dwelling aristocracy (although villa-building represents a partial move away from the city), particularly since feudal rent in the form of share-crops yielded a surplus in marketable commodities (wine, olives, silk). Nevertheless, the ideal city communicated in landscape terms the self-image of a feudal aristocracy rather than a merchant patriciate. The central *piazza*, for example, was dominated by church, signoral palace and military building and was for discourse and display. Markets were relegated to the periphery, symmetry and monumentality stated wealth, power and lineage rather than serving the needs of production and exchange which receive scant attention in the writings of ideal city theorists.

While this interpretation grounds the symbolic landscape in prevailing material conditions it fails to locate the production of symbolic order outside the realm of practical reason, to account for its structuring role, or to derive the *form* of the ideal city from the nature of the material forces and constraints seen as giving rise to it. Symbolic production must be regarded as more than the almost unmediated reflection of economic and class forces.

The ideal city as structured and structuring symbolic power

As a symbolic system, Renaissance humanism and its articulation in the form of ideal city plans contains a major contradiction. Humanism was secular and individualist, concepts of *virtù* and *ragione* were regarded in fifteenth-century Italian thought as a function of learning and the cultivation of human physical and intellectual faculties, thus open to all men. Yet the ideal city as a landscape is manifestly aristocratic and rank-ordered. It is an iconographic programme evoking a classical past and in its formal, monumental order requiring a ritualized form of behaviour which recalled an imagined heroic past rather than an egalitarian and individual future. This contradiction requires exploration in terms of the class struggles which were transforming Europe from a feudal and redistributive to a capitalist and market mode of life, and further, examination of that struggle as it took place in the realm of symbolic production itself.

The main site of symbolic production in redistributive feudalism lay in the social and specifically in its legitimation through the sacred rather than in material production.[22] An attack upon it had to be launched within that sphere, and this is where it was launched in fifteenth-century Italy. The debate within scholasticism discussed above was not formally intended to reject the accepted hierarchical ordering of the cosmos, but it did open the possibility of a radically new concept of human individuality upon which could be based a non-ecclesiastical humanism, supporting a secular view of the world, an attack upon rank and birth, and a scientific study of man and nature. All these were ideological tools in the hands of urban bourgeois for weakening the assumptions upon which feudal redistribution was founded, and they were developed at a time when this group was under increasing threat from a recharged feudalism. The widespread appeal of humanism across Europe is indicative of its structuring role in establishing the possibility of new mode of life. The debate remained within the area of symbolic production defined by a pre-capitalist mode of life, structured by it but structuring a new and different one. In landscape terms too, new ideas are expressed in homology with a centric social form. They focus upon the city and they turn to the iconography of sacred geometry – all roads leading to the axis and radiating again from the *fastigium* within a closed and regular form. These symbols may have roots in the repertory provided by human physiology, but their selection is culturally determined.

Renaissance humanism was originally developed, and its expressions produced, outside the landowning aristocracy by those of 'middle' origins[23] as part of their struggle against the former. Material conditions are implicated but do not structure the terms of the debate, although they affect its outcome. Because this humanist symbolic system was developed within the terms of the prevailing social order it was open to appropriation by those struggling to retain that order and their dominance of it. The struggle was won in northern Italy by the landowning class, and the individualist and secular aspects of Renaissance cosmosology were progressively whittled away. Humanist academies were aristocratized, *virtù* became a function of birth rather than practice, artistic expression became mannered and the ideal city became the highly formalized, aristocratic conception we associate with the 'grand manner' – readily appropriated for urban design by absolutist states elsewhere in Europe.

In the hands of a landowning nobility the ideal city became one aspect of their system of symbolic power, evoking a classical past whose virtues were imperial and aristocratic rather than republican and secular. The ideals of Renaissance humanism remained a moral order acceptable to a wide range of literate classes for whom it was meaningful in different ways. But its homology with the structure of the world as 'lived' and communicated by the Italian nobility assisted in legitimating their continued dominance. As a symbolic landscape, the ideal city communicated that world and its social order, sustaining cultural hegemony under the guise of a universal ideal. The ideal goes far further than the ideal city which is only one dimension of a whole symbolic order. But it is significant in that the plans for the ideal city locate symbolic power at the articulating point of the centric social order – in the form of the city itself.

This discussion is intended merely to suggest the lines along which an understanding of the symbolic in landscape might profitably move. More detailed study of individual landscapes would reveal that the structured and structuring role of symbolic power operated at different scales and variably according to local context. Nevertheless, it may suggest a way in which we might proceed to build theory without falling into the pitfalls of reductionism and idealism which have trapped so much of our discourse in historical geography.

Loughborough University of Technology, England

PART V

Theoretical Approaches in Historical Geography

On ideology and historical geography

A. R. H. BAKER

A retrospective view

It has proved difficult to start writing this essay, perhaps because it has been partially but directly prompted by the book which Gregory found it difficult to stop writing and which it is not easy to stop reading.[1] The problem also stems from the complex but changing characteristics both of historical geography and of ideology. No scholarly discipline or philosophy remains static and each reflects the cumulative complexity of the conditions of its conception and maturation. The study of historical geography is as richly diverse as the term ideology is robustly diffuse.[2]

It is important at the outset, therefore, to identify the principal meanings which have been attached to 'ideology' in order to minimize confusion in the subsequent discussion of ideology and historical geography. First, and strictly, an ideology is a form of social or political philosophy in which practical elements are as prominent as theoretical ones; an ideology is a system of ideas that aspires both to explain the world and to change it, a kind of programmatic understanding. Secondly, more loosely defined, an ideological approach is sometimes taken to mean any kind of action-orientated theory or any attempt to approach problems in the light of ideas. Thirdly, in Hegelian and Marxist philosophy the term ideology has been used pejoratively to imply 'false consciousness' on the part of people who have enacted historical roles assigned to them by forces which they did not understand and which could only be comprehended by an observer. More specifically, Marx used the term ideology to refer to a set of beliefs with which people deceive themselves. It is with ideology in this last sense, as unexamined discourse, and with science as ideology that Gregory's book is essentially concerned. But all three definitions of ideology – as programmatic understanding, as value-laden theory and as unexamined discourse – provide appropriate contexts in which to evaluate the practice of historical geography.

If we agree with Buttimer that charisma and context may be the root explanation of great ideas in human history,[3] then it does not become difficult to attribute a primary role in the development of historical geography to the ideas and influence of Carl Sauer and Clifford Darby, both of whom have exerted enormous charismatic impact directly through their own writings and teachings and indirectly through the efforts of their numerous pupils, but both of whom should also be viewed contextually as geographical revolutionaries intent on promoting a new orthodoxy as far as the purposes and practices of cultural and historical geography were concerned.[4] Some overall assessments of their roles and relations within geography have been essayed: jointly – and with others – they colonized and cultivated a distinctive niche within geography focused upon man's role in changing the face of the earth.[5] In their different ways, Sauer and Darby consciously strove to improve the quality of work in cultural and historical geography both methodologically and pragmatically while leaving to one side the more problematical philosophical questions. They tended to be more concerned with the practice than with the purpose of cultural and historical studies. Neither would probably have admitted the need for an explicit ideology. Indeed, Sauer claimed that it was possible for historical geography to be a value-free and objective study,[6] while Darby's approach was explicitly non-ideological in its pragmatic emphasis on the geographical intepretation of historical sources, seen *par excellence* in his studies not of the geography of England in the eleventh century or even in 1086 but of the Domesday geography of England.[7]

While cultural geography as practised in North America, in response largely to Sauer's advocacy, has been broadly based and interdisciplinary, it is now clear that a failing of much British historical geography until fairly recently has been its distinctiveness as an academic discipline in managing to survive almost entirely on enthusiasms and insights generated by its own practitioners without drawing much on concepts and methods developed in other fields.[8] Paradoxically, Darby's endeavours to create for historical geography a separate development could be considered to have been too successful: the discipline has flourished but somewhat artifically in intellectually isolated conditions which certainly cannot be expected – and probably should not be allowed – to persist. That this separatist view of historical geography endures is seen most strikingly in a recently published book which in many other respects might be considered as having been orchestrated as an alternative to Darby's *A New Historical Geography of England*: for Dodgshon and Butlin claim in their preface to *An Historical Geography of England and Wales* that 'historical geography will always have claim to problems and processes that are distinctly its own', although they offer no explicit discussion of what these problems and processes might be.[9]

There remains a marked reluctance on the part of some historical geographers critically to examine their own philosophies and practices. Since the mid-1960s, however, there has been a flurry of publications concerned with the methodology of historical geography and a reflexive critique is undoubtedly being undertaken, albeit by a minority of its practitioners.[10] While few historical geographers have felt a compelling need to make explicit their theoretical framework, an integral part of historical geography's false consciousness has been its focus upon *landscapes* transformed by men rather than upon *man* as an agent of landscape change, upon artefacts rather than upon ideas, upon actions rather than attitudes, upon external forms rather than internal processes. Ideologies structure time and space; landscapes are reflections of ideas as much as they are products of actions.[11] Studies in historical geography must logically therefore embrace ideologies as well as being themselves explicitly ideological. Furthermore, there is potential here for a significant *détente* – even the development of an *entente cordiale* – between historical geography and contemporary human geography stemming from an increasingly shared concern with geographies viewed historically.[12] But if more contemporary human geographers are prepared to accept strong advocacy by Slater and Brookfield for the adoption of an historical perspective and framework,[13] to what extent should historical geographers also accept their related advocacy for the adoption of a Marxist viewpoint?

Darby's *An Historical Geography of England before 1800*, a major milestone in the development of British historical geography, was published in 1936 as a series of cross-sections of England's geography at particularly significant periods in its history.[14] When a Marxist–Leninist historian, Yatsunsky, was reviewing the book, he unsurprisingly insisted that the periodization of historical geography should correspond with that of Marxist historical studies and that the subject should encompass the social aspects of the economy. Darby's book, although praised as the best example of work in the field of historical geography by bourgeois geographers, was said to suffer from a typically bourgeois approach, in that no mention was made of the class struggle.[15] Darby, who has responded directly to other kinds of criticisms – for example, by replying to critics of his Domesday geography[16] – chose to ignore Yatsunsky's comments in preparing his second major edited study of the historical geography of England, which retains the emphasis on landscape and economy which characterized its predecessor.[17] In a review article on patterns of popular protest, Baker observed that while there has been general acceptance by historical geographers of the aphorism of Clifford Darby – that all geography is historical geography, either actual or potential – there has been scant recognition of the adage of Karl Marx – that all history is the history of class struggle.[18] There is an obvious and logical necessity to relate these two views by considering what would constitute an historical geography of the class struggle. The beginnings of an exploration of this essentially uncharted territory have been undertaken in two conferences organized by the Historical Geography Research Group of the Institute of British Geographers, the first in 1977 on the Industrial Revolution and the English space-economy and the second in 1978 on the transition from feudalism to capitalism. Reports of these conferences indicate the, as yet, brief but memorable encounter of the British historical geographers with Marxian analyses and suggest that the relationship might well be worth pursuing.[19] This suggestion finds support within some recent writings on the historical geography of capitalism, such as those of Blaut and particularly of Harvey, in a volume of papers edited by De Koninck on historical materialism in geography, and in Cosgrove's claim that, if we are to understand and apply the findings of those geographers who have examined geographies of the mind, 'we must remove them from the realms of idealism, and place the dialectical method which they implicitly adopt within a materialist framework'.[20] It also finds support from a somewhat unexpected quarter in Day and Tivers' proposition that, whereas catastrophe theory provides a useful approach to the *description* of discontinuities in both the physical and the social sciences, 'the Marxist theory of dialectical materialism presents us with a suitable philosophical base for the *exploration* of such discontinuities'.[21] But much more substantial testimony is to be found within the works of Marxist historians.[22]

This is not the place or time to conduct at first hand a close examination of recent developments within social and economic history. Instead, attention will merely be drawn to Iggers's survey of new directions in European historiography.[23] This includes a detailed review of Marxian and modern social history, and opines that the emergence of a new social history, the product of many influences, including a distinct contribution from the merging of Marxism and social science, has been the most significant historiographical development in Britain and elsewhere in the last fifteen to twenty years.[24] This view is based on a general critique of the challenges offered by Marxists to non-Marxist historians and on a particular evaluation of the contributions made by Marxist historians in the U.S.S.R. and the German Democratic Republic, in Poland, in France and in Britain. As far as France is concerned, there has been a fruitful dialogue between Marxists and historians of the *Annales* school involving recognition that they share in common many concepts and methods.[25] Given the traditionally close links between history and geography in France, it is somewhat surprising that French historical geographers have apparently neither contributed to nor demonstrated any genuine awareness of this particular debate. Claval's recent critique of the development of ideas within the social sciences might indicate that such intellectual isolationism on the part of French geographers is at last being abandoned.[26] Within

Britain, there have been two distinguishable historical traditions relating to industrialization: one has involved an essentially favourable valuation of the effects of industrialization, based upon primarily materialistic criteria and the work of such historians as Clapham, Ashton and Hartwell; the other has involved judgement from a more humanistic perspective, insisting that material gain was more than outweighed by the price paid in terms of human misery and hardship, and finding support principally, but not exclusively, in the work of such socialist historians as the Hammonds, the Webbs and G. D. H. Cole, and more recently Edward Thompson and Eric Hobsbawm. To some extent, the former group of historians were writing a history of industrialization which would be acceptable to middle-class liberals and the capitalist orthodoxy, whereas the latter group were writing a history of industrialization from the viewpoint of the working class.[27] Although different, both groups could be involved in producing legitimate histories. Given Clapham's influence upon the young Darby and the latter's influence upon historical geography, it is particularly interesting to note that, on the basis of predominantly economic criteria, Clapham judged that industrialization had had a fundamentally beneficial effect on the lives of most Englishmen during the nineteenth century. Clapham's narrative success story and his assumption of material progress came to be mirrored in Darby's narrative account of man's successful taming of the English landscape. Darby established a tradition within British historical geography which was not only separatist and pragmatic, as already mentioned, but also materialistic and bourgeois in its orientation. While it would be possible to detect the emergence of interdisciplinary and theoretical threads within British historical geography, there has been little sign of an alternative tradition based on an idealistic and proletarian orientation parallel to that within social history. While British historical geography has its Claphams and its Hartwells, it can hardly be said to have its Thompsons and its Hobsbawms. Given the richness of the contributions to social history by Marxist historians, the time is long overdue for historical geographers to consider seriously Marxist methods of historical analysis and to ask to what extent it would be a constructive step to move towards a Marxian humanism.

A prospective view

This essay does not have sufficient space and time – nor its author sufficient knowledge and expertise – to present a comprehensive survey of those aspects of Marxism which might illuminate studies in historical geography. All that is essayed here is a preliminary exploration of what have been, to most historical geographers, *terrae incognitae*. In the broadest of terms and at a first glance, Marxism is likely to appeal to many historical geographers because it takes seriously the dynamics of historical change and of social groups in conflict and because of its overt concern for social justice: for these reasons it must also appeal to some contemporary human geographers.[28] But on closer inspection the diversity within even the main currents of Marxism acts as a brake upon its initial acceptance, and it becomes necessary to consider more critically some of the many components of a Marxist theory of history.[29] Five themes appear to deserve particular attention and each will be examined here briefly: first, history and historical geography as humanism; second, history and historical geography as particular practice; third, history and historical geography as generalization; fourth, total history and total historical geography; and fifth, history and historical geography as progress and praxis.

History and historical geography as humanism

History – and logically historical geography – must first and last be about people, only secondly about either periods or places. Marx came to reject 'history' or 'time' as an external force with an independent existence, just as increasingly geographers are coming, belatedly, to reject 'space' in the same terms. Fleischer has pointed out that as far as Marx was concerned

history does nothing, it 'owns tremendous wealth', it 'fights no battles'. Instead it is man, real, living man that does all this, owns and struggles; there is no such thing as 'history' that uses man as its means in order to attain its ends – as if it were a separate person – for history is nothing but the activity of man pursuing his ends.[30]

Similarly, it makes little sense to study historical geography from any viewpoint other than a humanistic one since it too is nothing but the activity of man pursuing his ends. Studies of, say, the geographical distribution of wealth are limited in meaning since wealth was created and distributed socially rather than geographically. Much historical geography has been based on a false consciousness which personified places which were nonetheless described without reference to the peoples who inhabited them. For Marx, the process of humanization also involved an increasing rationality, with rationality being understood not only in terms of more efficient organization of material and human resources for the purposes of production but in terms of the creation of, in Marx's words, 'those material conditions which alone can form the real basis of a higher form of society in which a full and free development of every individual forms the ruling principle'.[31] This involves a conscious organization of social production and distribution as much as it involves a conscious organization of that social production and distribution in space. At this point, questions about the social control of space and its resources and about the gradual coalescence of local, regional, national and supra-national societies are as much a part of the Marxist conception of history as they are of modern conceptions of geography.[32]

Essential to the process of the social and economic integration of space (not, let it be noted, the spatial integration of societies and economies, which is to put the cart before the horse) is the process of alienation. Marx considered various forms of negative alienation – between worker and the means of production, the products of his labour and labour itself; between man and man, man and his species, man and nature – while stressing also the more positive aspects of the search for various forms of non-alienated existence. Much geographical work, both traditional and modern, historical and contemporary, has in effect been focused upon man's alienation from nature and more specifically from his historical and geographical origins. As Samuels has put it:

the geography of alienation is a history of the search for roots, i.e. for places that bind and with which one can relate. Rootedness – the attachment of place, belonging – and the identification with places serves to illustrate that search. Localism, regionalism, nationalism, globalism, or any concrete expression of relationships at whatever scale is a 'positive' example of the search. The history of mankind is here always a geography of man's search for roots. The first man is, as it were, the man who invented a boundary to delimit *his* place, and human history is thereafter a history of boundary-making, maintaining, and changing.[33]

Existentialists and Marxists both seek a resolution to the dilemma of alienation in human history and geography,[34] so that there would seem to be a case worth exploring for the adoption and application of the concepts of existential Marxism by at least some historical geographers.[35]

History and historical geography as particular practice

For Marx, history was essentially concerned with the practices and activities of individuals and of social groups. The fundamental process at work historically and geographically has been, in his view, the contradictions created by the development of the 'material productive forces' and of the social relations associated with them. For Marx,

history is nothing but a succession of generations each of which exploits the material, capital and productive forces taken over from all its predecessors, hence on the one hand it continues the activity handed down to it under quite different conditions and on the other modifies the old circumstances with quite different activity.[36]

As envisaged by Marx, historical analysis involves reconstructing the systems of material production and of productive relations in terms of their tensions, antagonisms and contradictions since it is these which are seen as promoting change. A central theme in any Marxist historical analysis will, in consequence, be the class struggle and changing class consciousness. Although historical geographers have been much concerned with the impact of systems of material production upon changing landscapes, they have as yet paid scant attention to the role of social control and social conflict in the transformation of landscapes and the reorganization of space. To the reconstruction of regional consciousness in the past should be added the reconstruction of class consciousness, and in particular the reframing of such consciousness during the transition from feudalism to capitalism. Of course, Marx was here very much concerned with ideology, with false consciousness or the false image which a social class has of its own situation and of society as a whole:

distinction should always be made between the material transformation of the economic conditions of production which can be determined with the precision of natural science, and the legal, political, religious, aesthetic or philosophical – in short ideological – forms in which men become conscious of this conflict and fight it out. Just as our opinion of an individual is not based on what he thinks of himself, so we cannot judge of such a period of transformation by its own consciousness; on the contrary, this consciousness must rather be explained from the contradictions of material life, from the existing conflict between the social forces of production and the relations of production.[37]

This surely provides a firmer theoretical framework for studies by historical geographers, not only of past perceptions of landscapes and regions but also of the perceptions which social groups in the past had of each other? It certainly provides a rationale for integrating allegedly 'real' and 'imagined' worlds of the past, and for reconciling the observer's and the actor's view of the past.

Furthermore, Marx viewed history as being specific to particular places: at every stage of history there is 'a material outcome, a sum of productive forces, a historically created relationship to nature and of individuals towards each other', a sum-total of productive forces 'that is transmitted to each generation by its predecessor' and 'on the one hand is modified by the new generation but on the other itself prescribes its own living conditions and imposes upon it a definite development, a *special character of its own* – so that, in other words, circumstances make men just as men make circumstances'.[38] The specificity of historical-geographical development as propounded by Marx has certainly been echoed in recent geographical literature. For example, Harvey has advocated a 'materialist interpretation of ideas as they arise in particular places', Harris has suggested that those with historical habits of mind are prone to immersion in particular regions, and Gregory has cogently argued that geography should reclaim 'its traditional attachment to particular places and the people that live in them' and that 'we need to know about the constitution of *regional* social formations, of *regional* articulations and *regional* transformations'.[39] The concerns of historical geography are more properly with period and place than with time and space.

History and historical geography as generalization

Perhaps those who accept Lévi-Strauss's view of myths as 'machines for the suppression of time' – with myths being seen as a kind of collective dream capable of interpretation so as to reveal hidden meaning and having no location in chronological time – are also likely to argue conversely that history is a 'machine for the expression of time', with particular rather than universal significance and with specific rather than general meaning. But if myths are collective dreams then it would seem appropriate to regard histories as collective biographies: if myths are thought to express unconscious wishes which are somehow inconsistent with conscious experience, then perhaps histories might be thought to express conscious experience. In which case both myths and histories should be capable of interpretation so as to reveal hidden meanings: in the case of myths the meanings are likely to be essentially unchanging, whereas in histories they are likely to be essentially changing. Thus histories involve in broad terms a fundamental change from feudal, religious and hierarchical societies towards capitalist, secular and egalitarian societies. Whether or not this view is acceptable, it at least calls into question the unduly particularistic attitude of those who find themselves agreeing with Harris that the historical mind is contextual, not law-finding, for there is good logical reason to expect it to be both.[40] As Vance has pointed out:

It would be incorrect to hold that no regularity can be anticipated in the experiential (historical) approach to geographical analysis. Human behaviour is far from being unstructured and quixotic. It is subject to shared responses to common situations. At the same time, individual solutions to situations can be expected, and the study of the experience of man in shaping resolutions for problems has two logical concerns: that with the *commonly shared responses* and that with *exceptional acts*.[41]

That historical-geographical studies should be concerned with both particulars and generals finds support in the Marxist conception of history which requires a marriage between empirical and theoretical analysis. Marx's approach to society, while thoroughly historicist in its stress on change, is nevertheless normative.[42] Although history is nothing but the activity of men pursuing their aims it is also something that cannot, in Marx's view, be fully explained by men's pursuit of their aims. While history is the resultant of innumerable individual human aims and actions, these are often conflicting so that the outcome is generally different from and often actually opposite to that intended: so far as the end result is concerned, the Marxist argues that conscious motives are only of second-

ary importance, and that historical understanding requires examination of
the factors underlying the motivations.[43] History is made by men under
circumstances not always of their own choosing, since some are transmitted
from the past. Furthermore, man's actions create forces which at a point in
historical development come to operate independently of the will of
individual men and in fact come to control them. This makes it possible for
the Marxist to view the development of the economic formations of
society – that is, history – as a process governed by general laws. These
laws are, however, not laws in the sense of the natural sciences but laws of
social formations at specific points in their historical development. As
such, these laws are constructs won from reality which provide explanatory
theories for behaviour under particular historical circumstances. The
concrete historical situation is always more complex than the theory.[44]
Nonetheless, both generalizations and particularizations are integral to the
totality of history.

Total history and total historical geography

The Marxist stress on both the particular and the general finds echoes in
the emphasis which historians of the *Annales* school place upon *événe-
ments, conjonctures*, and *structures*. A further view which they share is that
the historical process needs to be studied in its totality.[45] This view will be
explored more fully elsewhere in a review of the relations between
historical geography and the *Annales* school of total history.[46] For the
present, it will suffice to note the greater impact as yet upon the
development of human geography of the analytical and empirical character
of American sociology than of the synthetic and historical character of
Marxist sociology. History and geography are quintessentially synthetic
disciplines: if the essence of geography is the study of regions, a kind of
place synthesis, then the Marxist argument would lend support to the view
that all geography must be historical in its perspective.

History and historical geography as progress and as praxis

The fundamental significance of a holistic concept of history and of
historical geography lies in its inclusion not merely of the past and the
present but also of the future, which it thus makes theoretically available
and practically real. A Marxist approach to history and to historical
geography carries with it a number of implications for its practice in the
future. Again, it is intended to consider these more fully elsewhere,[47] but it
will be convenient here to list them briefly:

(a) History as humanization incorporated within it a notion of progress.
For the Marxist, there are two criteria of progress: whether it increases

man's power over nature and diminishes men's power over other men. Historical geographers should, therefore, focus their attentions not only on man's developing control over nature but also on men's developing cooperation with or domination of men. Progress needs to be viewed not only in terms of material production but also of human emancipation.

(b) Logically, historical geographers should feel obliged to bring their studies through from the past to the present and to reject the artificiality of the distinction between the two.

(c) The Marxist approach sees the writing of history as an integral part of the making of history. There is ample scope for historical geographers to widen their perspective to include both the present and the future in very practical terms, through projecting their studies to a wider public and through accepting historical writing as, presumably, an instrument of the class struggle.

Advocacy of a move by historical geographers towards the adoption of a Marxian humanism is not an extremist view. It is instead a plea for balance, not only philosophically but also methodologically and technically. It is part of a search for an understanding and an experiencing of the past which can both be shared with others and contribute towards the making of a better history and a better geography.

University of Cambridge

Action and structure in historical geography

D. J. GREGORY

In his 'Foreword to Historical Geography' Carl Sauer claimed that human geography, unlike history, is a science that 'has nothing to do with individuals',[1] and in the postwar decades – with some noble exceptions – his presumptive opposition has proved to be unusually (if unconsciously) formative. In terms like these, of course, even historical geography, which Sauer once regarded as 'the apple of my eye', became resolutely ahistorical, committed to the excavation of patterns rather than processes and to the exhumation of places rather than people. On the rare occasions when the effectivity of human agency was admitted, its asymmetries were accepted and even endorsed: Darby's empty landscapes were 'made' by fistfuls of the prominent and the powerful, for example, while the ordinary men and women who were part of that 'making' – whose unremitting labours cleared the woods and drained the marshes, and the shape of whose lives was punched out by the contours of the new landscapes – slipped by largely unrecorded.[2] They were absent too when the register of the locational school was called: sometimes they filed through the playground in impassive columns or appeared at the gates in orderly crowds, but for the most part the historical syllabus carried on without them, a sequence of timeless geometries, and they became truants from their own past.

The details of this historiography need not detain us. They have been rehearsed many times, and derive from successive attempts to establish a distinctive location – a 'vacant space' – for historical geography. But none of this was uncontested. In geography Cole Harris's sensitive evocations of the 'historical mind' and in history Edward Thompson's coterminous celebrations of 'historical logic' stand as unequalled affirmations of a humanism which transcends disciplinary front-lines and sets its face against the incursions of a brutal mechanicism.[3] Its advances can be plotted on an intellectual terrain, of course, but its trenches snake their way out into a much larger domain which needs to be confronted at the very start, because its resonances inform the conception of historical practice which I want to discuss in this essay. In the late 1950s, 'watching the flames arise above Budapest', Thompson and many other socialist historians were profoundly moved by 'a common sense of political crisis': and it was *this*, he reminds us, which 'directed all of us, from different traditions, to certain common problems', and to understand these engagements 'you must commence, not within theory, but within the political world'.[4] The origins of Harris's critique were clearly different, but its destination was much the same. In particular, both men have been immensely suspicious of the theoretical systems of 'science' which marched hand in hand with the encirclements and closures of the Cold War. For Harris, the historical mind is 'contextual, not law-finding' or even 'law-applying', and he remains unconvinced 'that there are overarching laws to explain the general patterns of human life', while Thompson angrily denounces those who try to bring historical materials 'within the same criteria as those of physics' and who wrench the patterns of the past to fit the templates of some '*a priori* mental schematism'. History is a complex *empirical* field, and Harris insists that if the 'initially meaningless' is to become the 'understandable' then the historian must remain 'open to life as it is' rather than closed off by an unyielding, autistic theoreticism. So too, Thompson's historian has got to be 'listening' all the time, so that slowly he will be able to hear and eventually to understand the hollow echoes of the past, to discern rhythms and cadences in its faint babble of fragmentary sounds. Within Thompson's distinctive Marxian 'tradition', therefore, men and women are not to be reduced to Althusserian *Träger*, the mute bearers of structural determinations, but instead historical actors are to be understood as in some sense the authors of their own actions. To do otherwise, says Harris, is to 'override the humanistic side of Marx', and it is in precisely this tradition that Thompson once tried 'to rescue the poor stockinger' from 'the enormous condescension of posterity'.[5]

And yet, paradoxically, this recovery can be too complete, and history can become circumscribed by the collapse of actions into intentions.[6] The motivations and rationalizations of historical actors are an indispensable part of an authentic history, of course, but they are not its *essence*. This would be to limit historical reconstruction to an idealism which is incapable of explicating 'the escape of human history from human intentions and the return of the consequences of that escape as causal influences on human action' which is a chronic feature of social life.[7] As Marx himself recognized, social life is a *skilled* accomplishment, and his concept of praxis designated the modes through which men and women 'make' history: *but he also recognized that they do not do so under conditions of their own choosing*.[8] And Thompson, who is evidently further from Weber than Harris, knows this too: 'this agency will not be set free from ulterior determinate pressures nor escape determinate limits', and the challenge is thus to fashion 'a model [that can] encompass the distinctively human dialectic by which history appears as neither willed nor as fortuitous, as neither *lawed* (in the sense of being determined by involuntary laws of motion) nor illogical (in the sense that one can observe a *logic* in the social process)'.[9]

Thompson's solution is, at one level, a matter of style, of weaving what Olsson once called 'a net of words' somehow 'sensitive to the rhythm of that sound-dance that bends and moves without ever destroying the penumbrae between external and internal, subject and object, body and soul'.[10] And certainly one only has to turn to a book like *The Making of the English Working Class* to see how majestically Thompson mirrors the elusive and allusive cascade of human history. (Perhaps writing is our most neglected research skill?) He refuses to confer upon his reconstructions the spurious objectivity of historians whose pallid sentences, bare of adjectives and adverbs, display a past drained of the sensuous swirl of contingency and determination. Thompson's stylistic apparatus, in contrast, is drenched in emotive as well as denotive categories, and these are carefully scored to engage and animate the reader.

Our vote will change nothing, and yet in another sense it may change everything. For we are saying that these values, and not those other values, are the ones which make this history meaningful *to us* and that these are the values which we intend to enlarge and sustain in our own present. If we succeed, then we reach back into history and endow it with our own meanings: we shake Swift by the hand.[11]

Thompson's history presupposes a deliberately hermeneutic encounter with the text, therefore, which creates a constantly changing and ever-extending purchase on past and present alike.[12] In the process, however (and again paradoxically), the subjects become, as it were, 'de-centred'. Collages of evidences are built up, taken down and reworked; the fractured residues of historical actors, distributed through the historical archive, are recovered and reassembled, and *dramatis personae* made up to enact historical episodes whose containing script has a definite dramatic force and form. In *The Making*, for example, Thompson returns time and again to the working man, courageously displaying an extraordinary resilience in the face of the mounting exploitation and oppression of the early Industrial Revolution. We glimpse him in the flickering glow of burning mills, we eavesdrop on him in artisans' workshops, and we recognize his hand in desperate petitions to a deaf Parliament. We meet him so often, in fact, that he becomes the same man, *speaking through a hundred others*, whose presences and absences collectively disclose a disassociated 'structure': a cultural repertoire.

This is not a sign of Thompson's failure to respect the protocols of his discipline. On the contrary, what it gestures towards is precisely the 'radiating problems of historical determinism on the one hand, and of agency, moral choice and individual responsibility on the other' which he identifies elsewhere as his fundamental concern.[13] Indeed, it can be represented as an intrinsic element in the 'revival of narrative' in modern history which, as Abrams has shown, can be understood as an attempt 'to recover the movement of human agency as structuring'. But, as Abrams also makes clear, this loss of the subject and the conjoint recovery of structuration demands the incorporation of a more formal theoretical lexicon, both to make the narrative possible and to explicate the terms on which (and through which) it is realized. 'Explanation resides in an achieved sense of dramatic inevitability, an appreciation that, however surprising particular episodes in the drama may have been as they were presented, the plot as a whole viewed in retrospect rings true *as a structuring*.'[14] What this means, above all, is that narrative requires the theorization of 'the conditions of existence and the effectivity of the particular actions of particular agents': that is, the considered disclosure of a dialectic between action and structure.[15]

And in fact Thompson himself admits the importance of theoretical constructions to his (any) historical practice, and while his admission is (properly) nuanced and qualified it is nevertheless granted.

In every moment of our work we certainly need theory – whether in defining problems of the mode of production, or micro-economics, or the family, or culture or the state – and we need research which is both empirically and theoretically informed, and the theorised interrogation of what this research finds.[16]

Hence, at another level, Thompson's solution *is* a matter of theory (although – and this is essential – there is a vital reciprocation between theory and evidence), and he spells out his sense of the 'rule-governed structuration of historical eventuation' in terms which can, I think, be connected up to a more formal theory of structuration:

Societies (and a 'society' itself is a concept describing people within an imaginary boundary and actuated by common rules) may be seen as very complex games, which sometimes afford very material evidences as to their character (the pitch, the goals, the teams), sometimes are governed by visible rules (rule-books of law and constitution), and are sometimes governed by invisible rules, which the players know so deeply that they are never spoken, and which must be inferred by the observer . . .

The whole of life goes forward within 'structures' of such visible and invisible rules, which prohibit this action and assign a special symbolic significance to that . . .

When the rules of a game have been read or inferred, we can then assign each player his role or function in the game. He is (in terms of these rules) the game's carrier, an element within its structure – a half-back or a goalkeeper. In exactly this sense we can say that a 'worker' is the bearer of productive relations: indeed, we have already defined her in this way when we call her a 'worker' rather than a 'second violin'. But we must take the analogy further. For we do not go on to say that the goalkeeper is *being gamed*.[17]

Like all analogies, this must not be pressed too far, but it does indicate how Thompson intends that 'within these rules, players confront each other as creative agents',[18] so that their interactions, conscious or not, reconstitute or refashion the structures within which they take place. This analogical game can be generalized to argue, with Giddens, that social life displays an essential 'recursiveness', through which relations between actors are organized as *systems of interaction* by routinely drawing upon the semantic rules, resources and moral rules made available by *structures* of signification, domination and legitimation, in such a way that the successive and simultaneous engagement of interpretative schemes, facilities and norms necessarily reconstitutes or refashions the structures.[19] An example might make this clear. In speaking, I necessarily draw upon a pre-existing linguistic structure, and although I might not be able to specify the rules and resources which it makes available with any precision (particularly at levels below elementary grammar and syntax) its existence is nevertheless a *condition* of every intelligible speech act; and, symmetrically, these utterances necessarily reach back to reconstitute that structure, whose reproduction thus becomes an unintended *consequence* of every speech act.

The details of this scheme have been discussed elsewhere,[20] but here I want to suggest three reasons for providing this degree of theoretical formalization. In the first place, these theorems treat structures not as barriers to or constraints upon action, but instead as essentially involved in its production. To admit the existence of *unacknowledged* conditions and *unintended* consequences of action in this way demands a move towards a structural explanation distanced from conventional empiricism, and I take theoretical interrogation to be a necessary moment in such a movement. Clearly, Thompson's own work is not empiricist, and it is informed by and sustained through a definite system of concepts, but, as Johnston and others have shown, Thompson sometimes accords a privilege to the categories of 'experience' in ways which at least tremble on the edges of an empiricism which cannot effectively disclose the constitution of such structures.[21] At the same time, and in the second place, social life is not a simple working-out of deep-seated structural rules: actions are reflexive – they are motivated and rationalized – and as such they are essentially involved in the reproduction of social structures. Certainly, any attempt to mirror this movement between action and structure is a precarious struggle which can collapse at any moment, and Dawe has shown that the entire history of social theory (whatever its ostensible intentions) can be written

System:Structure	Theoretical system	Domain
Communication:signification	Theory of coding	Symbolic orders/modes of discourse
Power:domination	Theory of resource authorization	Political agents/institutions
	Theory of resource allocation	Economic agents/institutions
Sanction:legitimation	Theory of normative regulation	Legal orders/modes of sanction

Fig. 1. *The explication of social practice*

as a variation on 'the recurring theme of the negation of human agency'.[22] While it can provide no enduring guarantees, therefore, I take theoretical vigilance to be of strategic importance in safeguarding these interpenetrations. Of course, these elisions between action and structure have not been merely theoretical manoeuvres, and in the third place, as Dawe also indicates, they have a profoundly moral dimension and function as tacit 'ethical *prescriptions*'. I take this to mean that we must specify the ways in which our particular reconstructions inescapably inform determinate social and political practices.[23]

Giddens makes it clear that no social practice can be explicated in terms of a single rule or resource, 'rather, practices are situated within intersecting sets of rules and resources'.[24] Thompson frequently makes the same point: in *Whigs and Hunters*, for example, he found:

that law did not keep politely to a 'level' but was at *every* bloody level; it was imbricated within the mode of production and productive relations themselves (as property-rights, definitions of agrarian practice) and it was simultaneously present in the philosophy of Locke; it intruded brusquely within alien categories, reappearing bewigged and gowned in the guise of ideology; it danced a cotillion with religion, moralising over the theatre of Tyburn; it was an arm of politics and politics was one of its arms; it was an academic discipline, subjected to the rigour of its own autonomous logic; it contributed to the self-identity both of rulers and ruled; above all, it afforded an arena for class struggle, within which alternative notions of law were fought out.[25]

This makes it necessary to identify the set of theoretical systems which are *conjointly* involved in the explication of any social practice (Fig. 1).[26] These sort of tabulations are only gestural, of course, although they do reveal how desperately incomplete – even deficient – many of our 'explanations' have been. In particular, these equivalences do not in them-selves establish concepts of determination through which a hierarchy of effects between the different domains can be identified. This is especially important in the present context since, as Hall remarks, 'Marxists cannot be satisfied with [the] positing of an endless series of contingent "particu-larities"' because this would erect 'History' into an absolute, a 'final arbiter and judge' every bit as repressive as the absolutization of 'Theory' to which Thompson so passionately objects.[27]

Thompson is (rightly) sceptical about concepts of *economic* determina-tion, and dismisses the formulations of classical Marxism and (less accur-ately) newer, structural Marxisms as 'actively unhelpful', as invitations to an ulterior reductionism:

Marx's most extraordinary accomplishment was to infer – 'read' – 'de-code' – the only partly visible structure of rules by which human relations were mediated by money: capital. He often glimpsed, sometimes grasped, other invisible rules which we, after one hundred years, are – or ought to be – able to read more plainly. There were other, and significant, symbolic and normative rules which (in my view) he overlooked. Some of these were not within the view of his contemporary knowledge, and for such rules Political Economy had no terms.

'We may hypothesize,' he allows, 'that one "vocabulary" will "reappear" within the other, but we still do not know how, by what means or mediations.'[28] I think it follows from the theory of structuration that these 'reappearances' are generally not a matter of conscious translation which can be reconstructed through some kind of subjective voluntarism; neither are they entirely unconscious transformations which have to be disclosed through the abstract procedures of a structuralism. Rather, they have to be understood as arising at the intersection of actions and structures: that is, as constituted through *situated social practices*. Raymond Williams cap-tures this particularly clearly when he reminds us that 'any abstraction of determinism, based on the isolation of autonomous categories, which are seen as controlling or which can always be used for prediction is . . . a mystification of the specific and always related determinants which are the real social process – an active and conscious as well as, by default, a passive and objectified historical experience.'[29]

Unlike Sauer, I prefer to endorse Whittlesey's celebrated claim that 'All geography is historical.' What I have tried to illustrate in this essay is that its explication demands a careful restoration of the dialectic between action and structure, and that this entails a conjoint concern with the *aesthetic form* and *theoretical status* of our narratives. To be sure, this distances us from the traditional canons of historical geography: but it is perhaps time that their guns fell silent.

University of Cambridge

Historical geography as the evolution of spatial form

W. NORTON

Evolutionary approaches to spatial problems currently constitute one of the principal growth areas of geography, and historical geographers are in an advantageous position in this search for dynamic explanations. Jakle observed that the impetus towards spatial analyses derived largely from social scientists within geography and not from historical geographers.[1] Similarly, the current impetus towards the construction of dynamic theories and the adoption of a process-to-form approach is best represented outside historical geography. Chisholm has argued for dynamic rather than static theories, and Amedeo and Golledge have detailed the need for process-to-form reasoning.[2] Langton, in a review of the work by Amedeo and Golledge, has emphasized its importance to historical geographers.[3]

Process and form reasoning

Analyses of form are often unsatisfactory as a means of explanation, for all forms are necessarily the outcome of earlier forms and of process. A principal objection to a static analysis is the exclusion of process. Many attempts to relate these two have, first, described the form and, secondly, inferred the process. This procedure is an unreliable route to new knowledge, for a given form may result from any one of several processes, and hence such analysis does not permit the detection of process. Even in situations with descriptions at several points in time it is difficult to detect the mechanics of change. Recognizing the limitations of static analyses and of inferential procedures, much recent literature has argued that the best approach to explanation is to hypothesize process and then deduce form. Such a procedure is well suited to much of the subject matter of historical geography. Harvey has advocated such a framework for historical geography and, further, the theme has a sound basis in the change through time approach best exemplified by Clark.[4] A persuasive argument was

presented by Amedeo and Golledge: 'We expect that the spatial manifestations of processes (i.e. "form") will change from one time period to the
next and, therefore, the time factor must be explicitly included for any
complete modelling of a process and its spatial implications.'[5]

There are, however, a number of problems which may emerge in
attempts to apply such procedures. Four specific difficulties are noted.
First, and most fundamental, this approach requires awareness of both
previous forms, if appropriate, and generating processes. Unfortunately
the meaning of process may be unclear and information difficult to attain.
Two words often associated with process are 'ongoingness' and 'change',
and it may be interpreted as a succession of actions which lead eventually
to a result. The problem remains as to the means by which the initial
understanding of process is achieved. Three sources are suggested: available theory, comparable empirical studies and form analysis, although this
third source introduces the inference problem. Boots and Getis have
advocated a procedure named process-model-pattern which includes the
selection of a theory, specification of assumptions which constitute the
theory and, finally, evaluation of the output of the process model with
reference to the real world, thus allowing acceptance or rejection of the
model.[6] This method ensures that empirical form knowledge does not
influence the creation of the model.

A second problem recognizes that both process and form are liable to
change through time and are scale-dependent. A process, as considered
here, comprises variables and their interrelationships, and these may
experience continuous change.[7] Necessarily, an analysis of process requires
simplification and generalization in order to accommodate presumed
change. Further, there is not likely to be a sound reason to contend that a
given form indicates a final response to a suggested process. A form is
typically but a stage in an ongoing development. Ideal states, such as that
proposed by von Thünen for an agricultural landscape, are unlikely. Formulation is further complicated by the realization that processes operate at a
variety of scales. A causal process is liable to consist of a mix of local and
regional influences. In this respect there is not one clearly defined and
unchanging set of variables which may be interpreted as the basis for
spatial form evolution. The scale problem also complicates form
description; this is clearly acknowledged for point-pattern techniques.

Both of the problems noted so far refer to the critical question of
achieving a simplified yet appropriate version of the real-world process.
Given that a process is not easily observable in the sense that a form may
be, if evidence remains, it is clear that process formulation is a principal
task in the search for dynamic explanations.

A third problem notes that a given form may result from a variety of
different processes. This is of course a principal drawback to the procedure

of inferring process from form. Getis, for example, has emphasized that random forms do not necessarily imply random processes.[8] Deducing form from process minimizes this problem as there is, presumably, a sound theoretical or empirical basis for the use of a particular process.

Fourthly, a stochastic process is able to generate more than one outcome. This is critical because it introduces the idea of the real world being but one of many possibilities, and one which may, indeed, represent an unlikely outcome. Historical geographers may profitably analyse other, more or less likely, outcomes. Simulation is an appropriate technique for deriving outcomes and for assigning probabilities to the entire range, including that which occurred.

Although several problems are evident they do not represent deterrents to the adoption of a process-to-form approach. Indeed, they raise some intriguing questions concerning spatial form evolution which require consideration and which invite the use of simulation, the adoption of counterfactual arguments and the incorporation of a behavioral approach. Given that spatial form evolution is a legitimate concern of the historical geographer, there is a sound basis for adopting a process-to-form approach. An appropriate and established method for generating forms from hypothesized processes, that is, for operationalizing process models, is simulation. A simulation framework in turn easily incorporates counter-factual assertions, the use of which is well established in economic history particularly. Furthermore, the employment of counterfactuals may require the historical geographer to indulge in behavioural analyses. These links between simulation, counterfactuals and behavioural analyses are now developed further.

Simulation and historical explanation

Consider the problem of settlement location decision-making, for which an appropriate process model might comprise the following three variables: measures of distance from points of attractiveness, such as market centres and entry locations; measures of physical environmental quality relevant to the emerging economic landscape; and measures of institutional control such as the availability and cost of land. Quantification of these variables and assumptions about their interrelationships permits the simulation of forms from the hypotheized process. Simplified processes are liable to produce simplified outcomes. Furthermore, as noted, the outcome of a stochastic simulation is but one of a large number of possible outcomes. Assume an individual may make one of three possible location decisions, namely, A, B or C, and that the decision-maker evaluates these three and anticipates their probable consequences, namely, X, Y or Z. An assess-ment is made regarding the relative desirability of the perceived consequences, and the appropriate decision is made. It is possible that the anticipated results are incorrect to some degree. Hence there are X′, Y′ and Z′ which are the actual outcomes if the appropriate decision is made.

This simple example demonstrates the important point that historical decision-makers consider a variety of possibilities, only one of which becomes the 'past' and, indeed, that this past may depart from that which was anticipated. The outcomes of the remaining possible decisions are the 'might have beens' of historical geography. By amending the formulation of the process, either by attaching different values to variables or by incorporating a stochastic component, it is possible to observe the effects of alternative decisions, the might have beens. Such a procedure requires explicit use of counterfactual assertions and also requires an understanding of the past decision-making environment. This second requirement suggests that historical geographers approach what historians refer to as 'historical understanding'. Simulation, then, facilitates the explanation of human activities, for both the real and a variety of possible pasts may be produced. It is because we seek to explain why people act in a particular way that we elect to consider the unrealized possibilities. Both Baker and Prince have advocated the use of counterfactuals to extend the limits of inference and to assess the consequences of particular processes.[9]

In addition to enabling a consideration of possible outcomes, the use of simulation, combined with a counterfactual assertion, where appropriate, facilitates comparisons between evaluated outcomes and the corresponding actual outcome, given the necessary decision is taken. In this sense the accuracy of the evaluated outcomes may be assessed within the limitations of the simplified process framework. Such logic assumes that we are (a) able to achieve a degree of historical understanding, (b) able to observe the real world and (c) able to develop a process model. Comparable procedures are discussed by Todd and, to a lesser extent, by Porter and Forrester.[10]

Todd has argued that the conflict concerning historical explanation might be reconciled by use of a new methodology which accomplishes both the discovery of empirical facts and the historical understanding required by idealists.[11] Two features of historical writing, the use of counterfactuals and evaluative judgements, were considered, and a discussion of twelve historical studies demonstrated that both features were employed in all twelve instances. Further, Todd noted that historians employ reasoning comparable to science and that they rely on implicit psychological laws.[12] It is the lack of precision concerning these laws which obliges the historian to practise imaginative re-enactment. Reconciliation of the two views followed an analysis of the use of models and games. Models were seen as simplifications which necessarily involve the use of counterfactuals. Thus the procedure of historical explanation involved the gathering of facts, explaining with counterfactuals, and using the technique of sympathetic identification.

Porter has made a sophisticated attempt to integrate the covering law thesis and the genetic narrative by means of applying Whitehead's ideas of process to historical method.[13] The arguments in historical explanation stem from a desire by historians to be both scientific and aspire to literary creativity. Whitehead's interpretations may be used to both explain the changing relationships between cause and effect and to create a narrative. Such process-oriented explanations would not appear radically different from causal explanations but may seem rather static in comparison to flowing narratives. However, as Porter noted, the problem of accomplishing such a process explanation remains unsolved.[14]

Forrester has proposed a mode of explanation which could be used for both rational and irrational actions.[15] Given an act it is inferred that, of all the likely effects, one is the reason for the act being accomplished. If, however, it is difficult to regard one of the likely consequences as being the reason for the act then the historian may argue that the act was irrational. This is a novel form of explanation.

Counterfactuals

In historical geography, as in history and economic history, the use of counterfactuals is a basic component of a cause and effect analysis. For example, the suggestion that the settlement forms of nineteenth-century Ontario were influenced by government land policy presupposes that, in the absence of such policy, the settlement forms would have been different. Unfortunately, the explicit use of counterfactuals is confused. The proposed uses noted by Gould, and his classification into weak and strong counterfactuals, have been criticized by Climo and Howells, whose alternative ideas relating to possible world analysis have in turn been rejected by Hurst.[16]

The use of counterfactuals is typically associated with economic history where the initial impetus stemmed from a desire to judge the effects of economic policies. Simply expressed, the argument is that, to assess the consequences of a policy, it is necessary to consider the consequences of alternatives; 'there is, in fact, no way that cause and effect can be discussed without comparing the observed with the hypothetical'.[17] Similarly, McClelland has noted that to consider cause and effect one is required mentally to remove the cause and speculate on the results.[18] A rather different justification for the use of counterfactuals was noted by Conrad and Meyer.[19] If the universe is regarded as stochastic, then the historical process is not determined exactly. There are accidents in the process, and some of these are random and, therefore, alternative processes may have occurred. The procedure of simulation has been suggested by Murphy and Mueller as a means of operationalizing counterfactuals.[20]

Although of considerable potential value in historical geography, the issue of counterfactuals needs to be approached with caution. When it is asserted that 'If A, then B', in the knowledge that A did not occur, then it is evident that certain conditions must be satisfied. First, the occurrence of A needs to have been either a feasible alternative to reality or an alternative which, although unlikely, leads to interesting conclusions regarding the process as a whole. The incorporation of an unlikely event may increase understanding of those variables which did operate. Secondly, if we suppose A to have occurred, then it may be appropriate to consider what events might have led to this occurrence. It may be the case that the occurrence of A implies real changes in the overall process which, in turn, lead to the negation of 'If A, then B'.

There have been few contributions to historical geography which are explicitly counterfactual. One study examines the consequences of a counterfactual for frontier settlement in southern Ontario.[21] Spatial restrictions on location are removed, and the resultant forms are seen to vary notably from the 'real' forms initially, although the developing forms converge through time. Clark has provided a provocative discussion of the effects of the counterfactual assertion that Champlain discovered the mouth of the Hudson during his explorations of the Atlantic coast of North America.[22] The consequences for North American development and, specifically, for the political evolution of the French Empire and later for Canada are a significant departure from the real history.

Further uses of counterfactuals by historical geographers may profitably focus on the following three applications. First, to test hypotheses which associate an event, A, which we know did not occur, to a consequence, B. Such usage is appropriate where the counterfactual event or decision was a feasible or interesting alternative to the actual and where there is sound theoretical or empirical support for the subsequent occurrence of B. Secondly, counterfactuals may be used to determine whether or not an actual outcome would have occurred without a specified assumed cause. In this second usage the sensitivity of result, B, to event, A, is being tested. It may be that the result occurs regardless of the assumed cause. This is a principal use of the procedure by economic historians. In the first use above we are testing the hypothesis that 'If A, then B' in the knowledge that A did not occur. In the second use above we are testing the hypothesis that 'If not A, then B' in the knowledge that A did occur. In both of these cases the likelihood of a given form being generated by more than one process is being investigated. A third use of the counterfactual approach might consider the decision-making process. Analysis may show that particular results stem from different decisions and that the evaluated outcomes of the decision-makers appear to be at variance with what would have occurred.

For the historical geographer a principal advantage of the explicit incorporation of counterfactuals into analyses is that is offers one means of achieving a combination of the frequently diverse approaches of the positivist and the behaviouralist. In answer to the criticism that the possible worlds resulting from counterfactuals are spurious entities, Climo and Howells observe that conventional historical worlds are also possible in that they are typically derived from limited empirical data.[23] Further, they represent an interpretation of that data.[24] The distinction between such worlds and counterfactually derived worlds is a matter of degree, not of principle.

Conclusion

It appears that historical geography, interpreted as the evolution of spatial form, can readily incorporate several useful and related procedures. A process-to-form methodological framework has strong support in human geography and may be operationalized by means of simulation. Counter-factual arguments may be included, and these shed light on both the complexities of the process-to-form relationship and the decision-making behaviour of individuals. These developments in historical geography are closely aligned to (a) recent developments in history and economic history, particularly with reference to counterfactuals; (b) recent developments in human geography which argue for temporal explanations; and (c) a traditional view of historical geography as the study of change. Spatial form evolution represents one valid research theme for historical geography.

Acknowledgements

The author gratefully acknowledges the financial support provided by the Department of Geography, University of Manitoba, and by The University of Manitoba and Social Sciences and Humanities Research Council Fund Committee.

University of Manitoba,
Canada

PART VI

Historical Sources and Techniques

Historical geography and its evidence: reflections on modelling sources

J. B. HARLEY

> These papers and parchments, so long deserted, desired no better than to be restored to the light of day: yet they are not papers, but lives of men, of provinces, and of nations. . . . All lived and spoke, and surrounded the author with an army speaking a hundred tongues. . . . As I breathed on their dust, I saw them rise up.
>
> Jules Michelet, *History of France* (1835–67)[1]

Amidst a search for new philosophies, methodologies and techniques to vitalize the practice of historical geography, the independent study of historical evidence has been neglected. This essay contends that evidence in its own right should be an object of theoretical studies by historical geographers. After a preliminary discussion of attitudes towards evidence as revealed in recent writings by historical geographers, the argument considers the relevance of the classic linguistic model to an understanding of evidence, and finally reviews the implications of its adaptation to existing paradigms within historical geography.

The word evidence is defined as 'testimony or facts tending to prove or disprove any conclusion' and of giving grounds for belief. While some might be chary of historical geography ever reaching a conclusion – inasmuch as each generation reinterprets the past in its own light – the definition is probably acceptable and may be preferable to narrower terms such as sources, relics,[2] or traces.[3] Evidence, the 'history as record' which gives us indirect access to the past,[4] thus includes cultural and physical survivals which are many and various: words written on paper or parchment; words or symbols carved on stone or wood; maps, paintings and photographs; monuments and landscape evidences; artefacts dug up from the ground; and the living documents of oral history – as yet little used by historical geographers. This recites some of the more familiar types of evidence, all objects carrying meaning, which are in a constant state of accretion and attrition. If we assume, what is surely not controversial, that all historical knowledge depends on the existence of such relevant records, then no historical geography can be better than the evidence from which it is inferred.

A corollary to these initial premises is that the systematic study of the component parts of that record – in both the theoretical and technical realms – is a prerequisite to historical understanding. Evidences provide the only authentic language in which the truth of the past can ultimately be articulated. So far so good. But why then, it must be asked, does not the view gain wider acceptance that historical evidences – initially on their own terms – can form a rewarding research activity for the historical geographer? While any conservatism about the *range* of evidences appropriate to historical geography is fast disappearing, the thought of being too introspective about the nature of sources – to revert to that word – may still manage to conjure the spectre of Mr Gradgrind's letter to *The Times*.

Attitudes towards evidence

In establishing the place of evidence in the historical geographer's world, it helps to try to review current attitudes towards it. The mental equipment of the individual scholar has been described by one historian as his 'second record', and comprises his skills, range of knowledge, the 'set of his mind' and the substance, quality and character of his experience.[5] Such qualities are personal to each historical geographer, but something of our collective approach to the vital matter of evidence can perhaps be distilled.

A first observation is that there is no properly developed tradition within historical geography of editing original documents as a research or teaching activity. In this respect we differ from other historical disciplines such as economic, social and political history, the history of science, and of discovery and exploration, while the archaeological literature also contains a well-defined category specifically concerned with publishing the detailed records of excavation and collection. Doubtless historical geography has its documentary finds and key sites, but it does not report them as particularly newsworthy or in an 'impartial' manner so that they are fully accessible to other scholars.

Similarly, although it is an established canon of historical method to make clear the particular evidence on which specific inferences rest, some historical geography is noticeably coy in the critical description of evidence. Monographs are still being published which, although addressed to substantive themes, contain no organized discussion of their evidential base. Nor is the periodical literature always explicit in pointing to the nature of testimony for its assertions. The *Journal of Historical Geography* can serve to underline this contention. In its first four volumes (1975–8) there are, it is true, a number of 'source-based' studies, but the frontier of innovation with evidence is often seen in terms of its manipulative properties for machine-processing rather than in understanding other aspects of the nature of documents. This is not a value criticism of computerized methods (which can reveal new dimensions in evidence) but a comment on attitudes. More disturbing are those studies in which even a straightforward description of evidence is minimal. Short sections deal with 'Sources' or 'The Source Material'; bland statements such as 'a rich storehouse of material for research purposes' are intended to be reassuring; the odd documentary deficiency is rather casually treated in footnotes; but the approach is that of the inventory, and for serious historical purposes evidence is treated as prolegomena. This comment does not include papers written without recourse to primary material, but it is not difficult to diagnose symptoms of a lack of conviction in studying the historical record for its own sake. In the 1970s historical geography does not seem to have invariably heeded the second half of Pirenne's well-known advice that 'Without hypothesis and synthesis history remains a pastime of antiquarians; without criticism and erudition it loses itself in the domain of fantasy.'[6]

Nor do there appear to be many beacons to guide us across the methodological terrain. The discussion of evidence as a key to historical literacy is hardly ever elevated to the mainstream of philosophical and methodological debate in historical geography. Recent trends, with an emphasis on understanding and experiencing the past, may mark a rethinking of this position, espousing as they do 'more rigorous approaches to a wide variety of sources' and 'harder analyses of soft sources'.[7] Yet the general contention can be sustained. Historical geography lacks a proper philosophy of sources and fails to bring to them – as evidence *qua* evidence – those conceptual insights which are otherwise an integral part of approaches to the past.

It may be worth pausing to ask why historical geography finds itself in this position. Two circumstances, both rooted in paradigm fashions in human geography at large, may offer a partial explanation. First is the social-scientific tendency to polarize 'theoretical' and 'empirical' (and inductive and deductive approaches), and sometimes to regard them as exclusive rather than complementary categories. At its simplest the conventional view still dictates that an approach to an historical problem via a concept is nicely theoretical; approaches directly via sources are empirical. In the former, a linear research model, in which empirical evidence follows a statement of theoretical constructs, leads to a subconscious downgrading of the place of evidence in the inquiry.[8] On closer examination, however, it may be doubted if many purely empirical studies exist (that is to say, studies without any theoretical constructs, although we might dispute their validity). Theories can be equally empirically derived – that is to say, exhumed second hand in the library – and the image of studies relating to evidence obsessed only with 'facts' dies hard. The distinction is misleading. In recent years it may have been further perpetuated by the somewhat arbitrary division of historical geography into real, imagined and abstract worlds of the past.[9] It may be pointed out that a new form of evidence, such as that captured by Ronald Blythe's tape recorder in *Akenfield: Portrait of an English Village* (1969), can sometimes be as stimulating as a new theory.

A related viewpoint, expressed by historians as much as by historical geographers, is that evidence is somehow 'inert', 'static', or 'dead'. If this is taken to refer to some physical property, then a statement such as the 'records are after all only paper, over the surface of which ink has been distributed in certain patterns'[10] is acceptable. But by some form of lateral thinking the morbidity of dead documents is also transferred to the messages they convey. An American historian asserts

the record of the past never speaks for itself. . . . Putting it another way, the surviving records of the past are a set of dimensionless points. As such they lie outside history. It is the work of historians to draw lines connecting the records of the past, and thus bring the dimensionless points within the dimension of history.[11]

There are other variants on such metaphors. The historian peers through a curtain or screen of documents and tries to make out a landscape of past events: the curtain is somehow incidental to the life beyond. Now this argument might be defensible from some philosophical standpoints (from the tenets of historical relativism, for example), but in practice, partly through being misunderstood, it contains a vein of thought which fossilizes and trivializes evidence. Even where such emphasis is subliminal, by implying separation rather than interdependence, it may encourage a Jack-and-Jill approach to historical inquiry, that is, one in which having found our theory it is relatively easy to wind up a bucketful or two of evidence.

A second aspect of the development of historical geography may also be a contributory factor. As a relatively new and small discipline – at least in the wider spectrum – it may be questioned whether it ever reached maturity as a 'traditional' scholarly subject. Its practitioners, at first few in number, were in some cases late in discovering and giving priority to original evidences, and before this philosophy had rooted and flowered it was overtaken by the spread of scientific method in human geography.[12] The excesses – and exaggerated expectations – of 'logical' positivism, while prodding historical geography into a search for new ways of exploring, organizing and processing data from the past, also blunted historical sensitivity. Theories, ill-clad and poorly shod with evidence, migrated like paupers into the past, lured on by the prospect of factual El Dorados to validate universal truths. Narrowly statistical historical geography for its own sake has also tended to detract from what has been called the collective quality of the 'historical mind'.[13] In 1971 this tendency was picked up by Andrew Clark, appropriately enough in the context of a conference on historical geography and archives, when he asserted:

a consequence of emphasizing theory on the part of social or behavioural scientists has been the implication that we should de-emphasize facts, and that with de-emphasis, turn away from some of the meticulous training in their discovery, handling and interpretation . . . associated with the best historical scholarship.[14]

This trend could be easily exaggerated. But if it has occurred at all it is a matter for concern for historical geographers if they count themselves as independent scholars rather than belonging to some entirely subservient division of a social science human geography concerned with the past. Indeed, the perceived status of historical geography within human geography, as a subject which 'strictly speaking merely carries the geographer's studies into the past', or 'in which the data were historical but in which the method was geographical',[15] may contribute to any failure to engage completely with evidence. It could be argued that the tendency to react to each paradigm shift within human geography, the urge to become planners or politicians to satisfy the god of relevance, or to match the desire of research councils to perpetuate inquiry in their own image, serves to dissipate the scholarly energies of historical geographers. It is not inevitably a matter for rejoicing – as some commentators imply[16] – that human and historical geography are drawing closer together. The most fundamental contribution of historical geography may yet lie – whatever its broader philosophical or social purposes – in the maintenance of scholarly values, in the reading and understanding of evidence – a precious gift – and in an undogmatic approach to past societies and landscapes in their manifold interactions. If such qualities were part of an old orthodoxy then equally they ought to form part of any 'new, new historical geography'.

Modelling evidence

An identification of attitudes underpinning present practice does not in itself advance historical geography. A second path to progress is to locate those theories which are most likely to increase our understanding of evidence. In a recent paper Derek Gregory itemized the need for historical inquiry to provide a 'critique of the constructs which survive from and were routinely drawn upon by historical actors and a conjoint critique of the constructs which the historian himself brings to bear upon the past'.[17] To this structuralist agenda could be added the need to perceive and describe the internal structures and tendencies of the evidence we employ. This –

getting inside evidence – is different from modelling some historico-geographical structure which it is believed evidence may help to uncover, but for which that evidence may provide only partial and surrogate testimony. This is a vital distinction to the whole argument in this essay.

It is submitted that one group of theories probably has most to offer in a search for the nature of evidence. In essence these theories are variants of the communication model with the implication that many sources are metalanguages. They have a common origin in linguistics – in particular in the notions of structural linguistics[18] – a model which in turn has been extended to non-linguistic aspects of human culture. Not surprisingly, however, as far as a theory appropriate to historical evidence is concerned, most enlightenment appears to be derived from those disciplines which – while adopting the linguistic model – are focused as the principal object of their inquiry on major forms of human communication (most obviously language, but also extending to painting, cartography, etc.). Indeed, it is important to go back directly to these 'communication disciplines', notably linguistics, rather than to derive theory, as much of human geography has done, via second-hand adaptations within other social sciences.

Two simple and even obvious propositions of linguistics are especially relevant to the problem of evidence. First, it is assumed that language possesses a definable structure. Secondly, through the mechanism of that structure it is also assumed that language played a functional role in society. The implications of these two assertions for historical evidence will be considered in turn. The basic point about the communicative structure of language is that this patterning could also serve to model other evidences. Taking the example of speech, a number of constituent factors have been recognized as entities within the structure. In Jakobson's terminology such factors were six, set out as in the diagram below:

```
                          context
                          message
     addresser  – – – – – – – – – – – – – – – – –  addressee[19]
                          contact
                          code
```

They are explained by Hawkes as follows:

All communication consists of a *message* initiated by an *addresser*, whose destination is an *addressee*. But the process is not as simple as that. The message requires a *contact* between addresser and addressee, which may be oral, visual, electronic or whatever. It must be formulated in terms of a *code*: speech, numbers, writing, sound-formations etc. And the message must refer to a *context* understood by both addresser and addressee, which enables the message to 'make sense' . . . The central point to emerge from Jakobson's account of communication is that the 'message' does not and cannot supply all of the 'meaning' of the transaction, and that a good deal of what is communicated derives from the context, the code, and the means of contact. 'Meaning' in short resides in the *total* act of communication.[20]

It is the statement ' "Meaning" . . . resides in the *total* act of communication' which is potentially most important in drawing out the fuller sense of historical evidence. In many studies in historical geography, one or more of the six factors may have been neglected. The explicit study of codes is a case in point. A code can be regarded as a set of conventions or of descriptive rules for the coding and decoding of messages, yet, although historical geographers employ an increasingly wide range of evidences – both verbal and non-verbal – essential differences between codes are seldom considered. Even some of the more obvious distinctions – say between a written topographical description and a map – may alert us to their capability for influencing human thought and action. Thus written language is lacking in simultaneity and is sequential in its impact, while a map, a painting or indeed a landscape, can display and juxtapose its elements at the same time.[21] Equally, there is the vital question of who possessed the language (the code) in the past and who could read it. The concept of literacy can be applied to signs other than words: it is possible to talk about carto-literacy,[22] for example, or landscape illiteracy, as attributes which vary in time and area, and between societies and the classes and individuals which comprise them. How various languages were used, what were their uses, and how they affected individual and group decisions also affords understanding of the role of communication in processes of geographical change. Even this single aspect of code could breathe new life into the study of evidence.

The reconstruction of contemporary contexts of sources is equally important. Here it is hard to escape the conclusion that some studies presented as mainstream historical geography still tend to treat sources *ex situ* and thus miss additional meanings which are unlocked by revealing the social contexts in which sources have originated, and their links and dependencies with other sources. In studies where historical problems (rather than single sources) are the object of geographical reconstruction, these dependencies become especially important. On the one hand, it is easy to be seduced into believing that any one source is sufficient in relation to the questions being asked (especially where it may be suitable for mechanical or statistical analysis). On the other hand, by admitting a range of evidence we need to establish not merely good relevant evidence, but the best relevant evidence from a number of sources.[23] In much historical geography these wide contexts are sometimes implied but seldom fully classified.[24]

The lesson of the linguistic model is explicit about context. Its core appears in Saussure's definition of language as 'a system of interdependent terms in which the value of each term results solely from the simultaneous presence of the others'.[25] This requirement to examine the structure of language rather than merely its content can be extended to other 'source languages'. For example, with the cultural evidences of social anthropology – kinship networks, myths, rituals, etc. – Lévi-Strauss assumes their articulation is structured 'like that of a language'.[26] Isolated relics acquire meaning in context: 'every detail . . . is seen as part of a complex; it is recognised that details, considered in isolation, are as meaningless as isolated letters of the alphabet'.[27] It follows that one of the most important facts about *any* single source is not merely its 'hard data' (the potential dot on a map or point on a graph) but its interdependence with other sources relating to the same problem. Only thus can the purpose, relative importance and bias of isolated sources be revealed. The languages of the past are much as those of the present: it is often not so much what is said as the context in which it was uttered which may be of vital significance.

The other assumption of the linguistic model – interrelated to considerations of both code and context – is that it is a *functioning* system. In accepting as valid a structure in which a message is carried from an addresser to an addressee, an interactive 'live' process, it also follows that the message (not least when the evidence was created) was capable of exerting an influence. In this respect some of the ideas of literary criticism – at least since the publication of I. A. Richards's *Principles of Literary Criticism* in 1924 – may provide us with an instructive example. One key to a proper critical method is seen as a description of 'the psychological processes that take place in both writer and reader when a work is produced and appreciated'.[28] Literature had an impact which should be studied as well as its causes: qualities in objects were discussed not as independent facts, but in terms of their effects on persons who experienced those objects. This led in turn to a study of the communication process and meanings in literature which can influence states of mind.

Nor is such an approach to criticism limited to written language. Art historians – again following the linguistic model whether explicitly or implicitly – view art in terms of its role in contemporary communication. E. H. Gombrich's dictum that there should be a 'priority of context over expression in the theory and practice of interpretation' led him to define and assess the social purposes of art.[29] Portraits, for example, far from being merely 'decorative', were deliberately commissioned in Renaissance Italy to exert functions which could be private, political or religious.[30] And their value as historical evidence should similarly be gauged not only as content in the conventional sense, but also in terms of a means of communication with possible sociological impact.

These examples indicate how modern linguistics has provided a basis for the study of the 'totality of human communication'.[31] It has also led to the development of the general science of semiotics.[32] This has been defined as the 'science of signs', taking as its first premise that man's role in the world is quintessentially one of communication.[33] Its principal hypothesis, as set out by Umberto Eco, is that 'the whole of culture should be studied as a communicative phenomenon based on signification systems'.[34]

In view of the increasingly eclectic evidences employed by a problem-solving historical geography, semiotics could offer a central philosophical position – and a general theory – for reading, translating and using the languages of the past. It is almost infinitely extendable to the sources we employ. Written and spoken language, cultural evidences employed by anthropologists and painting have already been referred to. But clearly the concepts can be stretched to include other 'communication systems' furnishing historical evidence, notably maps[35] and landscape. With respect to landscape, a sentence from Hawkes serves to underline this potential as seen, not by an historical geographer but, it may be noted, from the standpoint of semiotics:

nothing in the human world can be *merely* utilitarian: even the most ordinary buildings organise space in various ways, and in so doing they signify, issue some kind of message about the society's priorities, its presuppositions concerning human nature, politics, economics, over and above their overt concern with the provision of shelter, entertainment, medical care, or whatever.[36]

Applications within historical geography

In view of the inadequacy of the published literature about evidence – not only in historical geography but in the philosophy of history in general[37] – linguistic and semiotic concepts could be systematically evaluated for their structuring potential. At its simplest the argument which has been advanced is that many of the evidences we employ are the result of some aspect of past communication. Whether denoted or connoted[38] in their surviving form, this was one of their fundamental historical purposes. It would be to miss the point to observe that human (and historical) geographers have long used communication theory to permeate their behavioural studies. This is true, but the theories have not been applied to evidence nor were they derived directly from linguistics. It remains to be seen how far the complex theories of codes and sign formation, the prolific alternative terminologies, and the elaborate typologies of signs generated by modern semiotics can be adapted without saddling the study of evidence with a set of fine-sounding but historically unproductive ideas. Perhaps the best analogy is to the initial development of systems theory within historical geography. Here the difficulties of testing systems models suggested that early euphoria about their potential was misplaced, but this did not give grounds for rejecting them out of hand as a 'means of conceptualising reality'.[39] So too with the general communication model for evidence provided by semiotics.

One application of the theory is to clarify the use of evidence in relation to existing paradigms within historical geography. Set against the communication model there are thus three distinct ways in which evidence has (or potentially might) be employed within the discipline.

Static studies of evidence

These employ the evidence and its content in the conventional sense. There is little to choose between a piece of research which maps a document at one point in time and that which graphs data in some form of a time series. One might be called synchronic and the other diachronic (terms borrowed from linguistics but employed more loosely in historical geography), but irrespective of technique they are static inasmuch as they retrieve only content from the communication process. This is a 'snapshot' which encapsulates the data in some form – the 'message' – but which may require a knowledge of code and context to reveal its full historical significance.

Genetic studies of evidence

These are concerned with processes by which evidence was created. In part it provides background knowledge for the present-day scholar to decipher the code, but it is also an integral part of the model, focusing on the addresser and context of communication. It is therefore concerned with the life-worlds of individuals who fashioned evidence, their state of knowledge, motives, mental and physical equipment, and the processes of transformation which evidence has undergone. Where the source language itself – such as landscape or maps – has also been a primary object of research, these stages have been exhaustively studied so that we know a great deal about the processes giving rise to the document at the particular moment of the snapshot. These vital stages in the communication process are also integral to the process of inference from document to event.[40] Only thus will we acquire the codes of the past senders of our messages.

Dynamic studies of evidence

These are viewed as part of change, and are the most neglected studies in historical geography. They are concerned with the impact in past periods of the evidence which confronts us today. In terms of the model, attention shifts to the addressee, and we may have to ponder the mental reception of evidence on the part of its past recipients. Messages were often recoded so that (as in the classic linguistic/structuralist model[41]) the nature of communication constantly underwent transformation and self-regulation.

These three types of study – static, genetic and dynamic – together attempt to recover structures by which different evidences were communicated in the past. Domesday Book can serve as an example. In the literature of historical geography its analysis has provided the most extensive and successful example of synchronic analysis. The 'geographical message' of the document has now been encapsulated in a scholarly panorama so that local and regional variations in English eleventh-century landscape and society can be identified. Scholars have also reconstructed the biography of this particular source and, through studies of the 'addressers', their 'codes', 'contacts' and 'context', have established much of the purpose and reliability of the documents. But historical geographers still have to answer the question, as Reginald Lennard and others started to,[42] as to what the effect was of Domesday Book upon and within eleventh-century English society. Were the final documents just 'pigeon-holed' like so many government reports of today? Or were they instruments of social control and an integral part of the process of geographical change as in the redistribution of landed estates? The answer – as with so many other documents and other evidences – is that they were links in the chain of change.[43] They were living entities as much as the 'static' data we map or graph.

The example of Domesday Book also enables us to return to the wider question of the place of semiotic theory in modelling evidence, and in establishing the proper role of this testimony in the historical geographer's understanding of the past. If we can now accept that an old book, document or map functioned in the past according to a definable structural sequence, then this must lead to revision of negative attitudes towards sources. Among the potential advantages of taking semiotic concepts more explicitly into our thinking and practice the following are suggested:

(a) inasmuch as the theory is concerned with evidence in general rather than with particular approaches, methods or techniques, it could cut across and help to rationalize various alternative strategies canvassed for historical geography in recent years.
(b) semiotic theory could also provide a unifying concept for evidences. It can apply to both verbal and non-verbal sources – not only to written language in various forms, but also spatial signs including maps, painting, sculpture, architecture, village layout and so on, and to myths, rituals and rites. Indeed, insofar as the theory asserts that any aspect of human activity

carries the communicative potential for serving or becoming a sign, it could be extended to include other cultural patterns and even acts of social behaviour.[44]

(c) that evidences – in their own right – can be interpreted in terms of a significant theory should remove from historical geography the false dichotomy between empirical and theoretical approaches. To find ourselves deciphering messages rather than excavating facts may sound to be a semantic distinction of little practical importance, but in leading to an understanding rather than just a rationalization of the past its intellectual ethos may be subtly different.

(d) the fact that by semiotic definition the internal structures of evidence possess autonomy and wholeness, are self-regulating and undergo transformation, also invalidates the notion that they are static and outside history.

(e) in the sense that as scholars *we* communicate with the sources and simultaneously try to recreate the way in which *they* formed part of a communication system involving people in the past, it could assist in making more explicit – and more articulate – the dialogue of past and present.

(f) elaborations of the theory could encourage a continuing search for inner meanings in evidence – between denotation and connotation in language, for example – and for the ambiguities and subtle symbolisms which may have their own substructures.[45]

Conclusion

Where do these comments leave our research strategies? While it may be wrong to infer that the changes of the last two decades have ever induced a crisis of scholarship in historical geography, they have certainly given rise to much heart-searching and left us with many dilemmas. This feeling was most clearly put by John Langton when he wrote of the 'challenging association between thorough and exciting scholarship and intricate and enjoyable theoretical speculation'; yet this association still 'resembled semi-conscious co-existence rather than full symbiosis'.[46] It is clear that work with the sources – even of a high theoretical and technical quality – is not in itself sufficient. Nor will a plea for the virtue of scholarship and the pursuit of knowledge for its own sake come to our rescue. The delightfully individualistic view of Richard Cobb that the only methodological equipment that most historians require lay in their archives – 'one just went to the records, read them, thought about them, read some more, and the records would do the rest'[47] – while quintessentially true is also insufficiently prescriptive for most of us. The records alone – even when classified and modelled in their own right – do not supersede the need for other philosophical and methodological explorations.

Perhaps the answer – both to remove the stigma that work with the intrinsic characteristics of evidence is somehow arid and old-fashioned, and to reconcile the apparently conflicting demands of theory and empiricism – is that every historical geographer should equip himself with two sets of discrete yet reciprocal models. One will provide initial structures for the substantive problem to be investigated; the other will model the relevant evidences. Both would be templates of the past. At the points where the two coincide some of the truth may be found.

Finally, a semiotic view of evidence could also be a recipe for a more humanist historical geography, which seeks understanding in terms of purposes rather than laws. Man's role in the world is essentially one of communication. Most of the evidences we use – whether of landscape, document, or other cultural icon – were fashioned by men, consciously and subconsciously, to communicate with other men, and to be used in some way by them. To treat them as less than part of the biochemistry of the past – and to insist that they provide only the mechanical means but not an object of theoretical inquiry – is to deny the very existence of a meaningful historical discipline. The quotation from Jules Michelet which prefaces this essay – despite a touch of gothic fantasy – also contains more than a grain of truth.

Acknowledgement

The author would like to thank Dr Hansgeorg Schlichtmann of the University of Regina for his helpful comments on an earlier draft of this paper.

University of Exeter,
England

Private archives as sources for historical geography

C. HALL

Methods and sources in historical geography

In its basic methodology, historical geography has followed the mainstream of geographical thought, and, like geography as a whole, shares much of its methodology with other social sciences. The transition from an idiographic to a nomothetic framework is apparent in much historical-geographical research of the past thirty years,[1] while the behavioural approach now being increasingly stressed in other branches of the discipline has long been recognized as fundamental in historical geography.[2]

In its use of primary sources, on the other hand, historical geography is necessarily distinctive from other branches of geography. Primary sources for studying the geography of the present are virtually unlimited. Lack of time or financial resources may in practice restrict data collection, but the information required by the geographer is potentially available. Indeed, the volume of data available in statistical sources, maps, aerial photographs and field work is today so immense that the geographer studying the present is often forced to use sampling techniques in order to reduce his material to manageable proportions. In historical geography, by contrast, there comes a time in most research – often before all the problems have been solved – when no more data seem to be available. On some topics, there may apparently be little information of any kind; on others, the material may be incomplete, lacking in detail, or suitable only for qualitative analysis. The search for new primary sources, and the development of techniques for their analysis, should therefore be a constant preoccupation of the historical geographer.

Considerable advances have been made in recent years in the use of non-documentary sources for historical geography. Landscape analysis in the field can yield vital information about the geography of the past. The oral tradition, used with caution, can be an important source of data, particularly of a qualitative nature.[3] For the study of prehistoric geography, the archaeological record is indispensable.[4] Written documents, however, remain the major primary source for most research in historical geography.

A high proportion of the documents used by historical geographers are of an official nature, compiled for the purposes of government and administration, and preserved precisely because of this function. Into this category fall many of the documents available in public archives, whether at the national, provincial or municipal level, as well as printed documents such as censuses and official reports. Valuable though the material obtained from these sources can be, it is often insufficient for thorough historical-geographical research. First, many of the data in public archives are of an aggregate nature. Although the geographer's final interest is in overall patterns, generalized information such as that contained in censuses may obscure important spatial variations. Secondly, documents in public archives tend to stress official points of view, while unofficial opinions and perceptions are unrecorded. Thirdly, many topics of interest to the historical geographer are, or were in the past, peripheral to official administration, and therefore little information about them is available in public archives.

The value of private archives

When studying present-day patterns, the geographer can fill in documentary lacunae with information from a variety of other sources, particularly detailed investigation in the field. The data which can be obtained for historical geography from observation and interviewing in the field are obviously much more limited. It is for this reason that the private papers of individuals, families, farms or firms can be such an important complement to the documents available in official repositories. Their use in historical geography has so far been fairly limited.[5] Interpreted with care, however, a carefully kept private record is often not only the historical geographer's best and only substitute for a personal interview or questionnaire, but also, paradoxically, more valuable than either of these insofar as it is not moulded by the researcher's own ideas.

Private archives are extremely varied in presentation and content, and the historical geographer must, of course, be selective of the material he uses. The records of a politician or playwright may contain little of relevance to his purposes, whereas the papers of an explorer, a farmer or a railway builder could make a valuable contribution to geographical research. In some European countries and in the United States of America, many collections of private papers are already in safe keeping. In other parts of the world, however, including most of the Latin American republics, the present owners of such archives are often unaware of their potential value for research. Many let irreplaceable collections of documents decay under the attack of mildew or rodents, and eventually throw the whole lot away. Historical geographers could do great service by helping to locate and preserve private papers for future use before the opportunity is lost for ever.

The historical geographer is particularly interested in all those records which deal directly with man–environment relationships and spatial organization, either at some specific point in time, or over longer periods, for the purposes of both synchronic and diachronic analysis. He can obtain this information from many types of documents, including diaries, correspondence, business accounts, inventories, maps and plans. Providing that they deal with topics of interest to historical geography, private archives are most useful when they comply with the basic requirements of all documentary sources: reliability, homogeneity and continuity. Private records may contain both qualitative and quantitative information, and the best permit detailed statistical and cartographic analysis.

Perhaps the greatest single value of private archives to the historical geographer is the direct contact which they afford with decision-makers whose experiences would otherwise have gone unrecorded. The running of a farm over a period of years, for instance, is not usually a topic of interest to official record-makers. Whereas the public archives may include only agricultural censuses and general reports about farming in a particular area, private archives can reveal in detail how farming was carried out, how land use changed over time, why the farmer chose one crop and not another, and how his decisions were related to the overall economic and social conditions of the time. In addition, private archives have the great advantage that they were generally kept only for the use of their owners. Whereas information supplied for official purposes or public consumption might be grossly distorted, private records are much more likely to be a true reflection of the writer's opinions and activities. They record anxieties and failures as well as expectations and success.

Farm archives in Costa Rica

Considerable use has been made of private farm archives in recent research on the historical geography of Costa Rica, Central America. These will be referred to briefly, to illustrate the sort of material which can be found in private papers, and the way in which these can be used to complement official documentary sources. Research began some years ago into the impact of coffee cultivation on the Costa Rican landscape.[6] One of the poorest and least settled frontier provinces of the Spanish Empire, Costa Rica was also among the first of the Latin American republics to develop a flourishing export economy based on the cultivation of coffee and later bananas. The spatial expansion of coffee-growing from about 1830 onwards, the interrelation between coffee production and colonization, and the impact of the export economy on the production of food crops, the development of the transportation network and the evolution of the central place hierarchy were investigated initially from official documentary sources. A large volume of data extracted from the Costa Rican National Archives, the Property Register, the Official Gazette and the publications of goverment departments provided the basis for a general analysis of the ways in which coffee cultivation was associated with geographical change in Costa Rica. The information contained in a series of private archives, however, was an indispensable complement to the official sources, and permitted detailed research into many problems which could otherwise be studied only superficially.

The first discoveries of private archives were made by chance, during the course of field work. Once their potential was apparent, it proved possible to locate others, and many more collections of documents could probably still be found. The von Schröter diary, kept by a German coffee-grower in the mid-nineteenth century, has given valuable insights into the problems faced by individual farmers in the 1850s. It highlights transportation problems at a time when Costa Rica's trade with Europe still relied on the long Pacific route, and shows how the 1856 war in Nicaragua against the filibuster, William Walker, and the subsequent introduction of cholera into Costa Rica, temporarily disrupted the whole export economy.[7]

Contemporary with the von Schröter papers are the earliest documents of the Tournón archives, which cover nearly a century of the development of one of the largest agricultural enterprises in the centre of Costa Rica. Using these archives together with the Property Register, Gertrud Peters has traced the complex processes by which the firm of Tournón gradually acquired land for large-scale coffee production in a region already densely populated and divided into peasant small holdings.[8] Fig. 1 shows how, between 1918 and 1955, the firm amassed 411 *manzanas* (284 hectares) in 43 separate farms, many of which in turn had been formed by uniting several smaller holdings. Many more diachronic analyses could be made from the Tournón archives.

The documents of Don Ezequiel Gutiérrez, kept from 1873 to 1911, are less voluminous than those of Tournón, but of exceptional quality for the purposes of historical geography. They refer to the formation and management of two farms. The earlier papers deal with the *hacienda* of Tuis, between 1873 and 1876. Although the statistical data are fragmentary, these documents are the only detailed record so far discovered of the cattle ranching which preceded the formation of coffee estates on the frontiers of colonization.[9]

Much more complete are the records of the *hacienda* of Cóncavas, dating from 1889 to 1911. Six volumes of inventories, financial accounts and diaries permit a quantitative study of the formation and development of a new coffee estate. The archives show how a coffee planter with new

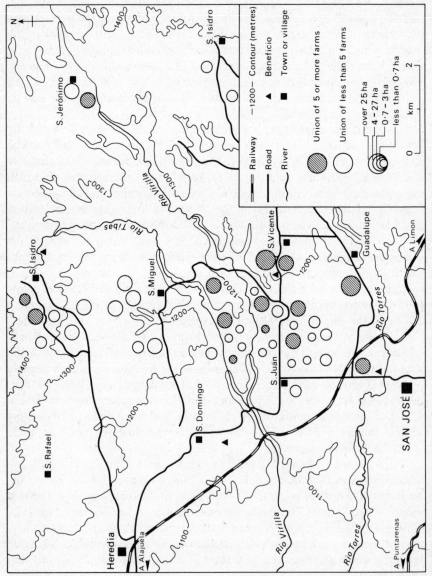

Fig. 1. Acquisition of coffee lands by the firm of Tournón, 1918–1955

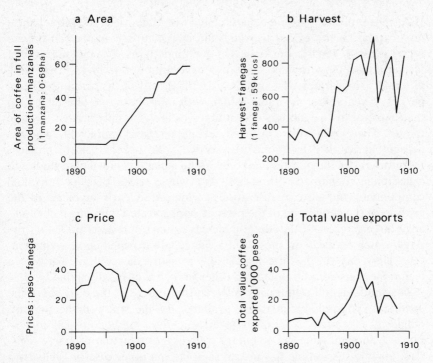

Fig. 2. *Coffee production of Cóncavas* hacienda, *1890–1910*

bushes coming into production each year weathered the economic crisis at the turn of the century (Fig. 2), while many farmers in the older areas of production were on the verge of ruin. They contain detailed information on employment and wages which corroborates the general impression of labour shortages obtained from official documents. They also include year-to-year reports of experiments in cultivation techniques, including the failure of attempts to introduce practices suitable to the temperate zone into a humid, sub-tropical environment.[10]

Methodological limitations

The limitations of private archives, however, must always be borne in mind. Like any other archival source, they contain a finite amount of material. Private archives rarely contain all the information the historical geographer would like to have at his disposal. Even judicious reading between the lines leaves many questions unanswered. Ultimately, the historical geographer still comes up against the eternal limitation of his data: the landscape which he is studying can no longer be observed in its entirety in the field, and except for the study of the recent past, he is unable to rely on oral sources.

A more serious problem, and one with important methodological implications, is the extent to which the information contained in private archives can be regarded as typical of overall patterns. The vast majority of farmers, entrepreneurs and travellers have not kept archives; most were illiterate. The farmer who made a careful record of his activities over a period of years was inevitably a man with more initiative and education than most of his neighbours. Farm archives are generally limited to large estates where relatively advanced techniques were employed, whereas peasant agriculture has gone unrecorded. The use of private archives therefore raises the question not only of the general value of case studies to a discipline concerned with society as a whole rather than its individual components, but also of case studies which are clearly atypical. In the analysis of the geography of the present, sophisticated sampling techniques have largely replaced the idiographic case study, and descriptions of 'the Argentinian *estancia*' or 'the Yoruba village' are frowned upon as unscientific. How can the historical geographer justify the continued use of a technique considered outdated in other branches of his discipline?

The fundamental differences between the sources at the disposal of the historical geographer, and those available for the study of the present, oblige the historical geographer to make certain methodological concessions. Although some documentary sources, for example property registers, may be susceptible to random sampling, in other cases it is clearly a choice between a single set of private papers or no information at all. The fact that the data contained in private records may not be entirely typical of overall conditions does not mean that the historical geographer should discard them. It does mean that he should use this type of material with particular care, always relating it to information from other sources. Initial analysis of private archives may lead to the publication of monographs about a single enterprise. This type of source-orientated study, however, is but a preliminary stage in the basically problem-orientated approach of modern historical geography. A description of an individual farm, out of context with region and period, is of little scientific value; used as a complement to other sources, private archives can yield detailed information unavailable elsewhere, and make a valuable contribution to the solving of wider problems in historical geography.

Acknowledgement

The author wishes to thank Srta Gertrud Peters for permission to reproduce Fig. 1.

San José,
Costa Rica

A Danish land survey from the seventeenth century

V. HANSEN

A major source for the study of Danish rural society in pre-enclosure times is Christian V's land survey of 1688. The historical and economic background to this remarkable document was that of the wars with Sweden which ended in 1660 with the surrender of the three rich provinces of Skåne, Halland and Blekinge to the victors, and a general economic decline in Denmark consequent upon the expensive military campaigns. The absolute monarchy had been introduced in 1660, and one of the first major royal orders was that demanding an outline of the nation's potential tax yield. However, the first attempt to produce an accurate land register (based on the available cadastres) proved less than useful, and it was for this reason that a new and complete survey was ordered which was accomplished between 1681 and 1683. After several years' deliberation the contents of the survey were confirmed by the government and ratified by the king in 1688. The resultant document was to become the basis for Danish tax assessments for the next 150 years, even after the passage through parliament of the enclosure acts in the late eighteenth century. Only in 1844 was it replaced by a register more suited to the new post-feudal conditions.

The 1688 land register comprised: a measurement of all farm land (even down to the single parcel) and an analysis of the composition of each furlong, its fitness for cultivation and its tax assessment. It also described the management system of the area and, in some cases, even the actual land use of individual parcels was documented. On a township basis, the share of each tenant (in terms of farm area, hay crop and cattle on the fallow) was ascertained, and finally the tax assessment for each farm or cottage was given.

The land register thus makes it possible to calculate the synchronic extent of tenancy, landownership, cultivated land and wasteland. Furthermore, the spatial distribution of different field systems can be mapped and correlated with a variety of morphological features, as well as with climate and soil regions. The survey also provides a key to understanding the distribution of villages and dispersed farmsteads. The survey as a whole has a number of undisputed merits, though also a series of related problems which can be summarized thus:

1. The survey covered the whole of the Danish monarchy lands (except the island of Bornholm).
2. The survey was completed by experienced surveyors and clerks in only two years (1682 and 1683). The survey of the Danish islands was completed in 1682, and in 1683 the much larger area of Jutland was surveyed. It is the general opinion of scholars that the survey in Jutland was less carefully conducted despite the appointment of several extra commissions consisting of experienced surveyors and clerks. Perhaps it is true to suggest that the field *measurements* themselves were less accurate overall, but by now the staff were more capable generally and the field-books often show more details of field *management* in Jutland than is common elsewhere – a distinct advantage to those studying the geography of seventeenth-century Denmark. Thus for example the parish of Tødsø was surveyed between 27 June and 6 July, though since work could not take place either on Sundays or rainy days the whole area was actually surveyed in only five and a half days, and this despite the fact that the actual land use of each strip was recorded. The field-book also contains a complete introduction to the management system of the parish.
3. The work was accomplished with few alterations to the instructions given to the commissioners. The instructions to the Jutland commissioners asked for a more detailed analysis (of significance to actual tax evaluation) in recognition of the much greater variation in soil type. More explicitly, the commissioners were asked to record deserted villages and fields created by sand-drift disasters which were at their height at the time. In such cases reductions in the tax assessment were granted.
4. Local farmers themselves testified concerning the management system and farming practices of their own areas. For this purpose only the more important farmers were canvassed in order to ascertain information for the whole county (though they were not asked about their own specific village). Ultimately, such farmers appear to have produced a just tax assessment, though this delicate task and its outcome is discussed further below.
5. Possible errors in the tax assessment were corrected and complaints investigated. Thus, for example, in a memorial of 1685, the number of classes of land quality was widened from four to six, with consequences for the taxation level, and a score of villages were surveyed anew. As a result of these and of local complaints, final assessment was approved by the fiscal chamber (*Rentekammer*) and ratified as Christian V's Land Register, 1688.

Clearly the local farmers who estimated the tax assessment of each field had a very delicate job to perform which could easily bring them into conflict with their fellow villagers. Unfortunately the field-books give no evidence of the methods used in their assessment, and neither do the instructions given to the commissions. This question has troubled many scholars and still requires a satisfactory answer, not least in connection with the detailed techniques used to characterize soil productivity which formed the basis of the tax evaluation.

Each furlong (or even part of a furlong) is detailed in terms of three characteristics: first, the soil composition (the amount of clay, sand and gravel as well as the humus content of the topsoil); secondly, the length of the rotation period (whether the specific field was sown yearly or whether there was a fallow period of one, three, six or nine years between the crops); and thirdly, the suitability of the furlong (either for a crop of rye, barley or mixed grains and whether the crop might be regarded as good or middle quality, or for a good middle or bad crop of oats, or for a good, middle or bad crop of buckwheat).

A pilot study into the correlations between the various measurements has demonstrated a high positive correlation between a good or middle crop (of rye, barley or mixed grains), a three-year rotation and at least some humus in the topsoil. At the other end of the spectrum, a similarly good correlation has been found between a crop of buckwheat, a rotation with three to nine years of fallow and no humus content. Moreover, there is a high correlation between these three variables and a fourth significant factor – distance from village. Problems remain, however, since no one has yet been able to determine whether a 'good barley cropland' in a three-year rotation with a suitable amount of humus actually carried a barley crop or whether this description was used as a way of expressing the tax assessment, particularly as this was the basis of the tax assessment itself.

Similar problems arise with the specification of an increasing number of fallow years in the same unenclosed field with increasing distance from the village. If this information is taken at face value then one is forced to assume the existence of a good many fences between furlongs with a different number of fallow years in each fenced portion. Since this could hardly have been the case in reality, the most likely explanation for the anomaly appears to be that more distant fields gave a poorer crop because they received little or no manure, and that the easiest way to indicate the lower productivity of these more distant fields was to adopt the formula of 'adding' several more fallows in the tax return. Such a solution would be in agreement with the widely accepted assessment principle adopted more generally. Normally the taxes were assessed according to the yearly cropped area, meaning that a three-field rotation of two cropping years and one year fallow (a two/one rotation) was taxed at the equivalent of two-thirds of a continuously cropped field. Thus, a two/three rotation paid only two-fifths of the full taxation, and a two/six rotation only one quarter. Therefore when one finds mention of a two/six rotation in a certain field, this might mean either that the rotation really included six years with fallow or that it was a field in a normal rotation with only one fallow year, but with such a meagre harvest that it should be valued as low as one quarter of a normal crop. The definitive answer to this problem has not yet been deduced. Only in those cases where a more detailed description of the rotation is given can one feel confident of the documents' unambiguous inferential capacities.

Nevertheless, despite such detailed problems, the Danish land register of 1688 is possibly the best source in Europe from which to attempt the synchronic reconstruction of a past rural geography on a national scale. With the generally accepted value of this source in mind (particularly its quantitative field measurements and qualitative details of agricultural practice) it is clearly up to the historical geographer to draw his own conclusions from this almost inexhaustible collection of documentary materials on the agricultural geography of Denmark.

The manuscript field-books (1,693 of them in total), together with the 101 volumes of abstracts, are housed in the Danish State Archive in Copenhagen, and are easily accessible to, as well as much used by, historians, geographers, place-name scholars and other students of the Danish rural past. Within this wide group of scholars the specific task of the historical geographer seems clear, namely, to bring both the temporal and spatial dimensions of the past into an overall synthesis of the economic, social and technological variables prevailing at that time, and interpret these in the light of the contemporary political situation (foreign policy as well as home policy). Such a programme is essential even if the task itself appears formidable.[1]

Such a programme highlights a number of important questions concerning the use of the land survey. For example, the question arises of the temporal representativeness of the survey – over what sort of time period can it be considered an accurate portrayal of Danish rural geography? To what degree would a changing political background or a different economic situation with changing market prices influence rural management systems, the relationships between landowner and copyholder or create major changes in the cultivated area? To what time periods, therefore, can the conclusions drawn from the survey be applied?

Supplementary records help to answer some of these questions, though in other cases scholars must resort to assumptions which rest upon knowledge of rural development more generally. As regards the management system, the best comparative sources are the reports from the local vicarages available from the time of the Lutheran reformation, and in several cases these detail how the land was tilled. Where such comparative cases occur, there appears to be little or no difference between these accounts and the survey of 1688. Similarly, a report of 1567 describes the distribution of the two- or three-field system on Sjælland, and again the management system appears identical to that recorded in 1688.

Changes in land ownership occurred quite often, but always between landlords and without any apparent consequence for the farming practices of the villagers themselves. However, the most extensive change in ownership took place when the crown took over most of the church land after the Reformation and distributed much of it to the nobility in repayment of debts. Clearly too, the manorial system was changing all the time, as old manors were extended and new ones created. In either case, landowners took the opportunity to reorganize land tenure away from the peasant land system of strip cultivation towards that of rationally consolidated holdings, with consequent farm and village desertion. The crown itself was an eager participant in this process and indirectly influential through its manorial policy. Fluctuations in grain prices also had a marked effect, creating about 2,000 deserted farms between 1525 and 1774 – over half of which occurred in Sjælland.[2]

Changes in the extent of cultivated land are also known to have occurred. In northern Jutland, virgin territory in low-lying areas was colonized in the sixteenth century, mostly as demesne land. In the same region, however, devastations caused by coastal erosion and by drifting sand in the sixteenth and seventeenth centuries robbed several farms and villages of their old farmland and even forced them to move their farmsteads to new locations. Even so, nothing comparable to the extensive reclamation works in Germany and the Netherlands on marshy areas and on heathlands took place in Denmark.

Such a general overview of changes in the rural geography of Denmark is well documented, but details are also required of the seasonal and daily variations in farm practices in specific areas and places. Attempts to produce studies of daily life through 'the eyes of contemporaries' are still comparatively rare. The ideal observer of such events would be a member of the local community or village council, since all decisions were taken in common as, for example, in the selection of a date for harvesting, or a date for fencing, or for releasing cattle to graze on the stubble. All these activities were officially regulated. Every Danish village had its own by-laws (*Vider og Vedtægter*) which had to be adhered to strictly. Surviving documents detailing these laws date from 1550, though they were made law in 1492 and doubtless have an even longer oral tradition going back to the introduction of the two- and three-field system with which they are strongly associated. From nearly two hundred of these surviving regulations, evenly distributed over the country, one gets a strong impression of the everyday workings of villages.[3]

This naturally leads us towards the question of how innovation both of ideas and of new technology came about within an essentially unreformed rural society and to the related issues of who innovated and to what extent the innovations were adopted. As a strong potential promoter of innovations one must consider the activities of the local court (*Herredsting*) where farmers met to resolve disagreements between neighbours or between townships and villages, as well as to exchange experiences of their daily work. The local market might have enjoyed a similar function since farmers here met townsmen and discussed farm produce, prices and qualities. Yet another agent of innovation might have been the village parson who, as perhaps the only learned man in the community (even if he might not have been an experienced agriculturalist), would through the force of example be able to transmit information about certain innovations and improvements. One might also point to the landlords as innovators on demesne lands, and certainly it is common to discover landlords taking up new methods both of cultivation and, even more commonly, husbandry. However, many landlords appear to have been uninterested in agricultural improvement on their demesnes, since their personal ambitions lay more often in the trading of land than in its tilling. Support for such a view comes from the fact that it is exceptional to find landlords creating by-laws until at least the eighteenth century.

The discussion thus far would naturally lead to the conclusion that innovation in agricultural practice was a very slow process and that the management and field systems depicted in the 1688 land register necessarily had very long established histories. There are indeed reasons to believe that the spatial distribution of the different field systems had very deep roots planted firmly in the different resource bases of the various regions. No doubt well-defined agricultural regions can be identified in the seventeenth century, reflecting an old-established adjustment to the local environment which would, in itself, constitute a formidable barrier to the flow of innovations. Yet, there is still one innovative force which may have operated throughout the centuries despite such barriers: Man's will to survive. Agricultural expansion as well as retreat finds its most obvious determinant in population change, irrespective of the cause of that demographic variable. It is well established that new farmland was taken in from waste or from meadowland in order to augment the existing arable. Similarly, distant fields were often abandoned following a decrease in available manpower owing to war, epidemic or starvation (following harvest failure). It might thus be suggested that strategies to meet such challenges were readily available and effected whenever circumstances were appropriate. However, such 'wounds' to the reproduction of society are known to have been healed in a surprisingly short period of time. Deserted farms were taken over by migrants from other parts of the country or perhaps more often by members of the underemployed groups of smallholders – a situation often revealed by biographical materials contained in parish registers. Thus it can be established that the widespread military actions and the occupation of the Swedish/Danish War of 1657–60 resulted in parts of Jutland in great losses of farm production as well as in cattle, bringing immense poverty to many parishes. Up to 40 per cent of farms were deserted in such areas by 1662. Only twenty years later these farms were once more occupied and in full production. Indeed, there is even evidence of overpopulation.[4]

Similarly, the consequences of the widespread plague in Sjælland in 1655–6 confirm that few farms were deserted, since 90 per cent of the deaths occurred amongst persons under sixteen years of age. The same tenants thus appear in the registers both before and after the plague. It is also evident from the register of tenant names in 1682, however, that most of the stock of copyholders had been renewed, though not by the normal practice of family inheritance (father to son). On the contrary, the new copyholders were either immigrants from other parts of the island (or from even farther away), or were smallholders or farm labourers from the parish itself. Thus had a 'lost generation' been filled.[5]

There has been much dispute amongst Danish scholars as to whether or not there was a stable rural population in the period from the Middle Ages through to the beginning of the nineteenth century. The number of farms certainly remained stable, though it would be wrong to deduce on this basis alone that there was also a stable population, since a farm might house two to three tenant families and possibly more. Any calculation of population must also take account of the rather neglected group of smallholders and cottagers which constituted not only the local reserve work force, but also the skilled craftsmen of the villages. In many areas of Sjælland and the other Danish islands, the 1688 land survey registers as many farm labourers as farm tenants, whilst in Jutland a division of tenancy is evident. Members of this lower rank showed a steady increase during the sixteenth and seventeenth centuries. Few of them had any farmland at all, and were fully dependent upon the landlord or upon the farmers to whom they gave their service in return for land. This increase in the labour force may well explain the extension of cultivated land which took place in the villages during the seventeenth century. This is well documented in the field-books of 1682–3 which tell, for instance, of a furlong which 'has lately been taken in from the meadowland' or of another furlong which 'has been taken in from the heath fifty years ago'.

It is well known from documents, from archaeological evidence, from field-names, from dating of ceramic remains found in the topsoil and from

V. Hansen

the analyses of soil phosphate content that a widespread shift in European settlement patterns took place in the Middle Ages as a result of population increase, and that this was followed by population decline, desertions and retractions in the late medieval period. The author is convinced, however, that nothing similar to this occurred in Denmark after the end of the medieval period, and perhaps even since the middle of the fifteenth century. Changes in population, in settlement structure and in agricultural practice since then have been but small waves upon an otherwise stable sea. In this sense the rural geography of Denmark, as expressed in the 1688 land register, may be valid not only for the latter part of the seventeenth century, but also more generally for over two hundred years prior to that.

University of Copenhagen,
Denmark

Cartographic representation of diachronic analysis: the example of the origin of towns

A. SIMMS

Introduction

A country's cultural identity depends largely on its collective historical biography. This puts a great responsibility on the biographer, because his awareness of historical events influences the perception which a people will have of their own past and the understanding that others will have of them. In this context historical-geographical maps have an important role to play insofar as they help to explain the historical meaning of change. They communicate evidence from a very complex set of sources.

There are at least two distinct categories of historical-geographical maps based on written documentary material. First are those maps whose aim is to use documentary evidence in order to produce a cross-sectional view of a particular region at a particular time; secondly, those maps which attempt to show an interpretation of historical change through time. These two categories correspond to the method of synchronic or diachronic analysis respectively. The first category of maps emphasizes primary documentation, and therefore 'they are timeless and completely independent of changing fashions of historical interpretation. On the other hand, maps which try to combine data for more than one particular period, development maps, necessarily contain a larger degree of judgement by the author.'[1]

The new *Atlas of Ireland* will include a map on the 'Origins of Principal Towns' (Fig. 1).[2] This map is an attempt to show the results of diachronic analysis. It was compiled in cooperation with the medieval historian Katharine Simms in order to show, in cartographical form, the rethinking which has recently been done on this topic in Ireland.[3] The map only includes those towns which at present have more than 3,000 inhabitants. It does not illustrate the total number of towns at any given historical period. This is a limitation imposed by the editor of the *Atlas*. On the other hand, it is only because of the limited number of towns (118) that the use of

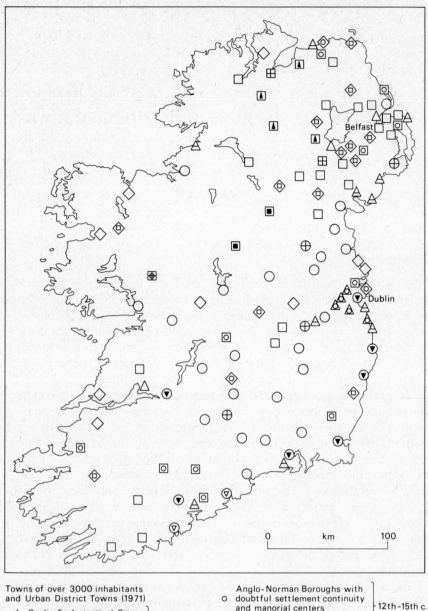

Towns of over 3000 inhabitants
and Urban District Towns (1971)

+ Gaelic Ecclesiastical Sites
▼ Viking Sea Ports   ⎫ Proto towns
▽ Presumed Viking Sea Ports ⎬ (9th-12th c.)

■ Gaelic Market Towns   ⎫ 15th c.
▲ Gaelic Castles   ⎭

○ Anglo-Norman Boroughs with
   doubtful settlement continuity ⎬ 12th-15th c.
   and manorial centers

◯ Anglo-Norman Towns
☐ Towns of the Tudor-Stuart
   Plantation Period   16th-17th c.

◇ Estate Towns   18th c.

△ New Towns (sea-side resorts,
   garrison towns and   19th c.
   railway junction towns)

△ New Towns and satellite towns 20th c.

Compilers: Anngret Simms, Katharine Simms

Fig. 1. *Origins of Irish towns with more than 3000 inhabitants in 1971.* Source: *after A. Simms and K. Simms. 'Origins of Principal Towns' in J. P. Haughton (ed.). Atlas of Ireland (Dublin, Royal Irish Academy, 1971)*

superimposed symbols was possible. Much work still needs to be done in this field, and the present map has to be considered as a pilot scheme.

Irish settlement history was strongly influenced by external colonizations.[4] It is for this reason that Irish historians, archaeologists and historical geographers become victims of a disorder referred to as 'invasion neurosis',[5] that is to say, that successive cultural changes were attributed exclusively to the arrival of new ethnic groups. The formation of towns were credited solely to the Vikings, the Normans and the English in succession, implying that urban civilization was more or less imposed on the Irish from outside by foreign conquerors. The following quotation reflects this judgement: 'Before urban life could take root on Irish soil a radically new cultural and economic milieu was needed and this could only come from outside.'[6] Unfortunately, this preconception was allowed to develop into an ideology of hostility against the urban way of life, which in my own experience, has been used by local government officials as an excuse for a lack of interest in the urban environment and in particular in the preservation of historic city-centres in Ireland. But recent excavations in the medieval centre of Irish towns, from the Viking and Norman period, have made a big difference not only to the understanding of the early phases of town-formation in Ireland but also to the willingness to accept towns as part of Irish history.[7]

Historical typology of towns

Quality changes in urban development are not easily recognizable in long-established areas; they are more pronounced in peripheral areas, where towns were created in relatively short time-spans as planned foundations.[8] Because of the repeated external colonizations in the course of Irish history and the resulting foundations of new towns, the qualitative changes in its urban system take on a revolutionary character and so dominate over the evolutionary ones.

The map is based on two variables: first, the definition of towns; secondly, the subdivision into periods significant for the formation of towns in Ireland.

As to the first variable, the overriding influence of repeated external colonizations made it particularly difficult to appreciate the element of continuity in Irish settlement history and to recognize the incipient forms of urban life in Ireland. Of course, such a recognition depends first of all on our definition of towns. As long as the study of urban history was a sector of legal history, the definition of a town was based on the existence of a charter and a constitution, as well as urban institutions. But medieval urban excavations in European towns have produced such rich archaeological material for early forms of urban life (objects of craftsmanship and trade) that we can now distinguish between two different types of medieval towns: the early medieval proto-town or pre-urban nucleus, and the fully fledged high medieval chartered town. We have learnt to realize that the hierarchy of criteria used in our definition of town must be rearranged for each distinct phase of town-formation. In short, a rigid definition has been replaced by a descriptive definition, that is to say, by a composite definition.[9]

But such a terminological distinction is missing on earlier maps showing the origin of Irish towns, for example on F. Aalen's map (1978) (Fig. 2), where the classification is restricted to Viking, medieval, Tudor and Stuart, estate towns and modern.[10] The clear impression that this map must create is that town-formation in Ireland was solely dependent on external colonization. In contrast, on the map of the origins of towns in the *Atlas of Ireland* a major distinction is made between proto-towns and towns (see Fig. 1). The proto-towns fall into three groups: Gaelic-ecclesiastical sites, Viking sea ports and Gaelic market towns. The Viking sea ports and Gaelic market towns were towns in all but the legal sense. The Gaelic-ecclesiastical proto-towns are a particularly Irish species, resulting from the important role played by the monasteries as central places in the early Irish period (5th–10th centuries).[11] But only those monastic settlements are classified as proto-towns for which there is clear documentary evidence of additional secular buildings. Because of the controversial nature of the category of Gaelic proto-towns the documentary evidence for two sites is reproduced in Appendix I.

As to the second variable, the important question is: which were the formative periods of town-formation in Ireland? This question leads us into a vicious circle, because the answer depends largely on our definition of towns, which in turn depends on the supposed time of their formation. On the basis of archaeological and documentary evidence the case has been made for the existence of proto-towns in Ireland before the coming of the Normans. These proto-towns were succeeded by the fully fledged constitutional towns, which the Normans introduced into Ireland. Their colonization, which began in 1169 and had its peak of territorial expansion c. 1250, led directly to a century of new-town building. B. Graham has recorded 174 boroughs for this period on the evidence of legally granted charters or burgage-land.[12] In the early thirteenth century, as a bait to settlers, Norman lords also granted charters to rural settlements, which never developed proper urban functions. These have been called 'rural boroughs'.[13]

The second important phase of new-town building came with the plantations of the sixteenth and seventeenth century, which were preceded by the reconquest of Ireland. These towns were primarily intended to be centres of anglicization and to act as an insurance against future rebellions

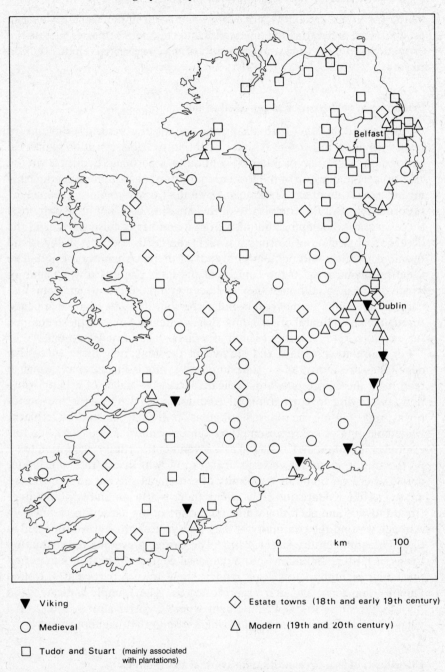

Fig. 2. *Origins of Irish towns with more than 1,500 inhabitants in 1971.* Source: *after F. H. A. Aalen,* Man and the Landscape in Ireland *(London, 1978)*

by the Irish.[14] In the eighteenth century landlords initiated the building of estate towns; and during the nineteenth and twentieth centuries we find the formation of new towns as a result of an increasingly industrialized society.[15]

Principles of cartographical representation

As illustrated by the Irish example, one of the central problems of town-formation in Europe is that of continuity. How can it be expressed cartographically? The problem of continuity is particularly difficult in the case of Ireland because of the formation of its urban system in an ethnically mixed area. A number of Irish towns owe their origin to more than one act of formation. But the complexity of the situation does not arise only from successive new beginnings but also from a number of false starts, and the desertion or decline of Norman towns in the north and west of the island owing to political and population trends in the late medieval period. The same problems arise in the context of the later planned towns, some of which diminished, although they had been granted full borough status and corporation rights in the Tudor–Stuart period. This may have happened through environmental or economic disadvantages. Some of these failures, for example, Gorey, were rescued at a later stage of development.[16]

For those towns which did survive in the long run, these successive beginnings are indicated by superimposed symbols on the map, which if read from the centre outwards indicate successive stages of urban forma-tion. According to cartographical tradition, the symbols for the proto-towns, representing the oldest settlement on the map, are shown in black, while later phases are represented by lighter symbols. Let us look at a few examples: Londonderry is shown as a seventeenth-century plantation town on the site of an earlier ecclesiastical proto-town. In contrast to London-derry, where we find only continuity of settlement site but no more, there are towns like Kildare and Kells where there is also continuity of buildings (round towers and enclosing walls) on the site of the earlier proto-town. In Armagh we find the continuity of the ecclesiastical proto-town reflected in the eighteenth-century street-plan.[17] The castles preceding the plantation towns of Ulster, and likewise the manorial centres of the Norman period preceding plantation towns or modern new towns (particularly around Dublin), must not be seen as proto-towns. They simply indicate valid reasons for siting the new settlement where a castle already stood or a village had grown up, and not anywhere else in the neighbourhood.[18]

Classification as a precondition for comparative studies

The problem of mapping urban origins is one of the great challenges for

German historians working in the field of urban history. There is a healthy respect for the complexity of the problem involved, for, in the words of E. Ennen: 'the first principle of historical-geographical mapping must be to make sure that a symbol on the map corresponds exactly to the different examples on the ground'.[19] In spite of the formidable task the historic atlases of the different counties in the Federal Republic of Germany include maps of the medieval urban system using different symbols for the different phases of town-formation.[20] The existence of these regional historical atlases is in itself an interesting phenomenon insofar as they show the effort of federal states to establish their own regional identity.

C. Haase and H. Stoob have discussed the methodological problems involved in mapping town-foundations.[21] They found that the best method of showing the accumulative growth of the urban system was to produce a number of distribution maps of town-foundations at formative periods. It is also possible to produce a composite map which shows for a particular region the date of origin for all towns by using different symbols for the different time periods. H. Stoob has mapped the formation of towns in Central Europe to A.D. 1250, on a scale 1:8 million, with approximately 1,500 entries.[22] He seems to have been the first to emphasize the importance of establishing historically meaningful periods for the forma-tion of towns rather than mapping their distribution century by century. According to Stoob, the period until A.D. 1150 marks the time when in Central Europe the phenomenon 'town' begins to crystallize. The period from 1150 to 1250 is taken as the time when the established old town was used as the model for a great number of newly planned towns. The period that followed until 1450 is that of the origin of small towns (*Kleinstädte*) and even smaller towns (*Minderstädte*). The period 1450–1800 is marked by an absence of new-town foundations, except for mining-towns, residen-tial towns of territorial lords and those built by religious refugees. After 1800 begins the important new phase of town-formation as a result of industrialization.

It is immediately obvious that the formative periods of town-formation in Ireland only coincide with those of Central Europe during the medieval period, when the colonization of the Vikings and the Normans linked Ireland culturally and economically to the continent. During later stages the development of Ireland's urban system was greatly influenced by Ireland's status as a colony.

A special edition of the *Deutsche Städte Atlas*, edited by H. Stoob, is in preparation with distribution maps for different aspects of urban history, including maps of urban origins and the expansion of existing towns at formative periods, as well as distribution maps of deserted towns at different periods.[23] Once these maps are published they will probably provide a helpful cartographical guideline.

All the continental examples discussed so far show successive phases of town-formation either by separate symbols on one map or on a number of different maps. The problem of trying to show the roots of early town-formation on one map was tackled by D. Denecke in his study of the origins of towns in Lower Saxony, many of which developed from an earlier village nucleus.[24] He mapped the development from the pre-urban state to the urban by using a combination of symbols which represent a generic sequence. Different pre-urban starters are identified, as for instance monasteries, bishop-seats, castles, fortified farmhouses, merchant settlements, mining settlements and foundries.

The example of urban origins in the area east of the Elbe is of particular interest in the Irish context, because it is also an area of mixed ethnic composition, where both German and Slav influences are of importance. The possible pitfalls of this situation become evident from a map compiled by W. Kuhn for Westermann's *Grosser Atlas zur Weltgeschichte*.[25] This map carries the title (in translation): 'German towns and towns founded on German town-law in the East'. On it the same symbol is used for both types of towns, and a false impression is created of the medieval expansion of German presence throughout the area. In no way is there any indication that a large number of these towns were built on sites of pre-existing Slavic strongholds or ecclesiastical settlements with proto-urban functions.[26]

The *Grosser Historischer Weltatlas*, published in Bavaria, avoids such a simplistic and therefore misleading presentation of the topic.[27] On two opposite pages we find maps, compiled by W. Schlessinger, showing the extent of West Slavic settlements *before* the medieval colonization of East Germany and the same territories *after* the German settlement. By using this method of facing pages the reader will understand that Lübeck, for example, is a German town from the twelfth century, located on the site of an earlier Slavic stronghold. Cracow is shown as a town laid out according to German town-law and containing a high proportion of German population until about A.D. 1400, and founded on the site of an earlier Slavic stronghold and Slavic ecclesiastical settlement.

The *Atlas zur Geschichte*, published in East Germany, includes a map on the origin and spread of towns in Central Europe.[28] This map is based on the terminological distinction between Slavic proto-urban settlements and later phases of town-formation. Successive beginnings are shown by placing symbols next to each other, a solution which is cartographically not very successful. For example, there are two little squares at Lübeck, one referring to the Slavic, the other to the German period, and the same for Cracow.

The last example is taken from a report by J. Herrmann on archaeological excavations in city-centres in East Germany.[29] It includes a map showing early stages of town-formations (Fig. 3). Towns are defined by

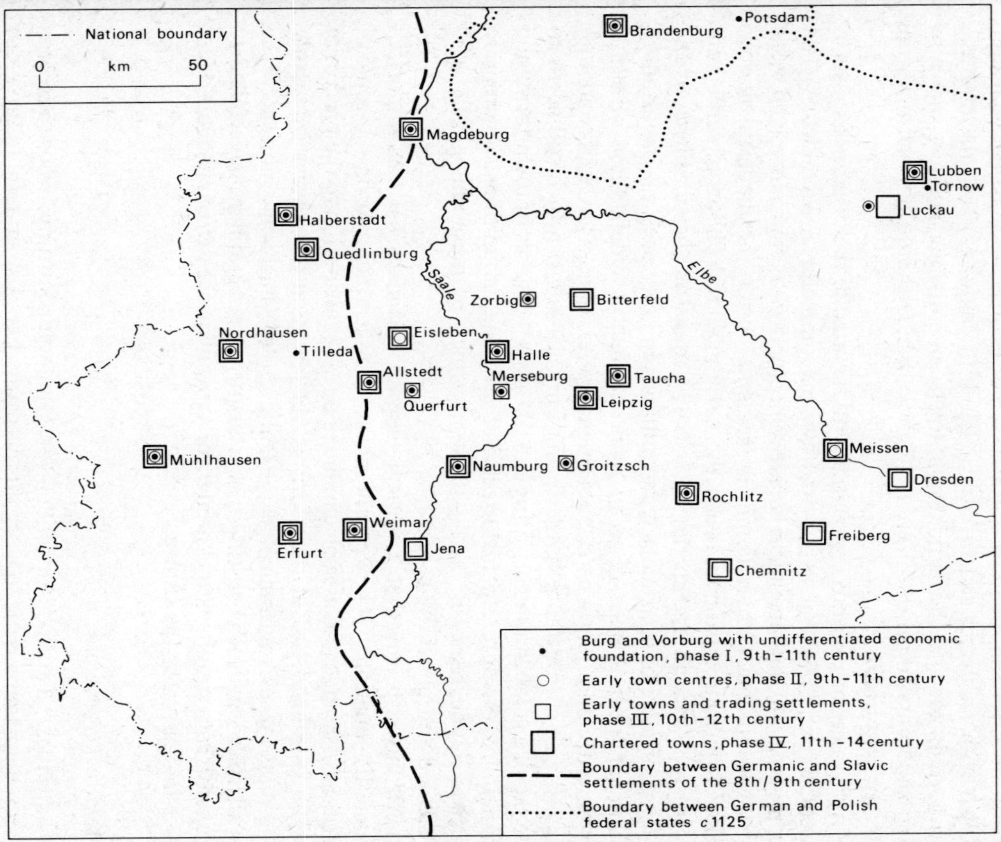
National boundary
0
km
50
Brandenburg
Potsdam
Magdeburg
Lubben
Tornow
Luckau
Halberstadt
Quedlinburg
Saale
Elbe
Zorbig
Bitterfeld
Nordhausen
Tilleda
Eisleben
Halle
Allstedt
Merseburg
Taucha
Querfurt
Leipzig
Mühlhausen
Naumburg
Groitzsch
Meissen
Dresden
Rochlitz
Weimar
Erfurt
Jena
Freiberg
Chemnitz
Burg and Vorburg with undifferentiated economic foundation, phase I, 9th–11th century
Early town centres, phase II, 9th–11th century
Early towns and trading settlements, phase III, 10th–12th century
Chartered towns, phase IV, 11th–14century
Boundary between Germanic and Slavic settlements of the 8th/9th century
Boundary between German and Polish federal states c1125

Fig. 3. *Origins of towns which have been archaeologically investigated in the German Democratic Republic.* Source: *after J. Hermann, 'Research into the Early History in the Territory of the German Democratic Republic' in M. W. Barley (ed.)*, European Towns: Their Archaeology and Early History *(London, 1977)*

implication as non-agrarian settlement centres. Four phases are distinguished in their development: (1) beginnings of non-agrarian centres in both Germanic and Slavic areas with non-specialized craftsmen (9th–11th centuries); (2) evolution of early urban centres with market charters and beginning of trade (9th–11th centuries); (3) beginnings of burgher-towns with merchants (10th–12th centuries); and (4) transition to the chartered town with an urban constitution (11th–13th centuries). On the map the important stages in the formation of towns on individual sites are shown by the superimposition of different symbols, which should be read from the centre outwards.

This map corresponds conceptually to the map of the origins of towns in Ireland (Fig. 1), yet the two were drawn up completely independently. The point is that in both instances we are concerned with ethnically mixed areas strongly influenced by colonial movements during the medieval period. Therefore comparisons between the early medieval phases of settlement history in Ireland and in the West Slavic areas on the periphery of the Germanic core are particularly meaningful. In both cases it is important to evaluate the influence of socio-economic factors independent of ethnic factors. But in order to carry out any successful comparisons and communicate them – for instance in the form of maps – 'a task which still needs to be tackled is the gradual working-out of the early phases of town-formation depending on different historical and economic conditions, in order to arrive by degrees, at a classification which is methodologically well founded and generally acceptable'.[30]

All this is to say that historical-geographical maps have an important semiotic function.[31] They communicate complex material on the topic of historical change and as such can make a real contribution to the process of rethinking history. But there are as yet few, and not always successful, attempts at cartographical representation of diachronic analysis. The criticism seems to be justified, that historical geographers have failed to develop cartographical techniques for showing processes of change.[32] Here is a challenge for the future.

Acknowledgements

I am indebted to the Alexander-von-Humboldt Stiftung, whose research fellowship enabled me to work on this essay. I am also grateful to Professor K. Fehn for granting me hospitality at the 'Seminar für Historische Geographie der Universität Bonn' and to Dr von der Dollen of the same Institute for his valuable discussion of my work.

APPENDIX I

Examples of source-material for the two Gaelic proto-towns of Armagh and Cavan (compiled by Katharine Simms, Institute for Advanced Studies, Dublin).

Name of Town: *Armagh*
Classification of origin: Gaelic-ecclesiastical proto-town with continuous occupation; Tudor–Stuart plantation borough

Suggested symbol:

Documentary or archaeological evidence: A.D. 870 house of the High King in Armagh mentioned (*Annals of Ulster*)
References to the 'streets' and thirds of Armagh (*Annals of the Four Masters* and *Annals of Ulster*, 1092, 1112, 1116, 1121, 1166)
Agreement between Archbishop John Mey and the citizens of Armagh in 1444 (P.R.O.N.I., Register of Archbishop Prene, Lib. 1, fo. 4)
Mention in 1587 of the following order: 'Her Majesty orders that . . . (a) . . . market shall be for ever held for her and her successors at Ardmagh on every Tuesday' (Cal. Pat. Rolls, Eliz., p. 123)
James I Town Charter (Cal. Pat. Rolls, James I, p. 255)
Any other comments: unlike the other Gaelic-ecclesiastical towns, which either became absorbed in Anglo-Norman boroughs (e.g. Kildare) or withered away (e.g. Clonmacnoise and Lismore) Armagh and Londonderry appear to have experienced some kind of continuous occupation under ecclesiastical jurisdiction throughout the Middle Ages.

Name of Town: *Cavan*
Classification of origin: Fifteenth-century Irish market town; Tudor–Stuart plantation borough

Suggested symbol:

Documentary or archaeological evidence: site of Franciscan friary founded by Giolla Íosa Ruadh O Reilly, king of Breifne (+ 1330) (A. Gwynn and R. N. Hadcock, *Medieval Religious Houses: Ireland* (London, 1970)
The O Reilly castle of Tulach Mongáin in vicinity said to have been built by Toirdhealbhach son of Seaán O Reilly, chief 1467–87 (J. Carney, *A Genealogical History of the O Reillys*, p. 12)
1468: O Reilly's residence ('baile') and the monastery of Cavan were burnt by Tiptoft, Earl of Worcester (*Annals of Ulster, sub anno*)
1479–80: Roll of the proceedings of the Irish Parliament, 19 & 20 Edward IV,

Complaint of the Anglo-Irish townsmen of Meath against 'divers markets' recently instituted by the Irish at Cavan, Granard and Longford 'in O Railly's country and in Offerrolls country' (*Statutes*, Edward IV, part II, ed. Morrissey, pp. 819–21)
1558: Charter of Maolmhordha O Reilly, prince of Breifne, granting an unoccupied street between the Market Cross and the highway leading into the north of the town to Bernard MacBrady, a merchant of Navan, in return for paving a street in the town of Cavan (Nat. Lib. Ireland MS D 10023, ed. G. MacNiocaill, Breifne I, no. 2, 1959, pp. 134–6)
1585: 'Dewties and Customs' of Breifne claimed by Sir Shane O Reilly included 'The dewties of the towne of Cavan also by the said custom, as rents, drink, and other dewties, now taken and not denied' (Lambeth Palace Lib. Carew MS 614, p. 162, printed by O Donovan, *Annals of the Four Masters*, V, 1806)
1607: Sir John Davies's letter to the Earl of Salisbury: 'We came the third day to Cavan, and pitched our tents on the south side of this poor Irish town' (H. Morley, *Ireland under Elizabeth and James I*, p. 374)
James I Town Charter (Cal. Pat. Rolls, James I, p. 180)

APPENDIX II

Selected sources for the compilation of the map: 'Origins of Principal Towns in Ireland' (Fig. 1)

R. A. Butlin, 'Irish Towns in the Sixteenth and Seventeenth Century' in R. A. Butlin (ed.), *The Development of the Irish Towns* (London, 1977)
G. Camblin, *The Town in Ulster* (Belfast, 1951)
J. T. Gilbert (ed.), *Historic and Municipal Documents of Ireland* (Dublin, 1870)
B. J. Graham, 'The Towns of Medieval Ireland' in R. A. Butlin (ed.), *Development of the Irish Towns* (London, 1977)
W. M. Hennessey and B. MacCarthy (eds.), *Annála Uladh, Annals of Ulster*, 4 vols. (Dublin, 1887–1901)
S. Lewis (ed.), *A Topographical Dictionary of Ireland*, 2 vols. and atlas (London, 1837)
G. MacNiocaill, *Na Búirgéisí*, 2 vols. (Dublin, 1964)
J. O Donovan (ed.), *Annála rioghachta Eireann, Annals of the Kingdom of Ireland by the Four Masters from the earliest period to the year 1616* (Dublin, 1851)
G. H. Orpen, *Ireland under the Normans, 1169–1333*, 4 vols. (Oxford, 1911–20)
A. J. Otway-Ruthven, *A History of Medieval Ireland* (London, 1968)

University College, Dublin,
Eire

A note on some documentary sources available for studying the historical geography of Japan

T. TANIOKA

Literary sources

Many documentary sources exist for studying the historical geography of Japan. While they have been used mainly by historians, Japanese historical geographers have also come to appreciate their usefulness. The oldest topographies (*Fudoki*) were produced by local administrations governed by the Emperor Genmyo in A.D. 713 and these survive for several provinces: Izumo province in the San-in region, Hitachi in Kwantô, Harima in Kinki, Bungo and Hizen in Kyûshû. Each *Fudoki* contains much of interest about physical geography, the history of place-names and the economy of the province concerned, so that they may be used as a basis for the reconstruction of the historical geography of the province. During the late-feudal age, detailed topographies were also compiled for the lords of the 66 provinces and two islands.

A collection of some 4,500 poems (*Manyo-shû*) compiled during the second half of the eighth century may be used with circumspection to reconstruct landscapes of the period. Similar anthologies are also available for the tenth to thirteenth centuries.

Detailed descriptions of land and water routes yield information not only about the routes themselves but also about the settlements along them. For example, the land and water route connecting the capital Heiankyo to the provincial Kokufu of Tosa in the Shikoku region may be traced in the travel diary *Tosa-nikki* which was compiled by the governor Kii between December 934 and February 935, and the Tôkaidô route linking the capital to the Kwanto region may be studied in the travelogue *Sarashina-nikki* which was written by a woman in about 1060.

Old encyclopaedias are also good sources on which to base reconstructions of ancient, mainly rural landscapes. The most famous is *Wamyo-shô* which was edited in the 930s and whose twenty volumes describe the communes or *Go* in each county and province.

Similarly, old statute books may be used to reconstruct patterns of ancient settlements: one such is the *Engi-shiki*, compiled between 905 and 927, which contains a volume describing 2,861 Shinto shrines and 3,132 gods. The oldest known census registers surviving are those made in 702 for nine villages, but during the late-feudal age every village and town compiled a census register and a geographical survey-book, constituting very valuable sources for studying Japan's historical geography.

Cartographic sources

Not only literary but also cartographic sources deserve attention. Some cadastral plans may have been made during the seventh century but have not survived. The oldest plans extant are of paddy fields on some manors of Tôdai-ji Buddhist temple and other temples in the mid-eighth century. Some aspects of the economic geography of certain provinces may be reconstructed from early taxation records which include maps and plans. Some aspects of spatial organization may be discovered in the twelfth-century cadastres (*Kenchû-châ*) and in sixteenth-century cadastres (*Kenchi-chô*).

Few small-scale maps exist of early Japan. There is only one general map of ancient Japan, which is said to be the work of a Buddhist priest during the seventh or eighth century. Some sixteenth-century maps imitate this one stylistically but in doing so restrict their use for historico-geographical studies. A map of each province (*Kuni-ezu*) was compiled during the seventeenth to nineteenth centuries, and portrays the names of all of the existing villages and towns, as well as some of the characteristics of a region's physical geography.

Other maps include route maps; a collection completed in 1821 of a series of about 300 maps carefully produced at scales of between 1:36,000 and 1:432,000 by the famous cartographer Tadataka; old town plans; and manorial plans and maps, the oldest of which dates from the eighth century.

The literary and cartographic sources available for studying the historical geography of Japan are voluminous and rich in information. They need to be much more thoroughly analysed for the light which they can throw upon historical changes in spatial organization.

University of Ritsumeikan,
Kyoto, Japan

Field evidence in historical geography: a negative sample?

A source critical study of an area with fossil forms in Östergötland, Sweden

M. WIDGREN

With a written history dating only from the beginning of the second millenium A.D., field evidence in the Scandinavian countries has played a vital role in describing and analysing settlement history. Abandoned settlements and fields have been studied by archaeologists and geographers. However, discussion of the sources – to what extent they provide a fair representation of the actual settlement forms and patterns – has only been dealt with indirectly. In his book *Fields in the English Landscape* Christopher Taylor described the problem in these terms:

the fields that remain for us to study have survived only because they lay on land which later people did not use intensively. Other and perhaps very different fields elsewhere have been totally destroyed by later activity and thus we have no evidence of them. . . . Therefore the fields that remain for us to study may not be representative, and by studying them we may produce only a distorted picture of what prehistoric fields actually looked like. We cannot solve this problem, but we must not forget that it exists.[1]

This paper investigates further the nature of this problem. It does not seek to provide the definitive answer to it.

Settlement desertion

Deserted settlements in marginal areas

From a source-critical point of view, deserted settlements and fields in marginal uplands pose different problems from those found in a living agrarian landscape. The expansion of settlement into marginal areas has been documented for many regions in Scandinavia, and two major periods can be established from the field evidence: A.D. 200–500 and A.D. 1000–1400. This expansion has been explained either in terms of popula-

303

tion increase, where the upland farms acted as a 'safety valve under pressure of population',[2] or as the spatial expression of a redistributive chiefdom structure which favoured the use of resources from wide areas.[3] The coincidence between settlement expansion and favourable climatic conditions has also been noted,[4] and thus deserted settlements and fields in marginal areas have been seen as an expression of demographic, social and climatological conditions. However, only indirectly can conclusions be drawn about settlement forms and farming systems in the lowland from the evidence of these marginal farms. The fact that marginal farms are so undisturbed by later activities – easy to record and investigate – might, however unconsciously, have distorted the scholarly image of a farm of this period.

Deserted settlements within a living agrarian landscape

Owing to general population movements or the more random process of desertion and new establishment almost all living agrarian landscapes contain a certain number of deserted settlements. In the past the desertion process, as well as the village layout before the desertion, can sometimes be discovered from documents and maps, thus allowing a full source-critical evaluation of the field evidence.[5] But the evaluation of the prehistoric evidence is more difficult. On the islands of Öland and Götland, in the Swedish province of Östergötland, and in the south-western parts of Norway an abundance of deserted farms and fields, dating from the period A.D. 0 to 500, can be found. The traces of this prehistoric landscape are found in the pasture land of present-day farms and form an underlying network of stone walls and settlement wholly unrelated to the contemporary landscape. When discussing the structure and density of this landscape analysis is needed not only of the remains themselves but also of their relation to the present farms, and of the processes which have changed and restructured the source material.

Source-critical studies dealing with prehistoric material have generally limited themselves to questions concerning the accuracy of representative artefacts – not of features in the landscape. Michael B. Schiffer has suggested an approach with wider application.[6] He stresses the importance of studying the processes in which material objects and structures are transformed from a behavioural state into the archaeological record, and the processes which transform the record. In a contemporary agrarian landscape all these processes are operating simultaneously. Settlements and fields are abandoned, new structures are erected and land reclaimed for cultivation. A full analysis of these processes would require continuous monitoring of the area from the abandonment of the farms to the present day, and the construction of a series of cross-sectional views. An understanding of the oldest cross-sections can only be gained through knowledge of the intervening processes.

Roman Iron Age sites in Östergötland

The area chosen for this study is the Skärkind sheet of the 1:10,000 map covering twenty-five square kilometres. Changes in the landscape which occurred after the abandonment of some of the farms in the sixth century are considered in order to evaluate the degree of accuracy of representation of the archaeological landscape. Four temporal cross-sections, together with a simplified soil map of the area, comprise the main materials of the study. All five maps have been stored on magnetic tape in the form of a matrix, where each cell of one hectare carries information about land use during the period.

In physical terms, the landscape is dominated by plains of clay deposits which cover approximately 6 per cent of the area. Till elevations of one to thirty hectares in area have accumulated around small patches of exposed bedrock, and some 35 per cent of the area is covered with such till. These elevations have always been attractive settlement sites because of their good drainage. The source for this cross-section is the geological map of the area to a scale of 1:50,000. A number of sources are available for the reconstruction of the agricultural geography of the region.

The landscape of A.D. 0 to 500

The remains of the agrarian landscape from the Roman Iron Age provides the basis for this map (Fig. 1). Field surveys in the area resulted in the discovery of two dwelling sites, bringing the total number of known settlements from that period to four. The traces of agricultural activity also included vast systems of stone walls – unrelated to the known historical landscape, but associated instead with the deserted Iron Age farmsteads of the prehistoric period. Altogether about twenty kilometres of prehistoric stone walls were found. Judging by these remains the landscape was characterized by single farmsteads linked together by systems of stone walls forming barriers against the unimproved land.[7]

Landscapes of the eighteenth, nineteenth and twentieth centuries

Cadastral maps from the period 1696 to 1769 allow a reconstruction of settlement and land use in the eighteenth century. Within the area there were ten vills (with two to five farms each) and five single farms – altogether 35 farms; 422 hectares of land were under the plough in a two-course rotation. The names of twelve settlements suggest a prehistoric

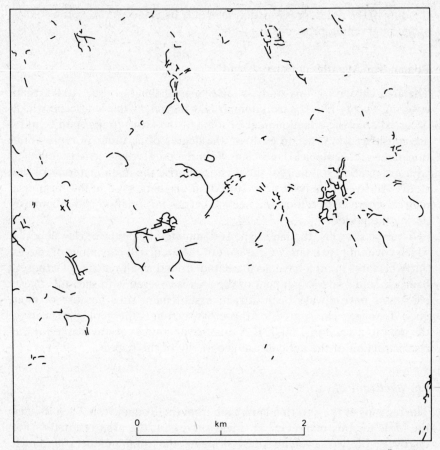

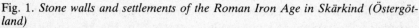

Fig. 1. *Stone walls and settlements of the Roman Iron Age in Skärkind (Östergöt-land)*

date (-*stad*, -*by* and others), while three single farms bear names of later origin (-*torp*) indicating an origin in the period A.D. 900–1200 (Fig. 2).

An economic map of the area in 1877 demonstrates that the *laga skifte* enclosure movement was of minor significance in this area. Only five of the 35 farms moved to new sites. But a considerable proportion of earlier meadow land was converted into cultivated fields.

A similar map of 1950 suggests that in comparison with the eighteenth century 800 hectares had been reclaimed for cultivation. These consisted chiefly of clay soils. The total number of settlements within the area decreased when compared with 1877 and only a few new settlements were established.

The four farms from the Roman Iron Age can be regarded as a sample

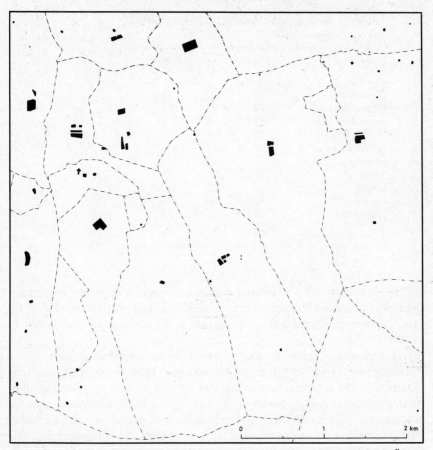

Fig. 2. *Eighteenth-century settlement and property boundaries in Skärkind (Öster-götland)*

drawn from the contemporary landscape, but the sampling process itself is clearly out of the researchers' control. We do not know if the sample is biased and we do not know how large the whole population was. One hypothesis is that the abandoned farms represent a secondary colonization from the main prehistoric settlement: the twelve settlements with prehistoric names, which still existed in the eighteenth century. The abandoned farms should then be seen as marginal farms within a non-marginal area, settled only during periods of expansion in the landscape. It follows that all conclusions about the general character of the agrarian landscape in the Roman Iron Age would therefore be biased. According to this hypothesis the abandoned farms were established later and on poorer soils. A pronounced difference in soils between the hamlets with prehistoric names and the deserted farms would support this assumption.

Table 1. *Soils around hamlets with prehistoric names*

Hamlet	Clay %	Till %	Bedrock %
Hässelstad	68	20	10
Lunnebjörke	61	35	2
Hestad	69	26	4
Ö. Alvestad	79	9	10
N. Alvestad	65	27	6
Kvästad	71	17	10
Viggeby	67	21	10
Backa	73	26	0
Hagelstad	63	36	0
Kätterstad	75	21	2
Total percentage	70	24	6

To test the hypothesis the soils within a radius of 500 metres around ten hamlets of prehistoric origin were investigated. The proportion of clay, till and exposed bedrock within the hypothetical farming area is shown in Table 1.

According to Table 2, the deserted farms enjoyed proportions of different soil-types within their boundaries. Thus no difference in the location of the deserted farmsteads can be seen in relation to the hamlets with prehistoric names. No support can be given to the hypothesis that the deserted farms are secondary to the hamlets with prehistoric names; rather the results imply that the area contains an abundance of possible dwelling sites, with the same prerequisites for farmstead location. Three farms from the Viking period or early Middle Ages also display the same distribution of soils within a 500 metre radius, and the variation between farms of different dates is slight. All the farmsteads incorporated between 58 and 79 per cent of clay land within their theoretical farming area.

Possible settlement sites

The number of possible dwelling sites within the area is not, however, infinite. The requirements for good drainage restrict the possible settlement area to the till or areas with a thin layer of soil upon bedrock – classified in the geological map as bedrock. Only 1,000 hectares of land out of 2,500 meet these requirements. Figure 3 shows the area of potential settlement according to this criterion.

The location of farms in relation to soils suitable for farmland further reduces the number of possible locations. Data on suitable combinations of

Table 2. *Soils around deserted farmsteads*

Farmstead	Clay %	Till %	Bedrock %
Dövestad	58	39	1
Augustenhill	69	27	2
Kopparslagarbacken	76	17	5
Kvästad Mellangård	64	24	10
Total percentage	67	27	5

soils can be gathered from the empirical observations in Tables 1 and 2. A sorting process was carried out with the help of a computer and only sites within reach of an appropriate combination of soils according to the results in Tables 1 and 2 were accepted. This search procedure produced a drastic reduction in the number of sites suitable for agrarian settlement (Fig. 3). The woodland in the south-east, together with many other parts of the area, was excluded from the potential settlement area because of its high proportion of till and bedrock. Of the original 1,000 hectares of land only 385 then remained. When sites less than three hectares in size were excluded 43 remained to be considered.

Settlement history of the sites

These sites will be examined in order to discover possible sites for farmsteads during the period A.D. 0 to 500. The analysis combines field observation and evidence from early maps. The possible settlement history of each potential site is evaluated on the evidence available. Fourteen sites showed no traces whatever of agrarian settlement, either in prehistoric or historical times. Only one of the farmsteads from the Roman Iron Age showed no trace of later occupation. Analysis of other settlement sites allowed identification of factors distorting the source material. One possible site is covered with graves from the period A.D. 600–1000. The destruction of an Iron Age cattle path by later graves is documented in the vicinity, and the discovery of Roman Iron Age settlement under later pagan burial grounds is a phenomenon well known to archaeologists in the area. The destruction of source material is thus already in evidence by the first century after the abandonment of the farms.

The gradual development around the hamlets with prehistoric names has probably eroded all trace of earlier structures. In early medieval times a period of inner colonization can be deduced from place-names, since the single farms with *-torp* names often have their boundaries described within the areas of earlier farms. Four such farms were established during the period. In one case the connection between the location of a *-torp* farm and

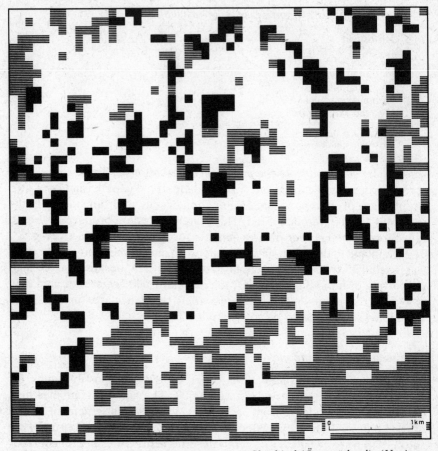

Fig. 3. *Theoretically possible settlement areas in Skärkind (Östergötland). (Horizontal shading indicates areas with till and bedrock; black shading indicates areas with till or bedrock within reach of an appropriate combination of farmland)*

remains of stone walls from an Iron Age farm is very evident. Two more might well have been built on earlier dwelling sites, while one farm from this period is located on the outlying land of the prehistoric settlement and was not responsible for the destruction of any earlier structures.

Similar settlement changes can be seen during the nineteenth century as a consequence of the *laga skifte* enclosure movement. Two of these farms were evidently located on Iron Age sites, but the earlier structures were preserved despite later occupation. For two other *laga skifte* farms a location on an earlier site is possible. Five settlements of recent origin have been located on what were potentially earlier dwelling sites.

The 43 possible sites are arranged chronologically in Table 3 according to their latest settlement or other earth works at the site.

Table 3. *Documented activities on the 43 sites*

Latest evidence of settlement	Number of sites	Roman Iron Age	Possible Roman Iron Age
No traces of agrarian settlement	14	–	–
Roman Iron Age farm	1	1	–
Burial ground A.D. 600–1000	1	–	1
Hamlets with prehistoric names	13	1	12
Farms with *-torp* names	4	–	3
Laga skifte farms	4	2	2
Other late settlement	5	–	5
Field survey impossible because of vegetation	1	–	1
Total	43	4	24

Conclusion

The analysis shows that two-thirds of the theoretically possible settlement sites were occupied during the different periods. In most cases the latest phases of occupation have altered the site to such an extent that the earlier history of the site cannot be interpreted from field observation. It is very probable that the establishment of new farms in the area has been encouraged both by the clearing of till from boulders, and by land reclamation carried out around earlier farm sites. A large proportion of the later establishments were thus located on Roman Iron Age sites. The total number of sites from that period is definitively more than four but less than 28. The analysis of soils around the four abandoned farms does not support the theory that they were marginal daughter settlements. They could thus be considered to constitute a small, but probably random sample of the past rural landscape.

University of Stockholm,
Sweden

Notes to the text

Notes to Ben-Arieh, 'Israel', pp. 3–9

1 G. A. Smith, *Historical Geography of the Holy Land* (London, 1894).
2 A. P. Stanley, *Sinai and Palestine in Connection with their History* (London, 1856).
3 E. Huntington, *Palestine and its transformation: Climate and Civilization* (London, 1915).
4 M. Avi-Yonah, *The Holy Land from the Persian to the Arab Conquests (536 B.C. to A.D. 640): A Historical Geography* (Jerusalem, 1951).
5 Y. Aharoni, *The Land of the Bible: A Historical Geography* (Philadelphia, 1967); Z. Kalai, *The Tribes of Israel, A Study in the Historical Geography of the Bible* (Jerusalem, 1967).
6 I. Schattner, *The History of the Map of Eretz-Israel* (Jerusalem, 1951).
7 D. H. K. Amiran, 'Development of Topographic Maps of Palestine', *Bulletin, Palestine Exploration Society* (1941), pp. 33–8; 'Jacotin's Map of Palestine', *Palestine Exploration Quarterly* (1944), pp. 157–63; 'Topographic Maps of Palestine from World War I', *Eretz-Israel Yearbook* (1953), pp. 33–40.
8 Y. Karmon, 'An Analysis of Jacotin's Map of Palestine', *Israel Exploration Journal* (1960), pp. 153–73; 244–53.
9 Y. Kedar, *The Ancient Agriculture in the Negev Mountains* (Jerusalem, 1967); and many other articles.
10 Y. Ben-Arieh, 'Pits and Caves in the Shephelah of Israel compared with Similar Pits in East Anglia', *Geography: Journal of Geographical Association* (1969), pp. 186–92.
11 M. Har-El, 'The Roman Road at Ma'aleh-Aqrabim', *Israel Exploration Journal* (1959), pp. 175–9; 'The Exodus Route in the Light of Historical-Geographic Research', *Geography in Israel* (1976), pp. 373–96; 'The Route of the Salt, Sugar and Balsam Caravans in the Judean Desert', *Geojournal* (1978).
12 Z. Ron, 'Agricultural Terraces in the Judean Mountains', *Israel Exploration Journal* (1966), pp. 33–49; 111–22.
13 S. Avitzur, *On the History of the Exploitation of Water Power in Eretz-Israel* (Tel-Aviv, 1960); *idem, Man and His Work: Historical Atlas of Tools and Workshops in the Holy Land* (Jerusalem, 1976).

14 D. H. K. Amiran, 'A Revised Earthquake-catalogue of Palestine', *Israel Exploration Journal* (1951), pp. 223–46; (1952), pp. 48–65.
15 S. Stern, 'The Development of the Urban Pattern of Haifa in the Years 1918–1947', Ph.D. dissertation, Hebrew University of Jerusalem, 1974.
16 Y. Ben-Arieh, 'A Geographical Approach to Historical Geography', *Studies in the Geography of Israel* (1970), pp. 138–60; 'Eretz-Israel as a Subject for Historical-Geography Study', *Social Research Review* (Haifa, 1974), pp. 5–26.
17 Y. Ben-Arieh, *The Rediscovery of the Holy Land in the Nineteenth Century* (Jerusalem, 1979); *A City Reflected in its Times: Jerusalem in the Nineteenth Century*, pt I: *The Old City* (Jerusalem, 1977); pt II: *The New City* (Jerusalem, 1979).
18 Ruth Kark, 'The Development of the Cities of Jerusalem and Jaffa, 1840–1914', Ph.D. dissertation, Hebrew University of Jerusalem, 1976; 'Jerusalem and Jaffa in the Nineteenth Century as an example of Traditional Near-East Cities', *Studies in the Geography of Israel* (Jerusalem, 1978), pp. 25–95. R. Reichav, 'Living and Dwelling Conditions in the Christian Monasteries in Wadi Qelt in the Judean Desert', M.A. dissertation, Hebrew University of Jerusalem, 1979.
19 Y. Ben-Arieh, *Jerusalem as a Religious City*, Discussion Paper No. 21, Department of Geography, York University (Toronto, 1978). S. Reichman, *From Foothold to Settled Territory, Jewish Settlement, 1918–1948: A Geographical Interpretation and Documentation* (Jerusalem, 1979). A. Shachar, *Traditional Urbanization* (Harvard University Press, in press). A. Gonen, 'Urbanization of the "Moshavoth" (Colonies) in Israel', *Studies in the Geography of Israel* (1978), pp. 31–44.
20 J. R. Gibson (ed.), *European Settlement and Development in North America: Essays on geographical change in honour and memory of Andrew Hill Clark* (Toronto, 1978).
21 G. Biger, 'Geographical Analyses of the Influence of the British Administration on the Development of Palestine 1917/18–1929/30', Ph.D. dissertation, Hebrew University of Jerusalem, 1979; *idem, The Role of the British Administration in Changing the Geography of Palestine, 1918–1929*, Occasional Paper, No. 35, Department of Geography, University College (London, 1979). Ruth Kark, *The Pioneer Jewish Settlement in the Negev until 1948* (Tel Aviv, 1974). Hilah Tal, 'Reappraisal of the Planning and the Development of the City of Be'er-Sheva, 1900–1965', M.A. dissertation, Hebrew University of Jerusalem, 1978. R. Aaronsohn, 'The Establishment of Two of the First Jewish Colonies in Palestine, 1882–1883', M.A. dissertation, Hebrew University of Jerusalem, 1978. Y. Catz, 'The "Achusah" (Absent Landlord) Settlements in Eretz-Israel, 1908–1917', M.A. dissertation, Hebrew University of Jerusalem, 1979. S. Sapir, 'The Anglican Missions and their Contribution to the Development of Jerusalem, 1880–1914', M.A. dissertation, Hebrew University of Jerusalem, 1979. N. Telman, 'The Contribution of the Germans (Excluding the Templars) to the Development of Palestine in the Second Half of the 19th Century', M.A. dissertation, Hebrew University of Jerusalem, 1979. Z. Shilony, *Changes in the Geography of Jerusalem Resulting From the First World War Outcomes* (in preparation).

Notes to Butlin, 'Britain', pp. 10–16

1 D. W. Moodie and J. C. Lehr, 'Fact and Theory in Historical Geography', *The Professional Geographer*, vol. 28 (1976), pp. 132–5.

2 H. C. Prince, 'Real, Imagined and Abstract Worlds of the Past', *Progress in Geography*, vol. 3 (1971), pp. 1–86; A. R. H. Baker (ed.), *Progress in Historical Geography* (Newton Abbot, 1972); *idem*, 'Historical Geography', *Progress in Human Geography*, vol. 1 (1977), pp. 465–74; *idem*, 'Historical Geography: Understanding and Experiencing the Past', *Progress in Human Geography*, vol. 2 (1978), pp. 495–504.

3 Baker, *Progress in Historical Geography*.

4 A. R. H. Baker, J. Hamshere and J. Langton (eds.), *Geographical Interpretations of Historical Sources* (Newton Abbot, 1970), p. 9.

5 W. G. Hoskins, *The Making of the English Landscape* (London, 1955); see also D. W. Meinig, 'Reading the Landscape' in D. W. Meinig (ed.), *The Interpretation of Ordinary Landscapes* (Oxford, 1979), pp. 195–244.

6 M. P. Conzen, 'Historical Geography at the I.B.G.', *Historical Geography Newsletter*, vol. 3 (1973), p. 27.

7 T. R. B. Dicks, 'Network Analysis and Historical Geography', *Area*, vol. 4 (1972), pp. 4–9; J. Langton, 'Networks and Roman Roads. Comments', *Area*, vol. 4 (1972), pp. 279–80; B. P. Hindle, 'Networks and Roman Roads. Comments', *ibid.* pp. 137–8; W. Zelinsky, 'In Pursuit of Historical Geography and Other Wild Geese', *Historical Geography Newsletter*, vol. 3 (1973), pp. 1–5; A. R. H. Baker, 'In Pursuit of Wilbur Zelinsky and Other Hysterical Geographers', *Historical Geography Newsletter*, vol. 4 (1974), pp. 17–19; J. A. Jakle, 'In Pursuit of a Wild Goose: Historical Geography and the Geographical Past', *Historical Geography Newsletter*, vol. 4 (1974), pp. 13–16.

8 J. Piaget, *Structuralism* (London, 1971).

9 Prince, 'Real, Imagined and Abstract World of the Past'.

10 R. C. Harris, 'Theory and Synthesis in Historical Geography', *The Canadian Geographer*, vol. 15 (1971), pp. 157–72.

11 Yi-fu Tuan, 'Geography, Phenomenology and the Study of Human Nature', *The Canadian Geographer*, vol. 15 (1971), pp. 181–92; *idem*, 'Structuralism, Existentialism and Environmental Perception', *Environment and Behaviour*, vol. 3 (1972), pp. 319–31.

12 H. C. Darby (ed.), *A New Historical Geography of England and Wales* (Cambridge, 1973).

13 A. R. H. Baker and J. B. Harley (eds.), *Man Made the Land* (Newton Abbot, 1973).

14 A. R. H. Baker and R. A. Butlin (eds.), *Studies of Field Systems in the British Isles* (Cambridge, 1973).

15 P. J. Perry (ed.), *British Agriculture, 1875–1914* (London, 1973); *idem*, *British Farming in the Great Depression* (London, 1973).

16 D. C. North and R. P. Thomas, *The Rise of the Western World: a New Economic History* (Cambridge, 1973).

17 R. Floud (ed.), *Essays in Quantitative Economic History* (Oxford, 1974).

18 W. N. Parker and E. L. Jones (eds.), *European Peasants and their Markets* (Princeton, 1975).

19 I. Wallerstein, *The Rise of the World-Economy* (New York, 1974).
20 Yi-fu Tuan, *Topophilia: a Study of Environmental Perception, Attitudes and Values* (Englewood Cliffs, 1974).
21 Yi-fu Tuan, 'Space and Place: a Humanistic Perspective', *Progress in Geography*, vol. 6 (1974), pp. 212–52.
22 D. Gregory, 'New Towns for Old: Historical Geography at the I.B.G.', *Historical Geography Newsletter*, vol. 4 (1974), p. 27.
23 M. Billinge, 'The Other Neighbours', *Historical Geography Newsletter*, vol. 6 (1976), p. 16.
24 J. B. Harley, 'Change in Historical Geography: a Qualitative Impression of Quantitative Methods', *Area*, vol. 5 (1973), pp. 69–74.
25 C. Lévi-Strauss, *From Honey to Ashes* (London, 1973); *idem, Structural Anthropology*, vol. 2 (London, 1977); B. Hindess and P. Hirst, *Pre-Capitalist Modes of Production* (London, 1975); *idem, Modes of Production and Social Formation* (London, 1977).
26 Yi-fu Tuan, 'Humanistic Geography', *Annals, Association of American Geographers*, vol. 66 (1976), pp. 266–76.
27 A. R. H. Baker, *Historical Geography and Geographical Change* (London, 1975).
28 D. Gregory, 'Re-thinking Historical Geography', *Area*, vol. 8 (1976), pp. 289–94.
29 Anne Buttimer, 'Grasping the Dynamism of Lifeworld', *Annals, Association of American Geographers*, vol. 66 (1976), pp. 277–92.
30 M. Castells, *La Question urbaine* (2nd edn, Paris, 1976).
31 R. Williams, *The Country and the City* (London, 1976).
32 K. Warren, *The Geography of British Heavy Industry since 1800* (London, 1976).
33 R. E. Glasscock, *The Lay Subsidy of 1334* (London: The British Academy, 1976).
34 I. H. Adams, *Agrarian Landscape Terms: a Glossary for Historical Geography* (London: Institute of British Geographers, 1976).
35 J. D. Hamshere and M. J. Blakemore, 'Computerizing Domesday Book', *Area*, vol. 8 (1976), pp. 289–94.
36 R. Dennis, 'Distance and Social Interaction in a Victorian City', *Journal of Historical Geography*, vol. 3 (1977), pp. 237–50.
37 M. Billinge, 'In Search of Negativism: Phenomenology and Historical Geography', *Journal of Historical Geography*, vol. 3 (1977), pp. 55–67.
38 A. R. H. Baker, 'Rhetoric and Reality in Historical Geography', *Journal of Historical Geography*, vol. 3 (1977), pp. 301–5.
39 B. S. Osborne (ed.), *The Settlement of Canada: Origins and Transfer* (Kingston, Ontario, 1976).
40 D. Gregory, *Ideology, Science and Human Geography* (London, 1978).
41 E. P. Thompson, *Whigs and Hunters* (London, 1975); *idem, The Poverty of Theory* (London, 1978).
42 R. H. Hilton, *The English Peasantry in the Later Middle Ages* (Oxford, 1975); *idem* (ed.), *The Transition from Feudalism to Capitalism* (London, 1976).

43 A. Macfarlane, *Reconstructing Historical Communities* (Cambridge, 1977); *idem, The Origins of English Individualism* (Oxford, 1978).

44 G. Crossick (ed.), *The Lower Middle Class in Britain, 1870–1914* (London, 1977); J. Foster, *Class Struggle and the Industrial Revolution* (London, 1974); G. Stedman-Jones, 'Working-class Culture and Working-class Politics in London, 1870–1900', *Journal of Social History*, vol. 7 (1974), pp. 460–508; *idem*, 'Class Struggle and the Industrial Revolution', *New Left Review*, vol. 90 (1975), pp. 35–69.

45 J. Langton, 'The Pathway of Progress in Historical Geography', *Journal of Historical Geography*, vol. 5 (1979), pp. 79–82; H. C. Prince, 'About Half Marx for the Transition from Feudalism to Capitalism', *Area*, vol. 11 (1979), pp. 454–8.

46 R. A. Dodgshon and R. A. Butlin (eds.), *An Historical Geography of England and Wales* (London, 1978); H. S. A. Fox and R. A. Butlin (eds.), *Change in the Countryside* (London: Institute of British Geographers, 1979); R. J. Dennis (ed.), *The Victorian City, I.B.G. Transactions*, New Series, vol. 4 (1979).

Notes to Billinge, 'Reconstructing societies', pp. 19–32

1 Both parts of this discussion – the critique/conceptual outline and the more empirical illustrations – are highly condensed versions of the original, lengthy argument to be found elsewhere in Mark Billinge, *A Cultural Geography of Industrialisation* (London, forthcoming). The fuller version not only explores issues which cannot be dealt with here, but also avoids the rather bald emphasis and rigid proselytizing of the current, brief exegisis. Given the exploratory nature of this chapter, and the more subtle contours of the forthcoming book, it is not intended that these notes be heavily bibliographical, that the illustrations be comprehensive or that the details of source locations be routinely charted as they would be in a more substantive paper. Thus only major or pivotal works will be cited and only issues demanding immediate clarification explored.

2 The methodological debate within historical geography has, of course, been raging for some considerable time now, and is by no means at or approaching quiescence. Over and above a marked tendency to reject on some grounds or other almost every conceivable philosophical position, and to ignore, in substantive papers, the difficulties raised by methodological discussion, few lines of agreement seem to have emerged. The precise details of these serpentine weavings need not long detain us here. For up-to-date summaries of these and other developments (together with comprehensive bibliographies) see: A. R. H. Baker, 'The Limits of Inference' in B. S. Osborne (ed.), *The Settlement of Canada: Origins and Transfer* (Kingston, Ontario, 1976); *idem*, 'Historical Geography', *Progress in Human Geography*, vol. 1 (1977); *idem*, 'Understanding and Experiencing the Past', *Progress in Human Geography*, vol. 2 (1978); *idem*, 'Historical Geography: a New Beginning?', *Progress in Human Geography*, vol. 3 (1979); and R. A. Butlin in this volume.

3 A. Giddens, *Central Problems in Social Theory* (London, 1979). This book, which follows and extends the arguments of his earlier *New Rules of Sociological Method* (London, 1976), is the clearest, best written and most constructive

of accounts of the problems facing those seeking to 'cut into' and expose the fabric of social life. Not least useful is Giddens's lengthy discussion of functionalist and Marxist sociology – the assumptions, methods and shortcomings of both. See *Central Problems*, pp. 49–95.

4 This tradition is a long and vigorous one. Adequately referencing its historiography is a gigantic and self-defeating task, but for recent examples of the genre see the papers by J. W. R. Whitehand; C. G. Pooley; M. Shaw and R. J. Dennis in J. W. R. Whitehand and J. H. C. Patten (eds.), *Change in the Town* (London: Institute of British Geographers, 1977). It cannot be stressed too strongly that these remarks refer only to work on British cities undertaken by British historical geographers.

5 See Giddens, *Central Problems*, pp. 49–76. Briefly, functionalism, like its otherwise totally antithetical counterpart Althusserian Marxism, emphasizes the determining power of structures (seen as structural categories) in the conditioning of human behaviour: that is, actors are seen as being directly controlled and directed by the structural roles into which 'society' binds them. Parsonian voluntarism, seeking to overcome such a deterministic stance, substitutes moral pressures for physical ones, whereby actors through learned conventions and behavioural norms operate in circumscribed ways. All these positions are unattractive both in their characterization of subject/object relations and in their marked inability to make conceptual room for a theory of action in which agency is emancipated and structures treated as resources to be drawn upon by skilled agents in the accomplishment of social goals. As Giddens again writes: '. . . whilst both systems of thought are concerned to overcome the subject–object dualism – Parsons via the action frame of reference and Althusser through his "theoretical anti-humanism" – each reaches a position in which subject is controlled by object. Parsons' actors are cultural dopes, but Althusser's agents are structural dopes of even more stunning mediocrity.' *Central Problems*, p. 52. See also R. J. Bernstein, *The Restructuring of Social and Political Theory* (London, 1976).

6 See, for example, A. M. Warnes, 'Residential Patterns in an Emerging Industrial Town', in B. D. Clark and M. B. Gleave (eds.), *Social Patterns in Cities* (London: Institute of British Geographers, 1973); R. Lawton and C. G. Pooley, 'The Urban Dimensions of Nineteenth-century Liverpool', *Social Geography of Nineteenth Century Merseyside Project: Working Paper no. 4* (Liverpool, 1975); L. H. Lees, 'Patterns of Lower-class Life: Irish Slum Communities in Nineteenth-century London' in S. Thernstrom and S. Sennett (eds.), *Nineteenth-Century Cities: Essays in the New Urban History* (New Haven, 1969); and R. S. Homes, 'Ownership and Migration from a Study of Ratebooks', *Area*, vol. 5 (1973). It should be noted that historical geographers have not been alone in taking this particular stance, or in falling for the easy 'explanations' offered by census-type socio-economic analyses. Urban historians no less have been insufficiently self-critical in their sociological assumptions.

7 R. J. Dennis, 'Distance and Social Interaction in a Victorian City', *Journal of Historical Geography*, vol. 3 (1977), p. 239. It should be said, in fairness, that Richard Dennis, together with David Ward ('Victorian Cities: How Modern?',

Journal of Historical Geography, vol. 1 (1975)) is one of the few historical geographers to take seriously the work of those such as Foster and Stedman Jones. For the original arguments of these exemplary nineteenth-century historians see J. Foster, 'Nineteenth-Century Towns: a Class Dimension' in H. J. Dyos (ed.), *The Study of Urban History* (London, 1968); J. Foster, *Class Struggle and the Industrial Revolution* (London, 1974); G. Stedman Jones, *Outcast London: a Study of the Relationships between Classes in Victorian Society* (London, 1971).

8 B. T. Robson, 'Foreword' to Clark and Gleave, *Social Patterns in Cities*, pp. vii–ix.
9 See Mark Billinge, *A Cultural Geography*.
10 Such a conclusion is, sadly, inescapable. The briefest of glances through the mainstream geographical journals will confirm the absence of serious discussions about class and the contribution of class relations to the shaping of the past. This is as true of substantive papers addressing what are in fact questions of class formation (not always explicitly recognized as such) as it is of abstract discussions of social change. In this sense, social historical geography appears to be in a bad way, since this reluctance to engage an issue widely perceived in other disciplines as an essential component of adequate 'explanation' is as dangerous as it is inexplicable. It would be hard to argue that its omission has been either beneficial or the result of more pressing concerns.
11 E. P. Thompson, 'The Peculiarities of the English' in R. Miliband and J. Saville, *Socialist Register, 1965* (London, 1965), p. 357.
12 Giddens, *New Rules*, pp. 93–129.
13 R. Williams, *Marxism and Literature* (Oxford, 1977), pp. 108–20. The nature and location of hegemony was amongst those issues most fruitfully debated by Perry Anderson and E. P. Thompson in their exchanges of the mid 1960s. The whole area of controversy was subsequently clarified by Poulantzas in what still remains an important and convenient *entrée* into the issues thrown up by those exciting exchanges. See P. Anderson, 'Origins of the Present Crisis', *New Left Review*, vol. 23 (1964); Thompson, 'Peculiarities'; and N. Poulantzas, 'Marxist Political Theory in Great Britain', *New Left Review*, vol. 43 (1967). The question of hegemony and its means of domination and control was, in modern terms at least, first explored by the imprisoned Antonio Gramsci, under circumstances of great difficulty. Translation of his important work was rather slow in appearing, though the flavour of both the contribution and the circumstances in which it was conceived can be found in A. Gramsci, *Prison Notebooks* (London, 1970). For nineteenth-century Britain as such, the best empirical treatment of these issues can be found in R. Gray, 'Bourgeois Hegemony in Victorian Britain' in The Communist University of London (ed.), *Class, Hegemony and Party* (London, 1977).
14 The rural preoccupation is undeniable. See H. S. A. Fox, *Register of Research in Historical Geography* (Belfast, 1976).
15 There is, of course, a huge literature on institutions of all kinds in the nineteenth century. For a reasonably comprehensive bibliography see Billinge, *A Cultural Geography*; for the mechanics institutes in particular see M. Tylecote, *The Mechanics Institutes of Lancashire and Yorkshire before 1851*

(Manchester, 1957); E. Storella, 'Oh What a World of Profit and Delight',
Ph.D. dissertation, Brandeis University, 1969 – strictly about the activities of
the Society for the Diffusion of Useful Knowledge, but containing much useful
information on Brougham's other brainchild; and in the Manchester context,
D. S. L. Cardwell (ed.), *Artisan to Graduate* (Manchester, 1974). For a more
general account of the institutional formation of mid-century and its relations to
broader social structures, see T. Tholfson, *Working Class Radicalism in
Mid-Victorian Britain* (London, 1976).
16 Gray, 'Bourgeois Hegemony'; Gramsci, *Prison Notebooks*.
17 For the empirical exemplification of this see W. E. Houghton, *The Victorian
Frame of Mind, 1830–1870* (London, 1957), and for the theoretical explication
Berstein, *Restructuring Social Theory*, pp. 171–236.
18 L. Stone, 'Prosopography', *Daedalus* (Winter, 1974), pp. 46–79.
19 Billinge, *A Cultural Geography*.
20 See L. Guelke in this volume.
21 See Tholfson, *Working Class Radicalism*, pp. 26–61, 124–55.
22 See for example the recent account in H. T. Dickinson, *Liberty and Property in
Eighteenth-Century Britain* (London, 1977). A number of interesting descriptions as well as perceptive analyses of the gentry and their ideological make-up
appear in J. B. Owen, *The Eighteenth Century, 1714–1815* (London, 1974),
especially in the sections on society and culture in the two half-centuries, pp.
123–69, 295–338. G. Mingay, *English Landed Society in the Eighteenth Century*
(London. 1963) gives a now somewhat dated account of the aristocratic
life-style, most marked by his inclination to present a more sober image of
England's political leadership. Mingay argues that the gentry on the whole took
their national responsibilities far too seriously to indulge in frivolous and
unproductive adventures ascribed by other authors. In this view, Mingay
remains unrepentant, despite considerable evidence to the contrary – see G.
Mingay, *The Gentry* (London, 1977).
23 Williams, *Marxism and Literature*, p. 111.
24 Giddens, *Central Problems*, pp. 65–9.

Notes to Prince, 'Modernization', pp. 33–43

1 N. Pevsner, *The Buildings of England: Hertfordshire* (London, 1953), pp. 235–6.
2 R. Strong, *The Renaissance Garden in England* (London, 1979).
3 W. Temple, *Upon the Gardens of Epicurus, or of Gardening in the Year 1685*
(London, 1692), p. 126, cited in J. T. Coppock and H. C. Prince (eds.), *Greater
London* (London, 1964), p. 345.
4 J. Evelyn, *Account of Architects and Architecture* (1697), cited in S. Piggott,
Ruins in a Landscape: Essays in Antiquarianism (Edinburgh, 1976), p. 118.
5 T. G. Smollett, *Humphrey Clinker* (1771), cited in Piggott, *Ruins in a
Landscape*, p. 119.
6 T. Fuller, *The Worthies of England* (1662), ed. J. Freeman (1952), p. 230, cited
in L. M. Munby, *The Hertfordshire Landscape* (London, 1977), pp. 141–2.
7 J. Summerson, *Architecture in Britain 1530 to 1830* (Harmondsworth, 1953), pp.
67–96.

8 Piggott, *Ruins in a Landscape*, p. 15.
9 'The Life of Anthony à Wood from the Year 1632 to 1672 Written by Himself' in *The Lives of those Eminent Antiquaries John Leland, Thomas Hearne and Anthony à Wood* (2 vols., Oxford, 1772), vol. 2, pp. 253–4, cited in D. Lowenthal and H. C. Prince, 'English Landscape Tastes', *Geographical Review*, vol. 55 (1965), p. 208.
10 H. Chauncy. *The Historical Antiquities of Hertfordshire* (2nd edn, London, 1826), vol. 1, pp. 248–9.
11 D. Defoe, *A Tour through the Whole Island of Great Britain* [1724–6], Everyman edn (1928), pp. 8–9.
12 S. Piggott, *William Stukeley: an Eighteenth-Century Antiquary* (Oxford, 1950), p. 25.
13 Pevsner, *Buildings of England: Hertfordshire*, pp. 57–8.
14 H. C. Prince, 'Georgian Landscapes' in A. R. H. Baker and J. B. Harley (eds.), *Man Made the Land* (Newton Abbot, 1973), pp. 153–66.
15 B. Jones, *Follies and Grottoes* (London, 1974), p. 169.
16 H. C. Prince, 'Parkland in the Chilterns', *Geographical Review*, vol. 49 (1959), pp. 18–31.
17 J. Evans, *A History of the Society of Antiquaries* (Oxford, 1956), p. 207.
18 *Ecclesiologist*, 4 (1845), p. 104, cited by Nikolaus Pevsner in J. Fawcett (ed.), *The Future of the Past* (London, 1976), p. 42.
19 J. Ruskin, *Seven Lamps of Architecture*, eds. E. W. Cook and A. Wedderburn (London, 1903–12), vol. 8, p. 245.
20 Evans, *A History of the Society of Antiquaries*, p. 309.
21 P. Henderson, *The Letters of William Morris* (London, 1950), p. 85.
22 Royal Institute of British Architects, *Sessional Papers, 1876–77*, p. 219.

Notes to Jaeger, 'Old Prussian landscapes', pp. 44–50

1 H. Mortensen, G. Mortensen, R. Wenskus and H. Jaeger, *Historisch-geographischer Atlas des Preußenlandes* (Wiesbaden, 1968–). Its drawing and printing is assisted by the Deutsche Forschungsgemeinschaft.
2 E.g. H. Mortensen and G. Mortensen, *Die Besiedlung des nordöstlichen Ostpreußens bis zum Beginn des 17 Jahrhunderts* (2 vols., Leipzig, 1937–8); H. Wunder, *Siedlungs- und Bevölkerungsgeschichte der Komturei Christburg 13–16 Jahrhundert* (Wiesbaden, 1968); P. Germershausen, *Siedlungsentwicklung der preußischen Ämter Holland, Liebstadt und Mohrungen vom 13 bis zum 17 Jahrhundert*, Wissenschaftliche Beiträge zur Geschichte und Landeskunde Ost-Mitteleuropas, no. 87 (Marburg/Lahn, 1969); K. Abe, *Die Komturei Osterode des Deutschen Ordens in Preußen, 1341–1525*, Studien zur Geschichte Preußens, vol. 16 (Köln, 1972).
3 E.g. *Preußisches Urkundenbuch*, eds. R. Philippi, C. P. Woelky, A. Seraphim, M. Hein, E. Maschke, H. Koeppen and K. Conrad, vols. 1–5 (Koenigsberg, 1882–1944; Marburg/Lahn, 1958–75).
4 M. Töppen, *Geschichte der Preußischen Historiographie* (Berlin, 1853; rep. 1973).
5 One of the first historical geographies in the German language has been the

work of Lotar Weber (*Preußen vor 500 Jahren* (Danzig, 1878)). He was a careful writer who made use of printed and unprinted sources, and his book is still helpful.

6 B. Schumacher, *Geschichte Ost- und Wastpreußens* (6th edn, Würzburg, 1977).
7 P. Johansen, 'Siedlungsforschung in Estland' in *Deutsche Siedlungsforschungen. Rudolf Kötzschke zum 60 Geburtstag* (Leipzig–Berlin, 1927), pp. 217–35; M. Hellmann, *Das Lettenland im Mittelalter*, Beiträge zur Geschichte Osteuropas, no. 1 (Münster/Köln, 1954).
8 Lieferung 3, map 'Vorgeschichtliche und mittelalterliche Wehranlagen' by R. Wenskus.
9 *Scriptores rerum Prussicarum*, eds. Th. Hirsch, M. Töppen and E. Strehlke (vols. 1–5, Leipzig, 1861–74; vol. 6, Frankfurt, 1968), vol. 1, pp. 50–2.
10 R. Wenskus, 'Kleinverbände und Kleinräume bei den Preußen des Samlandes' in *Die Anfänge der Landgemeinde und ihr Wesen, Vorträge und Forschungen VIII* (Konstanz/Stuttgart, 1964), pp. 201–54.
11 F. J. Byrne, 'Early Irish Society (1st–9th century)' in T. W. Moody and F. X. Martin (eds.), *The Course of Irish History* (Cork, 1967), pp. 43–60.
12 R. Wenskus, 'Kleinverbände und Kleinräume', pp. 228–41.
13 Lieferung 1 of the atlas. For the administration of the order see the works cited in Fig. 3, note 1 and R. Wenskus, 'Das Ordensland Preußen als Territorialstaat des 14 Jahrhunderts' in H. Patze (ed.), *Der deutsche Territorialstaat im 14 Jahrhundert, Vorträge und Forschungen XIII* (Sigmaringen, 1970), pp. 347–82.
14 Lieferung 1, map 'Verwaltung des Ordenslandes um 1400'.
15 Lieferung 3, map 'Der Gang derKirchengründungen in Altpreußen. Sonderkarte: Besetzte und unbesetzte Pfarr-kirchen Altpreußens in der 1. Hälfte des 16 Jahrhunderts'. Lieferung 2, map 'Die kirchliche Organisation um 1785'.
16 Details of the administrative sections of Polish Prussia in the second half of the sixteenth century are given in S. Herbst, M. Biskup and L. Koc, *Prusy Królewskie w Drugiej Połowie XVI W (Warszawa, 1960)*.

Notes to Koroscil, 'Soldier settlement', pp. 51–68

1 A. R. H. Baker (ed.), *Progress in Historical Geography* (Newton Abbot, 1972), pp. 207–302; see also *idem*, 'Historical Geography', *Progress in Human Geography*, vol. 1 (1977), pp. 465–74 and 'Historical Geography: Understanding and Experiencing the Past', *Progress in Human Geography*, vol. 2 (1978), pp. 495–504; B. S. Osborne (ed.), *The Settlement of Canada: Origins and Transfer* (Kingston, Ontario, 1976), pp. 169–210.
2 H. C. Darby, 'Historical Geography' in H. P. R. Finberg (ed.), *Approaches to History* (London, 1962), pp. 127–56.
3 D. W. Moodie and J. C. Lehr, 'Fact and Theory in Historical Geography', *Professional Geographer*, vol. 28 (1976), pp. 132–5.
4 M. Duverger, *An Introduction to the Social Sciences* (New York, 1964), pp. 96–102.
5 Microfilm File 25-F-1-25-F-752, Roll 1, 1915–1929, British Columbia Public Archives (PABC). 'B.C. Returned Soldiers' Aid Commission' (BCRSAC).
6 BCRSAC, The Provincial Secretary's Section (Victoria, 1917), p. 6.

7 PABC, Memorandum, Meeting BCRSAC, 30 June, 1916, pp. 1–3.

8 *British Columbia Statutes* (BCS), chapter 34, 1917.

9 *Canada Statutes*, chapter 21, 1917; see also Brewster Papers, Correspondence Inward, R. L. Borden to H. C. Brewster, PABC, 13 January 1917. For a survey of the Act see J. M. Powell, *Soldier Settlement in Canada, 1915–30*, Monash Publications in Geography, no. 7 (Victoria, 1979), pp. 1–37.

10 Canada, *Conference of Dominion and Provincial Governments* (Ottawa, 1918), pp. 1–7.

11 Canada, *Revised Statutes*, chapter 71, 1919.

12 BCS, chapter 80, 1918.

13 British Columbia, *Sessional Papers*, Land Settlement Board (BCSPLSB) (Victoria, 1918), L10; see also PABC, 'Premier's Papers', letter: Oliver to Nechako Valley Land and Development Company, 30 September 1919.

14 BCS, chapter 34, section 42, 1917.

15 BCSPLSB, Victoria, 1919.

16 BCSPLSB, 1921.

17 BCS, chapter 34, 1917.

18 BCSPLSB, 1921, T5.

19 BCSPLSB, 1923, Z5.

20 Simon Fraser University Library, Special Collections, *History of the B.C. Land Service* (1970), p. 16.

21 PABC, Pattulo Papers, Add. Mss no. 3, vol. 9, file 11, no. 159, no. 162. J. Bird, 'The History of Lister, B.C. 1919–1966', Vertical File, PABC, Lister.

22 BCSPLSB, 1920, M59.

23 *British Columbia Land Settlement Board Interim Report* (BCLSBIR), (Victoria, 1920), p. 27.

24 PABC, Add. Mss no. 1, vol. 6, file f, letter: Nelems to Smith, 31 December 1918, p. 1.

25 *ibid*. Nelems to Smith, p. 2.

26 PABC, letter: Boving to Smith, 23 January 1919.

27 'Soldier Farmers are Making Good', *Victoria Daily Colonist*, 23 May 1919, p. 5.

28 'Present Conditions at Merville Settlement', *Victoria Daily Colonist*, 20 January 1920, p. 13.

29 Bruce Alister Mackelvie Papers (1889–1960), Folder (8), Merville File, 1920, PABC.

30 'Settlers Speak Out', *Victoria Daily Times*, 6 February 1920, p. 3.

31 BCSPLSB, 1921, T6.

32 'Only Successful Soldier Settlements are in B.C.: Projects on Firm Basis', *Victoria Daily Times*, 22 March 1921, p. 8.

33 BCSPLSB, 1923, vol. 1, p. 27.

34 British Columbia, *Report of the Reappraisal Committee re Merville Lands* (Victoria, 1923), p. 17.

35 'Board Acquires Another Soldier Settlement Area', *Victoria Daily Times*, 11 June 1919, p. 9.

36 BCLSBIR (Victoria, 1921), p. 30.

37 PABC, Vertical File, Lister.

38 British Columbia, *Journals of the Legislative Assembly*, 21 March 1921, p. 7.

39 PABC, Bird, 'History of Camp Lister, 1919–1951', p. 4.
40 British Columbia, *Report of the Commission on Economic Conditions in Certain Irrigation Districts*, Special Collections, University of British Columbia, B.C. Government Paper, 1928, P.U. 13.
41 See T. Adams, *Rural Planning and Development* (Ottawa, 1917), pp. 207–16.
42 Canada, *House of Commons Debates, 1919*, vol. 4, 3863.
43 See A. W. Rasporich, 'Utopian Ideals and Community Settlements in Western Canada, 1880–1914', *The Canadian West* (Calgary, 1977), pp. 37–62.
44 J. Kolehmainen, 'Harmony Island: A Finnish Utopian Venture in British Columbia', *B.C. Historical Quarterly*, vol. V, no. 2 (1941), pp. 111–23.

Notes to Meinig, 'Imperial expansion', pp. 71–78

1 M. Hechter, *Internal Colonialism: The Celtic Fringe in British National Development, 1536–1966* (Berkeley, 1975).
2 J. Galtung, 'A Structural Theory of Imperialism', *Journal of Peace Research*, vol. 8 (1971), pp. 81–117.
3 C. V. Earle, 'Reflections on the Colonial City', *Historical Geography Newsletter*, vol. 4 (1974), pp. 1–17.
4 F. Jennings, *The Invasion of America: Indians, Colonialism, and the Cant of Conquest* (Chapel Hill, 1975).
5 B. S. Osborne and C. M. Rogerson, 'Conceptualizing the Frontier Settlement Process: Development or Dependency?', *Comparative Frontier Studies, An Interdisciplinary Newsletter*, no. 11 (1978); I. Wallerstein, *The Modern World-System, Capitalist Agriculture and the Origin of the European World-Economy in the Sixteenth Century* (New York, 1976).
6 J. M. Blaut, 'Geographic Models of Imperialism', *Antipode*, vol. 2 (1970), pp. 65–85; also *idem*, 'Imperialism: The Marxist Theory and its Evolution', *Antipode*, vol. 7 (1975), pp. 1–19.
7 E. H. Spicer, *Cycles of Conquest: The Impact of Spain, Mexico, and the United States on the Indians of the Southwest, 1533–1960* (Tuscon, 1962).

Notes to Galloway, 'Agricultural improvement', pp. 79–86

1 *American Husbandry* (London, 1775), published anonymously but usually attributed to Arthur Young.
2 Bryan Edwards, *The History, Civil and Commercial of The British Colonies in The West Indies* (London, 1783–1801).
3 William Beckford, *A Descriptive Account of The Island of Jamaica* (London, 1790).
4 M. L. E. Moreau de Saint Méry, *Description topographique, physique, civile, politique et historique de la partie française de L'Isle de Saint-Dominque* (Philadelphia, 1797–8).
5 Alexander von Humboldt, *Essaie politique sur L'Isle de Cuba* (Paris, 1826), and *Political Essay on The Kingdom of New Spain* (Edinburgh, 1811).
6 Robert Southey, *History of Brazil* (London, 1810–19).

7 Samuel Martin, *An Essay Upon Plantership* (Antigua and London, 1754 and various edns to 1802).

8 Dutrône La Couture, *Précis sur la canne et sur les moyens d'en extraire le sel essentiel* (Paris, 1790).

9 Le Citoyen Avalle, *Tableau comparatif des productions des colonies anglaises, espagnoles et hollandaises, de l'année 1787 à 1788* (Paris, An VII, 1799).

10 Francisco Arango y Parreño, *Obras* (Havana, 1952).

11 R. J. Shafer, *Economic Societies in the Spanish World, 1763–1821* (Syracuse, 1958).

12 *Mémorias Econômicas da Academia Real das Sciencias de Lisboa para o adiantamento da agricultura, das artes e da industria em Portugal e suas conquistas* (Lisbon, 1789–1815).

13 For the work of the Portuguese government in the encouragement of agricultural reform see J. H. Galloway, 'Agricultural Reform and The Enlightenment in Late Colonial Brazil', *Agricultural History*, vol. 53 (1979).

14 Fr José Matiano da Conceiçao Veloso, *O Fazendeiro do Brazil* (Lisbon, 1798–1806) and *O Fazendeiro de Brasil Criador* (Lisbon, 1801).

15 Von Humboldt, *Political Essay on The Kingdom of New Spain*, p. 256.

16 Luís dos Santos Vilhena, *A Bahia No Século XVIII* (Bahia, 1969), a republication of a MS completed in 1802 under the title 'Recopilição de Noticias Soterpolitanas e Brasilicas Contidas em XX Cartas'.

17 Von Humboldt, *Political Essay on The Kingdom of New Spain*, p. 15, and *Essai politique sur L'Isle de Cuba*, p. 235.

18 Ward Barrett, *The Sugar Hacienda of the Marquesas del Valle* (Minneapolis, 1970) and Ward J. Barrett and Stuart B. Schartz, 'Comparación Entre Dos Economias Acucareras Coloniales: Morelos México y Bahïa, Brasil' in Enrique Florescano (ed.), *Haciendas, Latifundios y Plantaciones en América Latina* (Mexico, 1975), pp. 532–72, Table 550.

19 Edwards, *History, Civil and Commercial*, pp. 166–7.

Notes to Robinson, 'Relating structure to process', pp. 87–98

1 See A. R. H. Baker, 'The Limits of Inference in Historical Geography' in B. S. Osborne (ed.), *The Settlement of Canada: Origins and Transfers. Proceedings of the 1975 British Canadian Symposium on Historical Geography* (Kingston, Ontario, 1976), pp. 169–182; H. C. Prince, 'Real, Imagined and Abstract Worlds of the Past', *Progress in Geography*, vol. 3 (1971), pp. 21–2; J. Langton, 'Potentialities and Problems of Adopting a Systems Approach to the Study of Change in Human Geography', *Progress in Geography*, vol. 4 (1972), pp. 126–79.

2 D. J. Robinson and M. M. Swann, 'Geographical Interpretations of the Hispanic American Colonial City: a Case Study of Caracas in the Late Eighteenth Century' in R. J. Tata (ed.), *Latin America: Search for Geographic Explanations* (Boca Raton, 1975), pp. 1–15; and also K. Waldron, 'A Social History of a Primate City: The Case of Caracas, 1750–1810', unpublished dissertation, University of Indiana, 1977. D. B. Rutman has suggested the use

326   Notes to pages 89–92

of urban density rather than age as a discriminator of urban growth: see 'People in Process: The New Hampshire Town of the XVIII Century', *Journal of Urban History*, vol. 1 (1975), pp. 268–92.

3 D. J. Robinson, *The Analysis of 18th Century Spanish American Cities: Some Problems and Alternative Solutions*, Department of Geography, Syracuse University, Discussion Paper Series, no. 4 (1975).

4 Students of Caracas are fortunate to have accurate and almost annual censuses of each urban parish between 1750 and 1820.

5 Waldron, *Social History*, pp. 25–7. For an extremely useful study of Venezuelan population change in the eighteenth century see J. V. Lombardi, *People and Places in Colonial Venezuela* (Bloomington, 1976).

6 Archivo Arquidiocesano de Caracas, Matrículas de las Parroquias de: Catedral; Altagracia; Candelaria; San Pablo; Santa Rosalía, 1809–10 and 1815–16. The earthquake hit the city on the morning of 11 April 1812, with an official toll of 2,000. Details are in A. Ibarra, *Tembladores y terremotos de Caracas* (Caracas, 1862).

7 These data were kindly provided by my student Katharine Altman, who at present is completing a thesis on the topic of migration within Caracas in the eighteenth century.

8 For changes in the housing stock see Table 2 of Robinson and Swann, 'Geographical Interpretations', p. 9.

9 Such mobility can be compared with that for other cultural contexts. See for example: S. Thurnstrom and P. R. Knights, 'Men in Motion: Some Data and Speculations about Population Mobility in Nineteenth-Century America', *Journal of Interdisciplinary History*, vol. 1 (1970–1), pp. 7–35; R. J. Hopkins, 'Occupational and Geographic Mobility in Atlanta, 1870–1876', *Journal of Southern History*, XXXIV (1968), pp. 200–13; L. A. Bissell, 'From One Generation to Another: Mobility in Seventeenth-Century Windsor, Connecticut', *William and Mary Quarterly* (1974), pp. 79–110; P. Laslett and J. Harrison, 'Clayworth and Cogenhoe', in H. R. Bell (ed.), *Historical Essays, 1600–1750: Presented to David Ogg* (N.W., 1963), pp. 157–84. An interesting contemporary study with implications for historical geographers is L. A. Brown and J. Holmes, 'Intra-urban Migration Lifelines: a Spatial View', *Demography*, vol. 8 (1971), pp. 103–12.

10 Summaries are provided in A. H. Johnson, 'The Impact of Market Agriculture on Family and Household Structure in Nineteenth-Century Chile', *Hispanic American Historical Review*, vol. 58 (1978), pp. 625–48; Linda L. Greenow, *Spatial Dimensions of Household and Family Structure in Eighteenth-Century Spanish America*, Department of Geography, Syracuse University, Discussion Paper Series, no. 35 (1977); D. J. Robinson, 'Population Patterns in a Northern Mexican Mining Region: Parral in the Late Eighteenth Century' in J. J. Parsons (ed.), *Geoscience and Man: Essays in Honor of Robert C. West* (in press); E. Kuznesof, 'Household Composition and Economy in an Urbanizing Community: São Paulo, 1765 to 1836', unpublished dissertation, University of California, Berkeley, 1976; L. L. Johnson and S. Socolow, 'Population and Space in Eighteenth-Century Buenos Aires' in D. J. Robinson (ed.), *Social Fabric and Spatial Structure in Colonial Latin America* (Ann Arbor, 1979), pp. 339–68; D.

Ramos, 'Marriage and the Family in Colonial Vila Rica', *Hispanic American Historical Review*, vol. 55 (1975), pp. 200–25.

It should be noted that the classification of household and family structure follows that outlined in P. Laslett (ed.), *Household and Family in Past Time* (Cambridge, 1972), pp. 28–32.

11 Waldron, *Social History*, pp. 141–59. It is necessary, as she argues, to devise a new class of households (non-kin extended) to include the slave-holding units that do not occur in the European cases. Whether Latin American households took in such extra units in phase with life-cycle changes is not yet known. See J. Modell and T. K. Hareven, 'Urbanization and the Malleable Household: An Examination of Boarding and Lodging in American Families' in T. K. Hareven (ed.), *Family and Kin in Urban Communities, 1700–1930* (New York, 1977), pp. 164–86.

12 Excellent examples include: D. Balmori and R. Oppenheimer, 'Family Clusters: Generational Nucleation in Nineteenth-Century Argentina and Chile', *Comparative Studies in Society and History*, vol. 21 (1979), pp. 231–61; and E. Kuznesof, 'Clans, the Militia and Territorial Government: The Articulation of Kinship with Polity in Eighteenth-Century São Paulo' in Robinson (ed.), *Social Fabric*, pp. 181–226.

13 Waldron, 'Social History of a Primate City', pp. 141ff., provides an excellent account of such urban controls, especially access to donations of public urban land.

14 With a total of between 20,000 and 30,000 persons, and vital records averaging almost 1,000 per year, the mobility of the population, and the problems of name-matching, it will require a considerable effort to undertake such an analysis. One of the key problems is the fact that the population turnover greatly reduces the chances of finding kin living in the city at subsequent dates. A useful digest of comparable nineteenth-century problems is C. Stephenson, 'Tracing Those Who Left', *Journal of Urban History*, vol. 1 (1974), pp. 73–84.

15 Details of Córdoba's structure are to be found in D. J. Robinson, 'Córdoba en 1779: ciudad y campaña' in R. Rey Balmaceda (ed.), *Homenaje a Federico Daus* (Buenos Aires, 1979), pp. 66–98.

16 The significance of the 'residential' bias in interpreting households and family structure has not passed unnoticed by those who have studied the history of the family in the past. In a critical review of Laslett's *Household and Family in Past Time*, Lutz Berkner argued that little could be deciphered from the synchronic data used in the Cambridge Group's files, since the development cycle of what he called the stem-family would not necessarily appear in significant proportions in any one cross-section. See L. Berkner, 'The Use and Misuse of Census Data for the Historical Analysis of Household Structure', *Journal of Interdisciplinary History*, vol. 5 (1975), pp. 721–38. His other major statement is 'The Stem-family and the Developmental Cycle of the Peasant Household; an Eighteenth-Century Austrian Example', *American Historical Review*, vol. 77 (1972), pp. 398–418.

Laslett and others have more recently elegantly disarmed Berkner, and punched a large hole in the developmental cycle hypothesis of the stem-family, by carrying out a large simulation study which effectively demonstrated that stem-families in the number suggested by Berkner are extremely unlikely to be developed under *any* demographic circumstances. Laslett also stresses that Berkner's definition of the stem-family does not, in fact, require co-residence, which destroys any basis for comparative analyses of classification schemes. There are also some significant problems with Berkner's Austrian family sources that remain unexplained. For details see K. W. Wachter *et al.*, *Statistical Studies of Historical Social Structure* (New York, 1978).

For evidence of American and French studies see E. Litwak, 'Geographic Mobility and Extended Family Cohesion', *American Sociological Review*, vol. 25 (1960), pp. 385–394; and C. Gokalp, 'Le Réseau Familial', *Population* (1978), pp. 1077–94. For Latin American colonial data, Johnson, 'Market Agriculture', p. 629, states that 'relatives did live in clusters'. Susan Socolow, in *The Merchants of Buenos Aires, 1778–1810* (New York, 1978), p. 74, demonstrates the significance of family and merchant clans in close proximity to each other. S. Blank's 'Patrons, Clients and Kin in Seventeenth-Century Caracas: a Methodological Essay in Colonial Spanish American Social History', *Hispanic American Historical Review*, vol. 54 (1974), pp. 260–83, does not, unfortunately, locate the persons within the city.

17 Sources included: Archivo Histórico de la Provincia de Córdoba, Sección Escribanías and Colonia: Censos; Archivo de la Curia Eclesiástica de Córdoba, Padrones y Registors Parroquiales. Several others have identified kin only on the basis of similar family names (name-grouping), however, and E. Malvido has pointed out the problems of Spanish American surnames which have a relatively limited range: E. Malvido, 'Problemas en la reconstitución de familias: Tula en la época colonial', Paper presented at International Congress of Americanists, Mexico City, 1974. In the present study only those who could be identified by name, age and relationship to a third person were positively linked.

18 Robinson, *The Analysis*, pp. 9–13. For a most instructive comment on the social significance of the facing-block see R. E. Reina, *Paraná: Social Boundaries in an Argentine City* (Austin, 1973), pp. 25–8, 94–112.

19 Instructive with regard to marriage is A. Lavrín and E. Couturier, 'Dowries and Wills: a Woman's Socio-economic Role in Colonial Guadalajara and Puebla, 1640–1790', *Hispanic American Historical Review*, vol. 59 (1979), pp. 280–304.

20 The only precise measurements that I could locate were median distances cited by D. R. Mills, 'The Residential Propinquity of Kin in a Cambridgeshire Village, 1841', *Journal of Historical Geography*, vol. 4 (1978), pp. 265-76; and M. Anderson, *Family Structure in Nineteenth-Century Lancashire* (Cambridge, 1971), p. 59. Mills has median values of 200–317.5 yards for various links, Anderson quotes 170 yards for Preston. The Córdoba median is 158 m which is less than Mills's elongated village, but quite close to urban Preston's figure. It is unfortunate that exact measures are not cited in A. Plakans, 'Identifying Kinfolk Beyond the Household', *Journal of Family History*, vol. 2 (1977), pp. 3–27. A useful computerized mapping technique for kin identified by name group is G. A. Collier, 'Computer Processing of Genealogies and Analysis of Settlement Patterns', *Human Mosaic*, vol. 3 (1969), pp. 164–74.

21 T. V. Hareven, 'Family Time and Industrial Time', in T. V. Hareven (ed.),

Family and Kin, pp. 187–207; and her 'The Family as Process: The Historical Study of the Family Cycle', *Journal of Social History* (1974). See also P. Glick, 'The Family Cycle', *American Sociological Review*, vol. 12 (1947), pp. 164–74.

22 The most detailed survey of *compadrinazgo* is to be found in D. V. Hart, *Compadrinazgo: Ritual Kinship in the Philippines* (De Kalb, 1977), which provides a much wider coverage than the title suggests. Classic Latin American studies include: S. W. Mintz and E. R. Wolf, 'An Analysis of Ritual Co-parenthood (Compadrazgo)', *Southwest Journal of Anthropology*, vol. 6 (1950), pp. 341–68; and G. M. Foster, 'Godparents and Social Network in Tzintzuntzán', *ibid*. vol. 25 (1969), pp. 261–78.

23 Hart, *Compadrinazgo*, pp. 179–203, cites the many other occasions.

24 The studies of marriage patterns in colonial Latin America must take into account the ritual relationships in specific communities. For an excellent summary see M. M. Swann, 'The Spatial Dimensions of a Social Process: Marriage and Mobility in Late Colonial Northern Mexico' in Robinson (ed.), *Social Fabric*, pp. 117–80. For Córdoba see also M. D. Szuchman, 'The Limits of the Melting Pot in Urban Argentina: Marriage and Migration in Córdoba, 1869–1909', *Hispanic American Historical Review*, vol. 57 (1977), pp. 24–50.

25 It is important to note that a third of both baptism and marriage records contain no specification of the residence of *padrinos*. It may be that where no information is given they were from the local parish, which would inflate the city figures to 86 and 74 per cent respectively. However, such figures would be mere speculation.

26 Hart, *Compadrinazgo*, pp. 141–58, and Robinson, 'Córdoba'.

27 For a comparative view see Balmori and Oppenheimer, 'Generational Clusters'.

28 Szuchman, 'The Limits', p. 25, cites them as 'indicators of social fluidity and rigidity'. Robinson uses marriage and baptism records to monitor interaction fields in eighteenth-century Yucatán in 'Indian Migration in Eighteenth-Century Yucatán' in D. J. Robinson (ed.), *Historical Populations in Latin America* (Vancouver, 1980).

29 See for example '. . . the first collaborative interdisciplinary effort to apply longitudinal questions to cross-sectional historical data' in T. V. Hareven (ed.), *Transitions: The Family and the Life Course in Historical Perspective* (New York, 1978), p. 13.

Notes to Lawton, 'Questions of scale', pp. 99–113

The range of material consulted has been very wide. Only those referring directly to points in the essay are noted here.

1 M. Fleury and L. Henry, *Des registres paroissiaux a l'histoire de la population* (Paris, 1956); E. A. Wrigley (ed.), *Identifying People in the Past* (London, 1973).

2 For a review see R. Lawton, 'Population and Society, 1730–1900' in R. A. Butlin and R. A. Dodgshon (eds.), *An Historical Geography of England and Wales* (London, 1978), pp. 313–66.

3 D. V. Glass and D. E. C. Eversley (eds.), *Population in History* (London, 1965).

4 E. A. Wrigley (ed.), *An Introduction to English Historical Demography* (Cambridge, 1966).

5 R. Lawton (ed.), *The Census and Social Structure* (London, 1978), esp. chaps. 1 and 2.

6 J. J. Clarke, *A History of Local Government in the United Kingdom* (London, 1955).

7 V. D. Lipman, *Local Government Areas in England, 1834–1945* (London, 1949).

8 D. Friedlander, 'Demographic Responses and Population Change', *Demography*, vol. 6 (1969), pp. 359–81.

9 J. I. Clarke, 'Population and Scale: Some General Considerations' in L. A. Kosinski and J. W. Webb, *Population and Scale. 1. Micro Population* (Edmonton, 1975) (International Geographical Union, Commission on Population Geography).

10 D. V. Glass, 'Changes in Fertility in England and Wales, 1851–1931' in L. Hogben (ed.), *Political Arithmetic* (London, 1938), pp. 161–212.

11 See, for example, N. Tranter, *Population Since the Industrial Revolution: the Case of England and Wales* (London, 1973), and C. M. Law, 'Local Censuses in the Eighteenth Century', *Population Studies*, vol. 23 (1969), pp. 87–100.

12 Lawton (ed.), *The Census and Social Structure*.

13 There was an experimental age enumeration in the 1821 census, but it is generally thought to be very inaccurate.

14 E. A. Wrigley (ed.), *Nineteenth-century Society: Essays in the Use of Quantitative Methods for the Study of Social Data* (Cambridge, 1972).

15 J. Langton and P. Laxton, 'Parish Registers and Urban Structure: the Example of Late-eighteenth-century Liverpool', *Urban History Yearbook, 1978* (Leicester, 1978), pp. 74–84.

16 A. Armstrong, *Stability and Change in an English Country Town: a Social Study of York, 1801–51* (Cambridge, 1974).

17 P. Spufford, 'Population Mobility in Pre-industrial England', *Genealogists Magazine*, vol. 17 (1973), pp. 420–9, 475–81 and 537–43.

18 R. Lawton, 'Population Changes in England and Wales in the Later Nineteenth Century', *Transactions, Institute of British Geographers*, no. 44 (1968), pp. 55–74.

19 W. A. Armstrong, 'The Use of Information about Occupation' in Wrigley (ed.), *Nineteenth-century Society*, pp. 191–310, and J. A. Banks, 'The Social Structure of Nineteenth-century England as seen through the Census' in Lawton (ed.), *The Census and Social Structure*, pp. 179–223.

20 T. McKeown, *The Modern Rise of Population* (London, 1976); R. Woods, 'Mortality and Sanitary Conditions in the "Best Governed City in the World": Birmingham, 1870–1910', *Journal of Historical Geography*, vol. 4 (1978), pp. 35–56.

21 R. Lawton and C. G. Pooley, 'Problems and Potentialities for the Study of Internal Population Mobility in Nineteenth-century England', *Canadian Population Studies*, vol. 5 (1978), pp. 69–84.

22 C. G. Pooley, 'The Residential Segregation of Migrant Communities in Mid-Victorian Liverpool', *Transactions, Institute of British Geographers*, New Series, vol. 2 (1977), pp. 364–82.
23 Wrigley (ed.), *Identifying People in the Past*.
24 I. Winchester, 'A Brief Survey of the Algorithmic, Mathematical and Philosophical Literature Relevant to Historical Record Linkage' in *ibid.* pp. 128–50.
25 Work completed includes studies of Edinburgh (by G. Gordon), Falkirk (M. Barke), Stirling (R. C. Fox), Sunderland (B. T. Robson), Halifax (A. Dingsdale), Huddersfield (R. J. Dennis), Wakefield (K. A. Cowlard), Hull (P. A. Tansey), York (A. Armstrong), Leicester (R. M. Pritchard), small towns in Leicestershire (S. A. Royle), Wolverhampton (M. Shaw), Cardiff (M. J. Daunton) and Merthyr Tydfil (H. Carter and S. Wheatley). *The Urban History Yearbook* (annually) contains regular reviews of work in progress.
26 R. S. Schofield and E. A. Wrigley (eds.), *Population Trends in Early Modern England* (forthcoming).
27 For example, R. Lawton, 'The Population of Liverpool in the Mid-nineteenth Century', *Transactions, Historical Society of Lancashire and Cheshire*, vol. 107 (1956), pp. 89–120.
28 Wrigley, *Nineteenth-century Society*, and Lawton, *The Census and Social Structure*.
29 M. Anderson *et al.*, 'The National Sample from the 1851 Census', *Urban History Yearbook, 1977* (Leicester, 1977), pp. 55–9.
30 R. S. Schofield, 'Sampling in Historical Research' in Wrigley (ed.), *Nineteenth-century Society*, pp. 146–90.
31 R. Lawton and C. G. Pooley (eds.), *Methodological Problems in the Statistical Analysis of Small-area Data*, Working Paper No. 2, Social Geography of Merseyside Project, Department of Geography, University of Liverpool 1973.
32 H. Carter and S. Wheatley, *Merthyr Tydfil in 1851: a Study of Spatial Structure (2). The Grid Square Base*, S.S.R.C. Project: The Social and Residential Areas of Merthyr Tydfil in the Mid-nineteenth Century (Department of Geography, U.C.W. Aberystwyth, 1978).
33 R. Lawton and C. G. Pooley, *The Social Geography of Merseyside in the Nineteenth Century*. Final Report to the S.S.R.C. (Department of Geography, University of Liverpool, 1976).
34 Kosinski and Webb, *Population and Scale*, p. 12.
35 Lawton and Pooley, 'Problems and Potentialities'.
36 Pooley, 'Residential Segregation'.
37 R. Lawton and C. G. Pooley, 'David Brindley's Liverpool', *Transactions, Historical Society of Lancashire and Cheshire*, vol. 125 (1975), pp. 149–68.

Notes to Bowden, 'Cities following disaster', pp. 114–126

 1 H. Landsberg, 'Comments', in W. L. Thomas, Jr (ed.), *Man's Role in Changing the Face of the Earth* (Chicago, 1956), pp. 436–7.
 2 M. J. Bowden, 'Downtown Through Time: Delimitation, Expansion, and Internal Growth', *Economic Geography*, vol. 47 (1971), pp. 121–35.
 3 M. J. Bowden, 'The Dynamics of City Growth: An Historical Geography of the

San Francisco Central District, 1850–1931', Ph.D. dissertation, University of California, Berkeley, 1967.

4 G. Roboff and K. Gelman, 'San Francisco Earthquake of 1906: Changes in Housing and Employment Patterns, 1905–11', unpublished paper (Worcester, Mass., 1975).

5 M. J. Bowden, 'Reconstruction Following Disaster: Commercial and Industrial Structure in Managua' in J. E. Haas (ed.), *Geographical and Sociological Perspectives on the Reconstruction of Managua, Nicaragua* (Boulder, 1975), pp. 2–16.

6 *San Francisco Relief Survey* (New York, 1913).

7 M. J. Bowden, 'Growth of the Central Districts in Large Cities' in L. Schnore (ed.), *The New Urban History* (Princeton, 1974), pp. 75–109.

8 Bowden, 'Dynamics of City Growth', pp. 477–560.

9 M. J. Bowden *et al.*, 'Reestablishing Homes and Jobs: Cities' in J. E. Haas, R. W. Kates and M. J. Bowden (eds.), *Reconstruction Following Disaster* (Cambridge, Mass., 1977), pp. 69–145.

10 M. J. Bowden, 'Reconstruction Following Catastrophe: The Laissez-faire Rebuilding of Downtown San Francisco after the Earthquake and Fire of 1906', *Proceedings, Association of American Geographers*, vol. 2 (1970), pp. 22–6.

11 M. J. Bowden, 'Persistence, Failure and Mobility in the Inner City: Preliminary Notes' in R. E. Ehrenberg (ed.), *Pattern and Process: Research in Historical Geography* (Washington, D.C., 1975), pp. 169–92.

12 C. M. Douty, 'The Economics of Localized Disasters: An Empirical Analysis of the 1906 Earthquake and Fire in San Francisco', Ph.D. dissertation, Stanford University, 1969.

13 Bowden *et al.*, *Reestablishing Homes*, pp. 79–91.

14 D. J. Amaral and M. J. Bowden, 'The Impact of the Disaster Reconstruction on the Residential Structure of Managua' in Haas *et al.*, *Geographical and Sociological Perspectives*, pp. 1–26, and Bowden *et al.*, *Reestablishing Homes*, pp. 139–45.

15 Unpublished data collected by Robert Bolin (1973–5), Institute of Behavioral Sciences, Boulder.

16 *San Francisco Relief Survey*, 1913; Bowden *et al.*, *Reestablishing Homes*, pp. 71–3, 84.

17 H. P. Friesema, 'Symposium on Disaster Impact on Selected Small Towns in the U.S.', unpublished papers, October 1975.

18 Bowden *et al.*, *Reestablishing Homes*, pp. 94–6.

19 'Managua Rebuilds Itself 10-times Larger, After Devastating Earthquake of 1972', *The Wall Street Journal*, 9 January 1978, p. 10.

20 Bowden *et al.*, *Reestablishing Homes*, pp. 102–8.

Notes to Denecke, 'Applied historical geography', pp. 127–135

1 Working on this paper I realized that the terminology of the historic landscape, its identification, recording and management are extremely vague and not precise enough for international cooperation in this field. Not only the different

languages but also the great number of disciplines, authorities and institutions and the rapid modernization of this complex field of study and practice form a considerable barrier to international understanding and create a confusion that is hard to penetrate. There are a few short and insufficient, but nevertheless very welcome, glossaries concerning this topic, for example in K. Hudson, *Museums for the Eighties* (New York, 1977), Glossary, pp. 185–90. An international terminological framework for a comprehensive glossary, elaborated by an international working group, would be very much appreciated.

2 D. Denecke, *Die historisch-geographische Landesaufnahme. Aufgaben, Methoden und Ergebnisse, dargestellt am Beispiel des mittleren und südlichen Leineberglandes*, Göttinger Geographische Abhandlungen, no. 60 (Göttingen, 1972), pp. 401–36; *idem*, 'Historical-geographical Regional Surveys. Methods, Procedures and Designs of Cartographic Recording' [examples from Southern Lower Saxony] in P. F. Brandon and R. N. Millman (eds.), *Recording Historic Landscapes, Principles and Practice*, Occasional Paper, Department of Geography, Polytechnic of North London (London, 1980).

3 Fossil prehistoric relics and sites are not considered in a historico-geographical survey, though the methods of the field survey are very similar to each other. They are recorded by a special archaeological (prehistorical) regional survey (*archäologische Landesaufnahme*) based on exhaustive field walking and an evaluation of museum inventories. Surveys of this kind have existed in Germany since 1926. For general problems and methods compare A. Tode, 'Organisation und praktische Durchführung einer allgemeinen archäologischen Landesaufnahme', *Vorgeschichtliches Jahrbuch*, vol. 3 (1926), pp. 10–21; H. Schirnig, 'Einige Bemerkungen zur archäologischen Landesaufnahme', *Nachrichten aus Niedersachsens Urgeschichte*, no. 35 (1966), pp. 3–13; J. Röschmann, 'Landesaufnahme, Möglichkeiten und Grenzen' in J. Röschmann, *Vorgeschichte des Kreises Flensburg* (Neumünster, 1963), pp. 109–16; H. G. Peters, 'Zur Methode der archäologischen Landesaufnahme', *Osnabrücker Mitteilungen*, no. 78 (1971), pp. 131–6; H. Jankuhn, 'Archäologische Landesaufnahme' in J. Hoops, *Reallexikon der Germanischen Altertumskunde*, 2nd edn, vol. 1 (Berlin, 1973), pp. 391–4.

4 G. Wolff, *Die südliche Wetterau in vor- und frühgeschichtlicher Zeit, mit einer archäologischen Fundkarte* (Frankfurt, 1913). The medieval period may be exemplified by G. Oberbeck, *Die mittelalterliche Kulturlandschaft des Gebietes um Gifhorn*, Schriften der wirtschaftswissenschaftlichen Gesellschaft zum Studium Niedersachsens, New Series, vol. 66 (Bremen–Horn, 1957); J. K. Rippel, *Die Entwicklung der Kulturlandschaft am nordwestlichen Harzrand*, Schriften der wirtschaftswissenschaftlichen Gesellschaft zum Stadium Neidersachsens, New Series, vol. 69 (Hannover, 1958); H. Kern, *Siedlungsgeographische Geländeforschungen im Amöneburger Becken und seinen Randgebieten. Ein Beitrag zur Erforschung der mittelalterlichen Kulturlandschaftsentwicklung in Nordhessen*, Marburger Geographische Schriften, no. 27 (Marburg, 1966); D. Denecke, *Methodische Untersuchungen zur historisch-geographischen Wegeforschung im Raum zwischen Solling und Harz. Ein Beitrag zur Rekonstruktion der mittelalterlichen Kulturlandschaft*, Göttinger Geographische Abhandlungen, no. 54 (Göttingen, 1969).

5 *Hessisches Gesetz zum Schutze der Kulturdenkmäler* (1974), Abschnitt 3, §§ 19 and 20.

6 G. Pritchard, 'Farming on Archaeological Sites in Norfolk', *Historic Landscapes: Identification, Recording and Management*, Occasional Paper, Department of Geography, Polytechnic of North London (London, 1978), pp. 88–90.

7 K. Raddatz, 'Zur Besiedlung der Leineaue bei Göttingen in ur- und frühgeschichtlicher Zeit', *Neue Ausgrabungen und Forschungen in Niedersachsen*, vol. 5 (1970), pp. 235–43.

8 D. Denecke, *Methodische Untersuchungen*, esp. map 'Das mittelalgerliche und frühneuzeitliche Wegenetz und die an ihm orientierten Anlagen nebst den Siedlungen und Wirtschaftsplätzen im Raum zwischen Solling und Harz und Materialkatalog', pp. 295–391; G. and E. Schröder, 'Spätmittelalterlich – frühneuzeitliche Kulturlandschaftsrelikte in der Umgebung von Güntersen (Kr. Göttingen)', *Göttinger Jahrbuch*, vol. 27 (1979), pp. 63–81.

9 Röschmann, *Vorgeschichte des Kreises Flensburg*; H. Aust, *Die Vor- und Frühgeschichte des Kreises Wesermünde* (Hamburg, 1979). See also the comprehensive references in Jankuhn, *Reallexikon der Germanischen Altertumskunde*, vol. 1, p. 394.

10 Denecke, *Methodische Untersuchungen*, Materialkatalog, pp. 295–391 and Übersichtskarte 1:50,000; E. Neuss, *Wüstungskunde des Saalkreises und der Stadt Halle*, pts 1 and 2 (Weimar, 1969–71); W. Janssen, *Studien zur Wüstungsfrage im fränkischen Altsiedelland zwischen Rhein, Mosel und Eifelnordrand*, pt 2 (Köln, 1975), Katalog und Faltplan 1 (Übersichtskarge 1:200,000): Wüstungen in der Eifel; D. Staerk, *Die Wüstungen des Saarlandes: Beiträge zur Siedlungsgeschichte des Saarraumes vom Frühmittelalter bis zur Französischen Revolution*, Veröffentlichungen der Kommission für saarländische Landesgeschichte und Volksforschung, no. 7 (Saarbrücken, 1976), Wüstungsverzeichnis, pp. 67–418 and Übersichtskarte; H.-G. Stephan, *Archäologische Studien zur Wüstungsforschung im südlichen Weserbergland*, Münstersche Beiträge zur Ur- und Frühgeschichte, vol. 10 (Hildesheim, 1978), pt 1, Wüstungsverzeichnis, pp. 198–283.

11 D. Denecke, 'Historische Siedlungsgeographie und Siedlungsarchäologie des Mittelalters. Fragestellungen, Methoden und Ergebnisse unter dem Gesichtspunkt interdisziplinärer Zusammenarbeit', *Zeitschrift für Archäologie des Mittelalters*, no. 3 (1975), Übersicht 3 and 4, pp. 21–5.

12 D. Denecke, 'Erzgewinnung und Hüttenbetriebe des Mittelalters im Oberharz und im Harzvorland. Erläuterungen zu einer Übersichtskarte', *Archäologisches Korrespondenzblatt*, vol. 8 (1978), Kartenbeilage: Mittelalterliche Gruben und Hüttenbetriebe im Oberharz, Mittelharz und Harzvorland. Another example is D. Düsterloh, *Beiträge zur Kulturgeographie des Niederbergisch-Märkischen Hügellandes: Bergbau und Verhüttung vor 1850 als Elemente der Kulturlandschaft*, Göttinger Geographische Abhandlungen, no. 38 (Göttingen, 1967), map I: 'Bergbauspuren und Steinbrüche' and map IIa: 'Fundstellen mittelalterlich – frühneuzeitlicher Eisenverhüttungsschlacken, Erzfundpunkte und Bergbauspuren' (1:50,000).

13 D. Denecke, *Glashüttenbetriebe im Leine- und Fulda-Werra-Bergland vom Mittelalter bis zur Neuzeit*, map (1:100,000) and additional diagram giving

selected historic data, compiled for the exhibition Archäologie des Mittelalters und der Neuzeit in Niedersachsen (1978–9), unpublished.

14 P. F. Brandon and R. N. Millman (eds.), *Historic Landscapes: Identification, Recording and Management*, Occasional Paper, Department of Geography, Polytechnic of North London (London, 1978).

15 A compilation of the laws of the protection of ancient monuments and historic buildings (*Denkmalschutzgesetze*) of all the *Länder* of the Federal Republic of Germany in force until recently and to date is given in G. Gaentzsch, 'Rechts- und Verwaltungsvorschriften' in Arbeitskrers Historische Stadtkerne der Deutschen UNESCO – Kommission (Bearb.), *Historische Städte – Städte Für morgen* (Köln, 1974), pp. 65–78.

In all of the *Länder* laws of the 1930s or even of the beginning of the century were still practised until new laws were enacted during the 1970s: Baden-Württemberg: Gesetz zum Schutz der Kulturdenkmale, 1971; Bayern: Gesetz zum Schutz und zur Pflege der Denkmäler, 1973; Berlin: Gesetz zum Schutz von Denkmalen in Berlin, 1977; Bremen: Gesetz zur Pflege und zum Schutz von Kulturdenkmälern, 1975; Hamburg: Denkmalschutzgesetz, 1973; Hessen: Hessisches Gesetz zum Schutze der Kulturdenkmäler (Denkmalschutzgesetz), 1974; Niedersachsen: Niedersächsisches Denkmalschutzgesetz, 1978; Rheinland-Pfalz: Landesgesetz über die Pflege und den Schutz der Kulturdenkmäler, 1978; Saarland: Saarländisches Denkmalschutzgesetz, 1977; Schleswig-Holstein: Gesetz zum Schutze der Kulturdenkmale, 1972.

16 Sir D. Walsh (chairman), 'Report of the Committee of Enquiry into Arrangements for the Protection of Field Monuments, 1966–1968', *Parliamentary Papers*, vol. 32 (London, 1969), pp. 739–825 (1–79).

17 A. Paech, 'Stellt die Teiche und Gräben der alten Oberharzer Wasserwirtschaft endlich unter Denkmalschutz!', *Unser Harz*, no. 26 (1978), pp. 63–6.

18 Landesvermessungsamt Nordrhein-Westfalen (Hrsg.), *Musterblatt für die topographische Karte 1:25,000* (Bad Godesberg, 1967).

19 Denecke, *Die historisch-geographische Landesaufnahme*, pp. 428–31, Table 5 and Fig. 10.

20 The substantial and comprehensive record kept by the division of the Archaeological Data Collection gives a 'Features List' comprising more than 470 features: British Ordnance Survey, *Publication and Map Revision, General Outline*, Appendix 1: Features List. For Switzerland, see H. Suter, 'Die Bestandsaufnahme der Kulturgüter in der Schweiz, eine Aufgabe der Eidgenössischen Landestopographie', *Schweizerische Zeitschrift für Vermessung, Photogrammetrie und Kulturtechnik*, no. 64 (1966), pp. 255–64.

21 R. M. Newcomb, *Planning the Past: Historical Landscape Resources and Recreation* (Folkestone, 1979).

22 D. Uthoff, 'Das historische Stadtbild als Wirtschaftsfaktor. Eine Fallstudie am Beispiel der Stadt Goslar' in *Denkmalpflege 1975. Tagung der Landesdenkmalpfleger in Goslar 1975* (Hannover, 1976).

23 Bavaria: H. Frei, *Der frühe Eisenerzbergbau und seine Gelände-spuren im nördlichen Alpenvorland*, Münchner Geographische, vol. 29 (Kallmünz, 1966), Figs. 4, 6, and Map 4: 'Ausschnitt-Kartierungen von Eisenerzschürffeldern; Bergisches Land: Düsterloh, *Beiträge zur Kulturgeographie*, Fig. 17: 'Obers-

prockhövel-Gennebreck, Nergbau- und Verhüttingspuren im Gelände; Hessia: E. Ernst, 'Stahlnhain – eine mittelalterliche Wüstung im Erlenbachtal' in E. Ernst and H. Klingsporn (eds.), *Hessen in Karte und Luftbild, Topographischer Atlas*, vol. I (Neumünster, 1969), Map, p. 111; Harz Mountains: Denecke, *Die historisch-geographische Landesaufnahme*, Fig. 8: 'Ausschnitt aus der Geländeaufnahme im Harz: Relikte des mittelalterlichen und neuzeitlichen Bergbaus im Lerbacher Eisensteinrevier, Grubenfeld Hohebleek'; Denecke, *Archäologisches Korrespondenzblatt*, vol. 8, Fig. 1, 'Grubenbezirk Rammelsberg im Mittelalter'; northern Lower Saxony: G. Schulz, 'Die Kartierung mittelalterlicher und frühneuzeitlicher Eisenschmelzplätze und Meiler in der Wietze-Niederung bei Isernhagen, Kr. Burgdorf', *Neue Ausgrabungen und Forschungen in Niedersachsen*, no. 7 (1972), pp. 308–33.

24 A very good example is the strategic landscape plan for Göttingen County. The plan was elaborated as a model and pilot study for further plans in Lower Saxony. In this plan for the first time *Altlandschaftsgebiete* were defined and proposals made to preserve them. D. Denecke, 'Altlandschaften und Kulturdenkmale, Übersichtsplan 6 und Katalog' in *Landschaftsrahmenplan Göttingen*, vol. 2, Erläuterungen (Göttingen, 1977), pp. 11–29.

25 Denecke, *Die historisch-geographische Landesaufnahme*, pp. 414f.

26 C. Dahm and U. Lobbedey, *Die Bergbausiedlung Altenberg* (Hilchenbach, 1979).

27 Newcomb, *Planning the Past*, esp. the example of 'A proposed outdoor historic site illustrating British field systems – Wormleighton, England', pp. 132–41.

28 Examples of detailed microsurveys of scatters of shards on sites of deserted and completely vanished settlements are given in: E. Kühlhorn, *Untersuchungen zur Topographie mittelalterlicher Dörfer in Südniedersachsen*, Forschungen zur deutschen Landeskunde, no. 148 (Bad Godesberg, 1964); W. Janssen, *Königshagen. Ein archäologisch-historischer Beitrag zur Siedlungsgeschichte des südwestlichen Harzvorlandes*, Quellen und Darstellungen zur Geschichte Niedersachsens, vol. 64 (Hildesheim, 1965), Taf. 20, 'Königshagen, der Wüstung'; Gesamtplan der Siedlungsreste auf dem Gebiet; D. Denecke, 'Die Ortswüstung Oldendorp bei Einbeck und die "Alten Dörfer" im Leinebergland', *Einbecker Jahrbuch*, vol. 29 (1970), pp. 20–3, esp. Fig. 3: 'Oberflächenfunde und Bodenmerkmale auf dem wüsten Siedlungsplatz Oldendorp'.

29 B. Meyer and U. Willerding, 'Bodenprofile, Pflanzenreste und Fundmaterial von neu erschlossenen, neolithischen und eisenzeitlichen Siedlungsstellen im Göttinger Stodtgebiet', *Göttinger Jahrbuch*, vol. 9 (1961), pp. 21–38. Raddatz, *Neue Ausgrabungen und Forschungen*, vol. 5.

30 D. Denecke, 'Die Rekonstruktion wüster Orts- und Hausgrundrisse mit Hilfe des Luftbildes. Methodische Untersuchungen am Beispiel der spätmittelalterlichen Wüstung Moseborn', *Nachrichten aus Niedersachsens Urgeschichte*, no. 43 (1974), pp. 69–84; D. Kirchner, 'Versuch einer Rekonstruktion des Ortsgrundrisses der Wüstung Friwole (Vredewolt), Gem. Hardegsen (Kr. Nort heim) mit Hilfe bon Handbohrungen', *Göttinger Jahrbuch*, vol. 26 (1978), pp. 67–91.

31 Since Hassinger began a building survey in Vienna in 1910, Dörries continued to develop this method for Göttingen, Northeim and Einbeck in Lower Saxony

in 1923, and other authors have continued these studies for some neighbouring towns. Modern surveys in connection with studies of social structure and architecture have been published by Lichtenberger for Vienna, Möller for Hamburg, Lafrenz for Lübeck and finally by Meynen for Cologne. A model for Britain is the comprehensive study by Conzen on Alnwick or the study by Hinton and Carpenter on Oxford. A national project comprising a total survey of all the cities and towns in Austria was started by A. Klaar. See: H. Hassinger, 'Kartographische Aufnahme des Wiener Stadtbildes', *Mitteilungen der Geographischen Gesellschaft in Wien*, vol. 58 (1915), pp. 6–8; H. Dörries, *Die Städte im oberen Leinetal, Göttingen, Northeim und Einbeck*, Landeskundliche Arbeiten des Geographischen Seminars der Universität Göttingen, vol. 1 (Göttingen, 1925); Denecke, *Die historisch-geographische Landesaufnahme*, pp. 406–8, Figs. 1 and 3; E. Lichtenberger, *Wien: Bauliche Gestalt und Entwicklung seit der Mitte des 19 Jahrhunderts* (Köln/Graz, 1966); I. Möller, *Die Entwicklung eines Hamburger Gebietes von der Agrar- zur Großstadtlandschaft, Mit einem Beitrag zur Methode der städtischen Aufrißanalyse*, Hamburger Geographische Studien, no. 10 (Hamburg, 1959); J. Lafrenz, *Die Stellung der Innenstadt im Flachennutzungsgefüge des Afflomerationsraumes Lübeck: Grundlagenforschung zur erhaltenden Stadterneuerung*, Hamburger Geographische Studien, no. 33 (Hamburg, 1977), pp. 81–103; H. Maynen, *Die Wohnbauten im nordwestlichen Vorortsektor Kölns mit Ehrenfeld als Mittelpunkt: Bauliche Entwicklungen seit 1845, Wechselbeziehungen von Baubild und Sozialstruktur*, Rheinisches Archiv, no. 104 (Bonn, 1978); M. R. G. Conzen, *Alnwick, Northumberland, a Study in Town-Plan Analysis*, Institute of British Geographers, no. 27 (London, 1969); D. A. Hinton and D. Carpenter, *Oxford Builders from Medieval to Modern* (Oxford, 1972); A. Klaar, *Baualterpläne österreichischer Städte*, ed. by Österriechischen Akademie der Wissenschaften, Kommission für die Historischen Atlas der Alpenländer (Wien, 1972).

32 An excellent model of a comprehensive and detailed architectural building survey is the 'Survey of London' of the Greater London Council, published since 1900 in to date 39 volumes covering a great number of the ancient parishes. There are also in Germany many survey schemes of local authorities. For methods employed and general information compare F. H. W. Sheppard, 'Sources and Methods used for the Survey of London', in H. J. Dyos (ed.), *The Study of Urban History* (1968), pp. 131–45. A comprehensive national documentation of historic buildings in the United States has been compiled in the active files of the Historic American Buildings Survey, Office of Archaeology and Historic Preservation, Library of Congress, Washington D.C.

33 One example based on modern survey methods is the selective survey that is being compiled for cities, towns and villages in Lower Saxony by Niedersächsisches Ministerium für Wissenschaft und Kunst, Denkmalpflege.

34 General publications: H. Foramitti and P. Leisching, *Wiederbelebung historischer Stadtviertel* (Köln/Graz, 1965); P. Ward (ed.), *Conservation and Development in Historic Towns and Cities* (Newcastle-upon-Tyne, 1969). Examples of local projects: A. R. H. Baker, 'Keeping the Past in the Present: The Preservation of French Townscapes', *Town and Country Planning*, vol. 37 (1969), pp. 308–11; Landeskonservator Rheinland (ed.), *Technische Denk-*

mäler, Arbeitersiedlungen, vols. 1 and 2, Arbeitshefte Landeskonservator Rheinland 1 and 3 (Köln, 1971, 1972); H. Hörmann, *Regensburg, Erneuerung einer alten Stadt* (Düsseldorf/Wien, 1967); T. G. Hassall, 'Urban Surveys: Medieval Oxford' in A. Rogers and T. Rowley (eds.), *Landscapes and Documents* (London, 1974), pp. 49–62.

35 W. Gallusser and W. Buchmann, 'Der Kulturlandschaftswandel in der Schweiz als geographisches Forschungsprogramme', *Geographica Helvetica*, vol. 29 (1974), pp. 49–70, esp.: 'Gebäudekonstruktionskartierung'; see also the publications of the group working on an 'Inventar der schützenswerten Ortsbilder der Schweiz'; D. Wieland, *Bauen und Bewahren auf dem Lande*, Deutsches Nationalkomitee für Denkmalschutz (Stuttgart, 1978).

36 P. Breitling, H. D. Kammeier and G. Loch, *Tübingen, erhaltende Erneuerung eines Stadtkerns*, Staatliche Denkmalpflege in Baden-Württemberg, Forschung und Berichte der Bau- und Kunstdenkmalpflege, vol. 1 (München/Berlin, 1971); V. Mayr (ed.), *Baualtersplan zur Stadtsanierung: Amberg*, Baualterspläne zur Stadtsanierung in Bayern, vol. 1 (München, 1972); G. Albers, P. Breitling and F. Bühler, *Stadtkernerneuerung und Entwichklungsplanung, Beispiel Altstadt Ulm: Studien und Modellvorhaben zur Erneuerung von Städten und Dörfern im Rahmen des Förderungsprogrammes des Bundesministeriums für Städtebau und Wohnungswesen*, Veröffentlichungen der Forschungsgemeinschaft Bauen und Wohnen, vol. 92 (Stuttgart, 1973).

37 Local examples: D. Benson and J. Cook, *The City of Oxford Redevelopment, Archaeological Implications* (Oxford, 1966); T. G. Hassall, *Oxford: the City beneath your Feet*, Archaeological Excavations in the City of Oxford, 1967–1972 (Oxford, 1972); M. Biddle and D. Hudson, *The Future of London's Past: a Survey of the Archaeologic Implications of Planning and Development in the Nation's Capital*, Rescue Publications, no. 4 (Worcester, 1973); V. Vogel, *Die archäologischen Ausgrabungen im Stadtkern von Schleswig*, Ausgrabungen in Deutschland, Monographien des Römisch-Germanischen Zentralmuseums, vols. 1 and 3 (Mainz, 1975); P. G. Fehring, 'Lübeck, Archäologie einer Großstadt des Mittelalters' in W. Neugebauer *et al.* (eds.), *Lübeck 1226, Reichsfreiheit und frühe Stadt*, Festschrift (Lübeck, 1976), pp. 267–98. General: C. M. Heighway (ed.), *The Erosion of History: Archaeology and Planning in Towns* (London, 1972).

38 Baker, 'Keeping the Past in the Present'.

39 Newcomb, *Planning the Past*, p. 143.

Notes to McQuillan, 'Interface', pp. 136–144

1 R. A. Kalnicky, 'Climate Change since 1950', *Annals, Association of American Geographers*, vol. 64 (1974), pp. 100–12; E. W. Wahl and T. L. Lawson, 'The Climate of the Mid-nineteenth Century United States Compared to the Current Normals', *Monthly Weather Review*, vol. 96 (1968), pp. 81–2; J. C. Knox, 'Human Impacts on Wisconsin Stream Channels', *Annals, Association of American Geographers*, vol. 67 (1977), pp. 323–42.

2 C. W. Thornthwaite, 'An Approach toward a Rational Classification of

Climate', *Geographical Review*, vol. 38 (1948), pp. 55–94. A significant contribution to understanding the nature of droughts is W. C. Palmer, *Meteorological Drought* (Washington, D.C., 1965). See also T. F. Saarinen, *Perception of the Drought Hazard on the Great Plains* (Chicago, 1966).

3 The sampling method is described in D. A. McQuillan, 'Adaptation of Three Immigrant Groups to Farming in Central Kansas, 1875–1925', unpublished Ph.D. thesis, University of Wisconsin, Madison, 1975, pp. 366–76.

4 R. W. Hecht, *Labor Used to Produce Livestock. Estimates by States, 1959* (Washington, D.C., 1963); R. W. Hecht and K. R. Vice, *Labor Used for Field Crops* (Washington, D.C., 1954).

5 J. C. Weaver, 'Crop Combination Regions in the Middle West', *Geographical Review*, vol. 44 (1954), pp. 175–200.

6 C. N. Castle, *Adapting Western Kansas Farms to Uncertain Prices and Yields* (Topeka, 1974).

7 Rather a lot of emphasis, some of it misplaced, has been given to the role of Mennonites in the introduction of hard winter wheat to Kansas: J. C. Malin, *Winter Wheat in the Golden Belt of Kansas, A Study in Adaptation to Subhumid Geographical Environment* (Lawrence, 1944), p. 167. In the sample townships of the study cited in note 3, Mennonites planted a larger acreage of corn than wheat in the early decades.

8 D. C. McQuillan, 'Farm Size and Work Ethic: Measuring the Success of Immigrant Farmers on the American Grasslands, 1875–1925', *Journal of Historical Geography*, vol. 4 (1978), pp. 57–76; D. A. McQuillan, 'The Mobility of Immigrants and Americans: a Comparison of Farmers on the Kansas Frontier', *Agricultural History*, vol. 53 (1979), pp. 576–96.

9 R. A. Bryson and T. J. Murray, *Climates of Hunger: Mankind and the World's Changing Weather* (Madison, 1977); H. H. Lamb, *Climate: Present, Past and Future* (London, 1972). In addition to the studies cited in note 1, see C. W. Sorenson, 'Reconstructed Holocene Bioclimates', *Annals, Association of American Geographers*, vol. 67 (1977), pp. 214–22; S. W. Trimble, *Man-induced Soil Erosion on the Southern Piedmont, 1700–1970* (Washington, D.C., 1974); G. Farmer, M. J. Ingram *et al.* (eds.), *Review Papers for International Conference of Climate and History* (Norwich, 1979).

10 A fine example of this cooperation is D. W. Moodie and A. J. Catchpole, *Environmental Data from Historical Documents by Content Analysis: Freeze-up and Break-up of Estuaries on Hudson Bay, 1714–1871* (Winnipeg, 1975).

Notes to Sporrong, 'Individualistic features', pp. 145–154

1 U. Sporrong, *Mälarlandskapen mellan historia och förhistoria*, Reports from Department of Human Geography, FARS no. 30 (Stockholm, 1976).

2 U. Sporrong, 'Medieval Traces in Today's Landscape', paper presented to the 1979 Permanent Conference for the Study of the Rural Landscape.

3 S. Göransson, 'Viking Age Traces in Swedish Systems for Territorial Organisation and Land Division' in T. Andersson and K. I. Sandred (eds.), *The Vikings*, Acta Universitatis Upsaliensis (Uppsala, 1978).

4 B. Berglund, 'Vegetation and Human Influence in South Scandinavia during

Prehistoric Time', *Oikos* (1969); D. Hannerberg, *Svenskt agrarsamhälle under 1200 år* (Lund, 1971).
5 H. Andersson and L. Redin, *Medeltidsstaden: stads-arkeologi i Mellansverige* (forthcoming).
6 A. R. H. Baker, 'Field Systems of Southeast England' in A. R. H. Baker, and R. A. Butlin (eds.), *Studies of Field Systems in the British Isles* (Cambridge, 1973), pp. 377–429; R. A. Dodgshon, 'The Early Middle Ages, 1066–1350' in R. A. Dodgshon and R. A. Butlin (eds.), *An Historical Geography of England and Wales* (London, 1978), pp. 95–100; B. Roberts, *Rural Settlement in Britain* (Folkstone, 1978); J. Sheppard, 'Metrological Analysis of Regular Village Plans in Yorkshire', *Agricultural History Review*, vol. 22 (1974).

Notes to Göranson, 'Land use', pp. 155–163

1 For interpretations of settlement history before A.D. 1050 here and elsewhere in this article, see for example S.-O. Lindquist, *Det förhistoriska kulturlandskapet i östra Östergötland* (Stockholm, 1968); U. Sporrong, *Kolonisation, bebyggelseutveckling och administration* (Lund, 1971), and U. Göranson, *Kulturlandskapsförändring och Samhällsutveckling* (Stockholm, 1977).
2 U. Sporrong, 'Bysamhället', *Svensk landsbygd* (Surte, 1973), p. 33.
3 *Ibid.* p. 16.
4 S.-O. Lindquist, 'Fossilt kulturlandskap som kulturhistorisk källa', *Västergötlands Fornminnesförenings Tidskrift 1975–1976* (1976), p. 157.
5 J. Ferenius, *Vårby och Vårberg* (Stockholm, 1971), p. 114.
6 B. Stjernquist, 'Das Problem der Grubenhäuser in Südschweden', *Jahrbuch des Römisch-Germanischen Zentralmuseums Mainz*, vol. 14 (1967), pp. 144–52.
7 B. Pamp, *Ortnamnen i Sverige* (Malmö, 1971), pp. 36–7, 41, 44.
8 L. Hellberg, 'Kumlabygdens ortnamn och äldre bebyggelse', *Kumlabygden* (Kumla, 1967), p. 358.

Notes to Egerbladh, 'Significance of time', pp. 164–179

1 A survey is given by P. Haggett, A. D. Cliff and A. Frey, *Locational Analysis in Human Geography*, vol. 1: *Locational Models* (London, 1977).
2 *Ibid.* p. 106; R. L. Morrill, 'Simulation of Central Place Patterns Over Time' in K. Norberg (ed.), *Proceedings of the IGU Symposium in Urban Geography*, Lund Studies in Geography, Series B: Human Geography, no. 24 (1962).
3 E. Bylund, *Koloniseringen av Pite lappmark t. o. m. år 1867*, Geographica, no. 30 (Uppsala, 1956), and *idem*, 'Theoretical Considerations Regarding the Distribution of Settlement in Inner North Sweden', *Geografiska Annaler*, vol. 42 (1960); J. C. Hudson, *Theoretical Settlement Geography* (mimeographed, University of Iowa, 1967); and *idem*, 'A Locational Theory for Rural Settlement', *Annals, Association of American Geographers*, vol. 58 (1969); S.-O. Lindquist, *Det förhistoriska kulturlandskapet i Östra Östergötland* (Stockholm, 1968).
4 All the settlement units are supposed *a priori* to need a given area expressed as circular domains. The process continues until all the land is occupied, and then

a separation by boundaries takes place, which is achieved in the model by using Thiessen polygons. The empirical base for the model is the development of central Sweden, but Lindquist claims it valid also for much later colonized areas. The boundaries in the latter case need not be formal, but informal limits for areas of interest. See Lindquist, *Förhistoriska.*

5 This process is called spread in Hudson's theory (Theoretical Settlement Geography and 'A Locational Theory'), but Bylund ('Theoretical Considerations'), names it 'clon-colonization', and Lindquist (*Förhistorika*), 'inner-colonization'.

6 Concerning Bylund's models in 'Theoretical Considerations', no patterns are implied by him, but the spatial consequences have been deduced and tested by G. Olsson, 'Complementary Models: a Study of Colonization Maps', *Geografiska annaler,* Series B, vol. 50 (1968).

7 Bylund, 'Theoretical Considerations', also considers effects on location and directions in the evolution of clusters by attractions and barriers.

8 Properly as a point = the site of settlement, and/or an area = land belonging to the unit: see Lindquist, *Förhistorika.*

9 As compact holdings with the farms at the centre are desirable in order to minimize transport costs, the dispersed pattern will be the most efficient. Whether a relocation is implicitly supposed in conjunction with abandonment of farms is not evident: see Hudson, 'A Locational Theory'.

10 This development is reflected in Swedish medieval laws and described also for other countries, for example V. Hansen, 'The Medieval Dispersal of Rural Settlement in Denmark as a Function of Distance from Primary Nucleations' in Buchanan, Butlin and McCourt (eds.), *Fields, Farms and Settlement in Europe* (Newry, 1976). For this kind of diffusion of settlement Chisholm has suggested four preconditions, of which changes in the landholding system might be the most important in industrialized areas: M. D. I. Chisholm, *Rural Settlement and Land-use: an Essay in Location* (London, 1962).

11 This unit was initially applied to an area to sustain a household at an early stage of agriculture, but over time a successively smaller part of this unit was enough for one household, which is reflected in rules concerning the division of holdings or the minimal size of a new holding. The Swedish equivalent is *mantal.*

12 The date of the first sedentary settlement is not known. Archaeological evidence is sparse, but ongoing research, mostly in the palaeoecological field, suggests that rural settlement units were founded somewhat earlier than the beginning of the fourteenth century.

13 Å. Holmbäck and E. Wessén, *Svenska landskapslagar: Södermannalagen och Hälsingelagen* (Uppsala, 1940), and *Magnus Erikssons landslag i nusvensk tolkning: Rättshistoriskt bibliotek* (Stockholm, 1962); Å. Holmbäck, 'Studier över de svenska allmänningarnas historia', *Uppsala universitets årsskrift* (1920, Juridik 1); I. Jonsson, *Finnbebyggelsens lokalisering i Hälsingland och södra Medelpad, Forskningsrapporter från Kulturgeografiska institutionen,* Uppsala Universitet, no. 10 (1968); and G. Prawitz, 'En 1300-tals avvittring i Hälsingland', *Svensk lantmäteritidskrift* (1943).

14 K.-G. Selinge, *Agrarian Settlements and Hunting Grounds: a Study of the Prehistoric Culture Systems in a North Swedish River Valley* (Stockholm, 1979).

15 M. R. J. Jarman, 'A Territorial Model for Archaeology: a Behavioural and Geographical Approach' in D. L. Clarke (ed.), *Models in Archaeology* (London, 1972). The time-distance according to Clarke is cited in E. Baudou, 'Den förhistoriska fångstkulturen i Västernorrland', *Västernorrlands förhistoria* (Motala, 1977).

16 The calculation is based upon maps printed in Bylund, *Koloniseringen*, and F. Hultblad, *Övergång från rennomadism till agrar bosättning i Jokkmokks socken* (Lund, 1968).

17 N. Arell, *Rennomadism i Torne lappmark* (Umeå, 1977).

18 J. E. Almquist, 'Det Norrländska avvittringsverket', *Svenska lantmäteriet, 1628–1928* (Stockholm, 1928); and Jonsson, *Finnbebyggelsens*.

19 Chisholm, *Rural Settlement and Land-use*.

20 Regarding units in inland location, however, factors other than agriculture might explain the small domains, for instance a high reliance upon fishing.

21 This evidence takes the form of mixed ownership in infields and/or outfields, periodical joint fiscal registration, or in a few cases, statements in court records referring to an earlier primary–secondary relationship.

22 Almquist, 'Det norrländska', and C. E. Enagrius, *Samling av lantmäteriförfattningar* (Stockholm, 1826).

23 T. Hahr, *Samling av författningar rörande skogsväsendet* (Stockholm, 1906).

24 G. Enequist, *Nedre Luledalens byar: En kulturgeografisk studie*, Geographica, no. 4 (Uppsala, 1937).

25 N. Wohlin, *Den svenska jordstyckningspolitiken i de 18e och 19e århundradena* (Stockholm, 1912).

Notes to Ukita, 'Cotton production', pp. 180–186

1 Kannokyoku, *Zenkoku Nosanhyo 1877* (Tokyo, 1879).

2 T. Ukita, 'The Cotton Production in Japan during the Edo Era', *Human Geography (Jimbun Chiri)*, vol. 7 (1955), pp. 266–83.

3 T. Ukita, 'Land Use in the Nara Basin in the Tokugawa Shogunate', *Geographical Review of Japan (Chirigaku Hyoron)*, vol. 30 (1957), pp. 927–46.

Notes to Guelke, 'Historical geography', pp. 189–196

1 R. G. Collingwood, *The Idea of History* (New York, 1956; first edn., 1946).

2 *Ibid.* pp. 206–9.

3 *Ibid.* p. 213.

4 T. G. Bergin and M. H. Fisch, *The New Science of Giambattista Vico* (New York, 1961), pp. 52–3.

5 Collingwood, *Idea of History*, p. 170.

6 L. Guelke, 'An Idealist Alternative in Human Geography', *Annals, Association of American Geographers*, vol. 64 (1974), pp. 198–9.

7 R. G. Collingwood and J. N. L. Myers, *Roman Britain and the English Settlements* (London, 1937), pp. 124–34.

8 L. J. Goldstein, 'Collingwood's Theory of Historical Knowing', *History and Theory*, vol. 9 (1970), p. 32.

9 Collingwood, *Idea of History*, p. 216.
10 *Ibid.* p. 215.
11 L. Rubinoff, *Collingwood and the Reform of Metaphysics* (Toronto, 1970), pp. 278–9.
12 Collingwood, *Idea of History*, p. 227.
13 Rubinoff, *Reform of Metaphysics*, p. 288.
14 D. W. Moodie and J. C. Lehr, 'Fact and Theory in Historical Geography', *The Professional Geographer*, vol. 18 (1976), pp. 132–5.
15 Guelke, 'An Idealist Alternative', p. 198.

Notes to Chambers, 'Images', pp. 197–204

1 This paper is a part of a much larger work. Here I limit myself to a critique of the historical geosophical literature of farming frontiers, especially the North American Great Plains.
2 The term 'geosophy' was coined by J. K. Wright in '*Terrae Incognitae*: The Place of the Imagination in Geography' in *Human Nature in Geography* (Cambridge, Mass., 1966), p. 83.
3 See, for example, the review article by R. Downs and J. Meyer, 'Geography and the Mind: An Exploration of Perceptual Geography', *American Behavioral Scientist*, vol. 22 (Sept.–Oct. 1978), p. 60.
4 Yi-fu Tuan, 'Discrepancies between Environmental Attitudes and Behavior: Examples from Europe and China', *Canadian Geographer*, vol. 12 (1968), p. 176.
5 I am aware that there are numerous formulations of the sociology of knowledge. Here I do not refer to Mannheim, or Berger and Luckmann, or any other scheme in particular. Rather, what is meant is that in a society different groups have different ideas, attitudes, values and images – that knowledge is not held in common.
6 This is *not* to distinguish elite from popular images, nor correct from incorrect images. Which images are required depends entirely upon whose behaviour we want to understand.
7 M. Bowden, 'Desert Wheat Belt, Plains Corn Belt: Environmental Cognition and Behavior' in B. Blouet and M. P. Lawson (eds.), *Images of the Plains: The Role of Human Nature in Settlement* (Lincoln, Nebraska, 1975), p. 192.
8 J. Tyman, 'Subjective Surveyors: the Appraisal of Farm Lands in Western Canada, 1870–1930' in Blouet and Lawson (eds.), *Images of the Plains*, p. 89.
9 D. Wishart, 'Images of the Northern Great Plains from the Fur Trade, 1807–43' in Blouet and Lawson (eds.), *Images of the Plains*, pp. 45–55.
10 M. P. Lawson, 'Towards a Geosophic Climate of the Great American Desert: The Plains Climate of the Forty-Niners' in Blouet and Lawson (eds.), *Images of the Plains*, pp. 101–13; R. Jackson, 'Mormon Perception and Settlement of the Great Plains' in Blouet and Lawson (eds.), *Images of the Plains*, pp. 137–47.
11 R. Jackson, 'Mormon Perception and Settlement', *Annals, Association of American Geographers*, vol. 68 (September 1978), pp. 317–334. In this article Jackson shows that Mormon leader Brigham Young decided where to settle in the western United States after discussing possible sites with fur traders.

12 J. M. Powell, *Mirrors of the New World: Images and Image-Makers in the Settlement Process* (Folkestone, 1977), pp. 64–5.

13 G. M. Lewis, 'Regional Ideas and Reality in the Cis-Rocky Mountain West', *Transactions of the Institute of British Geographers*, vol. 38 (June 1966), pp. 135–50.

14 M. Bowden, 'The Great American Desert and the American Frontier, 1880–1883' in T. Hareven (ed.), *Anonymous Americans: Explorations in Nineteenth-Century Social History* (Englewood Cliffs, 1971), pp. 48–79; *idem*, 'The Great American Desert in the American Mind: The Historiography of a Geographical Notion' in D. Lowenthal and M. Bowden (eds.), *Geographies of the Mind* (New York, 1975), pp. 119–47; *idem*, 'Desert Wheat Belt, Plains Corn Belt: Environmental Cognition and Behavior' in Blouet and Lawson (eds.), *Images of the Plains*, pp. 189–201.

15 Lewis, 'Regional Ideas', p. 137.

16 For example, see D. Lowenthal, 'The American Scene', *Geographical Review* (January 1968), pp. 61–88. Lowenthal seems to be unsure whether people make landscape conform to their ideals (p. 61), or if people's values are determined by their way of life and the environment (p. 88).

17 There is a logical limitation on the uses of images derived from acts. When we derive people's attitudes solely from records of their acts then we cannot explain those acts by using the images we have derived: a derived image cannot be used to explain the act it was derived from. (See W. James, *Pragmatism: A New Name for Some Old Ways of Thinking* (Cambridge, Mass., 1978), pp. 46, 126.) Yet geosophers have fallen into this trap. For example, Malcolm Lewis uses circular reasoning when he speculates on the Indians' perception of the prairie–forest boundary: see 'The Recognition and Delimitation of the Northern Interior Grasslands during the Eighteenth Century' in Blouet and Lawson (eds.), *Images of the Plains*, pp. 23–44, esp. p. 36.

18 R. L. Heathcote, *Back of Bourke: a Study of Land Appraisal and Settlement in Semi-Arid Australia* (London, 1965), pp. 62–78. Of course, rent is a synopsis of many factors (such as soil quality, availability of water and timber, access to markets) and from rent alone we cannot evaluate the relative importance of each of these factors.

19 Heathcote reports that even the Australian government came to realize that 'the ultimate test of evaluation was . . . the sale price of the land. . . . All pretence at the evaluation of land on purely natural merits has [to be] abandoned.' By implication, Heathcote's own use of land rents was also pretence, though he does not seem to recognize this. See *Back of Bourke*, p. 71.

20 This is a familiar problem in all of the social sciences, but it is compounded in historical inquiries because all historical documents, written or not, are records of the *consequences* of people's acts. Only in the present can we observe acts without attending to the consequences of acts.

21 The exception, of course, is that the taken-for-granted values expressed in everyday activities have no verbal record of intentions; they are unselfconscious.

22 For a good, short introduction to this model of man, see I. C. Jarvie, *Concepts and Society* (London, 1972), pp. 3–35; another treatment can be found in R.

Berkhofer Jr, *A Behavioral Approach to Historical Analysis* (New York, 1969), pp. 32–74.

23 See D. Carveth, 'The Disembodied Dialectic', *Theory and Society*, vol. 4 (Spring 1977), pp. 73–102, esp. p. 91. I am grateful to David Evans for bringing this article to my attention. For a view of the intentionality of past events that is very different from mine, see L. Guelke, 'An Idealist Alternative in Human Geography', *Annals, Association of American Geographers*, vol. 64 (June 1974), pp. 193–202.

24 Powell, *Mirrors of the New World*, pp. 25–6.

25 H. R. Merrens, 'The Physical Environment of Early America: Images and Image-makers in Colonial South Carolina', *Geographical Review*, vol. 59 (October 1969), p. 550.

26 For example, see: D. A. McQuillan, 'Territory and Ethnic Identity' in J. R. Gibson (ed.), *European Settlement and Development in North America* (Toronto, 1978), pp. 136–69; J. Rice, 'The Role of Culture and Community in Frontier Prairie Farming', *Journal of Historical Geography*, vol. 3 (1977), pp. 155–75; J. T. Lemon, *The Best Poor Man's Country* (New York, 1976), pp. xv, 42–6, 70; H. C. Brookfield, 'On the Environment as Perceived', *Progress in Geography*, vol. 1 (London, 1969), p. 71.

27 See R. C. Harris and L. Guelke, 'Land and Society in Early Canada and South Africa', *Journal of Historical Geography*, vol. 3 (1977), pp. 135–53.

28 On whether images are visual see Yi-fu Tuan, 'Images and Mental Maps', *Annals, Association of American Geographers*, vol. 65 (June 1975), pp. 205–13. In this article Tuan doubts that 'people walk about with pictures in the head, or that people's spatial behavior is guided by picture-like images and mental maps that are like real maps' (p. 213). By 'specific' I mean factual, analyzable and conscious – useful when making decisions by weighing alternatives. This I contrast with 'conceptual' which is general, thematic, synthetic and usually (though not always) unselfconscious. On the thematic nature of concepts and their role in the scientific enterprise (which in many ways is comparable to geographical exploration), see G. Holton, *Thematic Origins of Scientific Thought* (Cambridge, Mass., 1973), pp. 11–44.

29 See Yi-fu Tuan, *Topophilia* (Englewood Cliffs, 1974), pp. 193–9. Tuan writes that as people become accustomed to an environment their images of it become diffuse, implicit and inarticulatable.

30 Bowden in Blouet and Lawson (eds.), *Images of the Plains*, pp. 193–9.

31 Heathcote, *Back of Bourke*, pp. 166, 195–7.

32 J. Allen, 'An Analysis of the Exploratory Process', *Geographical Review*, vol. 62 (1972), pp. 13–39. For a philosophical approach to rationality as the ability to cope with novelty see S. Toulmin, *Human Understanding* (Princeton, 1972).

33 See J. Allen, 'Division of the Waters', *Journal of Historical Geography*, vol. 4 (1978), pp. 357–70.

34 K. Boulding, *The Image: Knowledge in Life and Society* (Ann Arbor, 1956), p. 79.

35 Carl Sauer wrote, 'Every human landscape, every habitation, at any moment is an accumulation of practical experience.' J. Leighly (ed.), *Land and Life* (Berkeley, 1963), p. 366. Similarly, Stephen Toulmin writes that the theory of

knowledge has lost touch with the 'historical procedures by which our practical knowledge is extended'. *Human Understanding*, p. 13.

36 Toulmin writes, 'Men demonstrate their rationality not by ordering their concepts and beliefs in tidy formal structures, but by their preparedness to respond to novel situations with open minds.' *Human Understanding*, pp. vii–viii, 83, 85.

37 Much of this section comes from conversations with Professor Fred Lukermann of the University of Minnesota.

38 F. A. Hayek, 'Scientism and the Study of Society' in J. O'Neill (ed.), *Modes of Individualism and Collectivism* (New York, 1973), pp. 27–67, quotation from p. 40. At least one geographer sees geosophy as dealing with problems of psychology: see Lewis in Blouet and Lawson (eds.), *Images of the Plains*, pp. 23–44 – a good example of how far this can go.

Notes to Claval, 'Image of France', pp. 205–11

1 L. Gallois, *Régions naturelles et noms de pays: Étude sur la région parisienne* (Paris, 1908).

2 R. Dion, *Les frontières de la France* (Paris, 1947).

3 P. Chaunu and R. Gascon, *Histoire économique et sociale de la France*, vol. I: *1450–1660, L'État et la Ville* (Paris, 1977).

4 G. Huppert, *L'idée de l'histoire parfaite* (Paris, 1973).

5 P. Goubert, *Centmille provinciaux au XVIIIe siècle* (Paris, 1968).

6 N. Elias, *Die höfische Gesellschaft*, translated as *La société de cour* (Paris, 1975).

7 N. Elias, *La Civilisation des moeurs* (Paris, 1975).

Notes to Senda, 'Perceived space', pp. 212–219

1 J. Needham and L. Wang, *Science and Civilisation in China*, vol. 3, pt 3: *The Science of the Earth* (Cambridge, 1959), p. 502.

2 K. Ashicaga, 'On the Planning of the Ancient Capital' in M. Ueda (ed.), *Tojyo (Ancient Capital)* (Tokyo, 1976), pp. 191–226.

3 K. Fujioka, *Kokufu* (Tokyo, 1969), pp. 17–35.

4 R. Kinoshita, 'On the Crossroad in *Kokufu*', *The Historical Geographical Review* (1977), pp. 5–32.

5 M. Senda, 'Structure in Ancient Space', *Geographical Studies, Nara Women's University*, no. 1 (1979).

6 M. Senda, 'Semiological Approach to Geographical Space and Mandala Pattern', *Abstracts for the Congress of the Human Geographical Society of Japan* (1979).

Notes to Cosgrove, 'Problems', pp. 220–230

1 M. Mikesell, 'Cultural Geography', *Progress in Human Geography*, vol. 1 (1977), pp. 460–4; C. O. Sauer, 'Foreword to Historical Geography' and 'The Morphology of Landscape' in J. Leighly (ed.), *Land and Life: A Selection*

from the Writings of Carl Ortwin Sauer (Berkeley, 1963), pp. 351–404 and 315–50.

2 L. Guelke, 'An Idealist Alternative in Human Geography', *Annals, Association of American Geographers*, vol. 64 (1974), pp. 193–202; *idem*, 'On Rethinking Historical Geography', *Area*, vol. 7 (1975), pp. 135–8; D. Gregory, 'The Discourse of the Past: Phenomenology, Structuralism and Historical Geography', *Journal of Historical Geography*, vol. 4 (1978), pp. 161–73; M. Billinge, 'In Search of Negativism: Phenomenology and Historical Geography', *Journal of Historical Geography*, vol. 3 (1977), pp. 55–67; A. R. H. Baker, 'Historical Geography: Understanding and Experiencing the Past', *Progress in Human Geography*, vol. 2 (1978), pp. 495–504.

3 D. Gregory, *Ideology, Science and Human Geography* (London, 1978), p. 172; and *idem*, 'Discourse of the Past', pp. 172–3.

4 D. Ley and M. S. Samuels (eds.), *Humanistic Geography: Prospects and Problems* (London, 1978); D. Cosgrove, 'Place, Landscape and the Dialectics of Cultural Geography', *Canadian Geographer*, vol. 22 (1978), pp. 66–72.

5 P. Wheatley, *The Pivot of the Four Quarters: a Preliminary Enquiry into the Origins and Character of the Ancient Chinese City* (Chicago, 1971), p. 478.

6 On the two forms of structuralism, see D. Gregory, 'On Rethinking Historical Geography', *Area*, vol. 8 (1976), pp. 295–9.

7 M. Sahlins, *Culture and Practical Reason* (Chicago, 1976), employs this term to cover all social theories which explicitly and implicitly formulate human culture out of practical activity and, behind that, utilitarian interest. The argument develops the thesis outlined in an earlier work: *Stone Age Economics* (London, 1974), where Sahlins provides empirical evidence for the substantivist position in economic anthropology of regarding economy as 'a category of culture rather than behaviour, in a class with politics or religion rather than of rationality or prudence: not the need-serving activities of individuals, but the material life process of society' (p. xii).

8 Sahlins, *Culture and Practical Reason*, p. 211: 'The peculiarity of Western culture is the institutionalization of the symbolic process in and as the production of goods, by comparison with a "primitive" world where the locus of symbolic differentiation remains social relations.'

9 Carl Sauer, *Land and Life*, p. 376, made exactly this point in 1941: 'even the current world market price for wheat is only an expression of cultural demand from a dominant purchasing group, not a real expression of the utility of the different grains'.

10 K. Polanyi, C. Arenberg and H. W. Pearson, *Trade and Markets in Early Empires* (Glencoe, 1958), pp. 243–70; L. Vallensi, 'Pour une histoire anthropologique: la notion de réciprocité', *Annales: Économies, Sociétés, Civilisations*, vol. 29 (1974), pp. 1309–19.

11 For a discussion of the problem of *Verstehen* see Billinge, 'In Search of Negativism', p. 60; and Gregory, 'Discourse of the Past', pp. 165–6. The problem is in some ways exemplified in the recent work of Cole Harris and Leonard Guelke, both of whom argue for a form of *Verstehen* in understanding past landscapes (R. C. Harris, 'The Historical Mind and the Practice of Historical Geography' in Ley and Samuels (eds.), *Humanistic Geography*, pp.

123–37; and Guelke, 'On Rethinking Historical Geography'), and yet whose substantive discussions of seventeenth-century colonial landscapes rely heavily upon assumptions of behaviour determined by practical reason (cheap lands and distant markets) with minimal attention to its symbolic constitution: R. C. Harris, 'The Simplification of Europe Overseas', *Annals, Association of American Geographers*, vol. 67 (1977). pp. 469–83; R. C. Harris and L. Guelke, 'Land and Society in Early Canada and South Africa', *Journal of Historical Geography*, vol. 3 (1977), pp. 135–53.

12 P. Bourdieu, 'Sur le pouvoir symbolique', *Annales: Économies, Sociétés, Civilisations*, vol. 32 (1977), pp. 405–11, ref. on p. 410.

13 Wheatley, *The Pivot of the Four Quarters; idem, City and Symbol* (London, 1967). Also J. Bird, *Centrality and Cities* (London, 1977), for a recent summary.

14 The subject of the ideal city is a broad one involving aspects like military fortification and utopian theories which are beyond the scope of this essay but would require treatment in any exhaustive study. For useful short summaries, illustrations and references to original treatises see J. C. Argan, *The Renaissance City* (London, 1969), and H. Rosenau, *The Ideal City: its Architectural Evolution* (London, 1974).

15 M. Eliade, *The Sacred and the Profane: The Nature of Religion* (New York, 1959), pp. 20–65.

16 Yi-fu Tuan, *Topophilia: a Study of Environmental Perception, Attitudes and Values* (Englewood Cliffs, 1974), pp. 150–72 and 13–29.

17 E. Cassirer, *The Individual and the Cosmos in Renaissance Philosophy* (London, 1963); E. Panofsky, *Studies in Iconography: Humanistic Themes in the Art of the Renaissance* (New York, 1972); R. Wittkower, *Architectural Principles in the Age of Humanism* (London, 1971).

18 Much of this discussion is based upon the recent attempt to provide a broad historical materialist survey of social formations during the emergence and decline of feudalism as a dominant mode of production in Europe: P. Anderson, *Passages from Antiquity to Feudalism* (London. 1978), and *idem, Lineages of the Absolutist State* (London, 1974). On feudal organization in Italy see P. J. Jones, 'Italy' in M. M. Postan (ed.), *The Cambridge Economic History of Europe*, vol. 1: *The Agrarian Life in the Middle Ages* (Cambridge, 1966), pp. 340–431.

19 D. Whaley, *The Italian City Republics* (London 1978), p. 128; P. J. Jones, 'Communes and Depots: The City States in Late Medieval Italy', *Transactions of the Royal Historical Society*, 5th Series, vol. 15 (1965), pp. 71–96.

20 E. Sereni, *Storia del Paesaggio Agrario Italiano* (Bari, 1974), pp. 247–52. For a more specific regional study see A. Stella, 'La crisi economica veneziana della seconda meta del secolo XVI', *Archivo veneto*, no. 58 (1956), pp. 17–69, esp. pp. 20–37.

21 For an example of this process in the Venetian terrafirma see A. Ventura, *Nobilità e popola nella società veneta del '500 e '600* (Bari, 1964).

22 Anderson, *Passages from Antiquity to Feudalism*, pp. 131–7, admits the difficulty of making sense of such a consistently significant cultural phenomenon as the Roman church whose 'autonomous efficacy' he claims was 'not to be found in the realm of economic relations or social structures . . . but in the

cultural sphere above them', and yet which played a central role in the transition of Europe (A.D. 400–800) from the ancient to the feudal mode of production. His difficulty results precisely from the reductionist stance he adopts in separating base and superstructure in this way and failing to see economic relations and social structures as culturally encompassed.

23 P. Burke, *Tradition and Innovation in Renaissance Italy* (London, 1974), pp. 50–61, has a useful analysis of the social and geographical origins of the Italian 'creative elite' of the fifteenth and early sixteenth centuries. While the artists, sculptors and musicians show a clear majority of 'middle' origins (i.e. neither peasants nor nobles), writers and humanists do more frequently have noble origins, unsurprisingly given the cost of university education. But ideas and cosmology were developed and communicated widely among the humanist 'elite' and it is questionable how far Burke's subdivisions have validity, as he himself admits.

Notes to Baker, 'On ideology', pp. 233–243

1 D. J. Gregory, *Ideology, Science and Human Geography* (London, 1978), p. 13.
2 H. C. Prince, 'Real, Imagined and Abstract Worlds of the Past', *Progress in Geography*, vol. 3 (1971), pp. 1–16; J. A. Jakle, 'Time, Space and the Geographic Past: a Prospectus for Historical Geography', *American Historical Review*, vol. 7 (1971), pp. 1084–1103; A. R. H. Baker (ed.), *Progress in Historical Geography* (Newton Abbot, 1972); H. C. Prince, 'Time and Historical Geography' in T. Carlstein, D. Parkes and N. Thrift (eds.), *Making Sense of Time* (London, 1978), pp. 17–37; M. Cranston, 'Ideology', *The New Encyclopaedia Britannica*, 15th edn, vol. 9 (1978), pp. 194–8.
3 A. Buttimer, 'Charism and Context: The Challenge of *la Géographie humaine*' in D. Ley and M. S. Samuels (eds.), *Humanistic Geography: Prospects and Problems* (London, 1978), pp. 58–76.
4 C. O. Sauer, 'The Morphology of Landscape', *University of California Publications in Geography*, vol. 2 (1925), pp. 19–54; *idem*, 'Foreword to Historical Geography', *Annals, Association of American Geographers*, vol. 31 (1941), pp. 1–24; H. C. Darby, 'On the Relations of History and Geography', *Transactions and Papers of the Institute of British Geographers*, vol. 19 (1953), pp. 1–11; *idem*, 'An Historical Geography of England: Twenty Years After', *Geographical Journal*, vol. 126 (1960), pp. 147–59; *idem*, 'The Problem of Geographical Description', *Transactions and Papers of the Institute of British Geographers*, vol. 30 (1962), pp. 1–14; *idem*, 'Historical Geography', in H. P. R. Finberg (ed.), *Approaches to History* (London, 1962), pp. 127–56.
5 R. D. Vicero (ed.), *Historical Geography Newsletter*, vol. 6, no. 1 (1976): an issue devoted to Carl O. Sauer and Andrew H. Clark; P. J. Perry, 'H. C. Darby and Historical Geography: a Survey and Review', *Geographische Zeitschrift*, vol. 57 (1969), pp. 161–78.
6 Sauer, 'Morphology of Landscape', p. 31.
7 H. C. Darby, *Domesday England* (Cambridge, 1977).
8 A. R. H. Baker, 'Historical Geography in Britain' in Baker (ed.), *Progress in Historical Geography*, pp. 90–110.

9 H. C. Darby (ed.), *A New Historical Geography of England* (Cambridge, 1973); R. A. Dodgshon and R. A. Butlin (eds.), *An Historical Geography of England and Wales* (London, 1978).

10 A. R. H. Baker, 'Historical Geography', *Progress in Human Geography*, vol. 1 (1977), pp. 465–74; *idem*, 'Historical Geography: Understanding and Experiencing the Past', *Progress in Human Geography*, vol. 2 (1978), pp. 495–504; *idem*, 'Historical Geography: a New Beginning?', *Progress in Human Geography*, vol. 3 (1979), pp. 560–70.

11 P. Claval, *Espace et pouvoir* (Paris, 1978); D. J. Gregory, 'Social Change and Spatial Structures' in Carlstein, Parkes and Thrift (eds.), *Making Sense of Time*, pp. 38–46; A. Giddens, *Central Problems in Social Theory* (London, 1979), pp. 198–233.

12 C. Harris, 'The Historical Mind and the Practice of Geography' in Ley and Samuels (eds.), *Humanistic Geography*, pp. 123–37.

13 D. Slater, 'The Poverty of Modern Geographical Enquiry', *Pacific Viewpoint*, vol. 16 (1975), pp. 159–76; H. C. Brookfield, *Interdependent Development* (London, 1975).

14 H. C. Darby (ed.), *An Historical Geography of England before 1800* (Cambridge, 1936).

15 R. A. French, 'Historical Geography in the U.S.S.R.' in Baker (ed.), *Progress in Historical Geography*, pp. 111–28.

16 Darby, *Domesday England*, pp. 375–84.

17 Darby, *A New Historical Geography of England*.

18 A. R. H. Baker, 'Patterns of Popular Protest', *Journal of Historical Geography*, vol. 4 (1975), pp. 383–7.

19 A. R. H. Baker, 'Rhetoric and Reality in Historical Geography', *Journal of Historical Geography*, vol. 3 (1977), pp. 301–5; M. P. Conzen, 'High Marx for British Historical Geographers?', *Historical Geography: a Newsletter for Historical Geographers*, vol. 8 (1978), pp. 26–7; J. Langton, 'The Pathway of Progress in Historical Geography', *Journal of Historical Geography*, vol. 5 (1979), pp. 79–82; H. C. Prince, 'About Half Marx for the Transition from Feudalism to Capitalism', *Area*, vol. 11 (1979), pp. 43–50; A. R. H. Baker, 'On the Historical Geography of France', *Journal of Historical Geography*, vol. 6 (1980), pp. 69–76.

20 J. M. Blaut, 'Where was Capitalism Born?', *Antipode*, vol. 8, no. 2 (1976), pp. 1–11; D. Harvey, *Social Justice and the City* (London, 1973); *idem*, 'Class-monopoly Rent, Finance Capital and the Urban Revolution', *Regional Studies*, vol. 8 (1974), pp. 239–55; *idem*, 'The Geography of Capitalist Accumulation: a Reconstruction of Marxian Theory', *Antipode*, vol. 7, no. 2 (1975), pp. 9–12; *idem*, 'The Political Economy of Urbanisation in Advanced Capitalist Societies' in G. Gappert and H. M. Rose (eds.), *The Social Economy of Cities* (Beverly Hills, 1975); *idem*, 'The Urban Process under Capitalism: a Framework for Analysis', *International Journal of Urban and Regional Research*, vol. 2 (1978), pp. 101–32; R. De Koninck (ed.), 'Le matérialisme historique en géographie', *Cahiers de Géographie du Québec*, vol. 22 (1978); D. Cosgrove, 'Place, Landscape and the Dialectics of Cultural Geography', *Canadian Geographer*, vol. 22 (1978), pp. 66–72.

21 M. Day and J. Tivers, 'Catastrophe Theory and Geography: a Marxist Critique', *Area*, vol. 11 (1979), pp. 54–8.

22 J. S. Cohen, 'The Achievements of Economic History: the Marxist School', *Journal of Economic History*, vol. 38 (1978), pp. 29–57.

23 G. G. Iggers (ed.), *New Directions in European Historiography* (Middletown, Conn., 1975). See also G. Eley, 'Some Recent Tendencies in Social History' in G. Iggers and H. Parker (eds.), *International Handbook of Historical Studies* (New York, 1980), pp. 55–70.

24 G. G. Iggers, 'Marxism and Modern Social History' in Iggers (ed.), *New Directions*, pp. 123–74.

25 P. Vilar, 'Histoire Marxiste, histoire en construction: Essai de dialogue avec Althusser', *Annales: Économies, Sociétés, Civilisations*, vol. 28 (1973), pp. 165–98: translated as 'Marxist History, a History in the Making: Towards a dialogue with Althusser', *New Left Review*, vol. 80 (1973), pp. 64–106.

26 P. Claval, *Les Mythes fondateurs des sciences sociales* (Paris, 1980).

27 Iggers (ed.), *New Directions*, pp. 155–72.

28 I. Wallace, 'Towards a Humanised Conception of Economic Geography' in Ley and Samuels (eds.), *Humanistic Geography*, pp. 91–108.

29 An impressive survey of the varieties of Marxism is: L. Kolakowski, *Main Currents of Marxism: its Rise, Growth and Dissolution*, 3 vols. (Oxford, 1978). A much briefer but nonetheless useful survey of Marx's ideas is: R. Aron, *Main Currents of Sociological Thought*, vol. 2 (Harmondsworth, 1968), pp. 111–82. For specific discussions of Marxism and history, see: H. Fleischer, *Marxism and History* (New York, 1973); W. H. Shaw, *Marx's Theory of History* (London, 1978).

30 Fleischer, *Marxism and History*, p. 17.

31 Iggers (ed.), *New Directions*, p. 127.

32 See, for a recent example: D. W. Meinig, 'The Continuous Shaping of America: a Prospectus for Geographers and Historians', *American Historical Review*, vol. 83 (1978), pp. 1186–1217.

33 M. S. Samuels, 'Existentialism and Human Geography' in Ley and Samuels (eds.), *Humanistic Geography*, pp. 22–40.

34 J.-P. Sartre, *Critique de la Raison Dialectique* (Paris, 1960), translated as *Critique of Dialectical Reason* (London, 1976); M. Poster, *Existential Marxism in Postwar France* (Princeton, 1975); *idem, Sartre's Marxism* (London, 1979).

35 It is intended to pursue this theme further in A. R. H. Baker and D. Gregory, 'Terrae Incognitae' in Historical Geography' in A. R. H. Baker, D. Gregory (eds.), *Explorations in Historical Geography* (forthcoming).

36 Quoted in Fleischer, *Marxism and History*, p. 21.

37 Quoted in Aron, *Main Currents of Sociological Thought*, p. 120.

38 Quoted in Fleischer, *Marxism and History*, pp. 21–2.

39 Harvey, *Social Justice and the City*, pp. 12–13; Harris, in Ley and Samuels (eds.), *Humanistic Geography*, p. 126; Gregory, *Ideology, Science and Human Geography*, p. 146.

40 Harris, in Ley and Samuels (eds.), *Humanistic Geography*, pp. 126–7.

41 J. E. Vance, *The Merchant's World: The Geography of Wholesaling* (Englewood Cliffs, 1970), p. 140.

42 Iggers (ed.), *New Directions*, p. 127.
43 Fleischer, *Marxism and History*, p. 29.
44 Iggers (ed.), *New Directions*, p. 126.
45 T. Stoianovich, *French Historical Method: the 'Annales' Paradigm* (Ithaca, 1976).
46 A. R. H. Baker, 'Historical Geography and the *Annales* School of Total History: an Exploration of Some Interdisciplinary Relations' in Baker and Gregory (eds.), *Explorations in Historical Geography*.
47 Baker and Gregory, '*Terrae Incognitae* in Historical Geography' in *ibid*.

Notes to Gregory, 'Action and structure', pp. 244–250

1 C. Sauer, 'Foreword to Historical Geography', *Annals, Association of American Geographers*, vol. 31 (1941), pp. 1–24.
2 H. C. Darby, 'The Changing English Landscape', *Geographical Journal*, vol. 117 (1951), pp. 377–94.
3 R. C. Harris, 'The Historical Mind and the Practice of Geography' in D. Ley and M. Samuels (eds.), *Humanistic Geography: Prospects and Problems* (London, 1978); E. P. Thompson, *The Poverty of Theory and Other Essays* (London, 1978).
4 E. P. Thompson, 'The Politics of Theory' in R. Samuel (ed.), *People's History and Socialist Theory* (London, 1981), pp. 399–400.
5 R. C. Harris, 'The Historical Mind'; Thompson, *Poverty; idem, The Making of the English Working Class* (London, 1963).
6 See, for example, L. Guelke, 'An Idealist Alternative in Human Geography', *Annals, Association of American Geographers*, vol. 64 (1974), pp. 193–202.
7 A. Giddens, *Central Problems in Social Theory: Action, Structure and Contradiction in Social Analysis* (London, 1979), p. 7.
8 See the discussion in A. Giddens, *New Rules of Sociological Method: a Positive Critique of Interpretative Sociologies* (London, 1976), pp. 126–7.
9 Thompson, *Poverty*, p. 353.
10 G. Olsson, 'Of Ambiguity: or Far Cries from a Memorializing Mamafesta', in Ley and Samuels (eds.), *Humanistic Geography*, p. 114.
11 Thompson, *Poverty*, p. 234.
12 See D. Gregory, 'The Discourse of the Past: Phenomenology, Structuralism and Historical Geography', *Journal of Historical Geography*, vol. 4 (1978), pp. 161–73.
13 Thompson, *Poverty*, p. 93.
14 P. Abrams, 'History, Sociology, Historical Sociology', *Past and Present*, no. 87 (1980), pp. 3–16.
15 This phrasing – for all Thompson's attacks on their work – is taken from A. Cutler, B. Hindess, P. Hirst and A. Husain, *Marx's Capital and Capitalism Today* (London, 1977); there are, of course, genuine differences between them and Thompson, but his polemic obscures some equally important points of contact: see P. Anderson, *Arguments within English Marxism* (London, 1980), and P. Hirst, 'The Necessity of Theory', *Economy and Society*, vol. 8 (1979), pp. 417–45.

16 Thompson, 'Politics', p. 405.
17 Thompson, *Poverty*, p. 344.
18 Anderson, *Arguments*, pp. 56–7.
19 Giddens, *Central Problems*.
20 *Ibid*; see also D. Gregory, 'Human Agency and Human Geography', *Transactions of the Institute of British Geographers*, vol. 6 (1981), pp. 1–18.
21 R. Johnson, 'Edward Thompson, Eugene Genovese and Socialist-humanist History', *History Workshop Journal*, no. 6 (1978), pp. 79–100ff.
22 A. Dawe, 'Theories of Social Action' in T. Bottomore and R. Nisbet (eds.), *A History of Sociological Analysis* (London, 1979), p. 390.
23 *Ibid*. p. 369. Taken together, these three claims correspond to what I earlier characterized as structural, reflexive and committed explanation: D. Gregory, *Ideology, Science and Human Geography* (London, 1978).
24 Giddens, *Central Problems*, p. 82.
25 Thompson, *Poverty*, p. 288; *idem, Whigs and Hunters: The Origin of the Black Act* (London, 1975).
26 Giddens, *Central Problems*.
27 S. Hall, 'In Defence of Theory' in Samuel (ed.), *People's History*, p. 383.
28 E. P. Thompson, *Poverty*, p. 344.
29 R. Williams, *Marxism and Literature* (Oxford, 1978), p. 87.

Notes to Norton, 'Historical geography', pp. 251–257

1 J. Jakle, 'Time, Space and the Geographic Past: A Prospectus for Historical Geography', *American Historical Review*, vol. 76 (1971), pp. 1084–1103.
2 M. Chisholm, *Human Geography: Evolution or Revolution?* (Harmondsworth, 1975), pp. 122–65; and D. Amedeo and R. G. Golledge, *An Introduction to Scientific Reasoning in Geography* (New York, 1975).
3 J. Langton, 'Review of "An Introduction to Scientific Reasoning in Geography" by Amedeo, D and Golledge, R. G.', *Journal of Historical Geography*, vol. 3 (1977), pp. 90–1.
4 D. W. Harvey, 'Models of the Evolution of Spatial Patterns in Human Geography' in R. J. Chorley and P. Haggett (eds.), *Models in Geography* (London, 1967), pp. 549–608; and A. H. Clark, 'Historical Geography' in P. James and C. F. Jones (eds.), *American Geography: Inventory and Prospect* (Syracuse, 1954), pp. 70–105.
5 Amedeo and Golledge, *Introduction to Scientific Reasoning in Geography*, p. 177.
6 B. N. Boots and A. Getis, 'Probability Model Approach to Map Pattern Analysis', *Progress in Human Geography*, vol. 1 (1977), pp. 264–86.
7 R. W. Wilkie, 'The Process Method versus the Hypothesis Method: A Nonlinear Example of Spatial Perception and Behavior' in M. H. Yeates (ed.), *Proceedings of the I.G.U. Commission on Quantitative Geography* (Montreal, 1974), pp. 1–31.
8 A. Getis, 'On the Use of the Term "Random" in Spatial Analysis', *Professional Geographer*, vol. 29 (1977), pp. 59–61.
9 A. R. H. Baker, 'The Limits of Inference in Historical Geography' in B. S.

354   Notes to pages 254–262

midOsborne (ed.), *The Settlement of Canada: Origins and Transfer* (Kingston, Ontario, 1976), pp. 169–82; and H. C. Prince, 'Time and Historical Geography' in T. Carlstein *et al.* (eds.), *Timing Space and Spacing Time*, vol. 1 (London, 1978), pp. 17–37.

10 W. Todd, *History as Applied Science* (Detroit, 1972); and D. H. Porter, 'History as Process', *History and Theory*, vol. 14 (1975), pp. 297–313; and M. Forrester, 'Practical Reasoning and Historical Enquiry', *History and Theory*, vol. 15 (1976), pp. 133–40.

11 Todd, *History as Applied Science*.

12 *Ibid.* p. 161.

13 Porter, 'History as Process', pp. 297–313.

14 *Ibid.* p. 313.

15 Forrester, 'Practical Reasoning', pp. 133–40.

16 J. D. Gould, 'Hypothetical History', *Economic History Review*, vol. 22 (1969), pp. 195–207; and T. A. Climo and P. G. A. Howells, 'Cause and Counterfactuals', *Economic History Review*, vol. 27 (1974), pp. 461–8; *idem*, 'Possible Worlds in Historical Explanation', *History and Theory*, vol. 15 (1976), pp. 1–20; and B. C. Hurst, 'A Comment on the Possible Worlds of Climo and Howells', *History and Theory*, vol. 18 (1979), pp. 52–60.

17 L. E. Davis, ' "And it Will Never be Literature" – The New Economic History: A Critique' in R. P. Swierenga (ed.), *Quantification in American History* (New York, 1970), p. 283.

18 P. D. McClelland, 'Railroads, American Growth and the New Economic History: A Critique', *Journal of Economic History*, vol. 28 (1968), pp. 102–23.

19 A. H. Conrad and J. R. Meyer, *Studies in Econometric History* (London, 1965), p. 33.

20 G. G. S. Murphy and M. G. Mueller, 'On Making Historical Techniques More Specific: "Real types" Constructed With a Computer', *History and Theory*, vol. 6 (1967), pp. 14–32.

21 W. Norton, 'Process and Form Relationships: An Example From Historical Geography', *Professional Geographer*, vol. 30 (1978), pp. 128–34.

22 A. H. Clark, 'The Conceptions of "Empires" of the St Lawrence and the Mississippi: An Historico-Geographical View with some Quizzical Comments on Environmental Determinism', *American Review of Canadian Studies*, vol. 5 (1975), pp. 4–27.

23 Climo and Howells, 'Possible Worlds', p. 19.

24 E. H. Carr, *What is History?* (Harmondsworth, 1961); and Prince, 'Time and Historical Geography', p. 31.

Notes to Harley, 'Historical geography', pp. 261–273

1 P. Thompson, *The Voice of the Past: Oral History* (Oxford, 1978), p. 43.

2 R. G. Collingwood *The Idea of History* (Oxford, 1946), p. 282.

3 G. J. Renier, *History its Purpose and Method* (London, 1951), pp. 87–105.

4 A. C. Danto, *Analytical Philosophy of History* (Cambridge, 1965), p. 88.

5 J. H. Hexter, *The History Primer* (New York, 1971), p. 80. Much has been made by philosophers of history of the influence on the writing of history of the

historian's own constructs. In the context of historical geography the problem was recently discussed, *inter alia*, by J. A. Ernst and H. R. Merrens, 'Praxis and Theory in the Writing of American Historical Geography', *Journal of Historical Geography*, vol. 4 (1978), pp. 277–90.

6 Quoted by Renier, *History its Purpose and Method*, p. 54.

7 A. R. H. Baker, 'Historical Geography: Understanding and Experiencing the Past', *Progress in Human Geography*, vol. 2 (1978), pp. 495–504.

8 R. Floud (ed.), *Essays in Quantitative Economic History* (London, 1974), pp. 3–4, warns against the pitfalls of such linear research models in a statistical context.

9 H. C. Prince, 'Real, Imagined and Abstract Worlds of the Past', *Progress in Geography*, vol. 3 (1971), pp. 1–86.

10 C. L. Becker, 'What are Historical Facts?' in H. Meyerhoff (ed.), *The Philosophy of History in our Time* (New York, 1959), pp. 120–37.

11 Hexter, *The History Primer*, p. 78.

12 True in British historical geography, this was also noted by Ernst and Merrens, 'Praxis and Theory', in American historical geography and, in a Canadian context, by R. C. Harris, 'Theory and Synthesis in Historical Geography', *Canadian Geographer*, vol. 15 (1971), pp. 157–72.

13 R. C. Harris, 'The Historical Mind and the Practice of Geography' in D. Ley and M. S. Samuels (eds.), *Humanistic Geography* (London, 1978), pp. 123–37.

14 A. H. Clark, 'First Thing First' in R. E. Ehrenberg (ed.), *Pattern and Process: Research in Historical Geography* (Washington, D.C., 1975), pp. 9–21.

15 H. C. Darby, 'On the Relations of History and Geography', *Transactions and Papers of the Institute of British Geographers*, vol. 19 (1953), pp. 1–11; the extent to which the approach became firmly rooted in British historical geography is illustrated by A. R. H. Baker, J. D. Hamshere and J. Langton (eds.), *Geographical Interpretations of Historical Sources: Readings in Historical Geography* (Newton Abbot, 1970), and numerous subsequent studies.

16 Baker, 'Historical Geography: Understanding and Experiencing the Past' notes this as a 'productive' trend. In the sense of new methodological tides flowing through historical geography – as the behaviouralist and humanistic approaches – this is true, but the present argument contends that it has not led, *pari passu*, to advances in understanding the nature of evidence.

17 D. Gregory, 'The Discourse of the Past: Phenomenology, Structuralism and Historical Geography', *Journal of Historical Geography*, vol. 4 (1978), pp. 161–73.

18 D. Robey (ed.), *Structuralism: an Introduction* (Oxford, 1973), pp. 1–2.

19 R. Jakobson, 'Closing Statement: Linguistics and Poetics' in T. A. Seboek (ed.), *Style in Language* (Cambridge, Mass., 1960), p. 353.

20 T. Hawkes, *Structuralism and Semiotics* (London, 1977), p. 83.

21 A. H. Robinson, 'The Uniqueness of the Map', *The American Cartographer*, vol. 5 (1978), pp. 5–7.

22 For a study of carto-literacy using one source see J. B. Harley and G. Walters, 'English Map Collecting 1790–1840; a Pilot Survey of the Evidence in Sotheby Sale Catalogues', *Imago Mundi*, vol. 30 (1978), pp. 31–55.

23 D. H. Fischer, *Historians' Fallacies: Towards a Logic of Historical Thought* (New York, 1970), p. 62.
24 For an exception see M. J. Freeman, 'The Stage-coach System of South Hampshire, 1775–1851', *Journal of Historical Geography*, vol. 1 (1975), pp. 259–81.
25 Hawkes, *Structuralism and Semiotics*, p. 26.
26 E. Leach, 'Structuralism in Social Anthropology' in Robey (ed.), *Structuralism*, p. 39.
27 E. Leach, *Culture and Communication: The Logic by which Symbols are Connected* (Cambridge, 1971), p. 1.
28 D. Daiches, *Critical Approaches to Literature* (London, 1956), p. 132.
29 E. E. Gombrich, 'The Evidence of Images' in C. E. Singleton (ed.), *Interpretation Theory and Practice* (Baltimore, 1969), p. 71; the fullest exposition is in the same author's *Art and Illusion: A Study in the Psychology of Pictorial Representation* (New York, 1960).
30 P. Burke, *Tradition and Innovation in Renaissance Italy: a Sociological Approach* (London, 1974), pp. 140–51; see also the levels of meaning identified by E. Panofsky, *Studies in Iconology: Humanistic Themes in the Art of the Renaissance* (Oxford, 1939).
31 Hawkes, *Structuralism and Semiotics*, p. 8.
32 *Ibid.* pp. 123–50. Semiotics is the North American term; in the European literature semiology is often employed.
33 Apart from Hawkes, a clear introduction will be found in T. A. Seboek, 'Semiotics: a Survey of the State of the Art' in T. A. Seboek, *Contributions to the Doctrine of Signs* (Bloomington, 1976), pp. 1–45.
34 U. Eco, *A Theory of Semiotics* (London, 1977), pp. 3–47.
35 The fullest statement on cartographic communication is in A. H. Robinson and B. B. Petchenik, *The Nature of Maps: Essays toward Understanding Maps and Mapping* (Chicago, 1976), pp. 23–42; but see also the reprinted essays: L. Guelke (ed.), *The Nature of Cartographic Communication*, Cartographica, no. 19 (Toronto, 1977); for an explicit adaptation of the language of semiotics see H. Schlichtmann, 'Codes in Map Communication', *The Canadian Cartographer*, vol. 16 (1979), pp. 81–97; and for a broader use of linguistics, C. E. Youngmann, 'A Linguistic Approach to Map Description', in G. Dutton (ed.), *First International Advanced Study Symposium on Topological Data Structures for Geographic Information Systems*, vol. 7: *Spatial Semantics: Understanding and Interacting with Map Data* (Cambridge, Mass., Laboratory for Computer Graphics and Spatial Analysis, Harvard University, 1978).
36 Hawkes, *Structuralism and Semiotics*, p. 134.
37 For a recent summary, but with relatively little about evidence *per se*, see R. F. Atkinson, *Knowledge and Explanation in History: an Introduction to the Philosophy of History* (London, 1978).
38 An important distinction in linguistics and semiotics. Denotation is normally taken to mean the use of language to mean what it says: connotation means the use of language to mean something other than what is said. Art historians sometimes substitute the terms manifest and latent content to imply the same distinction.

39 J. Langton, 'Potentialities and Problems of Adopting a Systems Approach to the Study of Change in Human Geography', *Progress in Geography*, vol. 4 (1972), pp. 127–79.
40 V. K. Dibble, 'Four Types of Inference from Documents to Events', *History and Theory: Studies in the Philosophy of History*, vol. 3 (1964), pp. 203–21.
41 J. Piaget, *Structuralism* (London, 1971), pp. 5–16.
42 R. Lennard, *Rural England, 1086–1135* (Oxford, 1959), pp. 22–39.
43 A number of recent studies in historical geography – for example of the process of agricultural innovation and improvement – reveal a new awareness of this dynamic face of evidence, although they are not articulated in a semiotic idiom: see, for example, H. S. A. Fox and R. A. Butlin (eds.), *Change in the Countryside: Essays on Rural England, 1500–1900* (London, Institute of British Geographers, 1979), especially the essays by J. R. Walton, 'Mechanization in Agriculture: a Study of the Adoption Process', pp. 23–42; and H. S. A. Fox, 'Local Farmers' Associations and the Circulation of Agricultural Information in Nineteenth-century England', pp. 43–63.
44 Hawkes, *Structuralism and Semiotics*, pp. 124–6.
45 *Ibid.* pp. 133–4.
46 J. Langton, 'The Pathway of Progress in Historical Geography', *Journal of Historical Geography*, vol. 5 (1979), pp. 79–82.
47 R. Cobb, *A Sense of Place* (London, 1975), p. 47.

Notes to Hall, 'Private archives', pp. 274–280

1 D. Harvey, 'Models of the Evolution of Spatial Patterns in Human Geography' in R. J. Chorley and P. Haggett (eds.), *Models in Geography* (London, 1967), pp. 549–608.
2 W. Kirk, 'Historical Geography and the Concept of Behavioural Environment', *Indian Geographical Journal*, Silver Jubilee Volume (1951), pp. 152–60.
3 J. Vansina, *Oral Tradition: a Study in Historical Methodology* (Harmondsworth, 1973).
4 A. Goudie, 'Geography and Prehistory: a Survey of the Literature, with a Select Bibliography', *Journal of Historical Geography*, vol. 2 (1976), pp. 197–205.
5 A. R. H. Baker, 'Rethinking Historical Geography' in A. R. H. Baker (ed.), *Progress in Historical Geography* (Newton Abbot, 1972), pp. 11–28.
6 C. Hall, *El café y el desarrollo histórico-geográfico de Costa Rica* (San José, 1976); C. F. S. Cardoso, 'The Formation of the Coffee Estate in Nineteenth-century Costa Rica' in K. Duncan *et al.* (eds.), *Land and Labour in Latin America: Essays on the Development of Agrarian Capitalism in the Nineteenth and Twentieth Centuries* (Cambridge, 1977), pp. 165–202.
7 Hall, *El café y el desarrollo histórico-geográfico de Costa Rica*, pp. 47, 54, 63.
8 G. Peters-Solórzano, 'La formación territorial de las grandes fincas de café en la Meseta Central: estudio de la firma Tournón (1877–1955)' (unpublished thesis, San José University, 1979).
9 C. Hall, 'The Tuis Archives: Cattle Ranching on the Frontiers of Colonization

in Costa Rica, 1873–1876', *Revista Geográfica* (Pan-American Institute of History and Geography), no. 86–7 (1977–8), pp. 101–17.

10 C. Hall, *Cóncavas, formación de una hacienda cafetalera, 1889–1911* (San José, 1978).

Notes to Hansen, 'A Danish land survey', pp. 281–288

1 An extract of the figures was published in Henrik Pedersen, *De Danske Landbrug* (The Danish farms, recounted on the basis of Christian the Fifth's Land Register 1688) (1928).

2 Gunnar Olsen, *Hovedgård og bondegård: Studier over stordriftens udvikling i Danmark i tiden 1525–1774* (Manor Farm and Tenant Farm: Studies in the Development of the Manorial System between 1525 and 1774) (København, 1957). In this work the author has assembled thousands of records from the archives.

3 Poul Bjerge and Thyge J. Söegaard, *Danske Vider og Vedtægter*, vols. I–III (1902–20), is a collection with comments on nearly 200 village by-laws.

4 Aksel Lassen, *Fald og Fremgang* (Setback and Advance), an account of the population development in Denmark, 1645–1960 (1965). A more popular report from the same author appeared in *1659, da landet blev øde* (1659, When the Land Became Deserted) (1959).

5 The death registers from two parishes on Sjælland (Sørbymagle and Kirkerup) contain 900 comprehensive biographies covering the years 1646 to 1713. These are here compared to lists of shareholders in 1662 and again 1682 from the land registers.

Notes to Simms, 'Cartographic representation', pp. 289–300

1 H. Jaeger, private communication, April 1979. Jaeger's reconstruction of Old Prussian landscapes from the maps of the *Atlas des Preußenlandes* is a good example of synchronic analysis based on primary documentary material.

2 A. Simms and K. Simms, 'Origins of Principal Towns' in J. P. Haughton (ed.), *Atlas of Ireland* (Dublin, Royal Irish Academy, 1979), p. 43.

3 R. A. Butlin, 'Urban and Proto-Urban Settlements in Pre-Norman Ireland' in R. A. Butlin (ed.), *The Development of the Irish Town* (London, 1977), pp. 11-27; T. G. Delaney, 'The Archaeology of the Irish Town' in M. W. Barley (ed.), *European Towns, Their Archaeology and Early History* (London, 1977), pp. 48–63.

4 At the suggestion of H. J. Nitz I have recently used the framework of colonization for the evolution of settlement in Ireland in the same way as D. W. Meinig (in this volume) used the framework of imperial expansion as a generic phenomenon for the history of settlement in North America. A. Simms, 'Irland: Überformung eines keltischen Siedlungsraumes am Rande Europas durch externe Kolonisationsbwegungen' in J. Hagedorn, J. Hövermann and H. J. Nitz (eds.), *Gefügemuster der Erdoberfläche. Festschrift zum 42: Deutschen Geographentag* (Göttingen, 1979), pp. 261–308.

5 J. Andrews, 'The Ethnic Factor in Irish Historical Geography', unpublished

manuscript of lecture delivered at the Conference of Irish Geographers (Dublin, 1974).

6 F. H. A. Aalen, *Man and the Landscape in Ireland* (London, 1978), p. 273.

7 B. O'Riordaín, 'High Street Excavations' in B. Almquist and D. Green (eds.), *Proceedings of the Seventh Viking Congress* (Dublin, 1976), pp. 29–37. The fact that the battle for the proper excavation and preservation of the Viking town in the centre of Dublin, involving (on the initiative of Prof. F. X. Martin) the courts in Dublin and Strasbourg, has taken on such dramatic proportions, is an outward sign for the change of consciousness that has recently occurred.

8 H. Stoob, 'Die hochmittelalterliche Städtebildung im Okzident' in H. Stoob (ed.), *Die Stadt. Gestalt und Wandel bis zum industriellen Zeitalter, Städtewesen I.* Werkstücke für Studium und Praxis aus dem Institut für Vergleichende Städtegeschichte in Münster (Köln/Wien, 1979), pp. 131–56, Map 136.

9 H. Schledermann, 'The Idea of the Town: Typology, Definitions and Approaches of the Study of the Medieval Town in Northern Europe', *World Archaeology*, vol. 2, no. 2 (1970), pp. 116–27; H. Jankuhn, W. Schlesinger and H. Steuer, *Vor und Frühformen der Europäischen Stadt im Mittelalter*, Abhandlungen der Akademie der Wissenschaften in Göttingen, phil.-hist. Klasse, 3rd Series, no. 83 (Göttingen, 1974); C. Haase, 'Stadtbegriff und Stadtentstehungsschichten in Westfalen: Überlegungen zu einer Karte der Stadtentstehungsschichten' in C. Haase, *Die Stadt des Mittelalters*, vol. 1 (Darmstadt, 1975), pp. 60–94; S. Reynolds, *An Introduction to the History of English Medieval Towns* (Oxford, 1977), p. 3.

10 Aalen, *Man and the Landscape in Ireland*, p. 274.

11 L. De Paor, 'The Viking Towns of Ireland' in Almquist and Green (eds.), *Proceedings of the Seventh Viking Congress*, pp. 29–38.

12 B. Graham, 'The Evolution of Urbanisation in Medieval Ireland', *Journal of Historical Geography*, vol. 5, no. 2 (1979), pp. 111–25.

13 R. E. Glasscock, 'Moated Sites and Deserted Boroughs and Villages: Two Neglected Aspects of Anglo-Norman Settlement in Ireland' in N. Stephens and R. E. Glasscock (eds.), *Irish Geographical Studies* (Belfast, 1970), pp. 162–77.

14 R. A. Butlin, 'Irish Towns in the Sixteenth and Seventeenth Centuries' in R. A. Butlin (ed.), *The Development of the Irish Town* (London, 1977), pp. 61–100.

15 F. H. A. Aalen, 'The Towns', chap. 10 in *idem, Man and the Landscape in Ireland*, pp. 269–312.

16 Private communication by K. Simms, April 1979.

17 E. R. Norman and J. K. S. St Joseph, *The Early Development of Irish Society: The Evidence of Aerial Photography* (Cambridge, 1969), p. 118.

18 If it were not for the emphasis on the chartered town we could have described Dublin, Limerick and Waterford simply as walled Viking towns and ignore the subsequent Norman charters, just as we ignore Dublin's Tudor, Stuart, Georgian and Victorian periods as concerning subsequent growth and not origins.

19 E. Ennen, 'Aufgaben der landschaftlichen deutschen Städteforschung aus europäischer Sicht', *Blätter für deutsche Landesgeschichte*, vol. 93 (1957), p. 13.

20 For example, in the case of the Saarland the distinction is made between towns before 1200, towns in the thirteenth century, towns in the fourteenth century,

market places before 1200, proto-urban settlements and settlements with a qualitative change from market place to town. H. Ammann and E. Meynen (eds.), *Atlas für das Land an der Saar* (Saarbrücken, 1965), p. 6.

The historical atlases of the Saarland, Schwaben, Pfalz, Baden-Würtemberg, Berlin-Brandenburg and Prussia include many maps on topics of settlement history, while the atlases of Hessen and Bayern put more emphasis on problems of territorial borders and constitutional history. For a critical review of the different regional historical atlases in Germany see K. Fehn, 'Historische Kartographie', *Blätter für deutsche Landesgeschichte*, vol. 112 (1976), pp. 362–82.

21 Haase, *Die Stadt des Mittelalters*, pp. 60–94. H. Stoob, 'Kartographische Möglichkeiten zur Darstellung der Stadtentwicklung in Mitteleuropa, besonders zwischen 1450–1800' in *Historische Raumforschung*, I, vol. IV, Forschungs- und Sizungsberichte der Akademie für Raumforschung und Landesplanung (Bremen–Horn, 1956), pp. 5–21, reprinted in H. Stoob (ed.), *Forschungen zum Städtewesen in Europa*, vol. 1 (Köln/Wien, 1970), pp. 1–42.

22 Stoob (ed.), *Die Stadt. Gestalt und Wandel bis zum industriellen Zeitalter*, p. 156.

23 H. Stoob is the editor of an edition of special distribution maps to accompany the *Deutsche Städte Atlas*. This work is supported by the Curatorium for Comparative Urban History, Münster. The first volume of the German town-atlas (10 maps) was published in 1973, the second is forthcoming.

24 D. Denecke, 'Die Ortswüstung Oldendorp bei Einbeck und die "Alten Dörfer im Leinebergland', *Einbecker Jahrbuch*, vol. 29 (1970), pp. 15–36.

25 H. E. Stier *et al.* (eds.), *Grosser Atlas zur Weltgeschichte*, Westermann Verlag (10th edn, Braunschweig, 1978), Map 78.

26 E. Maynen, 'Geographische und Kartographische Forderungen an die Historische Karte', *Blätter für deutsche Landesgeschichte*, vol. 94 (1958), pp. 38–64.

27 J. Engel *et al.* (eds.), *Grosser Historischer Weltatlas*, vol. II: *Mittelalter, Bayrischer Schulbuchverlag* (2nd edn., München, 1979), Maps 36 and 37.

28 Editorial Committee, *Atlas zur Geschichte*, vol. I, V. E. B. Hermann Haack (Gotha/Leipzig, 1973), Map 33.

29 J. Herrmann, 'Research into the Early History of the Town in the Territory of the German Democratic Republic' in M. W. Barley (ed.), *European Towns: Their Archaeology and Early History* (London, 1977), pp. 243–59, Map 245.

30 J. Herrmann, personal communication, 11 September 1979.

31 I would like to put in a plea that historical geographers should not only develop semiotic models for a better reading of historic maps (see J. B. Harley in this volume) but also devise semiotic models in order to achieve a better communication of documentary material in cartographical form.

32 W. Witt, 'Geschichte, Historische Geographie, Vorgeschichte' in *Thematische Kartographie: Methoden und Probleme, Tendenzen und Aufgaben* (Hannover, 1970), pp. 786–96; W. Plapper, 'Probleme der Genesedarstellungen' in *Untersuchungen zur Thematischen Kartographie*, Veröffentlichungen der Akademie für Raumforschung und Landesplanung (Hannover, 1969), pp. 43–52; G. Franz, *Historische Kartographie*, 2nd edn., Akademie für Raumforschung und Landesplanung, vol. 29 (Hannover, 1962); E. Arnberger, *Handbuch der*

thematischen Kartographie (Wien, 1966); H. Quirin, 'Vom Wesen der Geschichtskarte', *Geschichte in Wissenschaft und Unterricht*, no. 5 (1954), pp. 598–663; G. Franz and H. Jäger, *Historische Kartographie*, 3rd rev. edn., Veröffentlichungen der Akademie für Raumforschung und Landesplanung, vol. 29 (Hannover, 1978).

Notes to Widgren, 'Field evidence', pp. 303–311

1 C. Taylor, *Fields in the English Landscape* (London, 1975), p. 27.
2 B. Myhre, 'The Iron Age Farm in Southwest Norway', *Norwegian Archaeological Review*, vol. 6, no. 1 (1973), p. 29.
3 K. Odner, 'Ethno-historic and Ecological Settings for Economic and Social Models of an Iron Age Society: Valldalen, Norway' in D. L. Clarke (ed.), *Models in Archaeology* (London, 1972).
4 M. L. Parry, *Climatic Change, Agriculture and Settlement* (Folkestone, 1978).
5 Cf. for example S.-O. Lindquist, 'Fossilt kulturlandskap som agrarhistorisk källa', *Västergötlands Fornminnesförenings Tidskrift* (1975–6), pp. 125–8.
6 M. B. Schiffer, *Behavioral Archaeology* (New York, 1976), pp. 11–40.
7 For further reading on the Iron Age agrarian landscape in Östergötland see S.-O. Lindquist, *Det förhistoriska kulturlandskapet i östra Östergötland* (Stockholm, 1968), and M. Widgren, 'A Simulation Model of Farming Systems and Land Use during the Early Iron Age', *Journal of Historical Geography*, vol. 5, no. 1 (1979), pp. 21–32.

Select bibliography

Aalen, F. H. E., *Man and the Landscape in Ireland*, London, 1978
Amedeo, D. and Golledge, R. G., *An Introduction to Scientific Reasoning in Geography*, New York, 1975
Ammann, H. and Meynen, E. (eds.), *Atlas für das Land an der Saar*, Saarbrücken, 1965
Anderson, M., *Family Structures in Nineteenth-Century Lancashire*, Cambridge, 1971
Anderson, P., 'Origins of the Present Crisis', *New Left Review*, vol. 43, 1967
Lineages of the Absolutist State, London, 1974
Passages from Antiquity to Feudalism, London, 1978
Argan, G., *The Renaissance City*, London, 1969
Atkinson, R. F., *Knowledge and Explanation in History: An Introduction to the Philosophy of History*, London, 1978
Autorenkollektiv, *Atlas zur Geschichte, I,* V. E. B. Hermann Haack, Gotha/Leipzig, 1973
Baker, A. R. H. (ed.), *Progress in Historical Geography*, Newton Abbot, 1972
'Rethinking Historical Geography' in Baker, A. R. H. (ed.), *Progress in Historical Geography*
'Patterns of Popular Protest', *Journal of Historical Geography*, vol. 4, 1975, pp. 383–7
'The Limits of Inference in Historical Geography' in Osborne, B. S. (ed.), *The Settlement of Canada: Origins and Transfer*, Kingston, Ontario, 1976, pp.169–82
'Historical Geography', *Progress in Human Geography*, vol. 1, 1977, pp. 465–67
'Rhetoric and Reality in Historical Geography', *Journal of Historical Geography*, vol. 3, 1977, pp. 301–5
'Historical Geography: Understanding and Experiencing the Past', *Progress in Human Geography*, vol. 2, 1978, pp. 495–504
'Historical Geography: a New Beginning?', *Progress in Human Geography*, vol. 3, 1979, pp. 560–70
'On the Historical Geography of France', *Journal of Historical Geography*, vol. 6, 1980, pp. 69–76
and Butlin, R. A. (eds.), *Studies of Field Systems in the British Isles*, Cambridge, 1973

363

and Hamshere, J. D. and Langton, J. (eds.), *Geographical Interpretations of Historical Sources*, Newton Abbot, 1970

and Harley, J. B. (eds.), *Man Made the Land*, Newton Abbot, 1973

Barrett, Ward J. and Schwartz, Stuart B., 'Comparación Entre Dos Economiás Acucareras Coloniales: Morelos, Mexico y Bahïa, Brazil' in Florescano, Enrigue (ed.), *Haciendas, Latifundios y Plantaciones en América Latina*, Mexico, 1975, pp. 532–72

Ben-Arieh, Y., 'A Geographical Approach to Historical Geography', *Studies in the Geography of Israel*, 1970, pp. 138–60

A City Reflected in its Times: Jerusalem in the Nineteenth Century, Jerusalem, 1977 and 1979

Berkhofer, R. Jr., *A Behavioral Approach to Historical Analysis*. New York, 1969

Berkner, L., 'The Use and Misuse of Census Data for the Historical Analysis of Household Structure', *Journal of Interdisciplinary History*, vol. 5, 1975, pp. 721–38

Bernstein, R. J., *The Restructuring of Social and Political Theory*, London, 1976

Billinge, M., 'In Search of Negativism: Phenomenology and Historical Geography', *Journal of Historical Geography*, vol. 3, 1977, pp. 55–67

A Cultural Geography of Industrialisation, London, forthcoming

Blaut, J. M., 'Imperialism: the Marxist Theory and its Evolution', *Antipode*, vol. 7, 1975, pp. 1–19

'Geographic Models of Imperialism', *Antipode*, vol. 2, 1970, pp. 65–85

Blouet, B. and Lawson, M. P. (eds.), *Images of the Plains: The Role of Human Nature in Settlement*, Lincoln, Nebraska, 1975

Bourdieu, P., 'Sur le pouvoir symbolique', *Annales: Économies, Sociétés, Civilisations*, vol. 32, 1977, pp. 404–11

Bowden, M. J., 'Downtown Through Time: Delimitation, Expansion and Internal Growth', *Economic Geography*, vol. 47, 1971, pp. 121–35

'Growth of the Central Districts in Large Cities', in Schnore, L. (ed.), *The New Urban History*, Princeton, 1974, pp. 75–109

Brandon, P. F. and Millman, R. N. (eds.), *Recording Historic Landscapes, Principles and Practice*, Occasional Paper of the Department of Geography, Polytechnic of North London, London, 1980

Historic Landscapes: Identification, Recording and Management, Occasional Paper of the Department of Geography, Polytechnic of North London, London, 1978

Braverman, Harry, *Labor and Monopoly Capital: The Degradation of Work in the Twentieth Century*, New York, 1974

Brown, L. A. and Holmes, J., 'Intra-urban Migration Lifelines: a Spatial View', *Demography*, vol. 8, 1971, pp. 103–12

Burke, P., *Tradition and Innovation in Renaissance Italy*, London, 1974

Bylund, E., 'Theoretical Considerations Regarding the Distribution of Settlement in Inner North Sweden', *Geografiska annaler*, vol. 42, 1960, pp. 225–31

Cardoso, G. F. S., 'The Formation of the Coffee Estate in Nineteenth-century Costa Rica' in Duncan, K. *et al.* (eds.), *Land and Labour in Latin America: Essays on the Development of Agrarian Capitalism in the Nineteenth and Twentieth Centuries,* Cambridge, 1977, pp. 165–202

Carr, E. H., *What is History?* Harmondsworth, 1961
Clark, A. H., 'First Things First' in Ehrenberg, R. E. (ed.), *Pattern and Process: Research in Historical Geography*, Washington, D.C., 1975
  'Historical Geography' in James, P. and Jones, C. F. (eds.), *American Geography: Inventory and Prospect*, Syracuse, 1954, pp. 70–105
  'The Conceptions of "empires" of the St Lawrence and Mississippi: an Historico-geographical View with some Quizzical Comments on Environmental Determinism', *American Review of Canadian Studies*, vol. 5, 1975, pp. 4–27
Clark, B. D. and Gleave, M. B. (eds.), 'Social Patterns in Cities', *Institute of British Geographers, Special Publications*, no. 5, 1973
Claval, P., *Espace et pouvoir,* Paris, 1978
  Les Mythes fondateurs des sciences sociales, Paris, 1980
Climo, T. A. and Howells, P. G. A., 'Cause and Counterfactuals', *Economic History Review*, vol. 27, 1974, pp. 461–8
  'Possible Worlds in Historical Explanation', *History and Theory*, vol. 15, 1976, pp. 1–20
Cohen, J. S., 'The Achievements of Economic History: the Marxist School', *Journal of Economic History*, vol. 38, 1978, pp. 29–57
Collier, G. A. 'Computer Processing of Genealogies and Analysis of Settlement Patterns', *Human Mosaic,* vol. 3, 1969, pp. 164–74
Collingwood, R. G., *The Idea of History*, New York, 1956; first edition published 1946
Conrad, A. H. and Meyer, J. R., *Studies in Econometric History*, London, 1965
Cosgrove, D., 'Place, Landscape and the Dialectics of Cultural Geography', *Canadian Geographer*, vol. 22, 1978, pp. 66–72
Danto, A. C., *Analytical Philosophy of History*, Cambridge, 1965
Darby, H. C., 'On the Relations of History and Geography', *Transactions and Papers of the Institute of British Geographers*, vol. 19, 1953, pp. 1–11
  'An Historical Geography of England: Twenty Years After', *Geographical Journal*, vol. 126, 1960, pp. 147–59
  'Historical Geography' in Finberg, H. P. R. (ed.), *Approaches to History*, London, 1962, pp. 127–56
  'The Problem of Geographical Description', *Transactions and Papers of the Institute of British Geographers*, vol. 30, 1962, pp. 1–14
  (ed.), *A New Historical Geography of England and Wales*, Cambridge, 1973
Davis, L. E., ' "And it Will Never be Literature" – the New Economic History: a Critique' in Swierenga, R. P. (ed.), *Quantification in American History*, New York, 1970, pp. 274–87
De Koninck, R. (ed.), 'Le matérialisme historique en géographie', *Cahiers de Géographie du Québec*, vol. 22, 1978
Denecke, D., *Methodische Untersüschüngen zur historisch-geographischen Wege-forschüng im Raüm zwischen Solling und Harz, Ein Betrag zur rekonstruktion der mittelaterlichen Kulturlandschaft*, Göttinger Geographiesche Abhand-lüngen, vol. 54, Göttingen, 1969
  'Die historisch-geographische Landesaufnahme, Aufgaben, Methoden und Ergebnisse, dargestellt am Beispiel des mittleren und südlichen

Leineberglandes', Göttinger Geographische Abhandlüngen, vol. 60, Götting-
en, 1972, pp. 401–36

'Die Ortswüstung Oldendorp bei Einbeck und die "Alten Dörfer" im Leinebergland', *Einbecker Jahrbuck*, vol. 29, 1970, pp. 15–36

Dickinson, H. T., *Liberty and Property in Eighteenth-Century Britain*, London,
1977

Dion, R., *Les Frontières de la France*, Paris, 1974

Dodgshon, R. A. and Butlin, R. A. (eds.), *An Historical Geography of England
and Wales*, London, 1978

Downs, R. and Meyer, J., 'Geography and the Mind: an Exploration of the
Imagination in Geography', *American Behavioural Scientist*, vol. 22, Sept.–
Oct., 1978

Doyle, Don. H., 'The Social Functions of Voluntary Association in a Nineteenth-
century American Town', *Social Science History*, vol. 1, 1977, pp. 333–55

Earle, C. F., 'Reflections on the Colonial City', *Historical Geography Newsletter*,
vol. 4, 1974, pp. 1–170

Ehrenberg, R. E. (ed.), *Patterns and Process: Research in Historical Geography*,
Washington, D.C., 1975

Eley, G., 'Some Recent Tendencies in Social History' in Iggers, G. and Parker, H.
(eds.), *International Handbook of Historical Studies*, New York, 1980, pp.
55–70

Eliade, M., *The Sacred and the Profane: The Nature of Religion*, New York, 1959

Engel, J. *et al.* (eds.), *Grosser Historischer Weltatlas*, vol. II: *Mittelalter,* Bayrischer
Schulbuchverlag, München, 1979, 2nd edn.

Ennen, E., 'Aufgaben der landschaftlichen deutschen Städteforschung aus europäischer Sicht', in *Blätter für deutsche Landesgeschichte*, vol. 93, 1957, pp.
1–14

Fischer, D. H., *Historians' Fallacies. Towards a Logic of Historical Thought,* New
York, 1970

Forrester, M., 'Practical Reasoning and Historical Enquiry', *History and Theory,*
vol. 15, 1976, pp. 133–40

Foster, J., *Class Struggle and the Industrial Revolution*, London, 1974

Fox, H. S. A. and Butlin, R. A. (eds.), *Change in the Countryside*, London, 1979

Franze, G., *Historische Geographie*, Akademie für Raumforschung und Landesplanung, vol. 29, Hannover, 1962, 2nd edn

French, R. A., 'Historical Geography in the U.S.S.R.' in Baker (ed.), *Progress in
Historical Geography*, pp. 111–28

Gallois, L., *Régions naturelles et noms de pays: Étude sur la région parisienne*,
Paris, 1908

Galloway, J. H., 'Agricultural Reform and the Enlightenment in Late Colonial
Brazil', *Agricultural History*, vol. 53, 1979

Gibson, J. R. (ed.), *European Settlement and Development in North America:
Essays on Geographical Change in Honour and Memory of Andrew Hill Clark*,
Toronto, 1978

Giddens, Anthony, *Capitalism and Modern Social Theory: an Analysis of the
Writings of Marx, Durkheim and Max Weber*, Cambridge, 1971

New Rules of Sociological Method, London, 1976

Central Problems in Social Theory, London, 1979

Glass, D. C. and Eversley, D. E. C. (eds.), *Population in History*, London, 1965
Goldstein, L. J., 'Collingwood's Theory of Historical Knowing', *History and Theory*, vol. 9, 1970
Gombrich, E. H., 'The Evidence of Images' in Singleton, C. (ed.), *Interpretation, Theory and Practice*, Baltimore, 1969
Goranson, E., *Kulturlandshapsförandring och Samhällsutveckling*, Stockholm, 1977
Goudie, A., 'Geography and Prehistory: a Survey of The Literature, with a Select Bibliography', *Journal of Historical Geography*, vol. 2, 1976, pp. 197–205
Gould, J. D. 'Hypothetical History', *Economic History Review*, vol. 22, 1969, pp. 195–207
Gramsci, A., *Prison Notebooks*, London, 1970
Gray, R., 'Bourgeois Hegemony in Victorian Britain' in The Communist University of London (ed.), *Class, Hegemony and Party*, London, 1977
Gregory, D., *Ideology, Science and Human Geography*, London, 1978
'On Rethinking Historical Geography', *Area,* vol. 8, 1976, pp. 295–9
'The Discourse of the Past: Phenomenology, Structuralism and Historical Geography', *Journal of Historical Geography*, vol. 4, 1978, pp. 161–73
'Social Change and Spatial Structures' in Carlstein, T., Parkes, D. and Thrift, N. (eds.), *Making Sense of Time,* London, 1978, pp. 38–46
Guelke, L., 'An Idealist Alternative in Human Geography', *Annals, Association of American Geographers,* vol. 64, 1974
'On Rethinking Historical Geography', *Area*, vol. 7, 1975, pp. 135–38
(ed.), *The Nature of Cartographic Communication*, Toronto, 1977
Hall, C., *El cafe y el desarrollo histórico-geográfico de Costa Rica*, San José, 1976
'The Tuis Archives: Cattle Ranching on the Frontiers of Colonization in Costa Rica, 1873–1876', *Revista Geográfica*, Pan-American Institute of History and Geography, no. 86–7, 1977–8, pp. 101–17
Concavas, formacion de una hacienda cafetalera, 1889–1911, San José, 1978
Hareven, T. V., 'The Family as Process: the Historical Study of the Family Cycle', *Journal of Social History*, 1974
'Family Time and Industrial Time' in Hareven, T. V. (ed.), *Family and Kin*, New York, 1977, pp. 187–207
Transitions: The Family and the Life Course in Historical Perspective, New York, 1978
Harris, R. C., 'The Simplification of Europe Overseas', *Annals, Association of American Geographers*, vol. 67, 1977, pp. 468–83
'The Historical Mind and the Practice of Historical Geography' in Ley and Samuels (eds.), *Humanistic Geography*, pp. 123–37
'Theory and Synthesis in Historical Geography', *The Canadian Geographer*, vol. 15, 1971, pp. 157–72
and Guelke, L., 'Land and Society in Early Canada and South Africa', *Journal of Historical Geography*, vol. 3, 1977, pp. 135–53
Harvey, D. W., 'Models of the Evolution of Spatial Patterns in Human Geography' in Chorley, R. J. and Haggett, P. (eds.), *Models in Geography*, London, 1967, pp. 549–608
Social Justice and the City, London, 1973
Hawkes, T., *Structuralism and Semiotics,* London, 1977

Heathcote, R. L., *Back of Bourke: A Study of Land Appraisal and Settlement in Semi-Arid Australia*, London, 1965

Hechter, M., *Internal Colonialism: The Celtic Fringe in British National Development, 1536–1966*, Berkeley, 1975

Henretta, James, *The Evolution of American Society, 1700–1815: an Interdisciplinary Analysis*, Lexington, Mass., 1973

'Families and Farms: *Mentalité* in Pre-industrial America', *William and Mary Quarterly*, 3rd Series, vol. 35, 1978, pp. 3–32

Hermann, J., 'Research into the Early History of the Town in the Territory of the German Democratic Republic' in Barley, M. W. (ed.), *European Towns: Their Archaeology and Early History*, London, 1977, pp. 243–59

Hudson, J. C., *Theoretical Settlement Geography*, Mimeographed paper, University of Iowa, 1967

'A Location Theory for Rural Settlement', *Annals, Association of American Geographers*, 1969

Huppert, G., *L'Idée de l'histoire parfaite*, Paris, 1973

Hurst, B. C. 'A Comment on the Possible Worlds of Climo and Howells', *History and Theory*, vol. 18, 1977, pp. 52–60

Iggers, G. G. (ed.), *New Directions in European Historiography*, Middletown, Conn., 1975

Jacobson, R., 'Closing Statement: Linguistics and Poetrics' in Seboek, T. A. (ed.), *Style and Language*, Cambridge, Mass., 1960

Jakle, J., 'Time, Space and Geographic Past: a Prospectus for Historical Geography', *American Historical Review*, vol. 76, 1971 pp. 1084–1103

Jankuhn, H., 'Archaeologische Landesaufnahme' in Hoops, J., *Reallexikon der Germanischen Altertümskünde*, 2nd edn, Vol. 4, Berlin, 1973, pp. 391–4

Schlesinger, W. and Steuer, H. (eds.), *Vor und Frühformen der Europäischen Stadt im Mittelalter*, Abhandlungen der Akademie der Wissenschaften in Göttingen, phil.-hist. Klasse, 3rd Series no. 83, Göttingen, 1974

Jennings, F., *The Invasion of America: Indians, Colonialism, and the Cant of Conquest*, Chapel Hill, 1975

Johnson, L. L. and Socolow, S., 'Population and Space in Eighteenth-Century Buenos Aires' in Robinson, D. J. (ed.), *Social Fabric and Spatial Structure in Colonial Latin America*, Ann Arbor, 1979, pp. 339–68

Kanter, Rosabeth, *Commitment and Community: Communes and Utopias in Social Perspective*, Cambridge, Mass., 1972

Katz, Michael, *The People of Hamilton Canada West: Family and Class in the Mid-nineteenth Century*, Cambridge, Mass., 1975

Kirk, W., 'Historical Geography and the Concept of Behavioural Environment', *Indian Geographical Journal*, Silver Jubilee Volume, 1951, pp. 152–60

Kreitner, Philip C., 'Abandoned Theories: the Cooperative Commonwealth', *New Harbinger: a Journal of the Cooperative Movement* [now *Co-op: the Harbinger of Economic Democracy*], vol. 5, no. 3, 1978, pp. 29–38

Lafrenz, J., *Die Stellüng des Innestadt im Fluchennützüngsgefüge des Agglomerationsraumes Lübeck, Gründlagenforschüng zur erhaltenden Stadterrnenerang*, Hamburger Geographische Stüdien, no. 33, Hamburg, 1977

Lamb, H. H., *Climate: Present, Past and Future*, London, 1972

Langton, J., 'Potentialities and Problems of Adopting a Systems Approach to the Study of Change in Human Geography', *Progress in Geography*, vol. 4, 1972, pp. 126–79

Laslett, P. and Wall, R. (eds.), *Household and Family in Past Time*, Cambridge, 1972

Lawton, R., 'Population Changes in England and Wales in the Later Nineteenth Century', *Transactions of the Institute of British Geographers*, no. 44, 1968, pp. 55–74

(ed.), *The Census and Social Structure*, London, 1970

Leach, E., 'Structuralism in Social Anthropology' in Robey, D. (ed.), *Structuralism: an Introduction*, Oxford, 1973

Leighly, J. (ed.), *Land and Life: a Selection from the Writings of Carl Ortwin Sauer*, Berkeley, 1963

Lemon, J. T., 'The Weakness of Place and Community in Early Pennsylvania' in Gibson, James R. (ed.), *European Settlement and Development in North America: Essays on Geographical Change in Honour and Memory of Andrew Hill Clark*, Toronto, 1978, pp. 190–207

'The Urban Community Movement: Moving Toward Public Households' in Ley, David and Samuels, Marwyn (eds.), *Humanistic Geography: Prospects and Problems*, Chicago, 1978, pp. 319–37

Ley, D. and Samuels, M. S. (eds.), *Humanistic Geography: Prospects and Problems*, Chicago, 1978

Lindquist, S-O., *Det forhistoriska kulturlandskapet: Ostra Ostergotland*, Stockholm, 1968

Litwak, E., 'Geographic Mobility and Extended Family Cohesion', *American Sociological Review*, vol. 25, 1960, pp. 385–94

Lowenthal, S. and Bowden, M. (eds.), *Geographies of the Mind*, New York, 1975

McClelland, P. D., 'Railroads, American Growth and the New Economic History: a Critique', *Journal of Economic History*, vol. 28, 1968, pp. 102–23

Macfarlane, A., *The Origins of English Individualism*, Oxford, 1978

McQuillan, D. C., 'Farm Size and Work Ethic: Measuring the Success of Immigrant Farmers on the American Grasslands, 1875–1925', *Journal of Historical Geography*, vol. 4, 1978, pp. 57–76

Meinig, D. W., 'The Continuous Shaping of America: a Prospectus for Geographers and Historians', *American Historical Review*, vol. 83, 1978, pp. 1186–1217

(ed.), *The Interpretation of Ordinary Landscapes*, Oxford, 1979

Meynan, E., 'Geographische und Kartographische Forderungen an die Historische Karte', in *Blatter für deutsche, Landesgeschichte*, vol. 94, 1958, pp. 38–64

Mikesell, M., 'Cultural Geography', *Progress in Human Geography*, vol. 1, 1977, pp. 460–4

Moodie, D. W. and Catchpole, A. J., *Environmental Data from Historical Documents by Content Analysis: Freeze-up and Break-up of Estuaries on Hudson Bay, 1714–1871*, Winnipeg, 1975

and Lehr, J. C., 'Fact and Theory in Historical Geography', *Professional Geographer*, vol. 28, 1976, pp. 132–5

Morrill, R. L., 'Simulation of Central Place Patterns over Time', in Norborg, K.

(ed.), *Proceedings of the IGU symposium in urban geography*, Lund Studies in Geography, Series B, Human Geography, no. 24, 1962

Mortensen, H., Mortensen, G., Wenskus, R. and Kaeger, H., *Historisch-geographischer Atlas des Preußenlandes*, Wiesbaden, 1968

Murphy, G. G. S. and Mueller, M. G., 'On Making Historical Techniques more Specific: "Real Types" Constructed with a Computer', *History and Theory*, vol. 6, 1967, pp. 14–32

Newcomb, R. M., *Planning the Past: Historical Landscape Resources and Recreation*, Folkstone, 1979

Norton, W., 'Process and Form Relationships: an Example from Historical Geography', *Professional Geographer*, vol. 30, 1978, pp. 128–34

Odner, K., 'Ethno-historic and Ecological Settings for Economic and Social Models of an Iron Age Society: Valldalen, Norway' in Clarke, D. L. (ed.), *Models in Archaeology*, London, 1972, pp. 623–51

Olsson, G., 'Complementary Models: a Study of Colonization Maps', *Geografiska Annaler*, Series B, 1968

O'Neill, J. (ed.), *Modes of Individualism and Collectivism*, New York, 1973

Osborne, B. C. (ed.), *The Settlement of Canada: Origins and Transfer*, Kingston, Ontario, 1976

Osborne, B. S. and Rogerson, C. W., 'Conceptualizing the Frontier Settlement Process: Development or Dependency?', *Comparative Frontier Studies, an Interdisciplinary Newsletter*, no. 11, 1978

Parry, M. L., *Climatic Change, Agriculture and Settlement*, Folkstone, 1978

Perry, P. J., 'H. C. Darby and Historical Geography: a Survey and Review', *Geographische Zeitschrift*, vol. 57, 1969, pp. 161–78

Piaget, J., *Structuralism*, London, 1971

Pickvance, C. G. (ed.), *Urban Sociology: Critical Essays*, London, 1976

Plakans, A., 'Identifying Kinfolk beyond the Household', *Journal of Family History*, vol. 2, 1977, pp. 3–27

Polanyi, Karl, *The Great Transformation: the Political and Economic Orgins of our Time*, New York, 1944; Boston, 1957

Pooley, C. G., 'The Residential Segregation of Migrant Communities in Mid-Victorian Liverpool', *Transactions of the Institute of British Geographers*, vol. 2, 1977, pp. 364–82

Porter, D. H., 'History as Process', *History and Theory*, vol. 14, 1975, pp. 297–313

Poulantzas, N., 'Marxist Political Theory in Great Britain', *New Left Review*, vol. 43, 1967

Powell, J. M., *Mirrors of the New World: Images and Image-Makers in the Settlement Process*, Folkstone, 1977

Prince, H. C., 'Real, Imagined and Abstract Worlds of the Past', in Board, C. *et al.* (eds.), *Progress in Geography*, vol. 3, 1971, pp. 21–2

'Time and Historical Geography' in Carlstein, T. *et al* (eds.), *Timing Space and Spacing Time*, vol. 1, London, 1978, pp. 17–37

Relph, E. C., *Place and Placelessness*, London, 1976

Renier, G. J., *History: its Purpose and Method*, London, 1951

Roberts, B., *Rural Settlement in Britain*, Folkstone, 1978

Robey, D. (ed.), *Structuralism: an Introduction*, Oxford, 1973

Robinson, A. H., 'The Uniqueness of the Map', *The American Cartographer*, vol. 5, 1978
and Petchenik, B. B., *The Nature of Maps and Mapping*, Chicago, 1976
Robinson, D. J., *The Analysis of 18th Century Spanish American Cities: Some Problems and Alternative Solutions*, Department of Geography, Syracuse University, Discussion Paper Series, no. 4, 1975
and Swann, M. M., 'Geographical Interpretation of the Hispanic American Colonial City: a Case Study of Caracas in the late Eighteenth Century' in Tata, R. J. (ed.), *Latin America: Search for Geographic Explanations*, Boca Raton, 1975, pp. 1–15
Rosenau, H., *The Ideal City: Its Architectural Evolution*, London, 1974
Sahlins, M., *Culture and Practical Reason*, Chicago, 1976
Stone Age Economics, London, 1974
Sauer, C. O., 'Foreword to Historical Geography', *Annals, Association of American Geographers*, vol. 31, 1941, pp. 1–24. Reprinted in Leighly, J. (ed.), *Land and Life*, Berkeley, 1963, pp. 351–404
'The Morphology of Landscape', *University of California Publications in Geography*, vol. 2, 1925, pp. 19–54. Reprinted in Leighly, J. (ed.), *Land and Life*, Berkeley, 1963, pp. 315–50
Schiffer, M. B., *Behavioral Archaeology*, New York, 1976
Schledermann, H., 'The Idea of the Town: Typology, Definitions and Approaches of the Study of the Medieval Town in Northern Europe', *World Archaeology*, vol. 2, no. 2, 1970, pp. 116–27
Seboek, T. A., *Contributions to the Doctrine of Signs*, Bloomington, 1976
Senda, M., 'Semiological Approach to Geographical Space and Mandala Pattern', *The Abstracts for the Congress of the Human Geographical Society in Japan, 1979*, Tokyo, 1979
'Structure in Ancient Space', *Geographical Study, Nara Women's University*, no. 1, 1979
Sheppard, J., 'Metrological Analysis of Regular Village Plans in Yorkshire', *Agricultural History Review*, vol. 22, 1974
Simms, A. and Simms, K., 'Origins of Principal Towns' in Haughton, J. P. (ed.), *Atlas of Ireland*, Royal Irish Academy, Dublin, 1979, p. 43
Spicer, E. H., *Cycles of Conquest: The Impact of Spain, Mexico and the United States on the Indians of the Southwest, 1533–1960*, Tuscon, 1962
Sporrong, U., *Kolonization, bebyggelseutueckling och administration*, Lund, 1971
Stephenson, C., 'Tracing Those Who Left', *Journal of Urban History*, vol. 1, 1974, pp. 73–84
Stier, H. E. *et al.* (eds.), *Grosser Atlas zur Weltgeschichte*, Westermann Verlag, Braunchweig, 1978, 10th edn
Stoob, H., 'Die hochmittelalterliche Städtebildung im Okzident' in Stoob, H. (ed.), *Die Stadt Gestalt und Wandel bis zum industriellen Zeitalter*. Städtewesen I. Werkstücke für Studium und Praxis aus dem Institut für Vergleichende Städtegeschichte in Münster, Köln/Wien, 1979, pp. 131–56
Stoianovitch, T., *French Historical Method: the 'Annales' Paradigm*, Ithaca, 1976
Thompson, E. P., 'The Peculiarities of the English' in Miliband, R. and Saville, J. (eds.), *Socialist Register, 1975*, London, 1975

The Poverty of Theory, London, 1978

Thompson, P., *The Voice of the Past: Oral History*, Oxford, 1978

Todd, W., *History as Applied Science*, Detroit, 1972

Tuan, Yi-fu, 'Discrepancies between Environmental Attitudes and Behaviour: Examples from Europe and China', *Canadian Geographer*, vol. 12, 1968

Topophilia: a Study of Environmental Perception, Attitudes and Values, Englewood Cliffs, 1974

Space and Place: the Perspective of Experience, Minneapolis, 1977

Turner, Frederick J., *The Frontier in American History*, New York, 1920

Vansina, J., *Oral tradition: a Study in Historical Methodology*, Harmondsworth, 1973

Vicero, R. D. (ed.), *Historical Geography Newsletter*, vol. 6, no. 1, 1976: an issue devoted to Carl O. Sauer and Andrew H. Clark

Vilar, P., 'Histoire Marxiste, histoire en construction: Essai de dialogue avec Althusser', *Annales: Économies, Sociétés, Civilisation*, vol. 28, 1973, pp. 165–98

Wachter, K. W. *et al.*, *Statistical Studies of Historical Social Structure*, New York, 1978

Wallerstein, I., *The Modern World-system; Capitalist Agriculture and the Origin of the European World-Economy in the Sixteenth Century*, New York, 1976

Wenskus, R., 'Kleinverbände und Kleinräume bei den Preußen des Samlandes' in *Die Anfänge der Landgemeinde und ihr Wesen, Vorträge und Forschungen*, VIII, Konstanz/Stuttgart, 1964, 201–54

Wheatley, P., *The Pivot of the Four Quarters: A Preliminary Enquiry into the Origins and Character of the Ancient Chinese City*, Chicago, 1971

City as Symbol, London, 1967

Whitehand, J. W. R. and Patten, J. H. C. (eds.), 'Change in the Town', *Transactions of the Institute of British Geographers*, vol. 2, 1977

Widgren, M., 'A Simulation Model of Farming Systems and Land Use During the Early Iron Age', *Journal of Historical Geography*, vol. 5, no. 6, 1979, pp. 21–32

Williams, R., *The Country and the City*, London, 1976

Marxism and Literature, Oxford, 1977

Witt, W., 'Geschichte, Historische Geographie, Vorgeschichte' in *Thematische Kartographie, Methoden, und Problems, Tendenzen und Aufgaben*, Hanover, 1970, pp. 786–96

Wrigley, E. A. (ed.), *An Introduction to English Historical Demography*, Cambridge, 1966

(ed.), *Nineteenth-Century Society: Essays in the Use of Quantitative Methods for the Study of Social Data*, Cambridge, 1972

(ed.), *Identifying People in the Past*, London, 1973

Young, Alfred E. (ed.), *The American Revolution: Explorations in the History of American Radicalism*, De Kalb, 1976

Index

Abrams, P., 247
Adams, I., 316
administrative areas, 44–50, changes in, 99–100
Agrarian Landscape Research Group, 11
agriculture: archives in, 276–80; decision-making and, 136–44; innovation in, 79, 85
alienation, 239
Allen, J., 202
Amedeo, D., 251, 252, 353
Amiran, D. K., 4
Anchorage, 115, 118, 124
Ancient Monuments Protection Act, 43
Anderson, M., 331
Anderson, P., 348, 352
Annales school, 16, 236, 242
anthropology, and geography, 14
Arango y Parreno, F., 81
archaeological evidence, 128, 132–3
Armstrong, A., 330
Aron, R., 351
Ashton, W., 237
Atlas of Ireland, 289–300 *passim*
Atlas zur Geschichte, 296

Bacon, Francis, 35
Bacon, Sir Nicholas, 35
Baker, A. R. H., 11, 13, 14, 15, 254, 315, 316, 324, 325, 347, 350, 355, 357
Barbados, 86
Barrett, W., 85
Beckford, W., 80
Berkhampsted, 39
Berkner, L., 327, 328
Billinge, M., 13, 15, 316, 347

Bishop Morton's Palace, 35
Blandford Forum, 39
Blank, S., 327
Blaut, J. M., 78, 236, 324, 350
Blythe, R., 264
Boulding, K., 202–3
Bourdieu, P., 222
Bowden, M., 198, 199, 202
Brazil, 81, 82, 83, 86
Braudel, F., 16
British Columbia, 51–68
Brookfield, H., 234, 350
Brown, R., 193
Burke, P., 349, 356
Butlin, R. A., 13, 234, 329, 359
Buttimer, A., 14, 233, 349
bybildning, 155, 160; *see also* settlement
Bylund, E., 164–7, 170

Camden, W., 37
Camp Lister, 64–6
Canada, immigrant groups, 136–44
capitalism, 124
Caracas, 88–98; demographic history, 89; family structures, 91–4; population distribution, 89, 90
Carlstein, T., 349
Carr, E. H., 354
cartography, 44–50, 150; of Ireland, 289–300; of Israel, 4, 5, 8; of Japan, 302; as source material, 44–50, 129–31
Cassiobury, 35
Castells, M., 14
catastrophe theory, 236
causality, in history, 191
Cecil, Sir William, 35

373